To Mike Schwe...
Good Hu...

Bob Williams
12/4/10

For Mike,
Shoot straight +
Best wishes,
Joe Coogan

# AFRICA

# AFRICA
### Sporting Classics'

## *41 Adventures From*
## The *Dark Continent*

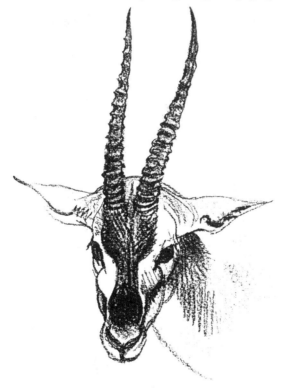

## *Illustrations by Bob Kuhn*

*A 30th Anniversary Presentation*
*from* SPORTING CLASSICS

AFRICA is published by SPORTING CLASSICS.

*Publisher & Editor: Chuck Wechsler*

*Creative Director & Designer: Ryan Stalvey*

*Illustrations by Bob Kuhn*

*Editorial Support: Matt Coffey & Etta Wilhelm*

*Production & Marketing: Duncan Grant, Lee Anne Futrell, Brian Raley Laura Wilhelm & Debbie Moak*

First Printing – 2010
Library of Congress Catalog Card Number – 20100936179
ISBN – 978-1-935342-11-3

# DEDICATION

*To Libby Kuhn, for 66 years the loving wife of animal artist Bob Kuhn, who passed away in 2007.*

# A NOTE FROM THE PUBLISHER

O ver the past three decades *Sporting Classics* has published more than 100 articles and columns on sport and wildlife conservation in Africa. This anthology, which commemorates the magazine's 30th anniversary, features the best of those stories.

Many talented, dedicated people made this book possible, particularly the authors who eagerly shared their stories. A special thanks to Libby Kuhn, her son Casey and daughter Karen, for providing more than 50 of Bob Kuhn's wonderful drawings of Africa's wild animals. I would also like to thank Dick Cabela for his compelling Introduction, and the staff at *Field & Stream*, who provided us with Bob Kuhn's painting for our dust jacket. The image originally appeared on the cover of their January, 1955 issue.

Jim Casada, the leading authority on sporting books, deserves accolades for his extensive and always thorough research of Africa-based stories and authors. Thanks to Ben Camardi and Harold Matson Co. Inc., who over the years have provided Robert Ruark's stories for our publications and to David Cabela for his literary contributions.

*– Chuck Wechsler, publisher*

# INTRODUCTION

*By Dick Cabela*

frica.

Most children can point it out on a globe. They probably know elephants and lions come from there. Some of them will never know more than that – a shame. Others, however, will develop a fascination with the "Dark Continent." Maybe they'll find a copy of *King Solomon's Mines* or lose themselves in an old *Tarzan* comic. These kids will fuel their innate sense of adventure with other classic tales and frequent expeditions into their backyards and beyond. The lucky ones will never lose that need to explore, and though they will gain wisdom with age, they will never truly grow up. For them, that one word is so much more than a geographical location. For them, Africa is a place where dreams live.

Driven by the hunter's passion to look into the eyes of a cape buffalo, follow the tracks of a bull elephant, or match wits with one of the great cats, some of our greatest writers have chronicled what Africa was to them. Many of their articles have appeared in *Sporting Classics* magazine over the past 30 years. And the best of those stories, both true-life and fictional, can be found on the pages that follow.

Much of my own fascination with Africa began with an early childhood wonder. But it was many of the writers in this anthology and their stories that steered that awe into something closer to an obsession. And when I finally found myself mesmerized by the lion's stare, or following an eland track for seven hours, or listening to the silence only a leopard can induce, I understood how those storytellers must have felt. They took past events and made them rise above the pages of a magazine to a place that exists somewhere between their minds and the reader's. They wrote stories that inspired hunters to dream about the unknown, and some of those hunters spent their lives reaching for the chance to create their own African memories.

Robert Ruark, Theodore Roosevelt, Peter Capstick, Ernest Hemingway – these men and others, these legends of outdoor literature, will live forever because they put into words what the rest of us felt. They followed their hearts to places that defy the effects of time to pursue animals that sometimes blur the definitions of hunter and prey.

I imagine the first hunting story, probably the first story ever told, happened around a slow-burning fire under a starry African sky. A perfect stalk on a kudu, a long tracking session for bongo, an unexpected encounter with a rhinoceros. The circumstances matter little now, but the way in which the hunter relayed his tale – his actions, his descriptions and his emotions – influenced future generations of storytellers who transformed it into an art.

When explorers first traveled to Africa something compelled them to write down their experiences. Is it possible that the echoes of those first fireside tales still whisper in the breeze? When you read these stories you will hear it, because these writers and adventurers tapped into Africa's ancient rhythm to make you feel as if it's the first story you've ever read.

Since 1987 I have hunted in Africa 30 times. I have been charged by elephant and rhino. I have collapsed after days of tracking eland. I have befriended some of the most genuine people on earth. And through it all, Africa has become like a second home.

These tales from the old masters and the contemporary voices of African hunting allow me to relive some of my own travels and fuel the desire to visit places I have not yet seen. They are more than words on a page – they are an inner look into some of Africa's greatest hunters pursuing its legendary game animals.

The stories in this book are from writers who define hunting literature. Writers whose stories will live beyond the sunset.

– *Dick Cabela, 2010*

# CONTENTS

## BWANAS & BARONS

## ON SAFARI

# FACING DEATH

# DEVILS & APE MEN

# BWANAS & BARONS

# The LUNATIC EXPRESS

*The Uganda Railway project was a monumental engineering challenge. Extending from Africa's east coast to Lake Victoria, the railroad had to cross vast expanses of thornbush, steep hills and plunging river valleys. Still, work progressed smoothly until the workers reached the Tsavo River, where all hell broke loose.*

By Jim Casada

In the 1890s Britain's far-flung empire covered a quarter of the globe, including a number of strange, out-of-the-way places. Of all its territories, perhaps none featured more geographical diversity than the vast reaches of British East Africa. This newly acquired territory, which had been explored by some of the great names in African discovery, encompassed the sultry, clove-laden island of Zanzibar, enormous mainland stretches of *bunda* (arid plains with nearly impenetrable thickets of thorn), the Great Rift Valley where *homo sapiens* had its beginning, Mount Kilimanjaro, and the lush tropics surrounding that immense inland sea, Lake Victoria.

In 1895 a handful of British politicians decided that what the region needed to make it economically viable was a railroad. These astute gentlemen, determined to make a truism of the widely held belief that only "mad dogs and Englishmen go out in the midday sun," moved their colleagues in Parliament to fund construction of the Uganda Railway. Designed to link Africa's barren east coast with the potentially rich territory around Lake Victoria, it was to become a stupendous engineering challenge.

To many, the enterprise was a hare-brained scheme that gave new meaning

3

AFRICA

to the word boondoggle, but it had cabinet-level backing and support from powerful politicians like Lord George Curzon. Anti-imperialists were outraged and in defeat, their leader, Henry Labouchere, read this bit of scathing doggerel to the bemused House of Commons:

*What will it cost no words can express;*
*What is its object no brain can suppose;*
*Where it will start from no one can guess;*
*Where it is going to nobody knows.*
*What is the use of it none can conjecture;*
*What it will carry there's none can define;*
*And in spite of George Curzon's superior lecture,*
*It clearly is naught but a lunatic line.*

But not even Labouchere could envision the single greatest disaster that would beset the builders of what author Charles Miller would style as "The Lunatic Express" in his book on the railroad project.

Construction progressed smoothly until the railroad reached the Tsavo River, which the engineer in charge of the Indian work gangs initially viewed as an ideal place for a permanent camp. He could not have been wider of the mark. For it was here, beginning in March of 1898, that the depredations of two huge male lions stopped the railroad for the better part of the year.

The gruesome exploits of the man-eaters, together with those of Lieutenant Colonel John Henry Patterson, the man who eventually took their measure, form one of the most fantastic tales in the annals of African adventure.

The very name Tsavo had negative connotations – its meaning in the language of the local Kikamba natives was "slaughter." In 1898 and on into 1899, the appropriateness of the term would become terrifying clear. In truth, the site was notorious among caravan leaders and natives long before the railway reached the river. Many caravan porters deserted at Tsavo. Legend had it that a certain evil spirit would entice the men away at night and after leading them down to the river, whisk them away. The area was also an old killing ground of the dreaded Masai warriors. Indeed, it had an aura of evil about it.

No sooner had the railroad established its camp when these ominous portents became grisly reality. Searchers looking for a missing coolie found only the man's skull and feet surrounded by a profusion of lion tracks. The spectre that would haunt Tsavo for many months had assumed substance. Further investigation uncovered other human skulls and skeletons scattered around the area.

Within days the phantom lions killed again. This time the flesh of a worker's face had been torn off, leaving the teeth exposed to form a horrible grinning expression. The hideous remains produced instant pandemonium among the coolies. Tsavo had, as the head engineer so pithily put it, become a "death hole."

It was at this fateful juncture that John Henry Patterson appeared on the scene. The Englishman was a slender, rather domineering individual full of the purposefulness and rectitude so characteristic of Queen Victoria's imperial servants. A trained engineer with extensive experience in railway construction, he had risen to his rank while in the Indian Army. Patterson was also an accomplished hunter and doubtless looked upon his posting to East Africa as a splendid opportunity to combine sporting pleasure and work.

At first Patterson gave little more than passing thought to the tales of man-eating lions. He optimistically expected to bridge the Tsavo and lay track on both sides of the river within a few months. All too soon, however, he found himself at center stage of the gripping drama.

In the latter part of March 1898, about two weeks after his arrival, servants awakened Patterson to inform him that one of his personal attendants, a muscular Sikh named Ungat Singh, had been carried bodily from his tent in a lion's jaws.

In his book, *The Man-Eaters of Tsavo*, Patterson provides graphic descriptions of the lions' kills. On this occasion, he came upon a trail marked by darkening spots of congealed blood, an indication that the cats had indulged in "their habit of licking the skin off so as to get at fresh blood." Following this macabre spoor, he encountered "a dreadful spectacle" – pieces of flesh, crushed bones and the victim's intact head "with the eyes staring wide open in a startled, horrified look." Patterson vowed on the spot to "rid the neighbourhood of the foul brutes." Little did he realize the immensity of his new task.

Patterson began hunting that very night, armed with a single-barreled Holland .303 rifle and a double-barreled 12-gauge shotgun loaded with a slug and buckshot. He took a stand in a thorn tree near the kill site, reasoning that the lions would return to feed on the remains. But after a few hours of waiting, he would learn that the lions' habits did not lend themselves to human powers of reasoning.

# AFRICA

In the depths of the night, distant roars and the shouts of natives told him the cats had taken another coolie. It was a scenario that would be repeated, with minor variations, time and again over the ensuing weeks and months. The felines seemed gifted with almost supernatural foresight, both as to Patterson's whereabouts and the location of defenseless men.

Sometimes the lions would go for a week or two without an attack; during other periods their violent incursions came night after night. Their sagacity and irregular habits made Patterson's task difficult, and more than once he confessed to emotions of "impotent disappointment." Meanwhile, an atmosphere of terror descended on Tsavo. Even when there were no attacks, the lions' guttural snarls and roars punctuated the darkness.

The coolies devised all sorts of measures to avoid the marauders. They built heavily fortified thorn barricades, called *bomas*, kept fires blazing throughout the night, posted night watchmen who banged on empty cans, and contrived all sorts of imaginative sleeping arrangements. Before long, the upper branches of every tall tree near the campsite was festooned with crude hammocks. One such tree splintered under its burden, tumbling the men into the midst of the prowling lions. All these expedients ultimately failed. No matter how secure a *boma* might seem, the lions would inevitably discover a weak link and claim yet another victim.

With unerring accuracy, the killer cats continued to second-guess their human adversaries, taking victim after victim. Even the hospital was not safe. Having forced it to relocate once because of their deadly forays, the lions soon discovered its new location and took another coolie. In this instance, they devoured their victim on the spot, leaving nothing but his skull and a few fingers. As Patterson noted, somewhat bizarrely, on one of the fingers "was a silver ring, and this, with the teeth (a relic much prized by certain castes), was sent to the man's widow in India." His action suggests that Patterson was also beginning to experience a bit of the eerie fatalism that plagued his coolies.

This became especially true following one sordid incident when the man-eaters, having taken yet another victim on a particularly dark, moonless night, consumed their prey within earshot of the hunter. "I could plainly hear them crunching the bones, and the sound of their dreadful purring filled the air and rang in my ears for days afterwards."

With such unwelcome diversions, it is small wonder that camp morale quickly disintegrated. Patterson's courageous, unstinting attempts to kill the lions helped at first, but as more coolies fell victim, despair gripped everyone. In desperation he took to stalking the lions in their thorny retreats during the day as well as maintaining his nighttime vigils.

Patterson had always been one for maintaining strict discipline, both in a personal sense and among his men. In fact, it says much for his powerful personality that he maintained order as well as he did. Most workers stuck to their tasks of bridge-building and track-laying, despite living in a state of siege. However, a few defiant coolies precipitated yet another crisis for the hard-pressed engineer.

Several malingerers, whom Patterson had previously exposed to public ridicule, hatched a plot to murder their taskmaster. Patterson got wind of the conspiracy and marched among the ringleaders unprotected. One of the bolder spirits actually attempted to seize him, but he avoided the attack. Patterson then leaped atop a rock and began to harangue the mob. He dared anyone to lift a hand against him. This mixture of bluster and bravery worked, for he was never again threatened.

The plucky Englishman needed more than raw courage to deal with his animal foes. The man-eaters had now been about their repugnant business for six months and showed no signs of ending their attacks. By September of 1898 they had become international news. In a well-intentioned if misguided attempt to resolve the crisis, Sir George Whitehouse, chief engineer for the Uganda Railway, authorized a reward of 200 rupees (equivalent to perhaps $3,000 today) for the skin of any lion taken within one mile on either side of the railway line.

The substantial reward, together with the promise of great fame for the successful hunter, made Tsavo a boom town. Wealthy English sportsmen rubbed elbows with opportunistic freebooters, while civil and military officers on leave arrived en masse. It was a circus devoid of comedy. Any lion, be it a cub or a lioness in advanced stages of pregnancy, became fair game. Patterson found the whole mess distasteful and felt hindered by the invasion of overzealous hunters. Meanwhile the man-eaters, now extraordinarily wise in the ways of men, continued to wreak havoc.

By now, Patterson was becoming desperate. He tried poisoning several donkey carcasses, but the lions scorned the tainted meat. One scheme would have succeeded, however, had Patterson not been plagued by the most rotten luck imaginable.

He ordered the coolies to build a massive trap, which generated considerable kibitzing among some Tsavo residents. The contraption was comprised of adjoining cages separated by steel bars fashioned from discarded lengths of rail. Patterson intended to serve as bait to lure the man-eaters into the adjacent cubicle. The trap also had an ingeniously designed mechanism that would lock in the beasts once they entered. Then, at point blank range, he could shoot the man-eaters. The workers camouflaged the device within a boma, but left a weak spot where the cats could enter.

Once the trap was complete, Patterson endured mosquitoes by night and the ridicule of his fellow Europeans by day. Fatigue eventually forced him to use volunteer coolies as bait, a decision that he would soon regret.

One of the man-eaters entered the cage and the door locked behind it. The panic stricken coolies in the adjacent enclosure emptied their rifles in the direction of the angry lion, but incredibly, every shot missed. One bullet, however, blew the lock off the door, allowing the man-eater to escape unscathed. Small wonder the superstitious workers regarded the beasts as devils!

On December 1, with Patterson nearing total exhaustion, the most crushing of all blows fell. Hundreds of workers converged on his tent and bluntly announced they would no long remain at Tsavo . . . that they had come to work for the government, not to become food for lions or devils. No sooner had they issued their proclamation than a materials train arrived on its return from the railhead enroute to Mombasa on the coast.

Hordes of coolies swarmed aboard like so many panicky lemmings, clutching to even the most precarious perches. The startled engineer, overwhelmed by this veritable onslaught of passengers, chugged away before Patterson could resolve matters. Tsavo was, practically speaking, abandoned. Only Patterson and a handful of brave coolies (or unfortunate souls who had missed the train) remained. The man-eaters had stopped a British railroad!

At this point, seemingly when matters could get no worse, Patterson got a break. Ironically, after the tumult and terror which had so long beset Tsavo, the end was almost anticlimactic. Shortly after daybreak on December 9, a Swahili native ran into Patterson's *boma* screaming "Simba." A lion had attacked a man and his donkeys near the river, killing one of the animals. Patterson snatched a gun and rushed out. In his haste, however, he had seized a borrowed double-barreled rifle. Nonetheless, he began stalking the lion. Just as the man-eater came into sight, Patterson's Swahili companion stumbled, spooking the lion into a patch of jungle.

At this moment of extreme frustration, Patterson had an inspired thought. He decided to drive the lion in much the same way he had hunted tigers in India. Summoning some men to serve as beaters, he arranged them in the classic horseshoe pattern. The beaters had barely started walking when Patterson, positioned atop a seven-foot anthill, saw a huge maneless lion. As he carefully drew a bead, the lion spied him and growled savagely. It was a formidable by unmissable target.

"I felt that at last I had him absolutely at my mercy . . . I pulled the trigger, and to my horror heard the dull snap that tells of a misfire." Before the lion could charge, Patterson fired the other barrel and heard the dull thud of a hit. The huge beast immediately plunged into a thorn thicket, where Patterson lost its trail.

A lesser man would have called it quits at that point, but nightfall found Patterson at a stand overlooking the donkey kill. After several hours "a deep long-drawn sigh – a sure sign of hunger – came up from the bushes." He immediately realized that he, not the dead donkey, was the object of the lion's attention. As the tension mounted, an owl, mistaking Patterson for a tree, actually brushed against him with its wings. It says much for his steel nerves and presence of mind that he did not fire in blind panic. Suddenly the lion appeared only several feet away. Patterson fired and the brute thrashed about before subsiding with a "series of mighty groans." One of the devils was no more.

At dawn the next morning eight men were needed to carry the lion, which measured nine feet eight inches from nose to tail. Other coolies triumphantly carried Patterson alongside. Congratulatory telegrams poured in and the world's press lauded his accomplishments. For the moment, Patterson was the *lion* of the *hour*. He knew, however, that the second man-eater remained at large and immediately began attempts to kill it.

One such attempt was tethering a trio of live goats to 250 pounds of steel rail. But the lion simply dragged the goats, weight and all, off into the bush for a leisurely repast. A few nights later Patterson managed to wound the man-eater, and for a time, thought the injury might prove fatal. Then, two days after Christmas, 1898, the killer reappeared, scaring a tree-full of coolies witless in an all-night siege.

Dusk the following evening found Patterson in the same tree. After several uneventful hours, he dozed off despite his best intentions to remain vigilant. He awoke with a start and an "uncanny feeling that something was wrong." A shadowy movement confirmed his instinct. It was "a most fascinating sight to watch this great brute stealing stealthily around us, taking advantage of every bit of cover as he came. His skill showed that he was an old hand at the terrible game of man-eating." Patterson fired his trusted Holland four times, scoring two hits before his quarry slipped into the *bundu*.

9

# AFRICA

At daybreak, accompanied by a gunbearer, he began tracking the lion. The pair came upon the badly wounded beast within a few hundred yards. As it charged, the hunter drove home yet another .303 slug. Still the lion came on. Patterson quickly turned to his gunbearer for his back-up carbine, only to see the native scrambling up a tree with the gun in tow. He had no choice but to join his gunbearer, and had it not been for the lion's broken hind leg, he would have never reached safety.

From the security of his perch, Patterson reloaded and fired again, dropping the man-eater. In his jubilation, he "rather foolishly," as he later admitted, leaped to the ground. The dying feline mustered strength for yet another charge, requiring two more shots before it fell barely five yards away.

The reign of terror was finally over. Now an ancient Kikuyu prophecy, which proclaimed that "an iron snake will cross from the lake of salt to the lands of the Great Lake," could be fulfilled. Every mile of this "iron snake" cost $9,500 – a fortune at the time. But the monetary expenses paled in comparison with the human and emotional prices exacted by the man-eaters. The deadly lions had killed 38 coolies and an estimated 100 Africans.

I n the *The Lunatic Express*, the best book on the railway project, Charles Miller writes: ". . . for a while (the lions) actually succeeded (in) gaining a notoriety customarily reserved for the dragons of medieval legend." If such was the case, Patterson emerged from the epic struggle as a modern-day St. George.

In the heroic engineer's eyes, however, completing his assigned goal was more significant than killing the man-eaters. With the work force back at full strength, Patterson and the Indian coolies bridged the Tsavo River by early February of 1899. His task was at an end. He had, with the stiff upper lip approach so admired by Victorians, "muddled through."

By way of a postscript, some mention should be made of Patterson's rather checkered subsequent career. *The Man-Eaters of Tsavo*, which did not appear until October 1907, was a best seller. Replete with an introduction by the famous African hunter, Frederick Selous, the book went through numerous editions and earned its author sizeable royalties. The feats it described also helped Patterson garner the job of Principal Game Ranger for the East African Protectorate (today's Kenya), a position he took after a stint in the Boer War and extensive travels. It was during his years as a game ranger that he produced another important sporting work, *In the Grip of Nyika* (1909 – *nyika* means wilderness).

Ironically, Patterson's second tenure in East Africa also aroused controversy, although much of it was suppressed or took place behind the scenes. While on a hunting safari with a couple identified only as Mr. and Mrs. B., what Patterson calls "a grave revolver accident" claimed Mr. B.'s life. As Colonial Office papers reveal, however, many Englishmen living in the region thought the "accident" was actually murder growing out of a love triangle. Interestingly, officials ordered Patterson home on "sick leave" as soon as he and Mrs. B. returned to Nairobi. The full truth likely will never be known.

Whatever might have transpired, Patterson weathered the controversy and later served in World War I. He became a staunch supporter of the Zionist cause and devoted most of his long life (he survived until 1947) to Jewish concerns. He championed a Jewish state in Palestine and wrote several books including With the Zionists in Gallipoli (1916), *With the Judeans in the Palestine Campaign* (1922), and *American Friends of a Jewish Palestine* (1941).

His accomplishments notwithstanding, Patterson did not even merit an obituary in *The Times* of London. His man-eating adversaries, for their part, have fared rather well at the hands of posterity. Their hides, while certainly not particularly attractive as trophies after years of exposure to the thorny *bundu*, were carefully preserved and remain the property of Chicago's Field Museum of Natural History. Likewise, thanks to Patterson's splendid book and other accounts, they have achieved a sort of lasting if perverse fame.

# Rogue Male

*How did the hero of Tsavo become the villain in East Africa's most enduring scandal? The true story behind Hemingway's Francis Macomber.*

*By Kenneth M. Cameron*

The great elephant rounded a clump of acacia and swung toward the two hunters. Drying blood made dark stains down its wrinkled shoulder and neck, but despite its wounds the big animal moved deceptively fast with that ambling gait that makes you misjudge its speed.

"Wait," the African professional hunter whispered.

The elephant rushed toward them – then abruptly it stopped, backed up several steps. Its ears came forward, moving like fans, listening for them. Hot, tiny eyes were red with hatred. It came again with a rush, only a couple of strides, backed away, rushed again.

The trunk went straight up, and the big male elephant screamed.

"Shoot!" the veteran cried, knowing the charge was coming now.

But the other man only stood there. His eyes were fixed on this thing that wanted to kill him; his mouth was a little open, foolish looking. He was holding a London-made double .450 express rifle, and as the elephant opened its mouth and screamed, he could have raised it and put a bullet up through the mouth and into the brain – but he did not.

13

# AFRICA

"For God's sake, shoot!"

But the amateur hunter could only stand there. He was trembling.

The veteran raised his own gun. It was the wrong gun for the task – an old military Martini-Henry carbine in .577/.450, its load behind the heavy ball hardly better than a shotgun's. But it was all he had. His face contorted with contempt for this man who stood transfixed beside him, he raised his gun and fired, then worked the breech to reload. The elephant recoiled a step as the ponderous bullet stuck, and it screamed and recovered and came on. A gunbearer, trying to dodge the charging elephant, almost fell under it. The veteran shot again, the whole world coming down to that dark, dusty mass of flesh. The Martini-Henry boomed like a kettledrum; the elephant bellowed and turned away from the bitter smoke and the noise and passed them, so close the man could feel the breeze of its rush. As the beast went by, it reached for the gunbearer with its trunk to rip him and trample him, but only knocked the cap off his head. It crashed into the acacias and disappeared.

The man with the Martini-Henry felt his heart thud and turn over. His knees were weak, and he could feel sweat starting under his arms. He glanced at the amateur, still clutching his express rifle, staring at the spot where the elephant had disappeared.

"Why don't you go wait with your wife," the professional hunter said. "I'll take care of the elephant. Alone."

He didn't wait for an answer. With a signal to one of the gunbearers, he walked into the acacias after the animal, and the black gunbearer in the ragged European clothes followed.

There would have been nothing for the hunter with the express rifle to say, anyway. Everything was too complicated by then, mostly because of his wife, and the affair he knew she was having with the professional hunter, here in the godforsaken bush.

The husband handed his rifle blindly to another gunbearer. He took a step and staggered, and sweat broke out all over him.

Thirty-six hours later he lay dead, his head burst apart by a bullet.

And his wife and the other man went on with the safari.

This real sequence of events happened in East Africa, in March, 1908. Twenty-six years later, the dean of professional hunters, Philip Percival, told the story – minus the real names – to Ernest Hemingway, who turned it into one of the classic short stories about Africa, *The Short Happy Life of Francis Macomber*. Twelve years after that, it was made into a motion picture called *The Macomber Affair*, starring Gregory Peck as the veteran hunter, Robert Preston as the husband, and a stunning Joan Bennett as the wife, whom Hemingway called a bitch. Except for its tacked-on and silly ending, it was the best movie Hollywood ever made from a Hemingway source.

Yet, when the movie was made, the identities of the real-life figures were kept secret. Ironically, the man whom Peck portrayed was actually living in Los Angeles when the movie was released.

Who was the veteran hunter? And who was the woman who, in Hemingway's version, put the bullet into the back of her husband's head? And was the husband the "nice jerk" of Hemingway, or was he the angry coward so brilliantly played by Preston? Or was he the "English lord" of the gossip that still goes around?

Sometimes, fact is not only stranger than fiction, but a lot more interesting as well. In this case, the veteran, the man played by the handsome Peck, was and still is famous for another of East Africa's greatest big-game feats. The book he wrote about it is still in print and is a hunting classic.

This man was John Henry Patterson. The book was *The Man-Eaters of Tsavo*, the tale of the man who saved the Uganda Railway from man-eating lions in 1898.

So how did this hero, a best-selling author, become involved in a scandal that generated the ugliest of campfire gossip? And how did he lose his East African career, and his reputation, because of it?

A great deal of nonsense has been written about John Henry Patterson – some of it by Patterson himself, who was a master of personal misinformation – so that his legend has come totally unstuck from his reality. In the legend, he is a well-to-do gentleman, an educated man (public school and Sandhurst, the British West Point), and above all a "sportsman."

In his legend, he is always Lieutenant Colonel Patterson, and that rank is always assumed to have been earned by his steady climb from his commissioning after Sandhurst. The legend assumes

15

that he was a military engineer, thus explaining his working on the Uganda Railway long enough to kill the lions before dashing off to volunteer for the Boer War.

In fact, Patterson was none of these things. He was not wealthy; he was not a Sandhurst graduate; he was not a British Army lieutenant colonel (not until World War I, at any rate); and he was not what the British then called a gentleman.

In fact, John Henry Patterson enlisted as a private in the British Army in 1885, after quitting his job as a groom in somebody's stable. He later gave so many versions of his birth date and place that it is impossible to pin them down, but he was probably 16 or so in 1885, an emaciated Irish kid with a first-rate mind, incredible courage and no future.

The Army became his mother and father – and his school. In 1886 he shipped for India, where he spent the next eight years with the Third Dragoon Guards. All the education he ever got was in the Army – the first and second class certificates of education, Lower Standard Hindustani, the sub-engineer's certificate. (Sorry – no Sandhurst.) He rose to the rank of sergeant and moved to the "unattached list," meaning that he served a civilian Indian department (railways) while remaining in the military. In 1897 he left the Army and signed on with the Uganda Railway as a junior assistant engineer, thus making his appointment with the lions and fame at Tsavo.

There is no question that he killed the lions, or that he did so heroically, if fairly stupidly. (He knew nothing about lion hunting and had virtually no help – he should have been killed.)

He left the railway in a fit of pique, forfeiting the cost of his passage both out and back, and returned to London to find himself in 1899 with a wife, no job and no prospects. He asked for his railway job back and was refused.

Then the Boer War crooked its finger at him.

Somehow – we shall never know how – Patterson got himself a commission in the gentlemanly Yeomanry. (Rather like an upper-class version of our National Guard, it became the Imperial Yeomanry when it served outside Britain. The Initials I.Y. were said by regulars to stand for "I Yield," although this was certainly not true in Patterson's case.) He must by then have talked like a gent and dressed like a gent; well, if it talks like one and walks like one . . .

In 18 months he rose from lieutenant to acting lieutenant-colonel of Yeomanry (not of the British Army), had his own command, and was awarded the D.S.O. for heroism. (You have to smile at the image of this former sergeant of dragoons leading a cavalry regiment made up of gentleman riders.) After the war ended he was an honorary lieutenant-colonel, with the permanent rank of captain, later major.

And then the legend began. From this point, Patterson reinvented his past to match the man he had become. Ireland faded further and further away in a romantic mist (he once gave his birthplace as London); his parentage took on more gloss (his death certificate lists his father's occupation as "general"); and through his new friends in the Yeomanry, he rose to a new position. This included, in 1907, his appointment as the Senior Game Ranger (warden) of the East Africa Protectorate – more or less modern Kenya.

In 1908, after only a couple months in his new position in Africa, Patterson organized a big safari to go into the unexplored country 300 miles north of Nairobi. His mission was to lay out a new eastern boundary for the Northern Game Reserve, which at that time filled most of modern Kenya's northern region. The area was inhospitable, mostly semi-desert; the route to it was lined by tribes still hostile to the British; and just to the north lay Abyssinia, home to large bands of heavily armed and quite ruthless raiders.

So Patterson invited two London friends to go along.

One of them was a woman.

J ames Audley Blyth was the younger son of Lord Blyth, one of the heirs to the Gilbey liquor fortune. Young Blyth had been an officer in Patterson's peacetime Yeomanry outfit, a Boer War veteran and a passionate horse breeder.

Ethel Jane Brunner Blyth was the daughter of Sir John Tomlinson Brunner, a self-made millionaire and a staunch financial supporter of the Liberal Party, then in power. Ethel (Effie) Jane was in her late 20s, wealthy in her own right, willful, handsome if not beautiful.

The Blyths had one child, which they left in England. They no doubt seemed a happy enough aristocratic couple; however, there was a worm in the rose, one that Patterson did not apparently know about: James was an alcoholic. Perhaps this East African safari was meant to dry him out (he had reportedly been hospitalized with d.t.'s not long before.) Perhaps it signaled an attempt to repair damage done to his marriage by his drinking. Whatever the goal, the safari became a recipe for disaster.

They set out from Nairobi in February, 1908. Patterson led on a gorgeous white Arabian, Abdullah, followed by his old dog, Lurcher. The Blyths were horse people and also rode. (One of the affinities between Patterson and Effie Blyth was their love of horses – his, of course, began when he was a groom. Another affinity was Effie's money, which she had and Patterson almost certainly desired.) They went north, then west to avoid the hostile areas, hunting a little as they went. James wrote a letter home, describing the terror of tracking a lion in grass higher than his head, moving with the safety off the double rifle, not knowing where the animal was.

Effie Blyth was the star of the safari. She turned out to be a brilliant shot who had no trouble handling a .450 express. The Samburu warriors, those gorgeous "butterflies" as the Masai call them, who prize carefully done hair, were stunned by Effie's long brown braids and eagerly touched her hair. Effie, wearing breeches like a man (most women in East Africa still hunted in skirts), rode and shot and dazzled.

And then James Audley Blyth got sick. First, he injured a foot; it healed over, abscessed, burst. He had to be carried on a litter. Effie and Patterson rode on ahead – together. James would get better for a day or two and totter around, even riding now and again, then he would sweat and shake, and they would have to carry him again. He probably got malaria at some point; his alcohol-weakened immune system staggered under the twin blows of the abscess and disease.

The safari had by then turned east and north and reached the Ewaso Nyiro River. Patterson led them along the river to Neumann's Camp (about where Samburu Lodge is now), where the elephant hunter Alfred Neumann had his base until his suicide two years before. There, Effie got sick and the dog Lurcher died. Patterson, in the dumps, tended to both Blyths – in their tent or in his own (who knows, perhaps he dreamed of a different arrangement).

Effie improved, and they went on. Twice, they discussed sending James back. But now they were so far way from any European contact that it was impossible to send this sick Englishman, who spoke no African languages, off by himself. Patterson may, in fact, have tried to make Blyth go back, leaving himself alone with Effie; surviving accounts are ambiguous on the point. The upshot was that all three of them went on, with an inevitable result.

Their rendezvous with tragedy was a place called Laisamis. It still has that name – a broad, gently rising flat surrounded by some shops and one-story buildings, in a rocky desert with a sand *lugga* trickling by and an Italian mission not far away. In 1908 there were no buildings and no missionaries, only some pools of water in the *lugga* and the great nowhere all around.

Two days before they reached Laisamis, they met the elephant. Patterson later said it was a rogue, a male made dangerous by isolation from the herd. James was riding that day, feeling a little better.

The three Europeans got down from their horses. Patterson told Effie to shoot, that it was her elephant – one of the few species she hadn't shot so far. She hit the bull twice with the .450, and it thundered into the bush. The two men went after it on foot while Effie stayed with the horses and the safari – a curious bit of sexism, as she would have been a far better companion in a tough situation than the sick Blyth. But by this time, a rivalry based on class and money and military rank may have developed between the two men, and Blyth may well have realized he was now competing for his own wife. So he took the express rifle and set out.

Then they met the elephant and Patterson hit it twice with his Martini-Henry, then sent Blyth back to camp and went after the elephant alone. The next hour was perilous confusion as Patterson tracked the elephant, while the elephant tracked the safari. The natives told Effie that Patterson had been killed by the bull; Patterson was told Effie had been killed, and when he at last caught up with the beast, it was anticlimactically dead from its wounds.

The only real victim of the elephant was Patterson's prized Arabian. In one of its charges, the bull had put a tusk through the horse's vitals.

That night the two men had a shouting argument, which Effie mediated. The ostensible subject was, apparently, the elephant's tusks: Patterson evidently wanted one as repayment for Abdullah. The real subject, not spoken, was nearer the heart and the loins.

But they patched it over and went on to Laisamis, where Blyth went out hunting and collapsed. Delirious and unable to stand, he was put to bed in his tent.

Effie spent that night – her first – in Patterson's tent.

In the morning Patterson exchanged a few civil words with James Blyth and then went to the center of the camp to oversee the loading. (There is no dispute on where he was.) Effie Blyth got up, dressed and crossed from Patterson's tent to her husband's.

After that, conflicting testimony, gossip and speculation take over. Two things happened for sure, but people differ about which happened first: Effie screamed, and a gun went off. She may have actually been in the tent, or she may have been in the doorway. And she may have exchanged a few words with her husband.

Then Effie ran from the tent, and Patterson along with his headman and the porters rushed in to find James Audley Blyth with a gaping wound in his head, and a .450 revolver. Later, in Nairobi, the porters all testified that the wound was in the back of Blyth's head, and the gun was in his hand. Patterson, however, first testified that the wound was in the temple, and both he and headman Mwenyakai bin Diwani – who seems to have been the first inside the tent – testified that Patterson picked up the gun and handed it to the headman.

At this point somebody must have put it back in Blyth's hand, because that was where the porters saw it, with the muzzle in the dying man's mouth – unless they somehow saw it the instant before Patterson handed it to the headman. Or perhaps Patterson or Mwenyakai put it back into Blyth's hand so the porters could see the way it had been. At any rate, it seems impossible that a dozen or so porters all saw precisely the same thing and reported it in precisely the same words after only a second or two of looking. Far more likely – hence their use of the same words later – was their being made to see, with somebody (Patterson?) standing there and saying, "See? The point (the word they all used) is in his mouth and his thumb is on the trigger."

At Patterson's direction, they burned all of James Audley Blyth's clothes and papers, and buried him in an intentionally shallow grave.

And Patterson took the safari north, sharing his tent with Effie for the six weeks it took them to get up to Marsabit and back to Nairobi.

T he ensuing scandal stunned Patterson and appalled Effie Blyth. Both left Nairobi after the most cursory of testimony, but they found no haven in London. Communication was good between the Protectorate and England, because many colonists had friends and relatives back home. By the summer Patterson was being accused in private of adultery and murder, with an official accusation of theft of government funds thrown in by the Nairobi administration (with good justification, it appears). The inquest (extra-legal, conducted by a Nairobi magistrate for lack of anybody else) gathered such testimony as it could, but there was no exhumation of the body, no visit to Laisamis, no forensic examination. Ironically, the Northern Game Reserve was outside normal jurisdictions, so there wasn't a legal mechanism for doing police work anyway.

An official verdict of suicide was issued; nonetheless, by the following year, as powerful a person as Winston Churchill was alleged to have said that he knew Patterson was guilty of theft, adultery and murder. (Churchill, undersecretary of the Colonial Office when Patterson was appointed, had made an East African trip just before the event and had friends there.)

Despite public exoneration in the House of Lords in 1909, Patterson had to resign his position, and he never went back to East Africa. Fate touched him again, however, when he took charge of the Jewish Transport Corps at Gallipoli (almost certainly a job given him because he had blotted his copybook). At this command he led the Jewish Legion in Palestine in 1918-19, which resulted in his enshrinement as a hero in modern Israel where his medals and uniforms are now in a museum.

Effie's wealthy father engineered a complete cover-up of her part in both the affair and the death, a whitewash so complete that Lord Crewe, then the colonial secretary, wrote to an acquaintance that he had endangered his immortal soul by lying. (It was Crewe who had to assure the House that no crimes had been committed.) Papa Brunner cut a deal that had Patterson resigning and shutting up about Effie's role in exchange for the official exoneration.

Contrary to what the legend and the gossip later said, Patterson and Effie did not marry. Patterson was an ambitious man, certainly not above dreaming of being Effie's second husband, a millionaire's son-in-law. But it never happened. They did not run away together, as some people have reported since. They probably did not even see each other after 1909.

# AFRICA

But in East Africa, the story survived, so vigorously that in 1934 professional hunter Philip Percival sat one night by the fire with an American client and told the moustached writer the story. And it clicked with Ernest Hemingway's ideas of courage and fidelity, and the tricky interplay between men and women.

Now, Phil Percival was the brother of Blayney, the man who lost his job as head of the game department to Patterson, and so he had good reason to despise Patterson. So it would not be surprising if his version made Patterson the villain. Yet that is not the way Hemingway wrote it: quite the contrary. Hemingway's Wilson, the professional hunter, is the terse arbiter of courage and male morality. Based on Bror Blixen and Phil Percival himself, Wilson is a model Hemingway man. And in making the husband the victim of a gun fired by the wife, Hemingway may have picked up something suggested by Percival – that it was Effie, not Patterson, who shot James Audley Blyth. To do so, however, Percival would have had to be privy either to the official inquest records (not impossible, as the Nairobi government was as porous as a burlap sack) or to gossip from the safari porters themselves. At any rate, Phil Percival passed on the story in a version that allowed Hemingway to make Patterson the moral center.

As to what really happened in those few seconds in the tent at Laisamis, only three people could have known: Effie Blyth, Patterson and the headman Mwenyakai – and they never told. Did Ethel Jane Brunner Blyth step into her husband's tent, raise a revolver and shoot him in the back of the head as he slept? Or did she walk in to find him feverish and raving, a gun in his hand, accusations spilling from a mouth that he himself stopped with the pistol barrel and the shot?

We shall never know. One tantalizing fact persists: a year after the public whitewash, Patterson still had a sword to dangle over Papa Brunner's head, one that caused Lord Crewe to refer to him as "dangerous" and ultimately to warn him off. This threat could have been merely the facts of his and Effie's affair. Or it could have been a fact that only Patterson and Mwenyakai knew – the location of the pistol when they entered the tent.

The Irish groom, the honorary lieutenant-colonel, the hero of Tsavo, died in Los Angeles in 1947, taking his threats and his secrets with him.

## THE STORY CONTINUES

Patterson's killing of the man-eating lions is told in *The Man-Eaters of Tsavo* (1907). His very biased version of the events surrounding Blyth's death are in his *The Lure of the Nyika* (1909). The story has been told in other versions than Hemingway's, including Francis Brett Young's novel, *Woodsmoke* (1924), and J.A. *Hunter's Hunter* (1952), where Hunter made the connection with the Hemingway short story but named no names.

The killing of the lions was the basis of the movie *Bwana Devil* (1953). A version of Patterson's work on the Uganda Railway inspired the 1959 film, *Killers of Kilimanjaro*.

The existing records of the actual events surrounding the Patterson-Blyth safari are scattered through a number of archives, including Britain's public Records Office, half a dozen British universities, and the Library of Congress in Washington, DC.

# GREAT ADVENTURE

*On March 23, 1909, Theodore Roosevelt and his son Kermit began the most fantastic safari ever attempted. For 11 months they hunted across east Africa, collecting specimens for the Smithsonian Institution's National Museum and enjoying the outdoor adventure of a lifetime.*

*By Peggy Robbins*

Well-known African explorer-hunter Carl Akeley, a contemporary of Theodore Roosevelt, had a simple answer as to why Roosevelt's African expedition was so enormously more successful than the expeditions of other hunters. "Few men," said Akeley, "could get so much out of a trip to Africa as Roosevelt could because few men could take so much to it." Indeed, the ex-president took with him a lifetime's experience as a hunter and practicing naturalist; he took an immense knowledge of Africa and its wildlife acquired from intensive book-study and from the personal counseling of hunters noted for their African safaris; he took the greatest amount of the best equipment ever assembled for such a venture; he took men superbly qualified to manage various phases of the expedition; and he took his own indomitable spirit, very alert mind and tremendous curiosity.

Long before Theodore Roosevelt's second term as president ended

# AFRICA

in March 1909, he decided to take a hunting trip through Africa as soon as he was free to do so. More than a year before he left the presidency, he wrote a friend: "I am already looking away from politics and toward Africa . . . I do not want to take the African trip as a mere holiday . . . I shall go on a regular scientific trip, with professional field taxidermists to cure the trophies and arrange for their transport back to this country."

About the same time, he wrote a famous British big game hunter, John Henry Patterson, for advice about the trip: "I shall be fifty years old . . . But I am fairly healthy and willing to work in order to get into good game country . . . Now, is it imposing too much on your good nature to tell me where I ought to go to get really good shooting?" Patterson complied.

On every possible occasion during 1908, Roosevelt invited to the White House men who had hunted or traveled on the "Dark Continent," and in so doing acquired information and advice from the leading African explorers of the era. By June 1908 he had worked out an itinerary that would cover about a year. He asked 18-year-old Kermit, his second son, if he'd like to take a leave of absence from Harvard the next year to make the trip. Kermit was delighted at the prospect. (Each of Roosevelt's four sons was introduced to hunting and wilderness life by their father, and each developed into a skillful hunter.)

The President engaged in intensive correspondence related to the acquisition of equipment and clothing, including "leather stockings, spine pads, wool socks, sun helmets, mosquito nets, hunting knives, waterproof matchboxes, compasses, portable bathtubs." Roosevelt's main outfits included heavy hobnailed shoes, tan army shirts and khaki trousers with leather-faced knees. One important decision was how many spectacles to carry. Through the years he had been having increasing trouble with his eyes, and from early 1908 on was almost blind in his left eye – a condition he did everything possible to keep secret until after the safari. He took nine pairs of glasses on the African trip.

Another decision was how much liquor to take. "I do not believe in drinking while on a trip of this kind," he wrote one of the men helping him with preparations. "I wish to take only the minimum amount of whiskey and champagne, which would be necessary in the event of sickness." During 11 months on safari he drank only six ounces of alcohol.

Both Roosevelt and Kermit gave grave consideration to selecting firearms for the safari. The father wrote his son: "I think I shall get a double-barrelled .450 cordite, but shall expect to use almost all the time my Springfield and my .45-70 Winchester. I shall want you to have a first-class rifle, perhaps one of the powerful new model 40 or 45 Winchesters. It would be a good thing to have a 12-bore shotgun that could be used with solid ball. You should also have a spare rifle . . . We would thus have four rifles and the shotgun between us . . . It is no child's play going after lion, elephant, rhino and buffalo. We must be very cautious; and we must always be ready to back one another up . . ."

Roosevelt wrote later: "My rifles were an army Springfield, 30-calibre, stocked and sighted to suit myself; a Winchester 405; and a double-barrelled 500-450 Holland, a beautiful weapon presented to me by some English friends. Kermit's battery was of the same type, except that instead of a Springfield he had another Winchester shooting the army ammunition, and his double-barrel was a Rigby. In addition, I had a Fox No. 12 shotgun; no better gun was ever made."

Roosevelt never went anywhere without taking selected books with him. Months before the African trip he made a list of about 60 titles, varying from the *Bible* to Poe and Mark Twain, which he wished to take "into the jungles of Africa." His sister, Corinne Robinson, had copies of all trimmed down, bound in pigskin, and packed in a specially constructed aluminum-and-oilcloth case. Roosevelt's "Pigskin Library" was a topic of much discussion in the America press – as was everything that leaked out about the president's forthcoming expedition. One newspaper editorial went too far as to tastelessly suggest that, considering the exciting life Roosevelt had already enjoyed, it would be appropriate for him to "meet his Maker" in some sensational manner in the wilds of Africa. The President thought that very amusing; his wife Edith did not.

In June 1908 Roosevelt conceived the idea of seeking sponsorship by the Smithsonian Institution's National Museum and wrote to Charles D. Walcott, secretary of the Smithsonian: "Now it seems to me that this opens up the best chance for the National Museum to get a fine collection, not only of the big-game beasts, but of the smaller animals and birds of Africa . . . I shall make arrangements in connection with publishing a book which will enable me to pay for the expenses of myself and my son. But I would like to get one or two professional field taxidermists, field naturalists, to go with us, who should prepare and send back the specimens we collect . . ."

Walcott, knowing how very poor the Museum's African zoological and botanical collections were, enthusiastically agreed. The Smithsonian selected Dr. Edgar Mearns, a U.S. Army naturalist, to accompany Roosevelt and agreed that Edmund Heller, a 26-year-old University of

# AFRICA

California professor chosen by Roosevelt, and naturalist Alden Loring of Owego, New York, would be Mearns' assistants. All were capable taxidermists. Arrangements were made so that funds for the three-man Smithsonian contingent would be supplied by private donations, with Andrew Carnegie the largest contributor. Roosevelt made an agreement with the scientists that no other member of the expedition was to do any writing whatsoever about it until his own accounts had been published.

He had no difficulty covering the expenses for himself and his son. Scribner's offered him $25,000 for a series of magazine articles to be sent from Africa, with the understanding they would later be published as a book. Before the President has time to accept, *Collier's* offered $50,000 and McClure's $60,000. He preferred *Scribner's*, which had published much of his earlier work; he asked *Scribner's* to up its bid to $50,000 and, when *Scribner's* agreed, signed a contract with the publisher, even though *Collier's* had raised its offer to $100,000.

Roosevelt became furious in late 1908 when he learned that certain reporters were trying to make arrangements to accompany him and send back dispatches. He fired off a letter to the Associated Press: It would be, he stated, "an indefensible wrong, a gross impropriety," to attempt any interference with his privacy; it would be "a wanton outrage" for any publication to make reports on his travels through Africa because such would adversely affect his "individual pleasure and profit." He issued a public statement pointing out that, at the time of the safari, he would be an ex-president, not a president, and that as such he demanded privacy. He assured the public that any statements attributed to him during his absence would be false. Roosevelt told his military aide, Archie Butt, that, if a certain newspaper man caught up with him in Africa for even a minute, his report of expenses to the National Museum would include: "Five hundred dollars for furnishing wine to cannibal chiefs with which to wash down a reporter of the *New York Evening Post*."

Months later, while he was inland in Africa, he became friendly with two wire service reporters who assisted him with mail and in editing his articles, and he allowed them to follow the expedition.

Many of Roosevelt's friends pleaded with him not to make the trip, with most basing their arguments on the much-publicized danger of deadly African sleeping sickness. Colonel Cecil Lyon, who had hunted with Roosevelt in the West, voiced a different opinion, however: "They don't know the Colonel. He may be in danger of wildebeests, rhinoceri, dik-diks, lions or snakes, but no one who ever saw him hunting would believe that sleeping sickness could ever catch up with him. *That* man's immune from that disease."

Roosevelt and Kermit had passage booked for Italy on the *Hamburg*, to leave from Hoboken, New Jersey, on March 23, 1909. By sailing date, Roosevelt had been ex-president less than three weeks; he was now, at his choosing, "Colonel Roosevelt," most often called simply, "The Colonel." He spent most of March 22 supervising the delivery and loading of the expedition's baggage – about 200 cases, each six by four feet, and each stamped, "Theodore Roosevelt, Mombasa, British East Africa."

At Roosevelt's direction, each of the food boxes contained, in addition to provisions endorsed by experienced African hunters, cans of Boston baked beans, California peaches, and tomatoes. An idea of the naturalists' equipment and supplies may be acquired from the fact that they included four tons of fine salt for curing skins.

The Colonel received many parting gifts, but none pleased him more than the last three: a small gold ruler with a concealed pencil in one end from the new president, inscribed, "Theodore Roosevelt from William Howard Taft – Good-bye, Good Luck and a Safe Return," delivered along with a personal letter from Taft by Archie Butt; a plaster cast of an elephant's head, marked for proper shooting, from Carl Akeley; and a rabbit's foot from John L. Sullivan.

The *Hamburg* pulled away from the pier, to be escorted across the harbor by a flotilla of gaily decorated vessels, while an enormous crowd cheered, flags waved and a band played *The Star-Spangled Banner*. Roosevelt, wearing an olive drab military uniform bearing a colonel's insignia and a military overcoat, stood on deck smiling and saluting with his beloved black slouch hat.

In Naples the Roosevelts transferred to another German ship, the *Admiral*. They crossed the Mediterranean to Port Said, steamed through the Suez Canal and on to Aden by way of the Red Sea. They continued on the Indian Ocean and followed the African coast to Mombasa, arriving there on April 21.

Arrangements for the hunt had been made through two of Roosevelt's English friends who were famous big game hunters: Frederick C. Selous and Edward N. Buxton. Selous had joined Roosevelt in Naples and was with the safari in Africa from time to time. The services of two long-time African residents, Scotsman R. J. Cuninghame and Australian Leslie

# AFRICA

Tarlton, also noted hunters, had been secured to assist on the entire safari; Cuninghame met the Roosevelts and Selous at Mombasa, and Tarlton awaited them in the interior.

The Colonel appreciated the warm welcome from the lieutenant-governor of British East Africa, but he was anxious to leave for the interior and did so the following day on the railroad that ran inland. So fascinated was he by the wildlife along the route that he spent the daylight hours perched on a seat built across the locomotive's cowcatcher, enjoying the slow ride through country that was "a very paradise for a naturalist."

At the little station of Kapiti Plains, 300 miles inland and a two-day trip from Mombasa, the safari and Tarlton awaited the Roosevelts. It was there, said the Colonel, that his "Great Adventure" *really* began. "As we drew up at the station," he wrote, "the array of porters and tents looked as if some small military expedition was about to start . . . A large American flag was floating over my own tent; and in the front line, flanking this tent on either hand, were other big tents for the members of the party, with a dining tent and skinning tent; while behind were the tents of the two hundred porters, the gunbearers, the tent boys, the *askaris* or native soldiers, and the horse boys or *saises* (All those numbered about 60, in addition to the porters.) In front of the tents stood the men in two lines; the first containing the 15 *askaris*, the second the porters with their headmen. The askaris were uniformed, each in a red fez, a blue blouse, and white knickerbockers, and each carrying his rifle and belt. The porters were chosen from several different tribes to minimize the danger of combination in the event of mutiny."

From Kapiti Plains the safari moved eastward, hunting along the way – zebra, wildebeest, hartebeest, gazelles, duiker, impala, reedbuck, steinbuck and dik-dik. Roosevelt has specified while planning the trip that it would "not be a game-butchering excursion, but instead a scientific expedition;" no animals would be shot except those needed for museum specimens or food; and that rule was followed. Except for a very few trophies kept by the Roosevelts, all ended up in the National Museum. The enormous job of preparing skins and bones for shipment to America continued constantly. As the safari moved, the Roosevelts and their companions, on horses, were followed by the long line of burdened porters and four huge, heavily loaded ox wagons, each drawn by a span of seven or eight yoke of the native, humped cattle. The Colonel had as personal attendants two gun-bearers, two "horse boys" and two "tent boys."

By the first of June the Roosevelts had reached Nairobi. There the naturalists made the first shipment of specimens to the United States and Roosevelt sent *Scribner's* the first four of the 14 articles he would write during the safari. The articles, varying in length from 5,000 to 15,000 words, were published in monthly installments beginning in October 1909. They covered everything from his encounters with dangerous big game animals to the "golden joys" of seeing and studying the brightly hued birds, butterflies and flowers.

At night, regardless of how tired he was from strenuous riding and hunting, the Colonel sat on a stool at his portable writing desk and, with a flickering lamp his only light, recorded the events and observations of the day. He had to wear a face shield of netting and gauntlets as protection from mosquitoes.

Kermit recalled later, "Father was invariably good-humored about it, saying that he was paying for his fun."

Roosevelt made three copies of each completed article. Keeping one, he sent the other two in blue canvas envelopes, by two different routes, to points from where they were sent on to *Scribner's*.

For six months the safari kept its main headquarters in Nairobi, but made extended trips in all directions to seek specific animals. Before embarking for Africa, Roosevelt had made a list of 21 animals he most wished to shoot: lion, elephant, rhino, buffalo, giraffe, hippo, eland, sable, kudu, oryx, roan, wildebeest, hartebeest, waterbuck, warthog, zebra, pallah, Grant's gazelle, bushbuck, reedbuck and topi. Before the safari was over he would bag them all – and others. Kermit had done nearly as well. Roosevelt wrote his oldest son, Theodore, Jr., that Kermit had developed into a splendid hunting companion, "a perfectly cool and daring fellow . . . a bold, skillful rider, always fearless and eager to work." That very day the boy had stopped a charging leopard at six yards, after the animal had mauled a porter.

The safari moved from Nairobi deeper into the interior, hunting in the Lake Victoria region and then farther north. On Christmas the Roosevelts were on the 160-mile overland trek from Victoria to Lake Albert Nyanza, which they reached on January 5, 1910. The remaining two months of their African travels were spent in successful pursuit of the huge, rare, square-mouthed or "white" rhinoceros in the wild, uninhabited Lado country on the White Nile and the giant eland in the Congo. They continued northward on the Nile and reached Khartoum on March 14, where the already greatly reduced expedition was disbanded. The Colonel and Kermit were met by Mrs. Roosevelt and daughter Ethel.

Theodore Roosevelt returned home in June to be honored by the greatest welcome New York had ever bestowed upon a native son. His African expedition had been an unqualified success; it had brought out of Africa a much greater and far more valuable collection than any other expedition and enriched the National Museum with more than 11,000 specimens – 4,897 mammals, 4,000 birds, 500 fishes and 2,000 reptiles. In addition, it had brought thousands of insects, shells and plants, and a great quantity of zoological, botanical and anthropological knowledge. Many of the species were new to science. Roosevelt had said, "I want Uncle Sam to have a better African collection than anybody else." He accomplished his purpose.

Roosevelt's score for the safari was 296 head of big game, including nine lions, eight elephants, 13 rhinoceros and six buffaloes; Kermit's was 216, including eight lions, three elephants, seven rhinoceros, four buffaloes, three leopards and two bongos.

His collected articles were published in the fall of 1910 as a book, *African Game Trails, An Account of the African Wanderings of an American Hunter-Naturalist*. It was dedicated to Kermit, "My Side-Partner in our 'Great Adventure.'" The *New York Tribune* called it "the book of the year"; the *Chicago Record-Herald* said it was the very best of outdoor literature, with "action, adventure, the excitement of the chase, and . . . stirs the imagination on every page"; and the *National Geographic*, in a six-page review, praised it as "an unusual contribution to science, geography, literature, and adventure." An immediate best-seller, it is still regarded as a hunting classic.

### AFRICAN GAME TRAILS

"The chase of the elephant," Roosevelt wrote in his *African Game Trails*, "entails more fatigue and hardship than any other kind of African hunting." He ranked the elephant hunting as slightly less dangerous than lion hunting, "though it makes far greater demands on the qualities of personal endurance and hardihood and resolute perseverance." He told of shooting his first elephant in August 1909, after days of pushing on foot through a mountainside forest in the rain, accompanied by fellow hunters, guides, and gun bearers:

*At last we came in sight of the mighty game. The trail took a twist to one side, and there, thirty yards in front of us, we made out part of the gray and massive head of an elephant resting his tusks on the branches of a young tree . . . We saw it was a big bull with good ivory. It turned its head in my direction and I saw its eyes; and I fired a little to one side of the eye, at a spot which I thought would lead to the brain. I struck exactly where I aimed, but the head of an elephant is enormous and the brain small, and the bullet missed it. However, the shock momentarily stunned the beast. He stumbled forward, half falling, and as he recovered I fired with the second barrel, again aiming for the brain. This time the bullet sped true, and as I lowered the rifle from my shoulder, I saw the great lord of the forest come crashing to the ground.*

*But at that very instant, before there was a moment's time in which to reload, the thick bushes parted immediately on my left front, and through them surged the vast bulk of a charging bull elephant, the matted mass of tough creepers snapping like packthread before his rush. He was so close that he could have touched me with his trunk. I leaped to one side and dodged behind a tree trunk, opening the rifle, throwing out the empty shells, and slipping in two cartridges. Meanwhile Cuninghame fired right and left, at the same time throwing himself into the bushes on the other side. Both his bullets went home, and the bull stopped short in his charge, wheeled, and immediately disappeared in the thick cover. We ran forward, but the forest had closed over his wake. We heard him trumpet shrilly, and then all sounds ceased.*

*. . . If we had been only after ivory we should have followed him at once; but there was no telling how long a chase he might lead us; and as we desired to save the skin of the dead elephant entire, there was no time whatever to spare . . . If the skin is to be properly saved, it must be taken off without an hour's unnecessary delay.*

*I felt proud indeed as I stood by the immense bulk of the slain monster and put my hand on the ivory. The tusks weighed a hundred and thirty pounds the pair . . .*

# Ring of Spears

*Theodore Roosevelt's grandest adventure was his year-long
safari in Africa shortly after his second term as president. Here,
we join Teddy's safari along the 'Nzoi River near the base of
Kenya's Mount Elgon. What ensues is vintage Roosevelt – his
observations of Africa's incredible natural diversity, an exciting
elephant hunt, and finally an eyewitness account of Nandi
warriors on a daring spear hunt for lions.*

By Theodore Roosevelt

The next day we moved camp to the edge of a swamp about
five miles from the river. Near the tents was one of the trees
which, not knowing its real name, we called "sausage-tree;"
the seeds or fruits are encased in a kind of hard gourd, the
size of a giant sausage, which swings loosely at the end
of a long tendril. The swamp was half or three-quarters
of a mile across, with one or two ponds in the middle,
from which we shot ducks. Francolins – delicious eating,
as the ducks were also – uttered their grating calls nearby; while oribi
and hartebeest were usually to be seen from the tents. The hartebeest,
by the way, in its three forms, is much the commonest game animal of
East Africa.

A few miles beyond this swamp we suddenly came on a small herd of
elephants in the open. There were eight cows and two calves, and they
were moving slowly, feeding on the thorny tops of the scattered mimosas,
and of other bushes which were thornless. The eyesight of elephants is
very bad; I doubt whether they see more than a rather near-sighted man;
and we walked up to within 70 yards of these, slight though the cover

was, so that Kermit could try to photograph them. We did not need to kill another cow for the National museum, and so after we had looked at the huge, interesting creatures as long as we wished, we croaked and whistled, and they moved off with leisurely indifference.

There is always a fascination about watching elephants; they are such giants, they are so intelligent – much more so than any other game, except perhaps the lion, whose intelligence has a very sinister bent – and they look so odd with their great ears flapping and their trunks lifting and curling. Elephants are rarely absolutely still for any length of time; now and then they flap an ear, or their bodies sway slightly, while at intervals they utter curious internal rumblings, or trumpet gently. These were feeding on saplings of the mimosas and other trees, apparently caring nothing for the thorns of the former; they would tear off branches, big or little, or snap a trunk short off if the whim seized them. They swallowed the leaves and twigs of these trees; but I have known them to merely chew and spit out the stems of certain bushes.

After leaving the elephants we were on our way back to camp when we saw a white man in the trail ahead; and on coming nearer whom should it prove to be but Carl Akeley; who was out on a trip for the American Museum of Natural History in New York. We went with him to his camp, where we found Mrs. Akeley, Clark, who was assisting him, and Messrs. McCutcheon and Stevenson who were along on a hunting trip. They were old friends and I was very glad to see them.

A year previously Mr. and Mrs. Akeley had lunched with me at the White House, and we had talked over our proposed African trips. Akeley, an old African wanderer, was going out with the especial purpose of getting a group of elephants for the American Museum, and was anxious that I should shoot one or two of them for him. I had told him that I certainly would if it were a possibility; and on learning that we had just seen a herd of cows he felt – as I did – that the chance had come for me to fulfill my promise. So we decided that he should camp with us that night, and that next morning we would start with a light outfit to see whether we could not overtake the herd.

An amusing incident occurred that evening. After dark some of the porters went through the reeds to get water from the pond in the middle of the swamp. I was sitting in my tent when a loud yelling and screaming rose from the swamp, and in rushed Kongoni to say that one of the men, while drawing water, had been seized by a lion. Snatching up a rifle I was off at a run for the swamp, calling for lanterns; Kermit and Tarlton joined me, the lanterns were brought, and we reached the meadow of short marsh grass which surrounded the high reeds in the middle. No sooner were we on this meadow than there were loud snortings in the darkness ahead of us, and then the sound of a heavy animal galloping across our front. It now developed that there was no lion in the case at all, but that the porters had been chased by a hippo. I should not have supposed that a hippo would live in such a small, isolated swamp; but there he was on the meadow in front of me, invisible, but snorting, and galloping to and fro. Evidently he was much interested in the lights, and we thought he might charge us; but he did not, retreating slowly as we advanced, until he plunged into the little pond.

Hippos are sometimes dangerous at night, and so we waded through the swamp until we came to the pool at which the porters filled their buckets, and stood guard over them until they were through; while the hippo, unseen in the darkness, came closer to us, snorting and plunging – possibly from wrath and insolence, but more probably from mere curiosity.

Next morning Akeley, Tarlton, Kermit and I started on our elephant hunt. We were traveling light. I took nothing but my bedding, wash kit, spare socks and slippers, all in a roll of waterproof canvas. We went to where we had seen the herd and then took up the trail, Kongoni and two or three other gun-bearers walking ahead as trackers. They did their work well. The elephants had not been in the least alarmed. Where they had walked in single file it was easy to follow their trail, but the trackers had hard work puzzling it out where the animals had scattered out and loitered along feeding. The trail led up and down hills and through open thorn scrub, and it crossed and recrossed the wooded watercourses in the bottoms of the valleys. At last, after going some ten miles we came on sign where the elephants had fed that morning, and four or five miles further on we overtook them. That we did not scare them into flight was due to Tarlton. The trail went nearly across wind; the trackers were leading us swiftly along it, when suddenly Tarlton heard a low trumpet ahead and to the right hand. We at once doubled back, left the horses, and advanced toward where the noise indicated that the herd was standing.

In a couple of minutes we sighted them. It was just noon. There were six cows, and two well-grown calves – these last being quite big enough to shift for themselves or to be awkward antagonists for any man of whom they could get hold. They stood in a clump, each occasionally shifting its position or lazily flapping an ear; and now and then one would break off a branch with its trunk, tuck it into its mouth, and withdraw it stripped of its leaves. The wind blew fair, we were careful to make no noise, and with ordinary caution we had nothing to fear from their eyesight. The ground was neither forest nor bare plain; it was covered with long grass and a scattered open growth of small, scantily leaved trees, chiefly mimosas, but including some trees covered with gorgeous orange-red flowers. After careful scrutiny we advanced behind an anthill to with in 60 yards, and I stepped forward for the shot.

Akeley wished two cows and a calf. Of the two best cows one had rather thick, worn tusks; those of the other were smaller, but better shaped. The latter stood half facing me, and I put the bullet from the right barrel of the Holland through her lungs, and fired the left barrel for the heart of the other. Tarlton, and then Akeley and Kermit followed suit. At once the herd started diagonally past us, but half halted and faced toward us when only 25 yards distant, an unwounded cow beginning to advance with her great ears cocked at right angles to her head; and Tarlton called "Look out; they are coming for us." At such distance a charge from half a dozen elephant is a serious thing; I put a bullet into the forehead of the advancing cow, causing her to lurch heavily forward to her knees; and then we all fired. The heavy rifles were too much even for such big beasts, and round they spun and rushed off. As they turned I dropped the second cow I had wounded with a shot in the brain, and the cow that had started to charge also fell, though it needed two or three more shots to keep it down as it struggled to rise. The cow at which I had fired kept on with the rest of the herd, but fell dead before going a hundred yards.

After we had turned the herd, Kermit with his Winchester killed a bull calf, necessary to complete the museum group; we had been unable to kill it before because we were too busy stopping the charge of the cows. I was sorry to have to shoot the third cow, but with elephant starting to charge at 25 yards, the risk is too great, and the need of instant action too imperative, to allow of any hesitation.

We pitched camp a hundred yards from the elephants, and Akeley, working like a demon, and assisted by Tarlton, had the skins off the two biggest cows and the calf by the time night fell. I walked out and shot an oribi for supper. Soon after dark the hyenas began to gather at the carcasses and to quarrel among themselves as they gorged. Toward morning, a lion came near and uttered a kind of booming, long-drawn moan, an ominous and menacing sound. The hyenas answered with an extraordinary chorus of yelling, howling, laughing and chuckling, as weird a volume of noise as any to which I ever listened.

At dawn we stole down to the carcasses in the faint hope of a shot at the lion. However, he was not here; but as we came toward one carcass a hyena raised its head seemingly from beside the elephant's belly, and I brained it with the little Springfield. On walking up it appeared that I need not have shot at all. The hyena, which was swollen with elephant meat, had gotten inside the huge body, and had then bitten a hole through the abdominal wall of rough muscle and thrust his head through. The wedge-shaped head had slipped through the hole all right, but the muscle had then contracted, and the hyena was fairly caught, with its body inside the elephant's belly, and its head thrust out through the hole. We took several photos of the beast in its queer trap.

After breakfast we rode back to our camp by the swamp. Akeley and Clark were working hard at the elephant skins, but Mrs. Akeley, Stevenson and McCutcheon took lunch with us at our camp. They had been having a very successful hunt; Mrs. Akeley had to her credit a fine maned lion and a bull elephant with enormous tusks.

From the 'Nzoi we made a couple days' march to Lake Sergoi, which we had passed on our way out; a reed-fringed pond, surrounded by rocky hills which marked about the limit to which the Boer and English settlers who were taking up the country had spread. All along our route we encountered herds of game; sometimes the herd would be of only one species; at other times we would come across a great mixed herd, the red hartebeest always predominating; while among them might be zebras, showing silvery white or dark gray in the distance, topis with beautifully colored coats, and even waterbuck. We shot what hartebeests, topis and oribis were needed for food.

All over the uplands we came on the remains of a race of which even the memory has long since vanished. These remains consist of large, nearly circular walls of stones, which are sometimes roughly squared. A few of these circular enclosures contained more than one chamber. Many of them, at least, are not cattle kraals, being too small, and built round hollows; the walls are so low that by themselves they could not serve for shelter or defense, and must probably have been used as supports for roofs of timber or skins. They were certainly built by people who were in some respects more advanced that the savage tribes who now dwell in the land; but the grass grows thick on the earth mounds into which the ancient stone walls are slowly crumbling, and nor a trace of the builders remains. Barbarians they doubtless were; but they have been engulfed in the black oblivion of a lower barbarism, and not the smallest tradition lingers to tell of their craft or their cruelty, their industry or prowess, or to give us the least hint as to the race from which they sprang.

We had with us an ox wagon with the regulation span of 16 oxen, the driver being a young colonial Englishman from South Africa – for the Dutch and English Africanders are the best ox-wagon drivers in the world. On the way back to Sergoi he lost his oxen, which were probably run off by some savages from the mountains; so at Sergoi we had to hire another ox wagon, the South African who drove it being a Dutchman named Botha. Sergoi was as yet the limit of settlement; but it was evident that the whole Uasin Gishu country would soon be occupied. Already many Boers from South Africa, and a number of English Africanders, had come in; and no better pioneers exist today than these South Africans, both Dutch and English. Both are so good that I earnestly hope they will becomes indissolubly welded into one people; and the Dutch Boer has the supreme merit of preferring the country to the town and of bringing his wife and children – plenty of children – with him to settle on the land. The homemaker is the only type of settler of permanent value; and the cool, healthy, fertile Uasin Gishu region is an ideal land for the right kind of pioneer home-maker, whether he hopes to make his living by raising stock or by growing crops.

A t Sergoi Lake there is a store kept by Mr. Kirke, a South African of Scotch blood. With a kind courtesy, which I cannot too highly appreciate, he with the equally cordial help of another settler, Mr. Skally – also a South African, but of Irish birth – and of the district commissioner, Mr. Corbett, had arranged for a party of Nandi warriors to come over and show me how they hunted the lion.

The Nandi are a warlike pastoral tribe, close kin to the Masai in blood and tongue, in weapons and in manner of life. They have long been accustomed to kill lions which become man-eaters or which molest their cattle overmuch; and the peace which British rule has imposed upon them – a peace so welcome to the weaker, so irksome to the predatory, tribes – has left lion killing one of the few pursuits in which glory can be won by a young warrior. When it was told them that if they wished they could come to hunt lions at Sergoi 800 warriors volunteered, and much heart-burning was caused in choosing the 60 or 70 who were allowed the privilege. They stipulated, however, that they should not be used merely as beaters, but should kill the lions themselves, and refused to come unless with this understanding.

The day before we reached Sergoi they had gone out, and had killed a lion and lioness; the beasts were put up from a small covert and dispatched with heavy throwing spears on the instant, before they offered, or indeed had the chance to offer, any resistance. The day after our arrival there was mist and cold rain, and we found no lions. Next day, November 20th, we were successful.

We started immediately after breakfast. Of course we carried our rifles, but our duty was merely to round up the lion and hold him, if he went off so far in advance that even the Nandi runners could not overtake him. We intended to beat the country toward some shallow, swampy valleys 12 miles distant.

In an hour we overtook the Nandi warriors, who were advancing across the rolling, grassy plains in a long line, with intervals of six or eight yards between the men. They were splendid savages – stark naked, lithe as panthers, the muscles rippling under their smooth dark skins. All their lives they had lived on nothing but animal food, milk, blood and flesh, and they were fit for any fatigue or danger. Their faces were proud, cruel, fearless; as they ran they moved with long springy strides. Their head-dresses were fantastic; they carried ox-hide shields painted with strange devices; and each bore in his right hand the formidable war spear, used both for stabbing and for throwing at close quarters. The narrow spear heads of soft iron were burnished till they shone like silver; they were four feet long, and the point and edges were razor sharp. The wooden haft appeared but a few inches; the long butt was also of iron, ending in a spike, so that the spear looked almost solid metal. Yet each sinewy warrior carried his heavy weapon as if it were a toy, twirling it till it glinted in the sun-rays. Herds of game, red hartebeests and striped zebra and wild swine, fled right and left before the advance of the line.

It was noon before we reached a wide, shallow valley, with beds of rushes here and there in the middle, and on either side high grass and dwarfed and scattered thorntrees. Down this we beat for a couple of

41

miles. Then, suddenly, a maned lion rose a quarter of a mile ahead of the line and galloped off through the high grass to the right, and all of us on horseback tore after him.

He was a magnificent beast, with a black and tawny mane; in his prime, teeth and claws perfect, with mighty thews and savage heart. He was lying near a hartebeest on which he had been feasting; his life had been an unbroken career of rapine and violence; and now the maned master of the wilderness, the terror that stalked by night, the grim lord of slaughter, was to meet his doom at the hands of the only foes who dared molest him.

It was a mile before we brought him to bay. It was a sore temptation to shoot him; but of course we could not break faith with our Nandi friends. We were only some 60 yards from him, and we watched him with our rifles ready, lest he should charge either us, or the first two or three spearmen, before their companions arrived.

One by one the spearmen came up, at a run, and gradually began to form a ring round him. Each, when he came near enough, crouched behind his shield, his spear in his right hand, his fierce, eager face peering over the shield rim. As man followed man, the lion rose to his feet. His mane bristled, his tail lashed, he held his head low, the upper lip now drooping over the jaws, now drawn up so as to show the gleam of the long fangs. He faced first one way and then another, and never ceased to utter his murderous grunting roars. It was a wild sight; the ring of spearmen, intent, silent, bent on blood, and in the center the great man-killing beast, his thunderous wrath growing ever more dangerous.

At last the tense ring was complete, and the spearmen rose and closed in. The lion looked quickly from side to side, saw where the line was thinnest, and charged at his topmost speeds.

With shields held steady and quivering spears poised, the men in front braced themselves for the rush and the shock; and from either hand the warriors sprang forward to take their foe in the flank. Bounding ahead of his fellows, the leader reached throwing distance; the long spear flickered and plunged. As the lion felt the wound he half turned, and then flung himself on the man in front. The warrior threw his spear; drove deep into the life, for entering at one shoulder it came out of the opposite flank, near the thigh, a yard of steel through the great body. Rearing, the lion struck the man, bearing down the shield, his back arched; and for a moment he slaked his fury with fang and talon. But on the instant I saw another spear drive clear through his body from side to side; and as the lion turned again the bright spear blades darting toward him were flashed of white flame. The end had come. He seized another man, who stabbed him and wrenched loose. As he fell he gripped a spear-head in his jaws with such tremendous force that he bent it double. Then the warriors were round and over him, stabbing and shouting, wild with furious exultation.

From the moment when he charged until his death, I doubt whether ten seconds had elapsed, perhaps less; but what a ten seconds! The first half-dozen spears had done the work. Three of the spear blades had gone clear through the body, the points projecting several inches; and these, and one or two others, including the one he had seized in his jaws, had been twisted out of shape in the terrible death struggle.

We at once attended to the two wounded men. Treating their wounds with antiseptic was painful, and so, while the operation was in progress, I told them, through Kirke, that I would give each a heifer. A Nandi prizes his cattle rather more than his wives, and each sufferer smiled broadly at the news, and forgot all about the pain of his wounds.

Then the warriors, raising their shields above their heads, and chanting the deep-toned victory song, marched with a slow, dancing step around the dead body of the lion; and this savage dance of triumph ended a scene of as fierce interest and excitement as I ever hope to see.

The Nandi marched back by themselves, carrying the two wounded men on their shields. We rode to camp by a roundabout way, on the chance that we might see another lion. The afternoon waned and we cast long shadows before us as we road across the vast lonely plain. The game stared at us as we passed; a cold wind blew in our faces, and the tall grass waved ceaselessly; the sun set behind a sullen cloud bank; and then, just at night-fall, the tents glimmered white through the dusk.

# A Man for All Seasons

*Carl Akeley hunted with Teddy Roosevelt, killed a leopard bare-handed, designed a movie camera for Eastman Kodak, helped build the Panama Canal, and you likely never heard his name.*

*By Roger Pinckney*

Carl Ethan Akeley, brave, proud, temperamental, relentless, driven . . . there is just no way to include all of his accomplishments in a sub-title. When you go into one of the outdoor super-stores and see the centerpiece of mounted animals, you can thank Carl Akeley. He was the father of modern taxidermy, the first man to display animals interacting in a replica of their natural environment. When you see a movie, you can think of him, too, as he set a Nairobi clockmaker to work designing the first wind-up drive for hand-cranked movie cameras. When Akeley was puzzling a way to plaster a framework to support elephant mounts, he came up with a pneumatic concrete gun, "shot-crete," we call it today. Bingo, that's the way they stabilized ditchbanks when they built the Panama Canal, the way we build "gunite" swimming pools.

Along the way, Akeley hunted and explored all across Africa, killed a leopard with his bare hands, got trampled by an elephant, and finally ended his days as an artist and environmentalist, a champion of the elephant and the mountain gorilla. He helped establish Africa's first national park, and his bronzes of African animals fetch considerable sums today.

# AFRICA

Strange are the ways of genius. Born in 1864, the son of a hardscrabble New York farmer, Akeley came to taxidermy at age 12 when he mounted his neighbor's canary. With eyes of glass beads pilfered from his mother's jewelry, the bird looked so alive, the neighbors claimed, "it could nearly sing." His next job was a big one indeed, P. T. Barnum's Jumbo, gone berserk and killed while charging a locomotive.

Of course, there were years in between. Only three of formal schooling, and an apprenticeship to Ward's Natural Science Establishment in Rochester, New York, a firm doing little-better-than-average work for circuses, medicine shows and newfangled natural history museums. His boss, Henry Ward, was an explorer in his own right, and primed young Akeley with his tales of the Dark Continent, being cast ashore in the Niger, rescued by an African princess intent on matrimony.

That was back in 1885, and times were good; the Gilded Age, they called it. Grover Cleveland was president and the silver dollar was God. More people could read than ever before; the public could afford magazines. Belgian King Leopold II had just proclaimed his domain over the Congo, Stanley had found Livingston, Sir Richard Burton had plumbed the source of the Nile, and sensational accounts of African adventure were a staple of the press in those days.

Good times or not, the average American ¬– then as now – could not afford a safari, or even a trip to the bogs of Ontario. Natural History Museums were a good second choice. From their advertisements they seemed almost circuses. "Exotic natural history, consisting of the most curious, exotic and beautiful . . . fishes, animals, shells, and other interesting objects . . ."

But taxidermy in those days was a crude art, at best. Hides were indifferently cured with salt, alum and arsenic, stretched onto wire frames stuffed with whatever was handy – rags, woodshavings or sawdust. Results were predictable. But Akeley changed all that.

Working with potter's clay, he replicated posture, muscle, every wrinkle of a living animal. A plaster cast was made of the model and a paper maché form made from that – the same techniques used today, except now we use fiberglass.

In 1891, riding the fame of the Jumbo mount, Akeley accepted a position at the Milwaukee Museum of Natural History and a commission from Chicago's Columbian Exposition to mount an Indian warrior with his mustang ponies. The ponies were real and even though the Indian was not, it brought Akeley even more notoriety.

The British Museum, whose specimens were in sorry shape, offered him a job. Akeley was on his way to a steamship in New York when he stopped at Chicago's Field Museum of Natural History. The museum was an endowment from Marshall Field, the Chicago dry goods magnate, a spin-off from the Columbian Exposition. Akeley's mustangs and Indian were there on exhibit and Akeley was an honored visitor.

By then Carl had a woman in his life, Delia Reiss – soon to be Akeley – a feisty Irish-American nicknamed Mickie, the wife of a hunting companion. A runaway at 13, child bride at 14, divorcee at 19, Delia and Carl must have been quite a scandal. But Mickie ducked the publicity, threw herself into Akeley's work, collecting rocks, moss, even leaves to add realism to his creations. Mickie supported his plans to move to London, and when the Field Museum tendered a better offer, she supported him when he changed his mind.

Akeley first went to Africa on a Field Museum expedition in 1896 and he spent his 32nd birthday there, holed up in the squalid and seething Arabian port of Berbea awaiting camels, supplies and wired money. His boss was Daniel Giraud Elliot, zoologist, explorer and writer. Though Akeley wrote regularly to Mickie, took copious field notes, and later dictated a book to a ghost writer, the best of that first expedition comes from Elliot's journal.

"The camel," Elliot wrote, "can kick like a Virginia mule. I can pay it no higher compliment. It can bite worse than a horse and buck in a way that would make a bronco ashamed of his efforts. He can run away whenever he feels like it and . . . then this sweet creature has a way of expressing his displeasure by thrusting its ugly nose in the rider's face, opening its cavernous mouth and bellowing a roar of disgust in such a fetid breath that the human is fairly blown into the middle of next month, his appetite lost for an indeterminable period."

That's the way things started, inland and uphill from the Gulf of

Aden through the deserts of Somaliland. Then things got worse. Akeley and Elliot got sick, they got lost, they were harassed by hyenas and intimidated by local militias. "Hell on earth," Elliot wrote, "barren rocks and hills covered with lava, a dreary waste of sand and low thorn bushes, scorpions big as lobsters, venomous snakes and all the hideous things no other land would have."

But Akeley managed to find his animals – wild asses, oryx, gazelles and kudu. He also wounded a lion, who worked its revenge on a mule, rather than the rider. The hides were fleshed out, rolled in salt, shipped back to the coast.

On the first safari, Akeley may have seemed a bumbling fool, but there were scrapes that showed us what he was made of – leveling his rifle at a native caravan that refused them aid, arresting two of his crew run amok, one for mayhem, the other for attempted murder. And then came the day in the highlands of the Maud when he went looking for an ostrich and found a leopard.

But first, Akeley shot a warthog. No problem, he needed one for the Field collection. He proceeded fruitlessly after ostrich, and upon his tramp back to camp at the end of the day, encountered a leopard feeding on his hog. "You have to kill a leopard right down to the end of its tail," Akeley later said. But he didn't. After four wild shots, he managed only to nick one rear paw.

The cat's charge sent Akeley sprawling, his rifle flying. No gun, no knife, he wrestled the beast down, pinning its front claws with his knees, staying clear of the rear ones, which were fixing to disembowel him. Jaws were another problem. Carl solved that by stuffing his arm down the animal's throat, the easiest part of the match, as the leopard had his hand in its mouth already. When he felt the cat's ribs start to pop, he knew he was home free.

But not quite. Back at camp, Elliot and the guides heard the shooting. "Either a dust-up with the natives, or a melee with an animal. In either case, it will be over before we get there." So they kept eating. Akeley staggered back in due time.

To his credit, Elliot was down with malaria, not drunk. His malaria and Akeley's eventual blood poisoning put an end to that first safari, good thing. Both of them got drunk on the way home and stayed that way, nursing ailments with regular doses of champagne, quaffed warm from tin cups. "A pretty mean drink," Akeley reckoned.

Asafari is a good thing to go on, a better thing to come home from, especially more or less in one piece. Trouble is, you will always try to go back. Carl Akeley returned four times, and the last safari killed him. But that would not be for another 30 years.

Back in the States, shredded and feverish, Akeley oversaw the mounting of his skins, some 200 mammals, 300 birds, numerous reptiles and half a barrel of fish. Nights, he went back to work on a long-postponed project, *The Four Seasons*, a diorama of whitetails in spring, summer, fall and winter. His African mounts notwithstanding, it was his most ambitious project to date, and it soon attracted the attention of the President of the United States.

Theodore Roosevelt promised Akeley that someday they would hunt Africa together. That promise would be a long time coming.

First, Akeley went back to Africa – to Kenya this time – on another Field expedition to collect elephants.

This elephant hunting is serious business. Six thousand pounds that can outsprint a Kentucky thoroughbred, and with senses like radar and maybe even ESP, elephants fear no natural enemy. They are peaceable enough, even loving to one another, but their fury knows no bounds when provoked. An elephant will not be content with just killing you, he will decorate the tops of nearby trees with hat-sized pieces of your carcass.

That's what Mickie was likely thinking when she saw that first bull. Yes, Mickie had joined the expedition and was toting a Mannlicher rifle, most likely a 6.5, hardly what you might call an elephant gun. But that long noodle of a bullet would penetrate, and if the shot were made with surgical precision, it would kill a tusker in his tracks, or nearly so. The "nearly so" got to Mickie. She bolted, but Akeley collared her, cussed her, turned her around.

They cut the root from a tusk and bloodied Mickie's face, a local tradition. They went on to take more elephants, cape buffalo, too, paring the skins, salting them down, wrapping them in canvas and shipping them overland down to Mombassa. That hunt was probably Akeley's most successful, the least traumatic of five safaris. But back home, there was trouble at the Field Museum.

# AFRICA

**M**arshall Field had died, leaving the museum with no major sponsor. The board let Elliot go as he was still suffering from his various African ailments, hired another curator who just couldn't find room or money to mount all of Akeley's five elephants. Carl quit in disgust and went to work for the American Museum of Natural History in New York.

The American Museum was supported by a virtual "who's-who" among the "Captains of Industry." And it was here that Akeley was to do his best work. In 1909 the museum sent him back to Kenya for more elephants and this time, the odds caught up with him. He was 9,000 feet up Mt. Kenya in a bamboo thicket in the rain when he set his rifle down to fire up his pipe. Bad choice.

There was no time to shoot. Akeley, who by then "knew more about elephants than any other white man," heard the brush break behind him. He wheeled and when he saw the bull upon him, he threw himself into the only place he might survive – between trunk and tusk. It was like flipping a dog a dollop of peanut butter, Akeley holding tight and the bull trying to shake him loose.

A runner brought the news down the mountain. Bwana was dead, or maybe not quite dead. Mickie roused the hands, but they would not go up the mountain in the dark. Mickie leveled her Mannlicher and was wondering how many native helpers she would have to shoot before the rest obeyed. But then, she came up with a better plan. She began jumping about, screeching and cursing, insulting them in as much of their language she knew – cowards, women, snakes, scorpions.

It worked. They found Carl about sunrise, nose, jaw, ribs broken, lungs punctured. The fashioned a stretcher from blankets and bamboo, and it took three full days to get him off the mountain, another three for a doctor to arrive. No hurry, he figured, since elephant maulings were always fatal.

Mickie was undone by the episode. "I just want to go home and keep house forever!" she blurted. Even Carl lost his nerve. But there was trouble of a different sort. Mickie had captured and tamed a young vervet monkey. She named it, fretted over it, pampered it, much the way childless rich women dote on lapdogs.

That monkey went everywhere Mickie went, slept on her cot. Carl and the monkey differed on many things, but shared one: they did not like each other. Mickie's devotion to the monkey – madness it sometimes seemed – led to argument, alienation, separation and eventual divorce.

But meanwhile, Akeley, feverish and broken, was dreaming. "I am always dreaming dreams," he wrote years later, "but most of them have been forgotten." But not this one. If he made it home alive, he would create an African Hall for the museum. He would design it himself, fill it with dioramas of game, with photographs of native people, with artifacts. He would bring wild Africa to America, before wild Africa was gone.

Besides the inspiration for the African Hall, that safari had another highpoint: A runner arrived in camp with a message from *Bwana Tumbo*, "Boss Belly," Theodore Roosevelt, himself.

They met as old friends, good American company in the African bush. After discussing politics, Akeley invited Roosevelt elephant hunting, a political move in itself, as a specimen collected by the former president would make good ink when Akeley set about garnering support for his African Hall. As it turned out, Roosevelt's elephant was too small and was never used, but Akeley neglected to mention that to anyone.

And then there was the lion hunt staged by the *Nandi*, one of the fiercest tribes in East Africa. British colonial authorities had put an end to the Nandi's raids of neighboring tribes, but still allowed their ritual lion hunting. The chief invited Akeley along, so long as he promised not to shoot, no matter how dire the circumstances. Carl carried his rifle anyway, and a cumbersome, hand-cranked movie camera.

Forty warriors armed with hand-forged spears and buffalo skin shields flushed a mature male from a patch of scrub, encircled it, began moving in, spears and shields to the ready. When the lion was provoked to charge, a warrior jumped into the circle, grabbed it by the tail. The lion was on him in an instant, jaws clamped around his throat, raking him with its front paws. Then the other warriors made their move, running the lion through with their spears. Akeley, struggling to keep up with the fracas, tripped over his tripod. The camera fell, ruining what would have been the most exciting footage ever yet filmed. His frustration at the loss led to the creation of the Akeley Camera, driven by clockwork, stabilized by gyroscope, with interchangeable telephoto lenses.

# AFRICA

**B**ack in New York in 1911 Akeley worked on his camera, promoted his African Hall while enduring the antics of Mickie's monkey who was shredding their apartment. After the monkey bit Mickie twice, Carl dropped the hammer: "Either the monkey or me." Mickie gave the monkey to a zoo, but left Carl anyway.

By then war had broken out in Europe. There was no money for the African Hall, and Mickie joined the American Expeditionary Force in France. Carl's world was in tatters, but there were two bright spots during those dismal years. The Signal Corps bought the camera, and Akeley turned to bronze sculpture.

Despite his "crash up" on Mt. Kenya, or maybe because of it, elephants were a favorite subject. His first, *Wounded Comrade*, remains his best known. It was followed by *Nandi Lion Spearing* and when he got into his "gorilla period," he created *Old Man of Mikeno* and finally *Chrysalis*, which created a furor among fundamental religionists as it showed a man emerging from the skin of a gorilla.

Akeley, pleased that his African Hall was finally showing progress, wanted to include gorillas in the collection, so on July 31, 1921, he left New York for the Virunga Mountains of the Belgian Congo. His first group of guides proved worthless, so Carl came back down, dismissed every one of them, then badgered the local sultan for others. He got them, started over.

Akeley shot his first gorilla at 10,000 feet, a 400-pound silverback male on a slope so steep he had to back his shoulder against a tree to keep the recoil from his .475 from blowing him off the mountain. He shot a female, who vaulted over a cliff in her death spasms, unleashing "an avalanche of gorillas" who followed her over the edge as they thought she knew the way to safety. At the bottom, his men speared a four-month-old infant when it was running for Akeley's arms. And that's when he figured he'd just committed murder.

So Carl Akeley, passionate always, added one more passion to his list. He would petition the Belgian government to protect the mountain gorilla. But it was as if when Akeley shot those gorillas, he had somehow killed himself. He would survive that safari, but not the next.

There would be other triumphs. He would encourage, direct and support Martin and Osa Johnson, the intrepid wildlife photographers. The African Hall would be built and it would bear his name. The Belgians would create Parc Albert, Africa's first national park. But Akeley was a dead man walking. He died in 1926, there among the mountain gorillas. He was buried there too, and native witch doctors pilfered his bones for their amulets, hoping somehow to catch the magic of this man for all seasons. Perhaps they did.

# THE LEGEND
# OF BWANA COTTAR

*The first American-born professional hunter in Africa, Charles Cottar would survive three leopard maulings and near-fatal attacks by elephant and buffalo to found the First Family of Safari.*

By Brian Herne

Charles Cottar was born in Iowa in 1874, the great-grandson of the first white settler in Cedar County. Before the turn of the century his family moved south by covered wagon, first to Kansas, then later to Oklahoma. The Cottars were among early homesteaders who staked out land in the Cherokee Strip when the Indian Territory was opened up for settlement. Charles modeled his early life after that of his trailblazing heroes, Daniel Boone and Davy Crockett, wearing his hair long in frontier fashion and hunting wild game with an old-fashioned musket. He soon grew into a brawny six-foot-four. His insatiable wanderlust, combined with his fast draw and dead aim, led him to Texas, then back to Oklahoma where he married and settled down for awhile, though his maverick thirst for adventure remained unquenched. In 1910 Cottar pulled up stakes and set off on a solitary mid-life pilgrimage to Darkest Africa. At the start of that fateful journey, none would have guessed that Charles Cottar was destined to gain fame as the first American-born white hunter in East Africa, and that his name would be indelibly etched in the annals of safari lore.

# AFRICA

The spark that fired Cottar's imagination and propelled him out of his own country and onto the shores of a primitive wilderness rose out of the blaze of publicity that heralded Teddy Roosevelt's 1909-10 hunting expedition in Africa. As newspapers around the globe trumpeted the myriad mysteries of Africa, Cottar vowed to see the land of King Solomon for himself. By the time Roosevelt's cavalcade had reach the white rhino country along Uganda's Nile Valley on the last leg of a 13-month trip, Charles Cottar had packed his guns and was on the high seas, steaming toward the tropical green waters of the Indian Ocean.

Cottar's voyage ended at the old Arab port of Mombasa, gateway to British East Africa where he boarded a railway carriage that would carry him 320 miles inland to the territory's capital. At Nairobi, the Oklahoma plainsman found himself in a dusty settlement where men still packed pistols, wore Stetsons and traveled by horseback or rickshaw. Among its powerful attractions for Cottar, Africa's frontier town had one feature that surpassed all others: it was smack in the middle of a sportsman's paradise. Lions strolled the back streets, while Cape buffalo wallowed in papyrus swamps near the celebrated Norfolk Hotel, and elephant often plundered vegetable gardens. From almost any place in the town countless wildebeest, Coke's hartebeest, zebra, Thomson's and Grant's gazelle, eland, warthogs and ostrich could be seen on the surrounding plains.

In Cottar's day there was no requirement that a white hunter accompany a visitor on safari. The only condition was that a basic game license be purchased. Lion and leopard were considered "vermin" and could be hunted by anyone prepared to gamble his life. Graveyard headstones bearing epitaphs such as "killed by a lion" or "killed by a buffalo" bore ample testimony to the bloody deaths suffered by greenhorns who tangled with the Big Five on their own. Yet danger was a magnet to Charles Cottar, and instead of a white hunter, he cut expenses by hiring an African *neapara* (headman).

The old *neaparas* were invaluable characters who had once marched at the head of slaving caravans or guided famous explorers to the interior. They kept the safari porters in line if need be, often with the strong-armed aid of a *kiboko*, a stiff whip made of hippo hide. But *neaparas* shared one failing: they were not hunters, and knew little about the habits of game, stalking or judging trophies. These tasks were left to gunbearers who came from specialized hunting tribes, such as the WaKamba.

At Nairobi railway station Cottar and his 30 African porters, along with three riding mules, a half-dozen pack donkeys, tents, chop boxes, kerosene lanterns, skinning knives, trophy salt, medical knives, bedding, machetes and axes were loaded on boxcars of a slow goods train bound for a station called

Kijabe. As the train rumbled to the edge of the Great Rift Valley at 6,500 feet, Cottar was stunned at the enormity of the panorama far below. Two extinct volcanoes studded the valley floor, surrounded by golden grasslands carved with dry streambeds lined with thickets of yellow-bared acacia. In the distance a blue haze of mountains beckoned.

Charles and his men followed a hand-drawn map supplied by Leslie Tarlton, the Australian white hunter who had outfitted his safari. Their route led to the sparkling freshwater lake at Naivasha, then beyond to a string of shallow soda lakes where every variety of bird and animal could be found. On the short-grass plains of Masailand, Cottar hunted rhino, then spoored Cape buffalo in brushy gorges at Hell's Gate. Charles marched to the 6,000-foot Laikipia Plateau, home to huge herds of game. As his safari edged around the forested slopes of the Aberdare mountains, Charles knew his search was over, and he had found the big game hunter's Holy Grail.

Back in Nairobi, Bwana Cottar, as he was now known, heard tales of giant tuskers deep in the rainforests of the Belgian Congo. The Congo was irresistible to hard-bitten adventurers who hankered to hunt for excitement and profit, without the bothersome expense of game licenses. On the west bank of the Nile at a place called Lado was a wedge of land that was the center of a territorial dispute between the Belgians and British. The poachers seized upon the dispute to operate in Lado, poaching ivory from under the noses of the Belgians, secure in the knowledge the British would ignore their shenanigans.

Poaching in the Congo was dangerous work, and several hunters died there. Frequent dust-ups with vigilant Belgian patrols sometimes ended in deaths or arrests. A famous poacher named Billy Pickering was killed by an elephant that tore his head off and then tramped his body to pulp. Another poacher by the name of Broom was shot dead by authorities. Belgian *askaris* had once wounded the greatest ivory hunter of all, Walter D. M. "Karamoja" Bell, as he sat in a canoe midstream in the Nile. Ironically, Bell was one of the few hunters in the Congo who was legitimate, having taken the trouble to buy licenses. The *askaris* paid a price for their temerity, for Bell returned fire with his 7mm rifle.

In the Congo's great Ituri forest, a region not much better known today than in Cottar's time, Charles made friends with the Efe pygmies. They alerted him to Belgian patrols and showed him how to hunt at close range in the thickest jungle. With their skillful help Cottar accumulated a sizable grubstake of ivory. But elephant and Belgian *askaris* were only part of the risk. Charles left the

# AFRICA

Congo with deadly *spirillum* tick fever. Comatose, he was carried by his native bearers more than 400 miles to the shores of Lake Victoria, and then 200 miles by train to Nairobi. He survived this extraordinary journey and recovered, but the effects of the disease remained with him to the end of his days. His life was saved only by the endurance and tenacity of his African safari crew.

For the next few years Cottar traveled back and forth between Africa and the United States. In 1915 he packed up his wife and nine children and left Oklahoma for good. A few miles northwest of Nairobi, Charles carved out a new homestead where he built a tropical bungalow-style house. The comfortable house was built on stilts, using wood and corrugated iron sheeting.

After the first World War, Charles founded his now famous Cottar's Safari Service. He returned often to hunt the game-filled plains of Masailand, and took to referring to the entire region as "Cottar Country." Those who entered his self-proclaimed territory did so at their own risk. His eldest daughter, Evelyn, recalled that he once "shot a few holes into the roof of a car that came in *his* country. They left in a hurry!"

Although Bwana Cottar was among the first to import Ford cars to Kenya, he favored riding mules for hunting. Charles built frames on his safari trucks and covered them with mosquito netting in order to transport his prized mules into big game areas. To reach certain parts of Cottar Country, it was necessary to leapfrog perilous "fly belts" inhabited by fierce tsetse flies whose bites were lethal to domestic stock, and sometimes to humans.

One day while hunting with a Winchester .30-06 for meat, Bwana came upon a leopard feeding on a guinea fowl. Cottar fired at the cat, but before he could reload the leopard swarmed all over him, biting him savagely on the shoulders and face. With his great strength, Cottar used his rifle as a stave to throw off the cat. To his amazement the leopard lay dead where it fell, having succumbed to his bullet. It would be the lightest of three leopard maulings he would experience.

Sometime later Cottar spotted another leopard in open country, and this time he ran it down on horseback. He lassoed the winded beast around the neck, then dismounted and hobbled its hind legs. Leaving the leopard to recuperate, he went to get his motion picture camera. Charles instructed his wife Anita to crank the film and his young son Mike to stand guard. Bwana planned to star in the first real-life action movie of a man tussling with a leopard.

As the camera rolled and Charles boldly advanced, the great cat, still hobbled, made a powerful lunge. Cottar swung up his rifle, but the snarling feline knocked him to the ground before he could shoot. Charles wrestled with the leopard and then fired a fatal shot. In those few short moments the cat had done great damage. Doctors told Cottar he had blood poisoning, and insisted on amputating his leg to save his life. He refused, and to everyone's surprise but his own, Bwana recovered. Anita never lived down the fact that the movie was out of focus and useless.

During his years as a white hunter, Charles and two of his sons offered unprecedented international hunts that began in Africa and ended in India or Indochina. He saw no difficulty in shipping his gunbearers and crews, along with safari vehicles and tentage, to the Far East. He once arrived at the foot of a nearly impassable mountain range in India. Cottar dismantled his cars and had them carried up the escarpments on the backs of elephants, then reassembled them on a plateau, ready for the hunt. These logistical exercises boggle the mind. Considering the great distances and modes of travel at that time, it was an unparalleled accomplishment in outfitting.

Over his long career, Cottar's fiery vitality and great strength saved him more than a few times in serious entanglements with dangerous game. His bullet once failed to stop the charge of a bull elephant in a thorny rendezvous. The enraged tusker grabbed Cottar and threw him into some brush, then unaccountably broke off the attack. Bwana escaped with a few broken ribs. Another time a buffalo knocked him down and gored him. Cottar lay on his back in the dust, while the buffalo shoveled him along the ground with its horns, trying to finish him off. Cottar got one foot on each side of the bull's neck and bracing his legs, he let the animal push him around until he could lever another shell into his .405 Winchester.

Although Cottar later suffered a stroke that partly paralyzed his left side, he continued to hunt with incredible energy for another 20 years. He also endured regular bouts of blackwater fever, an advanced and often deadly form of malaria. Doctors warned him that blackwater would kill him. Cottar ignored their warnings, convinced his end would come not from disease, but in the jaws of a lion. Elephant, buffalo and leopard had tried to kill him, and they had failed. He had not been horned by a rhino, but he dismissed old *faru* as being too ugly and too stupid to kill him. Although he had shot more than 50 lions, he was certain that one day a tawny cat would spring upon him from ambush when he least expected it. Bwana feared nothing on earth, yet he believed his days would end in a flurry of fang and claw, and he would die in writhing agony beneath the equatorial sun. Down the dangerous safari road, Cottar's gloomy prediction turned out to be off the mark, but not by much.

# AFRICA

During the monsoon rainy seasons in Africa, Cottar often returned to America to promote his safaris. In 1940 it seemed that God had smiled when he landed a rich contract for a lecture tour across the U.S. Cottar needed spectacular film for his tour, and with his eldest son Bud, he headed for Barakitabu (Difficult Road) in Masailand to set up *campi* at their favorite spot beside a shallow stream-crossing.

One morning as they hunted the green foothills of the Loita Range, they surprised an old rhino, which immediately charged. Bud fired, wounding the beast, which veered away into the dense brush. As his son pursued the rhino, Charles waited behind in the glade. All of a sudden the screech of tick birds pierced the stillness. Knowing the birds' cries signaled the presence of a rhino or buffalo, Charles quickly unshouldered his heavy wooden tripod. The brush crackled like gunfire as an angry rhino tore out of the thorns looking for trouble. It paused briefly, its head held high, its long horns tilted like lances at Bwana's mid-section. Charles kept his eye to the viewfinder and cranked away. As he rolled off the film, the rhino charged, boiling through the dust. It was exactly the kind of dramatic footage he so badly needed.

Charles figured he would film until the last one-hundredth of a second, then throw up his big .405 Winchester and drop the beast with a solid bullet in the brain. In worse case he could jump aside as the clumsy *faru* brushed past in his blind charge. When the thundering beast was on him, Cottar fired at point-blank range. The bullet struck muscle and bone, but the rhino was able to sweep his long horn upwards, ripping Bwana's thigh. The rhino's two-ton impact knocked the big man down, just as the *faru* fell mortally wounded across Cottar's legs. Yet the battering rhino had failed to loosen Bwana's grip on his rifle. Pinned down by the great thrashing body, Cottar rammed his rifle into the rhino and fired several more rounds.

Bud heard the gunshots and sprinted back to his father. He saw where the horn had opened Bwana's leg and passed through an artery. Bud fashioned a tourniquet to staunch the blood pumping from his father's thigh. Cottar's sun-shot eyes calmly gazed at a spiral of vultures with wings razoring the air, their shadows swooping doom over his tanned face. Cottar impatiently motioned toward the gunbearers who were tying a tarpaulin to shade him.

Mortally wounded, Charles commanded, "Tell them to stop. It's no use. I'm done for. Roll it back."

60

As he lay on Masailand's baked black-cotton soil, he fixed his blue eyes on the sky above Cottar Country. One hour later the 66-year-old hunter had bled to death.

On a Sunday afternoon Bwana's many friends paid their last respects at Nairobi's Forest Cemetery. His loyal African safari crews were there, too, and none had dry eyes. The *kali* old hunter had gone to meet his God *Ngai* on the frozen jagged peak of Mount Kenya.

Long after his death, Charles Cottar's legend lives on in the safari world. The dynasty he founded is now in its fifth generation. His eldest son Pat ("Bud") followed in his father's footsteps, accompanying the Duke and Duchess of York as well as renowned wildlife photographers Martin and Osa Johnson on their early safaris in Kenya. His middle son Mike was thought by colleagues and clients to be the finest hunter of his time. Among his noted clients was Woolworth Danahue, American dimestore heir. In July 1941, during a safari on the western Serengeti plains, Mike was charged by a buffalo that he shot at close range. In an incident that paralleled the death of Bwana Charles, the momentum of the wounded buffalo carried it forward and it fell on Mike. The talented hunter died soon afterwards of a ruptured spleen. Ted, the youngest son, left Africa to live in California, but occasionally returned to hunt throughout the 1950s.

In turn, Mike Cottar's only son, Glen, became a white hunter in 1956 during the glorious heyday of safari. For the next 40 years he pioneered expeditions into remote reaches of East Africa, Botswana, Zaire and Sudan. With his wife Pat, he developed tented photographic camps in some of the finest big game country. Glen died in 1996. Today, his only son, 36-year-old Calvin Cottar, maintains the fine traditions of Africa's First Family of Safari. His firm, Cottar's Safari Service, is named after that of his famous great-grandfather.

*Brain Herne was a leading professional white hunter in East Africa for more than 30 years. He is the author of five books, and has written numerous magazine articles about Africa. Brian's exciting classic,* White Hunters, the Golden Age of African Safaris, *was published by Henry Holt in June 1999.*

# I May Have to Shoot Him

*In this chapter from* West with the Night, *which Ernest Hemingway once described as "a bloody wonderful book," the courageous aviatrix relives her hunting days with the Baron von Blixen and their terrifying encounter with a bull elephant.*

*By Beryl Markham*

I suppose, if there were a part of the world in which mastodon still lived, somebody would design a new gun, and men, in their eternal impudence, would hunt mastodon as they now hunt elephant. Impudence seems to be the word. At least David and Goliath were of the same species, but to an elephant, a man can only be a midge with a deadly sting.

It is absurd for a man to kill an elephant. It is not brutal, it is not heroic, and certainly it is not easy; it is just one of those preposterous things that men do like putting a dam across a great river, one tenth of whose volume could engulf the whole of mankind without disturbing the domestic life of a single catfish.

Elephant, beyond the fact that their size and conformation are aesthetically more suited to the treading of this earth than our angular informity, have an average intelligence comparable to our own. Of course they are less agile and physically less adaptable than ourselves – Nature having developed their bodies in one direction and their brains in another, while human beings, on the other hand, drew from Mr. Darwin's lottery of evolution both the winning ticket and the stub to match it. This, I suppose, is why we are so wonderful and can make movies and electric razors and wireless sets – and guns with which to shoot the elephant, the hare, clay pigeons and each other.

The elephant is a rational animal. He thinks. Blix and I (also rational animals in our own right) have never quite agreed on the mental attributes of the elephant. I know Blix is not to be doubted because he has learned more about elephant than any other man I have ever met, or even heard about, but he looks upon legend with a suspicious eye, and I do not.

There is a legend that elephant dispose of their dead in secret burial grounds and that none of these has ever been discovered. In support of this, there is only the fact that the body of an elephant, unless he had been trapped or shot in his tracks, has rarely been found. What happens to the old and diseased?

Not only natives, but many white settlers, have supported for years the legend (if it is legend) that elephant will carry their wounded and their sick hundreds of miles, if necessary, to keep them out of the hands of their enemies. And it is said that elephant never forget.

These are perhaps just stories born of imagination. Ivory was once almost as precious as gold, and wherever there is treasure, men mix it with mystery. But still, there is no mystery about the things you see yourself.

I think I am the first person ever to scout elephant by plane, and so it follows that the thousands of elephant I saw time and again from the air had never before been plagued by anything above their heads more ominous than tick-birds.

The reaction of a herd of elephant to my Avian was, in the initial instance, always the same – they left their feeding ground and tried to find cover, though often, before yielding, one or two of the bulls would prepare for battle and charge in the direction of the plane if it were low enough to be within their scope of vision. Once the futility of this was realized, the entire herd would be off into the deepest bush.

Checking again on the whereabouts of the same herd next day, I always found that a good deal of thinking had been going on amongst them during the night. On the basis of their reaction to my second intrusion, I judged that their thoughts had run somewhat like this: A: The thing that flew over us was no bird, since no bird would have to work so hard to stay in the air – and, anyway, we know all the birds. B: If it was no bird, it was very likely just another trick of those two-legged dwarfs against whom there ought to be a law. C: The two-legged dwarfs (both black and white) have, as long as our long memories go back, killed our bulls for their tusks. We know this because, in the case of the white dwarfs, at least, the tusks are the only part taken away.

The actions of the elephant, based upon this reasoning, were always sensible and practical. The second time they saw the Avian, they refused to hide; instead, the females, who bear only small, valueless tusks, simply grouped themselves around their treasure-burdened bulls in such a way that no ivory could be seen from the air or from any other approach.

This can be maddening strategy to an elephant scout. I have spent the better part of an hour circling, criss-crossing and diving low over some of the most inhospitable country in Africa in an effort to break such a stubborn huddle, sometimes successfully, sometimes not.

But the tactics vary. More than once I have come upon a large and solitary elephant standing with enticing disregard for safety, its massive bulk in clear view, but its head buried in a thicket. This was on the part of the elephant, no effort to stimulate the nonsensical habit attributed to the ostrich. It was, on the contrary, a cleverly devised trap into which I fell, every way except physically, at least a dozen times. The beast always proved to be a large cow rather than a bull, and I always found that by the time I had arrived at this brilliant if tardy deduction, the rest of the herd had got another ten miles away, and the decoy, leering up at me out of a small, triumphant eye, would amble into the open, wave her trunk with devastating nonchalance, and disappear.

This order of intelligence in a lesser animal can obviously give rise to exaggeration – some of it persistent enough to be crystallized into legend. But you cannot discredit truth merely because legend has grown out of it. The sometimes almost godlike achievements of our own species in ages past toddle through history supported more often than not on the twin crutches of fable and human credulity.

As to the brutality of elephant hunting, I cannot see that it is any more brutal than 90 percent of all other human activities. I suppose there is nothing more tragic about the death of an elephant than there is about the death of a Hereford steer – certainly not in the eyes of the steer. The only difference is that the steer has neither the ability nor the chance to outwit the gentleman who wields the slaughter-house snickersnee, while the elephant has both of these to pit against the hunter.

The popular belief that only the so-called 'rogue' elephant is dangerous to men is quite wrong – so wrong that a considerable number of men who believed it have become one with the dust without even their just due of gradual disintegration. A normal bull elephant, aroused by the scent of man, will often attack at once – and his speed is as unbelievable as his mobility. His trunk and his feet are his weapons – at least in the distasteful business of exterminating a mere human; those resplendent sabers of ivory await resplendent foes.

Blix and I hardly came into this category at Kilamakoy – certainly not after we had run down the big bull or, as it happened, the big bull had run down us. I can say, at once with gratification still genuine, that we were not trampled within that most durable of all inches – the last inch of our lives. We got out all right, but there are times when I still dream.

On arriving from Makindu, I landed my plane in the shallow box of a runway scooped out of the bush, unplugged wads of cotton wool from my ears and climbed from the cockpit.

The aristocratically descended visage of the Baron von Blixen Finecke greeted me (as it always did) with the most delightful of smiles caught, like a strip of sunlight, on a familiar patch of leather – well-kept leather, free of wrinkles, but brown and saddle-tough.

Beyond this concession to the fictional idea of what a White Hunter ought to look like, Blix's face yields not a whit. He has gay, light blue eyes rather than sombre, steel-grey ones; his cheeks are well rounded rather than flat as an axe; his lips are full and generous and not pinched tight in grim realization of what the Wilderness Can Do. He talks. He is never significantly silent.

He wore then what I always remember him as wearing, a khaki bush shirt of 'solario' material, slacks of the same stuff, and a pair of low-cut moccasins with soles – or at least vestiges of soles. There were four pockets in his bush shirt, but I don't think he knew it; he never carried anything unless he was actually hunting – and then it was just a rifle and ammunition. He never went around hung with knives, revolvers, binoculars or even a watch. He could tell time by the sun, and if there were no sun, he could tell it, anyway. He wore over his closely cropped graying hair a terai hat, colorless and limp as a wilted frond.

He said, "Hullo, Beryl," and pointed to a man at his side – so angular as to give the impression of being constructed entirely of barrel staves.

"This," said Blix, with what could hardly be called Old World courtesy, "is Old Man Wicks."

"At last," said Old Man Wicks, "I have seen the Lady from the Skies."

Writing it now, that remark seems a little like a line from the best play chosen from those offered by the graduating class of Eton, possibly in the late twenties, or like the remark of a man up to his ears in his favorite anodyne. But, as a matter of fact, Old Man Wicks, who managed a piece of no-man's-land belonging to the Manoni Sugar Company, near Masongaleni, had seen only one white man in 16 months and, I gathered, hadn't seen a white woman in as many years. At least he had never seen an aeroplane and a white woman at the same time, nor can I be sure that he regarded the spectacle as much of a Godsend. Old Man Wicks, oddly enough, wasn't very old – he was barely 40 – and it may have been that his monkish life was the first choice of whatever other lives he could have led. He looked old, but that might have been protective colouration. He was a gentle, kindly man helping Blix with the safari until Winston Guest arrived.

It was a modest enough safari. There were three large tents – Winston's, Blix's and my own – and then there were several pup tents for the native boys, guri-bearers and trackers. Blix's boy Farah, Winston's boy, and of course my Arab Ruta (who was due via lorry from Nairobi) had pup tents to themselves. The others, as much out of choice as necessity, slept several in a tent. There was a hangar for the Avian, made out of a square of tarpaulin, and there was a baobab tree whose shade served as a veranda to everybody. The immediate country was endless and barren of hills.

Half an hour after I landed, Blix and I were up in the Avian, hoping, if possible, to spot a herd of elephant before Winston's arrival that night. If we could find a herd within two or three days' walking distance from the camp, it would be extraordinary luck – always provided that the herd contained a bull with respectable tusks.

It is not unusual for an elephant hunter to spend six months, or even a year, on the spoor of a single bull. Elephant go where men can't – or at least shouldn't.

Scouting by plane eliminates a good deal of the preliminary work, but when as upon occasion I did spot a herd not more than 30 or 40 miles from camp, it still meant that those 40 miles had to be walked, crawled or wriggled by the hunters – and that by the time this body and nerve-racking manuever had been achieved, the elephant had pushed on another 20 miles or so into the bush. A man, it ought to be remembered,

# AFRICA

has to take several steps to each stride of an elephant, and moreover, the man is somewhat less than resistant to thicket, thorn trees and heat. Also (particularly if he is white) he is vulnerable as a peeled egg to all things that sting – mosquitoes, scorpions, snakes and tsetse flies. The essence of elephant-hunting is discomfort in such lavish proportions that only the wealthy can afford it.

Blix and I were fortunate on our very first expedition out of Kilamakoy. The Wakamba scouts on our safari had reported a large herd of elephant containing several worthwhile bulls, not more than 20 air miles from camp. We circled the district indicated, passed over the herd perhaps a dozen times, but finally spotted it.

A herd of elephant, as seen from a plane, has a quality of an hallucination. The proportions are wrong – they are like those of a child's drawing of a field mouse in which the whole landscape, complete with barns and windmills, is dwarfed beneath the whiskers of the mighty rodent who looks both able and willing to devour everything, including the thumb-tack that holds the work against the schoolroom wall.

Peering down from the cockpit at grazing elephants, you have the feeling that what you are beholding is wonderful, but not authentic. It is not only incongruous in the sense that animals simply are not as big as trees, but also in the same sense that the 20th century, tidy and svelte with stainless steel as it is, would not possibly permit such prehistoric monsters to wander in its garden. Even in Africa, the elephant is as anomalous as the Cro-Magnon Man might be shooting a round of gold at Saint Andrews in Scotland.

But with all this, elephant are seldom conspicuous from the air. If they were smaller, they might be. Big as they are, and coloured as they are, they blend with everything until the moment they catch your eye.

They caught Blix's eyes and he scribbled me a frantic note; "Look! The big bull is enormous. Turn back, Doctor Turvy radios I should have some gin." Well, we had no radio – and certainly no gin in my plane. But just as certainly, we had Doctor Turvy.

Doctor Turvy was an ethereal citizen of an ethereal world. In the beginning, he existed only for Blix, but long before the end, he existed for everybody who worked with Blix or knew him well.

Although Doctor Turvy's prescriptions indicated that he put his trust in a wine list rather than a pharmacopoeia, he had two qualities of special excellence in a physician: his diagnosis was always arrived at in a split second – and he held the complete confidence of his patient. Beyond that, his adeptness at mental telepathy (in which Blix himself was pretty well grounded) eliminated the expensive practice of calling round to feel the pulse or take a temperature. Nobody ever saw Doctor Turvy – and that fact, Blix insisted, was bedside manner carried to its final degree of perfection.

I banked the Avian and turned toward camp.

Within three miles of our communal baobab tree, we saw four more elephant – three of them beautiful bulls. The thought passed through my head that the way to find a needle in a haystack is to sit down. Elephant are never within three miles of camp. It's hardly cricket that they should be. It doesn't make a hunter out of you to turn over on your canvas cot and realize that the thing you are hunting at suck expense and physical tribulation is so contemptuous of your prowess as to be eating leaves right in front of your eyes.

But Blix is a practical man. As a White Hunter, his job was to produce the game desired and to point it out to his employer of the moment. Blix's work, and mine, was made much easier by finding the elephant so close. We could even land at the camp and then approach them on foot to judge more accurately their size, immediate intentions and strategic disposition.

Doctor Turvy's prescription had to be filled, and taken, of course, but even so we would have time to reconnoitre.

We landed on the miserly runway, which had a lot in common with an extemporaneous badminton court, and within 20 minutes, proceeded on foot toward those magnificent bulls.

Makula was with us. Neither the safari nor this book, for that matter, could be complete without Makula. Though there are a good many Wakamba trackers available in East Africa, it has become almost traditional in late years to mention Makula in every book that touches upon elephant-hunting, and I would not break with tradition.

Makula is a man in the peculiar position of having gained fame without being aware of it. He can neither read nor write; his first language is Wakamba, his second a halting Swahili. He is a smallish ebon-tinted native with an inordinately wise eye, a penchant for black magic, and the instincts of a beagle hound. I think he could track a honeybee through a bamboo forest.

No matter how elaborate the safari on which Makula is engaged as tracker, he goes about naked from the waist up, carrying a long bow and a quiver full of poisoned arrows. He has seen the work of the best rifles white men have yet produced, but when Makula's nostrils distend after either a good or a bad shot, it is not the smell of gunpowder that distends

69

them; it is a kind of restrained contempt for that noisy and unwieldly piece of machinery with its devilish tendency to knock the untutored huntsman flat on his buttocks every time he pulls the trigger.

Safaris come and safaris go, but Makula goes on forever. I suspect at times that he is one of the wisest men I have ever known – so wise that, realizing the scarcity of wisdom, he has never cast a scrap of it away, though I still remember a remark he made to an overzealous newcomer to his profession: "White men pay for danger – we poor ones cannot afford it. Find your elephant, then vanish, so that you may live to find another."

Makula always vanished. He went ahead in the bush with the silence of a shade, missing nothing, and the moment he had brought his hunters within sight of the elephant, he disappeared with the silence of a shade, missing everything.

Stalking just ahead of Blix through the tight bush, Makula signaled for a pause, shinnied up a convenient tree without noise, and then came down again. He pointed to a chink in the thicket, took Blix firmly by the arm, and pushed him ahead. Then Makula disappeared. Blix led, and I followed.

The ability to move soundlessly through a wall of bush as tightly woven as Nature can weave it is not an art that can be acquired much after childhood. I cannot explain it, nor could Arab Maina who taught me ever explain it. It is not a matter of watching where you step; it is rather a matter of keeping your eyes on the place where you want to be, while every nerve becomes another eye, every muscle develops reflex action. You do not guide your body, you trust it to be silent.

We were silent. The elephant we advanced upon heard nothing – even when the enormous hindquarters of two bulls loomed before us like grey rocks wedded to the earth.

Blix stopped. He whispered with his fingers and I read the whisper. "Watch the wind. Swing round them. I want to see their tusks."

Swing, indeed! It took us slightly over an hour to negotiate a semicircle of 50 yards. The bulls were big – with ivory enough – hundred-pounders at least, or better.

Nimrod was satisfied, wet with sweat, and on the verge, I sensed, of receiving a psychic message from Doctor Turvy. But this message was delayed in transit.

One bull raised his head, elevated his trunk, and moved to face us. His gargantuan ears began to spread as if to capture even the sound of our heartbeats. By chance, he had grazed over a spot we had lately left, and he had got our scent. It was all he needed.

I have rarely seen anything so calm as that bull elephant – or so casually determined upon destruction. It might be said that he shuffled to the kill. Being, like all elephant, almost blind, this one could not see us, but he was used to that. He would follow scent and sound until he *could* see us, which, I computed, would take about 30 seconds.

Blix wiggled his fingers earthward, and that meant, "Drop and crawl."

It is amazing what a lot of insect life goes on under your nose when you have got it an inch from the earth. I suppose it goes on in any case, but if you are proceeding on your stomach, dragging your body along by your fingernails, entomology presents itself very forcibly as a thoroughly justified science. The problem of classification alone must continue to be very discouraging.

By the time I had crawled three feet, I am sure that somewhere over 50 distinct species of insect life were individually and severally represented in my clothes, with Siafu ants conducting the congress.

Blix's feet were just ahead of my eyes – close enough so that I could contemplate the holes in his shoes, and wonder why he ever wore any at all, since he went through them almost in a matter of hours. I had ample time also to observe that he wore no socks. Practical, but not *comme il faut*. His legs moved through the underbrush like dead legs dragged by strings. There was no sound from the elephant.

I don't know how long we crawled like that, but the little shadows in the thicket were leaning toward the east when we stopped. Possibly we had gone a hundred yards. The insect bites had become just broad, burning patches.

We were breathing easier – or at least I was – when Blix's feet and legs went motionless. I could just see his head close against his shoulder, and watch him turn to peek upward into the bush. He gave no signal to continue. He only looked horribly embarrassed like a child caught stealing eggs.

But my own expression must have been a little more intense. The big bull was about ten feet away – and at that distance elephant are not blind.

Blix stood up and raised his rifle slowly, with an expression of ineffable sadness.

*That's for me,* I thought. *He knows that even a shot in the brain won't stop that bull before we're crushed like mangos.*

# AFRICA

In an open place, it might have been possible to dodge to one side, but not here. I stood behind Blix with my hands on his waist according to his instructions. But I knew it wasn't any good. The body of the elephant was swaying. It was like watching a boulder, in whose path you were trapped, teeter on the edge of a cliff before plunging. The bull's ears were spread wide now, his trunk was up and extended toward us, and he began the elephant scream of anger which is so terrifying as to hold you silent where you stand, like fingers clamped upon your throat. It is a shrill scream, cold as winter wind.

It occurred to me that this was the instant to shoot.

Blix never moved. He held his rifle very steady and began to chant some of the most striking blasphemy I have ever heard. It was colourful, original, and delivered with finesse, but I felt that this was a badly chosen moment to test it on an elephant – and ungallant beyond belief if it was meant for me.

The elephant advanced, Blix unleashed more oaths (this time in Swedish), and I trembled. There was no rifle shot. A single biscuit tin, I judged would do for both of us – cremation would be superfluous.

"I may have to shoot him," Blix announced, and the remark struck me as an understatement of classic magnificence. Bullets would sink into that monstrous hide like pebbles into a pond.

Somehow you never think of an elephant as having a mouth, because you never see it when his trunk is down, so that when the elephant is quite close and his trunk is up, the dark red-and-black slit is by way of being an almost shocking revelation. I was looking into our elephant's mouth with a kind of idiotic curiosity when he screamed again – and thereby, I am convinced, saved both Blix and me from a fate no more tragic than simple death, but infinitely less tidy.

The scream of that elephant was a strategic blunder, and it did him out of a wonderful bit of fun. It was such an authentic scream of such splendid resonance, that his cronies, still grazing in the bush, accepted it as legitimate warning, and left. We had known they were still there because the bowels of peacefully occupied elephant rumble continually like oncoming thunder – and we had heard thunder.

They left, and it seemed they tore the country from its roots in leaving. Everything went, bush, trees, sansivera, clods of dirt – and the monster who confronted us. He paused, listened, and swung round with the slow irresistibility of a bank-vault door. And then he was off in a typhoon of crumbled vegetation and crashing trees.

For a long time there wasn't any silence, but when there was, Blix lowered his rifle – which had acquired, for me, all the death-dealing qualities of a feather duster.

I was limp, irritable and full of maledictions for the insect kind. Blix and I hacked our way back to camp without the exchange of a word, but when I fell into a canvas chair in front of the tents, I forswore the historic propriety of my sex to ask a rude question.

"I think you're the best hunter in Africa, Blickie, but there are times when your humour is gruesome. Why in hell didn't you shoot?"

Blix extracted a bug from Doctor Turvy's elixir of life and shrugged.

"Don't be silly. You know as well as I do why I didn't shoot. Those elephant are for Winston."

"Of course I know – but what if that bull had charged?"

Farah the faithful produced another drink, and Blix produced a non sequitur. He stared upward into the leaves of the baobab tree and sighed like a poet in love.

"There's an old adage," he said, "translated from the ancient Coptic, that contains all the wisdom of the ages – 'Life is life and fun is fun, but it's all so quiet when the goldfish die.'"

# Leopards are Different

*Of all the African big game animals,* Chui *the leopard is the most beautiful and exotic – even in death.*

**By Robert C. Ruark**

I t was a cold, clear night in the little camp at the Grummetti in Tanganyika. A sharp, winy night, like New England in the fall, with the stars distinct against the sky. The boys had built a roaring blaze out of dead thornbush logs. The dinner was responding kindly to a third cup of coffee. Everybody was tired. It had been a big day. There had been the immense waterbuck in the morning and the red-headed lion in the afternoon, and the business with the lioness and the cubs.

Suddenly the wind veered. A smell swept down on the breeze, a dreadful smell.

"O-ho," Harry Selby said. "Chanel No. 5, if you are a leopard. That delicious aroma would be your pig and your Grant gazelle. It may smell awful to you, but the bait has hit just about the right stage of decay to be better than Camembert to our noisy friend of the fig tree. I was never able to figure why the cleanest, neatest animal in the bush waits until his dinner is maggoty before he really works up an appetite. Let's see. We've had the bait up five days now. The boys say your pussycat's been feeding since yesterday. He ought to be through the pig now and working on the Grant. He ought to be feeling pretty cheeky about his vested interest in that tree.

"I don't know what there is about the tree," the professional hunter went on. "I think maybe it's either bewitched or made out of pure catnip. You can't keep the leopards out of it. It's only about five hundred yards from camp. I come here year after year, and we always get a leopard. I got one three months ago. I got one six months before that. There's an old tabby lives in it, and she changes boy friends every time. We'll go to the blind tomorrow and we'll pull her newest fiancé out for you – that is, if he's eaten deep enough into that Grant. That is, if you can hit him."

At this stage I was beginning to get something past arrogant. Insufferable might be the right word.

"What is all this mystery about leopards?" I asked. "Everybody gives you the old mysterious act. Don Ker tells me about the safari that's been out fourteen years and hasn't got a leopard yet. Everybody says you'll probably get a lion and most of the other stuff, but don't count on leopards. Leopards are where you find them. We got two eating out of one tree and another feeding on that other tree up the river, and we saw one coming back from the buffalo business yesterday. They run up and down the swamp all night, cursing at the baboons.

"You sit over there looking wise, and mutter about if we see him and if I hit him when we see him. You've been polishing up the shotgun and counting the buckshot ever since we hung the kill in the tree. What do you mean, if I hit him? You throw a lion at me the first day out, and I hit him in the back of the neck. I bust the buffalo, all right, and I get that waterbuck with one in the pump, and I knock the brain pan off that second Simba today okay enough, and I break the back on a running eland. What have I got to do to shoot a sitting leopard at thirty-five feet with a scope on the gun? Use a silver bullet?"

"Leopards ain't like other things," Harry said. "Leopards do strange things to people's personality. Leopards and kudu affect people oddly. I saw a bloke fire into the air three times once, and then throw his gun at a standing kudu. I had a chap here one time who fired at the leopard first night, and missed. We came back the second night. Same leopard in the tree. Fired again. Missed. This was a chap with all manner of medals for sharpshooting. A firecracker. Splits lemons at three-hundred and fifty yards, shooting offhand. Pure hell on running Tommies at six hundred yards, or some such. Knew everything about bullet weights and velocities and things. Claims a .220 Swift is plenty big enough for the average elephant. Already had the boys calling him One-Bullet Joe."

"So?" I inquired.

"Came back the third night. Leopard up the tree. Fired again. Broad daylight, too, not even six o'clock yet. Missed him clean. Missed him the next night. Missed him for the fifth time on the following night. Leopard very plucky. Seemed to be growing fond of the sportsman. Came back again on the sixth night, and this time my bloke creases him on the back of the neck. Leopard takes off into the bush. I grab the shotgun and take off after him. *Hapana* – nothing. No blood and no tracks. Worked him most of the night with a flashlight, expecting him on the back of my neck any minute. *Hapana chui* – no leopard. My sport quit leopards in disgust, and went back to shooting lemons at 350 yards."

"How do you know the marksman touched him on the neck?" I asked sarcastically. "Did he write you a letter of complaint to Nairobi?"

"No," Harry said gently. "I came back with another party after the rains, and here was this same *chui* up the same tree. This client couldn't hit a running Tommy at six hundred yards, and he couldn't see any future to lemon-splitting at 350. But his gun went off, possibly by accident, and the old boy tumbled out of the tree and when we turned him over there was a scar across the back of his neck, and still reasonably fresh. Nice tom, too. About eight foot, I surmise. Not as big as Harriet Maytag's, though. He was just on eight-four."

"If I hear any more about Harriet Maytag's lion or Harriet Maytag's rhino, Mr. Selby," I declared with considerable dignity, "it will not be leopards we shoot tomorrow. It will be white hunters, and the wound will be in the back. Not the first time it's happened out here, either. I'm going to bed possibly to pray that I will not embarrass you tomorrow. Evan if I am not Harriet Maytag, I still shoot a pretty good lion."

There was an awful row down by the river. The baboons set up a fearful cursing, the monkeys screamed, and the birds awoke. There was a regular, painting, wheezing grunt in the background, like the sound made by a two-handed saw on green wood.

"That's your boy, chum," Selby said brightly. "Come to test your courage. If you find him in the tent with you later on, wake me."

We went to bed. I dreamed all night of a faceless girl named Harriet Maytag whom I had not met and who kept changing into a leopard. I also kept shooting at lemons at three and a half feet, and I missed them every time. Then the lemons would turn into leopards, and the gun would jam.

# AFRICA

Everybody I had met in the past six months had a leopard story for me. How you were extremely fortunate even to get a glimpse of one, let alone a shot. How they moved so fast that you couldn't see them go from one place to another. How you only got one shot, and whoosh, the leopard was gone. How it was always night, or nearly night, when they came to the kill, and you were shooting in the bad light against the dark background on which the cat was barely perceptible. How if you wounded him you had to go after him in the black, thick thorn. How he never growled, like a lion, betraying his presence, but came like a streak from six feet or dropped quietly on your neck from a tree. How, if four guys went in, three always got scratched. And how the leopard's fangs and claws were always septic because of his habit of feeding on carrion. How a great many professionals rate him over the elephant and buffalo as murderous game, largely because he kills for fun and without purpose. And how unfortunately most of what you heard was true.

I had recently talked with a doctor who has sewed up three hunters who had been clawed by the same cat within the last six months. A big leopard runs only 150 pounds or so, but I had seen a zebra foal, weighing at least two hundred pounds, thirty feet above ground and wedged into a crotch by a leopard, giving you some idea about the fantastic strength that is hidden by that lovely spotted golden hide. I reflected that there are any amount of documented stories about leopards coming into tents and even houses after dogs and sometimes people and breaking into fowl-pens and leaping out of trees at people on horseback.

"A really peculiar beast," Harry had said when we jumped the big one coming back from the buffalo. "Here we find one in broad daylight right smack out in the open plain, when there are people who've lived here all their lives and have never seen one. Here is a purely nocturnal animal who rarely ever leaves the rocks or the river-edge, standing out in the middle of a short-grass plain like a bloody topi. They are supposed to be one of the shyest, spookiest animals alive, yet they'll come into your camp and pinch a dog right out of the mess tent. They'll walk through your dining room on some occasions, and spit in your eye. They're supposed to have a great deal of cunning, yet I knew one that came back to the same kill six nights in a row, being shot over and missed every time. But they're a great fascination for me, and for most people.

"The loveliest sight I've ever seen since I stared hunting was a leopard sleeping in a thorn tree in the late afternoon. The tree was black and yellow, the same color as the cat, and the late sun was coming in through the leaves, dappling the cat and the tree with a little extra gold. We weren't after leopard at the time, already had one; so we just woke him up and watched him scamper. He went up the tree like a big lizard."

I was getting to know quite a bit about my young friend Selby by this time. He was a professional hunter and lived by killing, or by procuring things for other people to shoot, but he hated use a gun worse than any man I ever met. He has the fresh face and candid eyes of a man who has lived all his life in the woods, and when he talks of animals his face lights up like a kid's in a toy store. He had nearly killed us all, a day earlier, coming back from a big *ngama* – lion dance party – in the Waikoma village. There were some baby francolin in the trail, and he almost capsized the Land Rover trying to miss them. What he liked was to watch animals and learn more about them. He refused to allow anyone to shoot baboons. He hated even to shoot a hyena. The only things he loved to shoot were wild dogs, merely because he disapproved of the way they killed by running their prey in shifts, pulling it down finally, and eating it alive.

"You're a poet, man," I told him. "The next thing, you'll be using the sonnet form to describe how old Katunga howls when his madness comes on in the moonlight nights."

"It would make a nice poem at that," Harry said. "But don't spoof me about leopards in trees. Wait until you have seen a leopard in a tree before you rag me. It's a sight unlike any other in the world."

When we got up that next morning, the scent of the rotting pig and the rotting Grant was stronger than ever. Harry sniffed and ordered up Jessica, the Land Rover. We climbed in and drove down the riverbank, with the dew fresh on the grass and a brisk morning breeze rustling the scrub acacias. As we passed the leopard tree there was a scrutching sound and a rustle in the bush that was not made by the breeze. A brown eagle was sitting in the top of the tree.

We made a daily ritual of this trip, after we had hung the bait the first day, in order to get the cat accustomed to the passage of the jeep. We also made a swing back just around dusk to get him accustomed to the evening visit. Always we passed close aboard the blind, a semicircle of thorn and leaves with a peephole and a crotched stick for a gun rest. Its rear was open to the plain and its camouflaged front faced the tree. By now it would seem that the leopard had been feeding on the two carcasses we had derricked up to an L-shaped fork about 30 feet above ground and tied fast with rope.

You could just define the shape of the pig, strung a little higher than the Grant, as they hung conveniently from another limb, in easy reach of the feeding fork. The pig was nearly consumed now, his body and neck all but gone and his legs gnawed clean to the hairy fetlocks. The guts and about twenty pounds of hindquarter were gone from the Grant. The steady wind was blowing from the tree and toward the blind, and they smelled just lovely.

Harry didn't say anything until he had swung Jessica around and we were driving back to the camp and breakfast. "You heard the old boy leave his tree, I suppose. I got a glimpse of him as we drove by. And did you notice the eagle?"

"I noticed the eagle," I said. "How come eagles and leopards are so chummy?"

"Funny thing about a lot of animals," Harry observed. "You know how the tick-birds work with the rhino. Rhino can't see very much, and the tick-birds serve as his eyes, in return for which they get to eat his ticks. I always watch the birds when I'm stalking a rhino. When the birds jump, you know the old boy is about to come bearing down on you. Similarly, you'll always find a flock of egrets perched on the backs of a buffalo herd. You can trace the progress of a buff through high grass just by watching the egrets.

"I don't know how they work out their agreements," Harry went on. "Often you'll see a lion feeding on one end of a kill and a couple of jackals chewing away on the other. Yet a lion won't tolerate a hyena or a vulture near his kill.

"Now, our friend, this leopard which you may or may not shoot tonight, or tomorrow night, or ever, has this transaction with the eagle. The eagle mounts guard all day over the leopard's larder. If vultures or even another leopard comes by and takes a fancy to old Chui's free lunch, the eagle sets up a hell of a clamor and old Chui comes bounding out of the swamp to protect his victuals. In return for this service the eagle is allowed to assess the carcass a pound or so per diem. It's a very neat arrangement for both."

We went back to camp and had the usual tea, canned fruit and crumbly toast. It was still cold enough for the remnants of last night's fire to feel good.

"We won't hunt today," Selby said. "We'll just go sight in the .30-06 again and you can get some writing done. I want you rested for our date with Chui at four o'clock. You'll be shaking enough from excitement, and

I don't want it complicated with fatigue."

"I will not be shaking from excitement or fatigue or anything else," I declared. "I am well known around this camp as a man who is as icy calm as Dick Tracy when danger threatens. In nearby downtown Ikoma I'm a household word amongst the rate-payers. I am Old Bwana Risase Moja, slayer of Simba, Protector of the Poor, Scourge of the Buffalo, and the best damn bird shooter since Papa Hemingway was here last. I promise you, you will not have to into any bush after any wounded leopard this night. I'm even going to pick the rosette I want to shoot him through. I intend to pick one of the less regular patterns, because I not want to mar the hide."

"Words," Selby said. "Childish chatter from an ignorant man. Let's go and sight in the .30-06. We'll sight her pointblank for fifty yards. They make a tough target, these leopards. Lots of times you don't have but a couple of inches of fur to shoot at. And that scope has got to be right."

"How come the scope? I thought you were the original scope-hater. At thirty-five yards I figure I can hit even one of those lemons you're always talking about with open sights, shooting from a forked stick."

Harry was patient, as if talking to a child. "This is the only time I reckon a scope to be actually necessary out here. The chances are that when that cat comes it will be nearly dark, well past shooting light. You won't even be able to see the kill with your naked eye, let alone the cat. The scope's magnification will pick him out against the background, and you can see the post in the scope a lot easier than you could see a front sight a foot high through ordinary open sights. And if I were you, I'd wear those polaroid glasses you're so proud of, too. Any visual help you can get you will need, chum."

We sighted in the .30-06, aiming at the old blaze on the sighting-in tree. Then we trundled Jessica back to camp, pausing on the way long enough to shoot a Thomson gazelle for the pot. It was a fairly long shot, and I broke his neck.

"I think I can hit a leopard, I said.

"A lousy little Tommie is different thing from a leopard," Harry replied. "Tommies have no claws, no fangs, and do not roost in trees."

"We slopped around camp for the rest of the morning, reading detective stories and watching the vultures fight the marabou storks for what was left of the waterbuck carcass. Lunchtime came, and I made a motion toward the canvas water bag where the gin and vermouth lived.

"Hapana," Harry said. "No booze for you, my lad. For me, yes. For Mamma, yes. For you, no. The steady hand, the clear eye. You may tend to bar if you like, but no cocktails for the Bwana until after the Bwana has performed this evening."

"This could go on for days." I grumbled. "Bloody leopard may never come to the tree."

"Quite likely," Harry remarked, admiring a small glass of lukewarm gin with some green lime nonsense in it. "The more for me and Mama. A lesson in sobriety for you."

A bee, from the hive in the tree behind the mess tent, dive-bombed Harry's glass and swam happily around in the gin-and-lime. Harry fished him out with a spoon and set him on the mess table. The bee staggered happily and buzzed blowsily.

"Regard the bee," he said. "Drunk as a lord. Imagine what gin does to leopard shooters, whose glands are activated by fear and uncertainty."

"Go to hell, the both of you. I'll eat while these barflies consume my gin."

The lunch was fine – yesterday's cold boiled guineafowl flanked by some fresh tomatoes we had swindled out of the Indian storekeeper in Ikoma, with hot macaroni and cheese that Ali the cook produced from his biscuit-tin over and some pork and beans in case we lacked starch after the spaghetti, bread and potatoes. Harry allowed me a bottle of beer.

"Beer is a food," he told me. "It is not a tipple. Now go take a nap. I want you fresh. I hate crawling after wounded leopards who have been annoyed by amateurs. It's so lonesome in those bushes after dark, the leopard waiting ahead of you and the client apt to shoot you in the trousers the first time a monkey screams."

I dozed a bit, and at four o'clock Harry came into the tent and roused me. "Leopard time," He said. "Let's hope he comes early. It'll give the bugs less chance to devour us. Best smear some of that bug dope on your neck and wrists and face. And if I were you, I'd borrow one of the Memsahib's scarves and tie it around most of my face and neck. If you have to sneeze, sneeze now. If you have to clear your throat or scratch or anything else, do it now, because for the next three hours you will sit motionless in that blind, moving no muscle, making no sound, and thinking as quietly as possible. Leopards are allergic to noise."

I looked quite beautiful with one of Mama's fancy Paris scarves, green to match the blind, tied around my head like an old peasant woman. We climbed into Jessica. Harry was sitting on her rail from the front-seat position. The sharp edge of her after-rail was cutting a chunk out of my rear. We went past the blind at about twenty miles an hour, and we both fell out, command-style, directly into the blind. The jeep took off, to return at the sound of a shot or at black dark if no shot.

I wriggled into the blind and immediately sat on a flock of safari ants that managed to wound me severely before we scuffed them out. I poked the .30-06 through the peep-hole in the front of the blind and found that it centered nicely on the kill in the tree. Even at four-thirty the bait was indistinct to the naked eye. The scope brought it out clearly. I looked over my shoulder at Selby, his shock of black hair uncluttered by shawl or insecticide. A tsetse was biting him on the forehead. He let it bite. My old 12-gauge double, loaded with buckshot, was resting over his crossed knees. He looked at me, shrugged, winked and pointed with his chin at the leopard tree.

We sat. Bugs came. Small animals came. No snakes came. No leopards came. I began to think of how much of my life I had spent waiting for something to happen – of how long you waited for an event to occur, and what a short time was consumed when the event you had been waiting for actually did come to pass. The worst thing about the war at sea was waiting. You waited all through the long black watches of the North Atlantic night, waiting for a submarine to show its periscope. You could not smoke. You did not even like to step inside the blacked-out wheelhouse for a smoke because the light spoiled your eyes for half an hour. You waited on islands in the Pacific. You waited for air raids to start in London, and then you waited some more for the all-clear. You waited in line at the training school for chow, and for pay, and for everything. You waited in train stations, and you sat around airports waiting for your feeble priority to activate – you waited everywhere. From the day you got into it until the day you got out of it you were waiting for the war itself to end, so that it was all one big wait.

Sitting in the blind, staring at the eaten pig and the partially eaten Grant and waiting for the leopard to come and hearing the sounds – the *oohoo-oohoo-hoo* of the doves and the squalls and squawks and growls and mutters in the dark bush ahead by Grummetti River – I thought profoundly that there was an awfully good analogy in waiting for a leopard by a strange river in a strange dark country. I began to get Selby's point about the importance of a leopard in a tree – waited for, planned for, suffered for – to be seen for one swift moment or maybe not to be seen at all.

These are the thoughts you have in a leopard blind in Tanganyika when the ants bite you and you want to cough and you nose itches and nothing whatsoever can be done about it. Five o'clock came. No leopard. *Hapana chui*, my head said in Swahili. I looked at Selby. He was scowling ferociously at a flock of guineafowl that seemed to be feeding right into the blind. With his hand he made a swift, attention-getting gesture. The guineas got the idea, and marched off. Selby pointed his chin at the leopard tree and shrugged. Now it was six o'clock. I thought about the three weeks I sweated out in Guam, waiting for orders to leave that accursed paradise, orders I was almost sure of but not quite. When they came, they came in a hurry. They came in the morning and I left in the afternoon. Six-thirty. *Hapana chui*.

I t was getting very dark now, so dark that you couldn't see the kill in the tree at all without training the rifle on it and looking through the scope. Even then it was indistinct, a blur of Lodies against a green-black background of foliage. I looked at Selby. He rapidly undoubled both fists twice, which I took to mean 20 more minutes of shooting time.

My watch said 12 minutes to 7, and it was dead black in the background and the pig was nonvisible and the Grant only a blob and even where it was lightest it was dark gray. I thought, *Damn it, this is the way it always is with everything. You wait and suffer and strive, and when it ends it's all wasted, and the hell with all leopards.*

Then I felt Harry's hand on my gun arm. Down the river to the left the baboons had gone mad. The uproar lasted only a split second, and then a cold and absolute calm settled on the Grummetti. No bird. No monkey. No nothing. About a thousand yards away there was a surly, irritable cough. Harry's hand closed on my arm, and then relaxed. My eyes were on the first fork of the big tree.

There was only tree to watch, a first fork full of nothing. Then there was a scrutching noise like the scrape of stiff khaki on brush, and where there had been nothing but tree there was now nothing but leopard. He stretched his lovely spotted neck and turned his big head arrogantly and slowly, and he seemed to be staring straight into my soul with the coldest eyes I have ever seen. The devil would have leopard's eyes, yellow-green and hard and depthless as beryls. He stopped turning his head and looked at me. I had the post of the scope centered between those eyes. His head came out clearly against the black background of forest. It looked bigger than a lion's head.

You are not supposed to shoot a leopard when he comes to the first fork. The target is bad in that light and small, and you either spoil his face if you hit him well or you wound him and there is the nasty business of going after him. You are supposed to wait for his second move, which will take him either to the kill or to a second branch, high up, as he makes a decision on eating or going up in the rigging. If he is not shot on that second branch or shot as he poises over the kill, he is not shot. Not at all. You can't see him up high in the thick of foliage. And Harry had said, "On a given night there has never been more than one shot at a leopard."

I held the aiming post of my telescopic sight on that leopard's face for a million years. While I was holding it the Pharaohs built the pyramids. Rome fell. The Pilgrims landed on Plymouth Rock. The Japs attacked Pearl Harbor.

And then the leopard moved. Only you could not see him. Where there had been leopard there was only fork. There was not even a flash or a blur when he moved. He disappeared.

Then he appeared on a branch to the left of the kill, a branch that slanted upward into the foliage at a 45-degree angle. He stood at full pride on that branch, not crouching, but standing erect and profiling like a battle-horse on an ancient tapestry, gold and black against the black. There was a slightly ragged rosette on his left shoulder as he stood with his head high.

The black asparagus tip of the aiming post went to the ragged rosette, and a little inside voice said, *Squeeze, don't jerk, because Selby is looking and you only get one shot at a –*

I never heard the rifle fire. All I heard was the bullet whunk. It was the prettiest sound I ever heard. No, not quite the prettiest. The prettiest was the second sound, which said *blonk*. That was the sound the leopard made when he hit the ground. It sounded like a bag of soft cement dropping off a roof. *Blonk*. No other sounds. No moans. No growls. No whish or swift, bounding feet on bush.

A hand hit me on the shoulder, bringing me back into the world of living people.

"*Piga*," Harry said. "*Kufa*. As bloody *kufa* as a bloody doornail. Right on the button. He's dead as a bloody beef in there. We were as near to losing him as damn to swearing, though. I thought he'd never leave that bloody fork and when he went I knew he was heading up to the crow's nest. You shot him one-sixtieth of a second before he leaped, because I could just make out his start to crouch. You got both shoulders and the heart, I'd say, from the way he came down. Aren't they something to see when they first hit that fork, with those bloody great eyes looking right down your throat and that dirty big head turning from side to side! You shot him very well, Bwana Two Lions. Did you aim for any particular rosette like you said?

"Go to hell twice," I said. "Give me a cigarette."

"I think you've earned one," Harry said. "Then let's go retrieve your boy. I'll go in ahead with the shotty-gun. You cover me from the left. If he's playing possum in there, shoot him, not me. If he comes, he'll come quick, except I would stake my next month's pay that this *chui* isn't going anywhere. He's had it."

Harry picked up the old 12-guage and I slipped the scope off the .30-06 and slid another bullet into the magazine. We walked slowly into the high bush, Harry six steps ahead and I just off to the left. I knew the leopard was dead, but I knew also that dead leopards have carved chunks out of lots of faces. Selby was bobbling the shotgun up and down under his left shoulder, a mannerism he has when he wants to be very sure there is nothing on his jacket to clutter a fast raise and shoot. We needn't have worried.

*Chui* – my *chui* now – was sleeping quietly underneath the branch from which he had fallen. He had never moved. He was never going to move. This great, wonderful golden cat, eight foot something of leopard, looking more beautiful in death than he had looked in the tree, this wonderful wide-eyed, green-yellow-eyed cat was mine. And I had shot him very well.

"You picked the right rosette," Harry said. "Grab a hind leg and we'll lug him out. He's a real beauty. Isn't it funny how most of the antelopes and the lions lose all their dignity in death, while this blighter is more beautiful when he's in the bag than he is in the tree? Look at those eyes. No glaze at all. He's clean as a whistle all over, and yet he lives on filth. He eats carrion and smells like a bloody primrose. Yet a lion is nearly always scabby and fly-ridden and full of old sores and cuts. He rumples when he dies, and seems to grow smaller. Not Chui, though. He's the most beautiful trophy in Africa."

"How does he compare with Harriet Maytag's leopard?" I asked, rather caustically, I thought.

"Forget Harriet Maytag, chum," Harry said. "I was only kidding. As far as I'm concerned, you are not only Bwana Simba, Protector of the Poor, but a right fine leopard man, too. Here come the boys. Prepare to have your hand shaken"

The boys ohed and ahed and gave me the old double-thumb grip, which means that the Bwana is going to distribute largesse later when he has quit bragging and the liquor has taken hold. We piled the big fellow into Jessica's back seat and took off for camp. Mama nearly fainted when we took the leopard out of the back and draped him in front of the campfire. The wind had changed again and she had heard no shot. When the boys left in the dark with the Rover, she had assumed they were going to pick us up.

The leopard looked lovelier than ever in front of the campfire. His eyes were still clear. His hide was only gorgeous. Even the bullet hole was neat. He was eight feet and a bit, and he was a big tom. About one-fifty on an empty stomach.

"Tail's a big too short for my taste thought," Harry said. "Harriet's had a longer tail."

"Harriet be damned. After you're through with the pictures, mix me a martini."

Harry took the pictures. He mixed me a martini. I drank it and passed out – from sheer excitement, I suppose, because I hadn't had a drink all day.

The next evening when Harry and Mama went down to see about the female, with cameras, she had already acquired another tom. This leads me to believe that women are fickle.

The tom came in across the plain, which leopards never do, and passed within a few feet of the blind. He growled mightily as he bounded past. The Memsahib gave up leopard photography. She said that Selby was obviously deaf, or he would have heard the leopard coming through the grass.

*Originally published in* Field & Stream, *April 1953. Reprinted by permission of Harold Matson Co., Inc.*

# A GREAT AND
# TAINTED GENIUS

*After Bimini, Ernest Hemingway followed big fish to Cuba, went on safari in Africa where he survived tooth and claw and two plane crashes, then settled in the hills of Idaho where he shot antelope and pheasants and mallards and finally, himself.*

*By Roger Pinckney*

Way up in the Sawtooths, the day comes creeping on the wind. The aspens rattle and the stars fade as the first light hits the great jumble of peaks and tells you how this place got its name. The wind ghosts up the mountain and whispers stories to those with ear and heart to hear. Stories of the Ancient Ones, the Sheep Eaters. Stories of the cavalry and miners and cowpokes and swindlers and bums and magnates. And finally the story of a man who loved this place, then came back here to die.

Ernest Hemingway. We love his work and puzzle over the man, this great and tainted genius. When we know the story, our puzzling ferments and ages like good wine, and it becomes smoky and sweet with an aftertaste like the morning wind in the Idaho hills.

No ordinary man and certainly no ordinary story. There's the greatest writer of the last century and wanderings across the continents with gun and rod, and it begins in 1951 just outside Havana in a ramshackle stone farmhouse on a hill overlooking the sea.

# AFRICA

Locals call it la Finca Vigia, the view farm. Little wonder. Below is the surging Caribbean, breaking upon a labyrinth of coral. Beyond is the Gulf Stream, home to trophy billfish and tuna and dolphin and great toothy wahoo.

Behind the house is a sunny patio and a swimming pool, where Ernest Hemingway swims laps while a woman reads a magazine and sips her gin and tonic. Ernest Hemingway is lately famous and very prosperous from *The Old Man and the Sea*, the book about a Cuban fisherman and a big fish that sold 50,000 copies in its first three weeks and is now selling 1,500 copies a day.

The woman is Mary Welsh Hemingway, a fine sliver of the Scandinavian gene pool from far northern Minnesota. She is tall, blonde, gutsy, formerly a war correspondent for *Time* and *Life* magazines. It's her third marriage, his fourth.

Mary sighs, proclaims her boredom. Ernest Hemingway breaks his stroke and stands to catch his breath. "Let's hunt birds in Idaho," he says.

Ernest Hemingway was a man of his word. He could coolly squeeze the trigger before charging African game. He could fight a blue marlin four times his weight for a full day with a flask of rum but without a jigger of complaint. He could hike and ski and wingshoot and drink and box to put most men to shame. But with women, he was a little shaky.

Which was why Ernest Hemingway knew Idaho. He went there in 1939, when he was between wives and looking for a place to hole up and write. Sun Valley is where Averell Harriman, president of the Union Pacific, built a ski resort to boost wintertime ticket sales on his railroad. As a publicity ploy, Harriman invited the rich and famous, threw in free rooms and sumptuous meals, then used the celebrities names in various advertising blitzes. Ingrid Bergman came, so did Robert Taylor and Clark Gable.

Harriman set Hemingway up in Room 206 where he wrote mornings and ventured forth to hunt and fish in the afternoons. Between times, he posed for publicity pictures. The man behind the lens was Lloyd "Pappy" Arnold, a serious outdoorsman who introduced Hemingway to another hunter, resort publicist Gene Van Guilder, and to Taylor "Beartracks" Williams, the area's best-known guide.

Pheasants cackled in the hills and mallards dipped into the backwaters of Silver Creek and the Big Wood River. Gene, Beartracks, Pappy and Papa Hemingway, as he increasingly called himself, went after them at every opportunity. Hunting ducks one Sunday morning, Gene Van Guilder was killed by a blast from a mis-handled shotgun. Hemingway, abed and nursing a hangover, was spared watching his friend die. He delivered the eulogy, reading at the windy gravesite words he had typed the night before. " . . . best of all he loved the fall. The leaves yellow on the cottonwoods. Leaves floating on the trout streams and above the hills, the high blue windless skies. Now he will be part of them forever."

Hemingway returned to la Finca Vigia to work on For Whom the Bell Tolls, but in the fall of 1941 he was back in Idaho. Beartracks Williams introduced him to the Old Timer, known by no other name, who hauled Arnold and Williams and Hemingway to his bug-infested shack in the Pashsimeroi Valley – Shoshone for "water and the one place of trees." There around the campfire the men heard the Old Timer's stories, tales of Custer's death at the Greasy Grass, and the Wagonbox fight, where sixty-seven woodcutters faced down two thousand Sioux.

The men chased antelope for two days without success. The third day out, they spooked a herd up into a blind canyon. There was only one way out and Hemingway saw it, ran for it, first on horse, later on foot, clambering over rocks while clutching his battered Springfield .30-06. He made it just in time. "They came streaming over the hump," he later wrote. "I picked the biggest buck and swung ahead of him and squeezed gently and the bullet broke his neck." Arnold saw it all and told the story for years.

But high society was calling. Down the mountain at Sun Valley, Gary Cooper and Robert Taylor were waiting to talk to him about the movie potential for For Whom the Bell Tolls, which had sold a half-million copies. And then there were the bars, the heated pools and roulette wheels.

After declining an invitation to speak at a book convention in New York City, Hemingway took off in the other direction. On December 4th, he was gazing into the depths of the Grand Canyon. The news of Pearl Harbor reached him when he was crossing the border into Mexico. So Ernest Hemingway, wounded in the first war, went to war again, first chasing German submarines in the Caribbean aboard his beloved Pilar, then covering the Normandy invasion, finally winning a Bronze Star as a leader of a troop of French partisans who fought their way into Paris considerably ahead of the U.S. Army.

After the war, there was la Finca again. He was far offshore, fishing the Gulf Stream when the radio crackled with the news he had won the Pulitzer Prize. Hollywood was calling by the time he got to shore. He celebrated by buying a yellow Plymouth convertible and planning a trip to Africa. He had been there 20 years before and his book, *The Green Hills of Africa*, had been a modest success. Now he had the money and the time and he was going back.

# AFRICA

And now there was Mary Welsh Hemingway, his fourth, last, and best wife. The first leg of the African trip took them to hotels and bars in Key West, New York and Paris, and then on to hotels and bars and bullfights in Spain. In Mombasa, they were met by Phillip Percival, who had begun his career guiding Teddy Roosevelt in 1909 and served Hemingway equally as well in 1933. They struggled uphill to Kenya, some 6,000 feet above the sea.

There at Percival's farm, the campfires were blazing. There awaited six tents, four trucks, 700 pounds of food, two dozen cases of whiskey, double rifles, double shotguns and .22s for taking camp meat. There was N'gui, the gunbearer, who would not shirk his duty when charged by lion or elephant; M'kao, the skinner and tracker who could read signs in the earth at a full run; M'thoka, the hunting car driver; ebony and bony M'windi, too old to do much else, who washed clothes and cleaned tents; and so on down the ranks until there were twenty-two Wakamba tribesmen ready to head off up the Salengai River.

"It was a green and pleasant country," he wrote, "with hills below the forest that grew thick on the sides of the mountain, and it was cut by the valleys of several watercourses that came down out of the thick timber on the mountain . . . and it was there by the forest edge that we waited for the rhino to come out."

But by odd coincidence, the first rhino came looking for him. A Kenyan warden stopped them on the road. A poacher had wounded a rhino, now sorely aggrieved and eager to trample the next person he met. Would Bwana like a crack at him?

Indeed, Bwana would. He uncased his Westley Richards .577 double, popped two rounds into the chambers, slipped a few more into his pockets, and took up the trail. The beast charged and Hemingway got off two quick shots, the nearest from 12 yards. The rhino careened off into the dust and gathering gloom. Hemingway spent a restless night, but in the morning the trackers found the beast, the bullet holes where Hemingway wanted.

Now they had their first trophy and lion were next. They shot two zebras, hauled the carcasses to likely spots, and set up baits. The local Masai heard the shooting and drifted into camp, greeting the hunters and their Wakamba crew by striking the ground with the butts of their long home-forged spears and saying "Jambo, Jambo." The taciturn and unflinchable Masai were much amused when Hemingway began plugging holes in half dollars and shooting cigarettes from their hands with his .22. Impressed, they disclosed the real reason for the visit. Lions had been killing their cattle. Would Bwana care to thin them out?

Once again, Ernest Hemingway was happy to oblige. A week later he took a poke at a big male in the half-light of dawn. Through they heard the bullet whock home, there was no roar and little blood, and the lion vanished into the brush. Percival joined the posse to root him out. A long harrowing hour and four shots later, the lion was dead, though Hemingway did not kill it.

Hoping for magic and a change of luck, Hemingway cut a sliver from the cat's backstrap, ate it raw. The Masai set up a great wail. Though they would open a cow's veins and lap blood like vampires, a white man eating lion flesh was too much for their sensibilities.

Whatever luck Hemingway had hoped would follow that bloody snack did not materialize. A week later he missed a Cape buffalo in the Kimana River Swamp, in the shadow of Kilimanjaro. He switched to his worn and trusty Springfield – the same rifle that took the running antelope and made three dozen one-shot kills on his first safari – and bagged a zebra and a gerenuk. But then he started missing again. Mary shot a kudu at 245 yards with a 6.5 Mannlicher, but Hemingway's bad luck continued. He fell out of the Land Rover, battering his head and throwing out a shoulder.

But life offers compensations, as Teddy Roosevelt noted in 1909 when he went on safari instead of moving into the White House. A half-century later, another one of Percival's clients set out to prove it once again. Hemingway – as fine a wingshot as ever – took lesser bustards and francolin and guinea fowl and sandgrouse almost daily.

Hemingway's work with the rogue rhino and the cattle-killing lion earned him the status of honorary Kenyan warden, with powers of investigation and arrest. He toured the countryside, responding to elephant raids on cornfields, and lion and hyena predation on donkeys and cattle. He knocked a leopard out of a tree and went after it on his belly with a Winchester pump-gun, shooting at close range until "the roaring stopped." *Look* magazine ran a picture of the bearded Bwana and old Chui, the spotted one.

And then there was Debba, the winsome Wakamba girl from the nearby shamba. Hemingway, typically outrageous, mentioned his lustful thoughts to Mary, who wryly suggested old M'windi give Debba a bath first. Hemingway waited until Mary flew up to Nairobi to do some shopping. She came back to find her bed broken, and the Greatest Living Writer in the English Language practicing with a spear and running about in shorts dyed various shades of Masai gray, pink and ochre.

Hemingway's run of bad luck only got worse. On January 21, 1954, he and Mary boarded a Cessna 180 at West Nairobi airport for sightseeing and photography above the White Nile and the Great Rift Escarpment. Three days later while circling low over a spectacular waterfall, the pilot clipped a telegraph cable, severing the radio antenna and most of the rudder. They made it another three miles before plowing into the thorn trees.

The pilot was jostled but otherwise unhurt. Ernest had a mild concussion, another injured shoulder and Mary was in shock. The trio struggled up a hill, built a fire and was spotted by a river streamer the following day. By then, news had flashed around the world that Ernest Hemingway was missing somewhere in Uganda and presumed dead.

The steamer deposited them at Lake Albert, where they boarded another aircraft – a decrepit De Havilland bi-plane – bound for the hospital at Entebbe. They never made it off the ground. Mary and the pilot shinnied out a tiny shattered window. While flames licked toward the fuel tanks, Hemingway rammed and kicked and butted his way through a jammed side door.

He was alive, but badly hurt. He was bruised and burned, but worst of all, his fractured skull was leaking blood and cerebral fluid. And it was still 140 miles to the hospital, two days by potholed and rutted Ugandan roads. Halfway there, they stopped for food and drink, and sympathetic bar patrons poured gin into Hemingway's open head wound, proclaiming the superiority of Ugandan bush medicine and predicting a speedy recovery.

But it was not to be. Ernest Hemingway, suddenly old at fifty-four, was never quite the same. He suffered flashes of black anger and irrational outbursts. And there were deep and recurring depressions, delusions of both grandeur and persecution. After briefly recuperating in Nairobi, where he claimed he was treating his burns with lion fat, and fishing on the Indian Ocean where he caught little, Hemingway returned to Europe. There he consorted – as best as he was able – with an old but very young lover, the lovely Adriana Ivancich, whom he had bedded years before in Cuba.

E ventually Hemingway made it back to la Finca Vigia, where he fished with Ava Gardner, Hollywood's hottest that year, after hours trolling her around the Havana nightspots, provoking a minor frenzy among young Latino night-lifers.

Mary remembered the early morning of October 28, 1954. She had slept alone, which was her custom, when her husband crawled in alongside and woke her with a throaty whisper. "I've won the thing."

"What thing?"

"The Swedish thing," he murmured.

Ernest Hemingway had won the Nobel Prize for Literature. But the black mood that had settled upon him was taking its toll. "I'm thinking of telling them to shove it." But he reconsidered. "Hell, it's $35,000. A man can have a lot of fun with $35,000."

And he did. He went back to Idaho. But there were other considerations. Hemingway had lately written, "I am a man without politics. This is a great defect but it is preferable to arteriosclerosis." But he was an American in a country where Castro and Batista were waging a bitter civil war. After a nervous patrol of government conscripts assassinated one of his favorite dogs, Hemingway headed north by northwest.

By then Hemingway was too famous and Sun Valley too touristy. The defunct mining town of Ketchum was just across the river. Mary recalled " . . . wooden boardwalks on either side of the two blocks long mainstreet, which was also Highway 91 heading toward Alaska . . . there was no bank but all the bars cashed checks. Canned milk and pinto beans and homegrown cabbage . . . in the only grocery store, whose front window displayed not merchandise, but a long row of slot machines."

The high-country climate suited Hemingway, who was finally limbering up after his two plane crashes so that he could swing on a bird once again. The Hemingways shot mallards and pintails, chukars, pheasants and sage grouse. They even chanced another airplane ride, that took them far up into the mountains – in a howling snowstorm – to hunt mule deer.

Up in Idaho, they still talk about those days. Patti Struthers, now in Albuquerque, was a teenager who remembers a big man with a charisma that filled every room he walked into. Still, she was afraid of him. "There was something about him that I did not like." Was it sex? Maybe so. "He spent some time with one of my girlfriends," Struthers says. "She seemed to be alright with it, but it gave me the creeps." Complex as always, Hemingway taught Patti's mother how to handle a shotgun.

At 81, Margaret Struthers' recollections are still vivid. "It was a double sixteen he had bought for his boys. We went out to the range and I got good enough to kill ducks we flushed from the irrigation ditches. Ernie would lay out a plan and we'd crawl on 'em. Nobody dared stand and shoot till he gave the word." And despite his legendary penchant for alcohol and recklessness, Margaret Struthers remembers a man who brooked no drinking until the limit was filled, the guns unloaded and cased. "He was very careful about that."

Hemingway and Margaret's brother, Bud Purdy, tried to introduce live pigeon shooting to Idaho, a sport Hemingway enjoyed in Cuba. The lack of sufficient pigeons proved no obstacle. The men used magpies, a bird rated by local ranchers as somewhere between a crow and a buzzard. There was a ten-cent bounty on them in those days, and Hemingway figured it would pay for the shells. Bud Purdy engineered the traps, which looked like giant lobster pots and often netted a hundred or more birds when baited with a sheep carcass. "We'd send the kids in to sack 'em up," Purdy recollects. "They didn't mind too much."

The magpies were released from a gunnysack, one bird at a time. "There was a shooter and a backer at each side," Bud says. "The backers couldn't fire until the shooter got off two rounds." Hemingway and Purdy were often joined by Gary Cooper, Jimmy Stewart, and once even by the Shah of Iran. Hemingway usually won, and one year was presented with a Magpie Trophy that proudly sat on the desk in his Ketchum home.

Meanwhile, there was trouble back in Cuba. Batista had fled and Castro and his band of bearded revolutionaries were in Havana and the first "Yanqui go home" graffiti was appearing on the city's walls. La Finca was in bad shape. The Hemingways went back, ordered maintenance and repairs. That chore finished, it was time for fishing. Hemingway and other international sport-fishermen organized a billfish tournament and invited Fidel Castro as a sign of good will. Castro won, though Hemingway, watching through binoculars, thought he saw one of Castro's security goons at the reel, a flagrant violation of the rules. Nevertheless, in the absence of irrefutable proof, he had to present Castro with the trophy. Hemingway, who loathed any sort of phoniness, left Cuba for the last time.

On November 30, 1960, one George Seviers was admitted into the Mayo Clinic at Rochester, Minnesota, for treatment of high blood pressure. Seviers had been flown in from Ketchum, and while refueling at Rapid City, he had attempted to walk into a whirling propeller. Seviers was also being treated for chronic depression. But it was a ruse to throw off the press. The real George Seviers was a medical doctor and still at home in Ketchum. The man in the Mayo Clinic was his patient, Ernest Hemingway.

His doctors ordered electroshock therapy, where a patient is strapped down and jolted with near-fatal charges. Hemingway seemed to respond well, and after a few weeks, was following his doctor home for meals, drinks and trapshooting. But electroshock therapy has one great and debilitating side-effect – the loss of memory. Hemingway wept when he could not remember the name of the swamp where he had missed that Cape buffalo back in 1953.

Then came a final indignity. Hemingway had been invited to the inauguration of John F. Kennedy, but was too ill to attend. The President had sent a copy of *The Old Man and the Sea*, asking for a line or two and an autograph. Hemingway stared at the page for most of the afternoon. The man who had written a dozen books and perhaps a thousand shorter pieces, the man who had won both the Pulitzer and Nobel prizes, could not think of a single line for the President of the United States.

Back in Ketchum, on July 2, 1961, Ernest Hemingway rose early. He padded to his gun cabinet, chose a fine Boss Pigeon Grade, put the barrels to his forehead and snatched both triggers.

He was buried in Ketchum's cemetery. His epitaph on a memorial erected by his Idaho friends was the one he had written for Gene Van Guilder back in 1939. "Best of all he loved the fall. The leaves yellow on the cottonwoods. Leaves floating on the trout streams and above the hills, the high blue windless skies. Now he will be part of them forever."

But the question haunts us still. How could he do it? He had fame, boats, cars, guns, women, whiskey, the best shooting and fishing on earth. How could this man who had repeatedly foiled death in war and love and sport do this to himself?

Hell, how could he do this to us?

Out in the Sawtooths, the day ends early as the sun slips behind the jumbled peaks. A coyote howls as the last of the light ricochets off the tallest mountains. The shade creeps, then rushes, and the lonesome sky deepens from blue to purple to violet to beyond human sight. The first pinprick stars glimmer and the valley cools and the wind eases back down the slopes, rattling the aspens like Ezekiel's dry bones. Ezekiel's bones prophesized, but the aspen do not and the question remains on the wind.

And you turn from this place and you think he was old and sick and could no longer do what he lived and loved to do. And he did it with a fine twenty-bore. He did it in style.

Maybe that's answer enough.

# SABLES ARE
# HARD TO HIT

*In this article for Outdoor Life, Jack O'Connor revels in the
name given him by the natives, Medala Pala Pala ("Old Man
Who Can't Hit a Sable," but in the end he manages to silence his
African critics by taking a fine bull.*

By Jack O'Connor

Native Africans who work for safari companies
have an apt and often unflattering way of naming
sportsmen. Almost never do they call them by
their proper American or European names, as
these names are as strange, meaningless, and
as difficult to pronounce for them as their own
names are for the sportsmen.

So when my wife, Eleanor, and I were
hunting in Mozambique with two friends, we all got names. Dr. Sib
West, a Willows, California, dentist was very lucky. He had a tape
recorder with him. The camp boys were impressed and called him
Mister Music Box. Fred Huntington, a reloading tool manufacturer
who for the purposes of the trip had dieted down from a blubbery
245 pounds to a lean, hard 241 and who was proud of his new
figure, was simply called Mafuta, the fat man. My wife, who has
always fancied herself the strong, silent type, a sort of a female Gary
Cooper, was shocked when she learned that the natives called her
Scotia – the little woman who talks all the time.

# AFRICA

In spite of my years, I have always thought of myself as a sprightly, shopworn college boy, but the camp lads named me Medala – the old man. I have always considered myself a fair shot, but they soon emended my name to The Old Man Who Can't Hit a Pala Pala. And in this there lies a story.

The concession, or coutada, run by Mozambique Safarilandia on the Save River in Portuguese East Africa swarms with exotic types of African antelope both great and small, including greater kudu, nyala, waterbuck, impala, reedbuck, bushbuck, wildebeest, eland, steenbok and oribi. There are also sable, the big black antelope with the scimitar-shaped horns, but at first my wife and I had a hard time finding them, and I had a harder time hitting one.

In Mozambique, sable are called *pala pala* by the natives, the same word used by the Swahili-speaking inhabitants of Tanganyika, a strange circumstance since Swahili is not used in Mozambique. The sable is in size about midway between a mule deer and an elk. Cows and young bulls are brown, but old bulls are jet black, hence the name. From reports I had heard I expected to see bulls with exceptional heads in Mozambique, but if there are big heads in the country, they are not on the Save River. We certainly didn't run into any. But that is getting ahead of the story.

We picked up a couple of handsome bull nyala very quickly, then knocked off a bushpig, warthog, waterbuck and a buffalo. All the time we had our eyes out for sable. Almost every day we saw their long, pointed tracks, but never the sable themselves. Fred and Sib each brought in a sable early in the trip, but for ten days we didn't lay eyes on one.

All this piqued us somewhat but did not break our hearts. Eleanor and I had both shot sable previously in Tanganyika. We had taken good bulls in 1959, and when I was on my first African hunt in 1953, I had shot a beauty with horns 44¼ inches around the curve. This, I believe, was the largest taken in Tanganyika that year.

For all his spectacular beauty, the sable is generally not the most difficult of animals to come by, once the hunter is in sable country. Sable run in herds of up to 40 animals. Since both bulls and cows have long, sharp horns and know how to use them, they have no need to be as wary as more defenseless animals. Even a lion shows great respect for the horns of the sable, and more than one hunter who has approached too close to a wounded sable has been impaled on those needle-sharp horns.

We had been hunting about ten days in what was generally considered good sable country before we ever saw one. Then one morning when we were cruising around in a four-wheel drive hunting car with Harry Manners, our white hunter, we saw our first herd. It was almost a mile away in the brush across an open, dusty plain. Our binoculars didn't show us much, but we could see black bulls as well as brown cows. We decided to investigate.

We left the hunting car about 400 yards from where we had seen the sable. Because Harry insisted, I took my .375. Eleanor tagged along with her 7x57. Harry led us upwind toward the herd. Presently, we saw a movement ahead of us in the brush. It was a cow. Then we saw two or three more cows and a young bull. We had the wind on the herd, so we worked to our left to see if we could find a shootable bull. We did, but he was behind a cow and all I could see was his head and his hindquarters.

"I think he will go 40," I told Harry.

"I doubt it," he said. "The biggest sable ever shot around here went 40 and it was bigger than this one."

"He's shootable, though," I said.

"Very much so," Harry agreed.

The grass was high there at the edge of the forest and the brush was fairly thick. The bull sable was about 200 yards away. I found myself a good tree, put my left hand over a branch and rested the fore-end of the .375 on it. When I got a clear shot at the bull, I'd let him have it.

But the bull wasn't cooperating. He and the cow walked together across an opening with the cow's body still shielding the bull. Then they stopped behind some thick brush. The bull stayed there, but the cow moved on. All I could see was the bull's head.

Watching through my scope, I waited, and waited and waited. Finally, I decided to hold where the bull's shoulder should be and see if I couldn't put a 300-grain Silvertip bullet through the brush.

# AFRICA

When the .375 bellowed, I saw small limbs, twigs and leaves fly, but the whole herd of sable took off, running through the forest to our left.

"Think he's hit, Harry?" I asked.

"I doubt it," Harry answered.

We followed for about 300 yards and presently Harry, who was ahead, held up his hand. "There's the bull," he whispered.

I edged forward. The bull was looking in our direction, facing us, but again he was concealed by brush except for his head. I estimated where the center of his chest should be and took a rest on a branch. Again the .375 bellowed and leaves and twigs rained down.

The bull whirled and ran off. The next time we saw him he was over 400 yards away, galloping along with the herd as good as new. We went back and examined the ground where he had been standing. No blood. Apparently two clean misses. I am sure that was the best bull we saw in Mozambique. He might not have gone 40, but he didn't miss it by far.

Until then I had knocked over everything I had shot at, almost always with one shot, and our two gunbearers, Joe and Julius, had even done a little bragging about their old man's shooting. But as we rode back to the Zinave camp by the river, the atmosphere was thick with gloom.

A couple of days later I took another pop at a sable, a lone bull this time. But I was jinxed. I could see the sable's body, though there was a fair amount of brush between me and the bull. He was about 200 yards away and I had a good solid position, but when I fired, he galloped off.

I couldn't believe my eyes, but as I stood there staring I suddenly noticed, about 100 yards away, the limb of a tree slowly bending towards the ground. I walked over to it and found that I had just about shot the limb in two. I felt a little better. I didn't have the sable, but at least I had an alibi. So that's how I became known as The Old Man Who Can't Hit a Pala Pala.

On the Save, it is the custom not to hunt on Sunday – or at least not very hard. It is the day off for the white hunters. Harry had his wife and little boy with him, and Wally Johnson's wife was there in camp at the time mourning the death of their pet dog. It had been pulled into the river and devoured by an enormous crocodile.

On that particular Sunday, Eleanor and I slept late. We saw Fred and Sib at breakfast, then went back to our hut to read, write some letters and make some notes. Presently, I heard the roar of a hunting car. Fred, Wally and Sib were off to do a little photography and to pop off an impala for camp meat. I had borrowed a book from Harry, so I settled down to read and maybe take a snooze. I was pounding my ear an hour later when Harry knocked at our door.

"Come on," he said. "Grab your rifles, you two. Wally has located a fine herd of sable on this side of the river."

We found them easily. There were about 50 of them and they were strung out over a wide, grassy plain near a waterhole. Among them were several shootable bulls, but the glasses told us that nothing would be very close to 40 inches.

"Well," said Harry, "the best bull looks to me to be the second from the right, but the one farthest to the left is also good. Who's going to take one?"

"It's mamma's turn," I said. "I've booted two chances, and I think she's just about the gal to break our sable jinx.

"All right, Eleanor," Harry said. "You'd better take Jack's .375 and we'll get going."

"I loathe .375s with a purple passion," Eleanor said. "I shot one once and I couldn't lift my arm for a week."

"She'd better take her 7mm, I said. "She'll hit it in the right place, but with the .375 she might not."

Harry shrugged. "Well, have it your way," he said.

It was an easy stalk. The sable were real back-country animals and they had hardly bothered to look at the hunting car. Harry and Eleanor walked perhaps 150 yards and climbed an anthill. As I sat in the car watching, I could see her take a good prone position and put her 7mm to her shoulder. Harry was watching the sable through his binoculars. I'd guess they were about 250 yards from where Eleanor lay.

I put my own glass on the bull. I heard the sharp crack of the 7mm. The bull sagged at the front quarters, then began a desperate, blundering run. He traveled in a little circle not over 50 yards in circumference. Then he plunged down into the grass.

I joined Harry and Eleanor by the sable, where Harry was measuring the head.

"Well," he said. "Old One-Shot Eleanor and her little peashooter have both lived up to their reputations."

Eleanor grinned at me. "The first step in getting a sable is to hit it!" she said. "It's all very simple to those who know."

The head was nice-looking but measured only 36 inches, about par for a trophy sable on the Save, but small compared with the 41 to 44¼-inch sables we had shot in Tanganyika and also small compared with the sable we were later to take in Angola. The kudu on the Save have magnificent horns and are as big as horses, but the sable simply don't grow large.

W e saw our next sable under conditions that could happen only in Mozambique. We had left camp before sunup that morning, as we had a long way to go. It was midwinter there far below the equator and we were chilly even in light down jackets. When we got to the river to be ferried over to the hunting car in a dugout canoe, steam was rising in the cold air from the smooth surface.

We drove off with the fantastic shapes of baobab trees outlined black against the pink flare of the sunrise. Below us the river was rose and silver. Waterbucks stood tall and stately along the trail and hordes of the little Angola impalas scurried across in front of us.

The sun was well up, but it was still early when we drove through a long valley filled with high grass and tall fever trees with feathery tops and green trunks. The valley was spotted with waterbucks, zebras and elands.

Then the track left the valley and started winding up to a high, dry plateau. We were almost on top when, to our left, four big greater kudu bulls stared at us for a moment, then started trotting up the hill. At the same time, a big bull sable galloped out from behind a bush and headed for the crest. He frightened an excellent bull nyala, which also took off.

There, in view at the same time, were three of the great African antelope trophies – trophies for which many a man has hunted hard for weeks. It would have been possible for a very good, very fast shot to have a kudu, sable and nyala from that one spot. Harry stopped the car so we could glass the kudu. They were jittering around, still in sight.

"I still don't believe it!" Eleanor said. "Kudu, sable and nyala all at once!"

"Nothing over fifty," Harry said, watching the kudu.

"I've seen plenty of places where a man would hunt hard for a week and be lucky if he saw one bull kudu that went fifty," I told Harry.

"Not here," he said. "Well, shall we go on and see what happened to our sable?"

We pulled up on top and saw that the dusty track ran through a grove of tall, beautiful trees. The sable had followed the road and we could see his fresh tracks in the dust.

Because we had frightened him with the car, we left it by the road and took off on foot. We saw the sable again, but just once. He had gone on through the woods and was standing about a quarter of a mile away out into the midst of an open plain, looking back in our direction. He saw us as soon as we saw him and ran off at a gallop. We watched him until he disappeared into the bush a mile away.

"Well, goodbye sable," Harry said. "See how wild he was? There's a lot of game up here on the plateau, but also a lot of poaching."

We saw a big herd of sable that day on an open plain about a mile away. But they were as wild as the lone bull. They dived into the brush the instant we drove in sight, and all we saw of them after that was the cloud of dust they raised as they raced to safety.

A day or so later we had climbed a little hill so we could look around when Joe, the gunbearer, hissed, "*Pala pala*." Below us and not over 100 yards away was a herd of sable, but there was not a shootable head in the bunch.

Our break came unexpectedly. We had crossed the river one cold morning and were headed back to the plateau where we had seen the big, spooky herd. An exceptional bull waterbuck, which we watched with binoculars for a few minutes, delayed us.

We were about to drive off when Joe jumped as if he had sat on a pin. "*Pala pala!*" he whispered.

I followed his pointing finger and, through a long avenue in the scrubby trees, I saw a sable walk into sight and disappear, then another and another. The glasses showed sable all over the place.

"Well," I said. "I'm not going to louse it up this time."

"Take the 7mm Magnum," Eleanor said. "That hell-roaring .375 is jinxed!"

Taking the 7mm Magnum, I crawled out of the car, and with Eleanor and Harry began a long circle that would bring us close to the herd with the wind right.

Half an hour later I was ready to shoot. There were about five sable, two bulls and three cows, in the space between a couple of trees, and for once I had a good clear shot at the largest bull. He was not very far away, probably not 200 yards. Since the grass there was short and sparse, I sat down, got in a tight sling, took a deep breath, released about half of it and started my squeeze. The Model 700 Remington Magnum cracked and I heard the solid thump of what sounded like a hit in the rib cage. All the sable vanished in the brush.

Joe and Julius hurried ahead and instantly found a blood trail. A very confusing circumstance was that the blood we saw was not plentiful and it looked like that from a muscle wound. If ever I had called a shot, it had been that one. The intersection of the cross-wires in the Redfield 4X scope had been exactly behind the foreleg and about halfway down from the backbone when the rifle went off. Since the bullet should strike about four inches high at 200 yards, the shot should have been smack through the lungs.

That herd of sable had come in from the remote back country to be nearer the water of the Save River. They were not used to being hunted and had quickly got over their fright. We caught up with them within three quarters of a mile.

"Hell," said Harry. "That's not the sable you shot at!"

Then I saw the young bull that had been with the herd. Apparently the 175-grain bullet had gone through my bull and had wounded the young one, as he had a long, shallow flesh wound across the rump. No wonder the blood looked as though it had come from muscle.

So we retraced our steps and went back to the place where the sable had been. There we found another blood trail, and this time it was the bright, frothy blood of a lung shot. We followed it not more than 100 yards and found the big bull lying under a tree. The bullet had hit just where I had called it. Like Eleanor's, my sable's horns went about 36 inches – not big as sables go, but good enough for the Save River country.

That took care of our sable jinx. From that time on we saw sable almost every day. No longer was I The Old Man Who Cannot Hit a Pala Pala. I was just the Old Man.

*Originally published in* Outdoor Life, *July, 1965. Reprinted with permission of* Outdoor Life.

# A MARVELOUS LIFE

*At age 14 John Sutton would survive a charging black rhino and years later a severe mauling from a leopard to enjoy an unmatched career as a professional hunter, guiding famous sportsmen and even royalty to some of the greatest Africa trophies ever taken.*

By J. Douglas Johnson

*Editor's Note:* This article is based on several interviews with noted professional hunter John Sutton and his wife, Angela, over four years beginning in 1992. Sutton died in the Nairobi Hospital on August 4, 1997, of complications resulting from an angiogram procedure done in mid-June.

We had been going for over an hour, following tracks and drops of blood. I called a halt. At that moment I couldn't see properly. The forest was very wet and very dense. I stepped up on this spreading root of a big polo tree and tried to look over the top of some thick bushes. All of a sudden there was a growl. Branches moved. Have you ever had a spotted, fur-sided tennis ball fly right at your face? That wounded leopard moved faster. I actually thought he was going for my gunbearer. I swung to take him, if I could before he got to Mutuku. What the animal did was use every bit of cover and come out underneath my gun. I fired over him. So close! He grabbed me by the left chest. The worst thing was not the bite, but those claws. They were like razors. He ripped my arms to shreds in seconds.

"His jaws clamped onto a diary in my shirt pocket over my heart. That little book saved my life. After slicing me up, the leopard ran off and several hours later another professional hunter followed it and found it dead. I got carted off to the hospital to have my muscles sewn back together.

"When I finally got back home, I looked at my diary and thought, 'Gosh this is difficult to open.' The leopard's teeth had almost met through the pages and glued them together. There were holes from January 1st to December 24th. It's still sitting around the house as a memento. It's also why I'm able to tell you this story.

"Our ethics or unwritten laws demand that if an animal is wounded, no matter how dangerous, we never let it suffer. We've got to find it. Then you really have to rely on the professional. This sort of thing is always very tense. We knew we were going to have a confrontation at almost point-blank range. It is well known that experienced big game hunters have extraordinary instincts. When I called a halt, instinct told me I was very close to the animal. I certainly was."

John Sutton was a consummate storyteller who collected his trove of spellbinders over 70 years of living in East Africa and nearly a half-century, 46 years to be exact, as a professional hunter. Any fracas with a wild animal that he had not experienced, his guide friends shared with him in vivid detail.

Although I feel like I knew him well, I never actually met the man. In the spring of 1992, Will Hudson, then manager of Pathways International, encouraged me to seek John's advice for planning a fishing trip in Africa. John and I got acquainted on the telephone – first a call to Nairobi, then New York, Florida and New Jersey. It was best to connect with John when he was on one of his annual business trips to the U.S., where he met with former and future clients. I talked with him last in 1996, and with his wife, Angela, in August of '97.

John was invariably less harried here in the States than when he planned trips in his Nairobi office or when he was on one of his "traditional tent safaris" in Kenya or Tanzania. There is no big game hunting in Kenya at present, so John specialized in wingshooting, wildlife viewing and special interest, adventure-type safaris.

"My Ker & Downey sporting visitors are a very fine group and I have tremendous friends in the U.S.," John told me. "I go around talking to people who have been on safaris with me, some of them many times. In so doing I find others who are interested in Africa's wildlife. I'm not anxious to do hundreds of safaris, just some really good ones. When we did a lot in Kenya, before big game hunting closed in 1977, we had a varied clientele. They were mostly Americans, a lot of Germans, quite a number of Scandinavians and Italians, the occasional Brit and Frenchman. Now the market is almost entirely American."

John spoke in a calm, deliberate baritone that would make you hold your fire if he whispered, "Wait, wait until you get a clear shot." He sprinkled his conversation with enough "chaps" to assure you he was from another culture.

Sutton had been with Ker & Downey longer than anyone. For the uninitiated, Ker & Downey holds the Mercedes Benz reputation among African outfitters for tented safaris. For over five decades it has been the biggest company of its kind. Since 1946 messages to "Gamefields Nairobi," their cable address, have clattered in from palaces, mansions, executive office suites and film studios around the world. Business soared in the '60s and '70s. "Gamefields" still reaches the Ker & Downey office, but times have changed. Now, their fax and e-mail get most of the traffic.

I've been very lucky. I've had a marvelous life," John said. "During my lifespan I've seen the greatest changes in Africa."

Sutton was born in Kenya in 1927, to English parents. His great uncle, J.J. Toogood, came from England to South Africa in the 1800s, then moved north to Kenya. He founded the first branch of the Standard Bank, now Standard Bank PLC, with branches countywide. John's father followed his uncle out in 1909. In the early days the family farmed "vast acres of ground" in the Nakuru area, a part of the Great Rift Valley. Later, John personally owned and developed a beautiful farm on the northern slopes of the Aberdare mountains.

"Sixty years ago Africa was an Eden," he recalled. "There was wildlife everywhere. As youngsters we used to ride out on horseback and play with the animals. We'd herd them around and chase them away. We hunted to protect the crops, to feed our camps and ourselves. When we were not shooting during the day, we were probably out at night with a spotlight to keep wildlife from trampling and eating everything. We had no other means of keeping the game off the land. I am not proud of all that I tracked and killed back then, but the experiences gave me the most incredible insight into the animals."

John was 14 when he killed his first major trophy. As he told it:

"A friend and I decided we needed some excitement. For a few shillings a local Maasai agreed to guide and track for us. We armed ourselves with an old .303 Lee Enfield and a double-barreled .375 that we felt would cover any hostilities. The tracker took us to an extra-thick patch of brush, where a bull and a cow rhino were known to live. The cow had a reputation among the locals for a somewhat mean disposition. This was not exaggerated!

"We came up against them when we peered down a tunnel in a dense thicket. My friend fired first, as agreed, hotly followed by a round from me. Suddenly he jumped sideways into the bush. I was left with an empty gun, no chance to reload, and the frightening sight of a 2,200-pound black rhino charging at point-blank range. I have never forgotten the vision of that horn! Somehow I managed to hurl myself out of the way as the rhino thundered past. We regrouped and, somewhat shaken, found the rhino I had shot. It was dead.

"We returned home a good deal wiser and very thrilled with our success, but our elation was shortlived. Our fathers were visited by the District Commissioner to discuss the legality of our hunt. Neither of us had licenses. We couldn't even apply for them until we were 18. After a severe dressing down, the Game Warden let us go, on the grounds of being irresponsible children. The situation was very different then. There were plenty of rhino. The land was untamed.

"When I came out of the army after World War II," John continued, "I went to manage a big tract of ground. I got very bored with that in a hurry. I had to make a change. I knew Jack Block, who was a partner in Ker & Downey. I phoned him one day in late 1951 and said, 'I have this wildlife background. I know about the safari experience and I'd love to know if you'd take me on.' Jack said, 'Absolutely. Certainly. But you must understand that in spite of your background, you have to go through an apprenticeship.'

"It was very tough. They wouldn't let you go out unless you were highly competent in all sorts of fields. The way they did it, of course, was pay me nothing and let me be a safari transport driver. We had British trucks, two-wheel-drive Bedfords. I had to know all about the trucks, the tents and safari equipment, and do all sorts of jobs before they would even allow me to take somebody hunting. 'Dogsbodying,' it's called."

Sutton willingly accepted the grunt work as a form of dues needed to launch his professional hunting career. And what an impressive career he would have. From 1951 through much of 1997, Sutton would meet many famous people and guide clients to some remarkable trophies. He helped lead a safari for Princess Anne and Prince Charles, and a separate camel safari for the Prince in 1971. In the '80s Sutton reopened tourism and hunting for Ker & Downey in Tanzania and Botswana.

Six of John's clients gained the exclusive "Hundred Pounder Club" for taking elephants with tusks weighing 100 pounds or more. Two of those hunters were women. A magnificent bongo with 32 7/8-inch horns downed by W. MacDonald qualified Sutton for the coveted Shaw and Hunter Trophy in 1965. It was presented by the East African Professional Hunters Association for "the most outstanding trophy of the year shot with a paying client whilst on safari."

That brief tribute may make the accomplishment sound simple, but Sutton assured me it was not. "The bongo is rated internationally as the most difficult animal to hunt. One of the few places you'll find them is in the Aberdare mountains at high altitude, from 7,000 to 12,000 feet, in dense, leafy undergrowth or thick clump bamboo. Bongo are extremely wary, with exceptional eyesight, hearing and scenting. The only way to have any reasonable chance of success is tracking silently, at a snail's pace, in wet weather. This invariably brings you dangerously close and in amongst elephants, buffalo and rhino.

"Once I was in the lead and concentrating very heavily on some bongo tracks when I became aware of a large, sharp rhino horn sticking out from a bush where I was about to put my foot. He became aware of me at the same moment. He had been lying down broadside, so we gave each other equal frights. He reared up, snorting heavily. I managed the most amazing leap backward. To my good fortune, he elected to leave the scene with a great crashing of bushes."

Most of Sutton's early clients were trophy hunters, but in the '50s a new breed of customer started to arrive. Film companies became important, and challenging, clients. Clark Gable, Grace Kelly, Ava Gardner and husband Frank Sinatra came to shoot *Mogambo*. This was John's first film-work, and the entire crew, more than 400 people in all, were housed under canvas.

"Normally, when we worked on a film, our firm supplied equipment and I was the chief consultant. There is that, but there is so much more to it. There is being involved with the director and the creative side of his script. There is contributing information about local customs, animal behavior and how to achieve various scenes. All very rewarding."

Ker & Downey supported and guided the cast and crew on Ashanti with Michael Caine, Peter Ustinov and Telly Savalis. K&D outfitted *Sheena, Queen of the Jungle*, and *The Color Purple*. Sutton also contributed to ABC's *The American Sportsman* in 1976 and he organized the outfitting for shooting *Gorillas in the Mist* starring Sigorney Weaver. "*Out of Africa*, with Meryl Streep and Robert Redford, was my favorite," Sutton revealed. "I picked most of the settings, and it is the only film that truly represents my feelings about the quality and greatness of my Africa."

Sutton also met Ernest Hemingway during the author's hunting trips in 1953 and '54 with Ker & Downey. Years later, much of Robert Ruark's novel, *Something of Value*, was gathered and written while he lived on Sutton's farm.

N o question, hunting has changed a great deal, even since the days of Ruark and Hemingway," Sutton admitted. "We used to hunt very hard and we enjoyed it. It was an experience. Pulling the trigger was just the finale; the rest of it – the outdoor life, camping under canvas, the game-viewing and tracking, the stimulation – was something you could really talk about. We were very close to the earth and all the feelings that go with it. We understood the animals. It was a fascinating life.

"I used to spend nine months of the year out on safari. One year I was gone ten months just traveling all over the place. We had no boundaries. The British influence was very great, so we never had any passport problems. It was a different world. But we still try to recapture those feelings. It is very personalized when you are in the type of camp we run – like being on a ship. You become very close companions. And the intense excitement, immense horizons, majestic animals, teeming waterholes and classes sunsets are still out there.

"I design itineraries of varied interest, including wildlife viewing and photography and bird-shooting," John added. "The possibilities are endless and it's all customized."

(This writer experienced an unforgettable fishing safari with Sutton's associate, Henry Henley. We helicoptered 10,000 feet up to a lake on the side of Mount Kenya where we caught fearless, 24-inch rainbows. Then at sea level on the Indian Ocean, we sailed out of famed Malindi where sailfish tail-walk right off the beach. Next, we set out to do what had never been done before: land a Nile perch on a flyrod. Nile perch weighing over 500 pounds have been recorded, but the one I caught at Lake Victoria, the first ever on a flyrod, was only two pounds, two ounces. It opened the Nile perch Freshwater Fly Rod category in the *International Game Fish Association's World Record Book*. One entry for me and two for Henley. Wonderful adventure!)

Contemplating the future of hunting in Africa, John Sutton shook his head. "I'm heavily involved in conservation circles as a trustee of the African Wildlife Foundation and a council member of The East African Wildlife Society. We do have problems. The biggest threat to the animals is human development. Even poaching is a product of that. There are just too damn many people. In time, they could eliminate the animals, which would eliminate hunting. People invade the habitat, develop it, and clash with the animals.

"My main point is: If you have a really good game management concept and include your wildlife as a natural resource of the country and you get your local people involved, then there's a chance for the wildlife to exist. Once you tell a landowner all he is allowed to do is protect wildlife on his land, while it eats all his grass, which interferes with his ability to send his kids to school or to feed them, then the game is gone. The aesthetic side of wildlife, that alone is not enough to conserve it.

"Africans place different cultural values on wildlife from us Westerners. They are also much more practical in their outlook. If they are given a value on an animal, and they can take advantage of it, they'll make sure it continues to exist. That is to their own benefit. It's the only way to get any foreign exchange or earnings or value on an animal. As one pragmatist put it, 'If it pays, it stays.'

"Part of that pay comes from hunting. Hunters will go where the ordinary tourists, viewers or photographers will not. And they will pay a lot more than the standard tourist visiting the game parks. If you permit a hunter to harvest an animal for a heavy fee, it is a sensible idea. Otherwise, that animal is going to be killed for no reason and no money. And the traffic of hunters keeps poachers away. Theirs is a secret business and they won't come around where they will be seen or even shot.

"I think a lot of things have improved," Sutton told me in our last interview in 1996. "There was a decimation of wildlife, particularly elephants and rhinos, going on fairly recently. In Kenya and Tanzania, they have almost brought poaching to a halt. Of course, a lot of the reason is because of the endangered species act. Some profitable trade has been knocked out of poaching. That is an enormous help, apart from which the Kenya government, for example, has recruited and trained exceptionally good men to protect the animals. And they make a tremendous effort.

"Many 'professional hunters,' as they are most popularly called now, have become photographic guides. They're damn good naturalists. They can help scientists and really educate new visitors in the ways of the bush. They know the plants and animals. They know about wildlife movements and habitat. On the top of it, we have started to develop another breed of guide who does not have any hunting background at all."

Maybe the days of darkest Africa are gone. Maybe the white hunter of fact is passing into fiction. But there is still the lure of a tented safari. Stories are still being told around the campfire, and you can still see magnificent beasts and incomparable sunsets on the savanna. And in the Sutton home 12 miles west of Nairobi at the edge of the Ngong Hills, that leopard-chewed diary is still there, a memento to an incomparable hunter and conservationist who thrived among the wild animals of his Kenya for seven decades.

*A Note from Angela Sutton –*
*August 29, 1997*

We had a *kwaheri* (Swahili for "goodbye") for John in our garden on August 15th, attended by almost 300 people of all races and creeds and from many walks of life. It was a cheerful occasion, which was helped because I was able to greet everyone with a smile. It finally ended at 10:30 p.m. John would have loved every minute!

There were various tributes, ending with Henry Henley saying Joyce Grenfell's poem: *If I should go before the rest of you, Break not a flower nor inscribe a stone, Nor when I am gone, speak in a Sunday voice, But be the usual selves that I have known. Weep if you must, parting is hell. But life goes on, so sing as well.*

Tomorrow, the 30th, about 30 of us will go to the Rift Valley and scatter John's ashes (John's wish) and have a picnic lunch. This will be the final farewell, and again we will have a happy few hours, which is what John would wish. And is very much my desire.

Although John was interested and involved in so many aspects of conservation in East Africa, he held very dear his role with the African Wildlife Foundation (AWF). He became a trustee in 1985, and then was recognized as Trustee Emeritus in 1993. He conscientiously attended board meetings in Washington D.C., the last in April this year.

One of his passions and convictions was that there must be more qualified and motivated African nationals brought into conservation. He promoted this in many ways, particularly though his support of bird-shooting in Kenya.

# ON SAFARI

# NIGHT SWEATS

*In the clarity of day, mid the Tanzania bush, you steel yourself against what can happen. It's in the deep, small, sweaty hours of the night that the honesty arrives.*

*By Mike Gaddis*

To hell with Bob Ruark. To blazes with Hemingway, Capstick, Percival, Boddington, the whole and bunch of them. It's enough that I struggle with the demons of my own conscience, at a thing at which I have been reasonably successful for the better part of my years. The more damnable that I must be over-burdened by their cumulative misgivings as well. By all they have said. So effectively they have built and amplified into diabolical aura, a presence which is outrightly flesh-and-blood, formidable without question, but blameless. Yet it is done, and impossible to ignore. Or to come to on my own.

It's three o'clock on a muggy Tanzania morning, in a bush camp, and today I am to hunt buffalo, and it's greatly their fault that I'm lying sleepless under canvas against a sweat-drenched pillow, uncertain whether the prickling of my skin is more the mosquitoes or the fear.

While the damned irony is, it's a thing I've pined most my life to do.

# AFRICA

"The Lukula," Sean Kelly, my PH, asked of the pilot, "how is it?"

The man, clad in khaki, gestures with the quaking flat of his hand. "Tricky," he said of the primitive airstrip, "even if the ele's haven't trampled it."

Minute-to-minute, Africa is built of intrigue. It accrues from the beginning.

We had chartered out of Dar, two hours airtime in a Cessna 206 for our tent camp on the Luwegu River in the depths of the Selous. An hour earlier I had sat in the lobby of the Colosseum Hotel, gear stacked alongside, sipping a colonial tea, mincing through Swahili from the local paper and relishing the unfolding unknown. Waiting for Sean to drop by, and the two of us to be off in what I fancied a safari-laden lorry. While others, obviously safari-bound too, waited there as well, weighing the suspense in the air or traded by, jabbering nervously. It wasn't the Norfolk in Nairobi, and it wasn't 1950, but it had felt like it, and it was East Africa.

"Hope you're ready for the heat," Sean said as we left. "It'll be God-awful, bloody hot."

Are you ever?

Nevertheless, the drone of the small plane had been life as I would have it, the ubiquitous tin-tops of the city melting away to the oblivion of the bush, ten-thousand feet below, the push of the horizon stretching ever and on. It was hot and close in the cockpit, the small overhead vent a bare lifeline. But beneath, the wildness grew into great sandy river corridors, sucked almost dry by drought – hanging on by ribbons, by meager, withering lakes and lagoons. On their flanks, low miombo woodlands, dark, thick and deep. Intermittently loomed chalky sketches of spooky-white and skeletonized leadwood trees, abandoned by water over time, to die and be preserved for a human eternity. As here and there across the immensity of the landscape, a far-flung vista of rolling hills and high tawny plains, tall plumes of smoke lifted from smoldering fires. It was October, and it wanted to rain, but hadn't yet.

Magical, legendary, the Selous, spilling off the tongue with the same alluring intrigue as the Okavango, the Kalahari or the Serengeti. The Se-loo . . . Old Africa, raw Africa, or nearest you can get. A remote 50,000- square kilometers, the largest and wildest big game reserve in the world. Teeming herds of buffalo. Lion. Hippo. Leopard. Africa's last great stronghold of elephant.

Remnants of the same ivory that brought Frederick Courtenay Selous to legend in the last of the 19th century, and ultimately to his death in its defense, in the 20th – below Sugar Mountain, at Beho Beho, by the Rafiji. So respected was the English hunter/explorer and author that his demise by German sniper fire was lamented as "ungentlemanly" by enemy Commandant Loettow von Vorbeck.

"One day I will be a hunter in Africa," Selous had said as a student to his headmaster at Rugby, who found him sleeping on a cold floor in his nightshirt. "I'm hardening myself to sleep on the ground." He had kept the promise, to be acknowledged greatest of them all.

"The man not even the elephants could kill," claimed the Matebele tribal chiefs.

In 1922 the Selous was named for him, and he is buried here, originally under a simple wooden cross, beneath a tamarind tree, in an inhospitable region loved by lion, hippo, elephant and rhino. A fit ending for a man so untamed.

"All that history," I remarked to Sean. He grinned.

"We'll make our own," he said.

"I'll get you so close you can smell his aasshh," Sean had promised, when first we had spoken of this hunt. He was good to his word.

It was only mid-morning of the first day, and for the last hour we had been slip-sliding along through stifling-thick bush, playing the wind, within 30 yards of the herd. Trying to get ahead of them, trying to sort out the bulls. Having a hard time doing it. The old, hard bulls were at the front, contrary to their classic pattern. We had tracked them since bare day, the spoor strengthening. Until Allan, our tracker, had stuck a finger in fresh, loose dung, and I in turn, and it came back warm and pungent.

Once, Sean had stopped abruptly, listening painfully. Then had shook his head. "A rumbling, I thought," he whispered. He listened a moment longer before we stole on.

A minute later we blundered into a feeding elephant, almost impossible to detect in the thick, matted brush. We almost didn't. Only Sean, at the last moment, before the agitated bull whirled and flared, and Allan, ten yards close, hurried past me to the rear, eyes wide with alarm. We had quickly backed away, facing the threat, rifles up and ready. I could see only gray, towering pieces of his hide. Fortunately, he did not press the issue.

Now, we had slammed stop again. Suddenly, Sean had snapped his fingers and immediately we had frozen, sinking slowly to our knees.

# AFRICA

Around us, whisper close, the unsuspecting herd was about its foraging ritual, drifting gradually along a *koronga*. In the thick cover, the whole of them was huge and daunting; even the cows were black and menacing. You could hear the low rumble of their stomachs, the gruff grunts and stiff *harruummphs* of their jostling as they shoved one another aside. The unsettling bleat of a calf.

Twenty yards ahead stood a bull, maybe 38 or 39 inches in the horn, better than average for the Selous. Massive and thick, sable and sinister. He was bullying the brush with his helmet. I could smell his ass, the thick, permeating stench of the runny green dung that plastered his buttocks. It condensed on the anxiety-laden air like warm dew on a cool blade of grass. I was worrying what would happen when he found us.

I shifted slightly. The bull raised his head, searching. Sean lowered his binoculars, raised a finger to his lips, cautioning me. Here was the perfect situation, and I knew it. I was getting ready, fighting my nerves, expecting Sean to order the moment of truth.

My heart was pounding, and I was working to talk it down. The heat was steamy and cruel. The soldier ants were under my gaiters again, the burning sting of their bites a needling aggravation at my ankles. Sweat poured down my face, welling in smarting eyes, and my legs were cramped and searing from sitting on my haunches for long, merciless minutes.

Reassuring myself with the presence of the big double rifle, my thumb waited on the safety. The shrill, single note of some strange bird rose three times, punctuating the suspense.

Before I had left home I had pledged to a friend who had hunted Africa and knew I was going, "that should I get back, I'd give him the account." And he had said casually to me, "Oh, you'll be back – a lot would have to go wrong for it to happen . . . to get killed by a buffalo."

It didn't feel like a lot would have to happen. It felt like damn little would have to happen.

"Good," Sean whispered finally, "bloody nice sweep and kick-backs. But soft, still."

I shouldn't have been relieved as we backed away, but I was.

We made a couple more loops to the front of the herd, with nothing more promising, then left them on their way to bed.

L ater, we came upon a hippo, a grumpy, pompous old bastard on a grassy plain, a surprisingly long way from water.

"Damn surly brute, the hippo," Sean had said. "Bump them on dry land and they'll as likely come. Rarely mock charge on land."

*Midst the bravery of a buffalo hunt,* I thought, *it would not be elegant to be trampled by a hippo.*

"I'd rather not like to shoot one," Sean said, skirting the possibility. Already that year, there had been two.

This one we could avoid, didn't have to shoot. There would be others.

Lunch done, I'm mellow, and Africa's all around; Andrea had tall glasses of chilled apple juice waiting when we pulled in – "Jambo, Bwana" – could you ever tire of it? Porkchops, corn-on-the-cob, a pasta salad, some chopped squash, a grilled cheese sandwich, filled us out about right.

Now, we're on our backs napping, or trying too. Until we meet again at three, to make a plan. Camp's hard on the riverbank, and my tent's shaded and wonderfully livable, but it's still hot as a whore in a Quonset hut, the air temp pushing 45 degree C. The humidity so thick you could cut and stack it.

So I'm watching the bull elephant on the sandbar across the way, ponderously thrashing the water, periodically lifting his trunk to shower himself. The small bands of waterbuck that will become a daily pattern, walking and grazing the river's edge. The yellow-green crocs sleeping semi-dead against the gray-blue of the water, under the caress of the sun.

Afternoons will become a matter of chance . . . of getting lucky. It's too late to take up a track, but maybe we'll catch the buffalo coming to water. Mostly not, but the reccies I will come to anticipate, as they will be filled with adventure nonetheless.

That first afternoon – cruising and hoping – was without buffalo, much as the others would be. But elephant are everywhere. Yellow baboon. Wildebeest. Impala. Bushbuck. A tribe of warthog. Charcoal bunches of waterbok. A multi-colored aviary of song and water birds.

I am close to pulling the big double from its case only once. The makeshift trail we follow narrows to a mere gap between the bush. The car slows. It happens in the twitch of an instant. Out of the thickets – point blank – barrels an elephant, a half-grown bull, eyes narrowed to small black coals, ears flared, trunk raised, trumpeting. He is bent on coming through us all.

"Haaa! Sean yells once. "HAAA!" Twice. He's still coming.

# AFRICA

My hand grabs the waist of the stock, my fingers around two thick cartridges in my vest. At last, the angry bull slams to a halt, a few feet away, the fine, choking dust boiling and wrapping around us. He shakes his head, starts back, turns again.

"HAAA!"

Reluctantly he retreats, leaving me quaking.

*My God*, I'm thinking. *Even the teenagers.*

Trailing out of the riverbottom, dusk is sweet with the breath of monkey-apple. It reminded me of jasmine, cloying the evening air around a southern country home place back in the States.

"There's our problem," Sean said, pointing to the full moon. "They're layin' up, the buffalo, these hot days. Waiting for the cool of the dark. Just not getting to the river in time."

Distantly in the twilight rose the fanatic chuckle of a hyena. The wallowing crash of a hippo from the river. The car lurched, as Nbliasi jerked it free of a honey-bear hole. Night was falling. Camp and dinner was a pleasant, swelling under-thought.

"Well," Sean said, "it's been a hell of an opener. You almost walked up the asshole of an elephant, were in the stinkin' midst of buffalo, and got mock-charged by a juvenile tembo."

We looked at each other and grinned. "A grand hell of an opener," I agreed.

Use enough gun," the Man had said. I'd taken him to heart. Forewarned is forearmed. So I carried almost the largest, and certainly the best, in the world. A back-actioned, Holland & Holland round-bodied sidelock, in 3-inch, .500 Nitro Express, regulated for traditional 570-grain Kynochs. A beautiful, fearsome thing, and the only way I had ever wanted to shoot a buffalo. The only way I would allow myself to hunt them. Close-on, with a Holland double.

Any big double from a premier maker is an incomparable mix of grace, beauty and awe. The awe comes from a heavy caliber like the .500, the beauty from bespoken, Old World-quality craftsmanship. But the grace – the "coming-in" of a fine double – is a delicate and almost indescribable matter of form and feeling, parlayed from something apart. A mince of history, happening, legend and longing. No one does "grace" better than Holland.

With every clunk of heavy cartridges into huge hollow chambers, each a cavern of eternity, grows another welcome reassurance.

But sooner than later, you must take again, your pillow. Try to sleep.

Now again, I'm alone with myself. It's the black edge of morning, the night sweats are back, and the demons are at me again. After the dark, piercing honesty of the buffalo bull, point-on this morning, I am riddled once more with uncertainty. It's a far different thing to know the only fear between you and the creature you have pitted yourself against is your own. Bravery wears easily until it is called to test.

Ruark might have told the whole of it. You're prodding a fight you better be able to finish. The beast you are badgering didn't invite you here. It's more than the glare of owing him money. It's more closely that you've loaned the mortgage on your life, and that he is fully willing and able to foreclose.

In the end, it is a given. The courage and strength of the buffalo will not abandon him. Of yourself, the surety is less certain. You have to kill him. Or if he is to live, be of truth to himself, he must kill you. Die in the trying.

It is important for a man to do a thing well, even if it is killing. The honor of a feat is the measure of how you do it. If it comes to it, it is better for a man to die in body than in his mind.

Men search for comparables. There is no comparable to a buffalo.

Sean and I have hunted together twice before. The morning of the second day, before we were off, he picked up the big Holland. "I didn't know who I was happier to see," he said, "you or this rifle."

"Dance with the one you're with," I said.

He laughed. Sean's a stalwart young man of unusual good humor, utterly dependable, of a good South African family who values honor. He had his unscoped Dakota .458, a gun that already could tell many tales. I knew of no one I'd rather have backing me.

I ask him if the notches in his ears registered the number of hippos he's had to dispatch. He winced. "The bloody sun," he says, "has teeth."

I pull on my hat. Africa is a land of many perils.

The sun was still sleeping when we cut the first track. Twice we had to circle, the spoor confused in a tangle of elephant tracks. But Samuel and Allan work it through. By eight o'clock we were with the herd, playing the same game as before. Loop-de-loop, to gain the front. To get ahead of the bulls. On our haunches at 25 yards, trying to see what was there. In cover so thick it was almost suffocating. Exciting stuff.

You could smell them, feel them. Taste them, almost, if my mouth hadn't been so dry from the nerves. If not only the ploy with the buffalo, but the incessant vigil for hippo. You could never let down, not for a moment. But it was a fool's game with the herd. They were moving too fast. We couldn't get ahead of them in the dense cover, kept seeing the same animals. Finally, after two-and-a-half hours slap-middle of them, they slowed, and we were able to almost manage the fore.

There were the mature bulls. One hard old warrior, though only about 34 inches. He glared. It was if he had the measure of me in the split of a second, knew the truth of me more than even I ever had, and I could not stop the twitch of my stomach. The rest plodded on; we couldn't really make them out.

We backed away, out of the bush, over parched and cracked grasslands pocked deeply by the travel of elephant and hippo. The going to higher ground was treacherous. There we waited for the car.

"*Bahati*," Sean exclaimed, shaking his head. "You see how it is, Myke, working the herds this way in this thick cover? *Bahati*. Pure luck. Pure blind, Aussie luck.

"It robs us of our skill. We can't move fast enough to get ahead of them. Pure luck, stumbling onto a good, mature bull. We did everything perfectly, but they were moving too fast. We need a group of old bulls, where we can use our skills."

He looked away, then back.

"*Kali*, the old ones," he said. "Very sharp, very wary. They will face the danger, not run from it.

"*Kali*," he said again, "but we can beat them.

"Maybe we'll find us an ancient, old scrim-cap," he said.

I have seen them before, the old and hard and mud-caked sons-of-Satan with the worn or splintered horns, that are past herd sovereignty. That must fend as a few, or on their own. Gnarly, proud, eccentric and ill. They give you shivers.

We crossed the first spoor of lion that afternoon. And leopard. A huge male, by the stride, over seven feet. "My favorite hunt," Sean says, "the cats."

"And why?" I said.

"More of the mind," he declared.

We passed the monolithic, ragged tower of stone that housed the craggy face of the Man-In-The-Rock. On our way to Lookout Hill. Past Little Tabletop Mountain. A bellwether of the hunt, The Old Man, Sean had ventured. To me, he seemed stoic as ever. Again, there were no buffalo. Again, the big gun did not clear its case.

But we were not so desperate as the Botswana party Sean told me of, which found itself eight days into safari void of even a fresh track. The client, worn and disgusted, peevishly directed the PH to ask of his Bushman tracker, "Where are all your buffalo?" Which the PH dutifully translated, and the little man – a river Bushman, not a San – thought for a time, said "Tell your client, if he's asking where my cattle are, I can tell him of each and every one. If he wants to know where God's cattle are, he must ask Him."

Another evening had run lean, but the morning had been good, quiver-tight against another herd. We'd spotted a kudu bull, about a mile away, under a mahogany tree. A pack of wild dogs resting from their evening's hunt, on a grassy green island.

On the way home now, we saw in the dust the spoor of lion again, and bushpig, and little, wandering ticky-tacky trails where the francolin had walked. At every dampening rose swirling storms of butterflies, lemon and lime. Behind us the sun was dying over the river, bleeding molten orange onto glimmering water. Waterbuck fed peacefully along ocher sandbars. Elephant loitered, great and gray, on shadowy-yellow shores.

Dusk was closing, as we stopped the car, gazed back over it all one last time.

"Another shitty day in Africa," Sean said.

A *nd what was the truth of me*, I wondered? Night was back, and the heat and the sweat. The long, dark, piercing and sleepless hours between midnight and bare dawn.

I asked myself, again, why this is so much a thing I must do? Kill a buffalo. I could be lying safely home in bed, against the warmth of my wife, eight thousand miles west of this place. On one plane I know exactly why I am here. On another, it's ambiguous, strangely threaded to the remorse of my first boyhood squirrel. Stemming back to the burden of taking a life. At some point of honesty, I tell myself, in a lifetime of hunting, it has become a moral necessity that I risk my own. If I will ask him to die, I must be ready to do the same.

But there's more and I know it. The mettle of a man can be tested only at the pinnacle of his fear. There are two reasons a man comes to the moment of killing a lion, a buffalo, an elephant or a grizzly. The first is that he would gain the respect of other men his kind. The greater is that he would augur his own. What he can take away of himself.

# AFRICA

It is not just the fear, but the doubt, its constant companion. It drives a man to cipher the sum of his life and living, and the older he gets the more desperate he becomes. To find a truthful measure.

Ultimately, it is the fate of every civilized man to know within himself that he can pretend bravery, and most likely, never have it truly called to test.

Between a man and a buffalo, there is no pretense.

Each day we have come a bit closer. Today is the day I am to know.

On our bellies, in the sweltering red sand, Sean, Samuel, Allan and I had gauged at length a very good bull yesterday. Thirty-seven inches probably, beautifully configured. Heavy bosses, graceful flip-backs. In sparse forest this time, making it hard to close. We were 60 yards far, for a double and iron sights. Doable, but dicey. He had angrily tossed his head, turned away twice. If I hurt him, he would not again. At a point, I was almost sure we would try to take him, and it was harder than I wished to push aside the fear.

We had passed, finally, hoping for bigger, but I could not deny with myself that with the relief came also another quiver of doubt.

This morning, only a short time before, we had encountered the lions. Not the old man, skulking successfully, but his lionesses. Lying in the yellow grass, their eager ears and burning eyes only vaguely perceptible. They had left me thinking, that on the ground should they want, they could easily take you unaware, come like splintered lightning.

My mind was still uneasy as we made our way to a promising buffalo woods below the soaring river cliff called Lookout Hill. We never got there.

"Mbogo." Samuel. The mere breath of the word and the air stiffens. The polarity of the hunt swings dead sober. Foreboding travels your body like electricity through a hot wire.

They are more than a kilo away, five bulls standing distantly on the yellow slope of a swelling hill. Sean and Samuel are off the car, binos at work, waging their measure. I raise my own glasses and my heart throttles. Even from here, they are bloody massive.

Sean motions me down. "Get your rifle." My stomach runs queasy. Allan hands him his own.

There is a broad *koronga*, another ridge, between us and the buffalo. The herd is in view now, scattered along the long hill, above the bulls.

"One of them is very good," Sean says, as Samuel steals quietly off, down the deep slope into the *koronga*, Sean tight behind him, me glued to Sean.

"We must be very careful," Sean has warned, "there's a herd of elephants ahead of us. We've got to get around them. Rouse them and it's over."

In my palm the heavy Holland has never felt better. Two big softs chambered home. But it's Ruark again, Capstick . . . and my heart's pounding like the south stroke of a sledgehammer. I knew it at my soul this time. All the midnight desperation was about to come down to a few piercing seconds of reckoning.

"Divide him into thirds no matter how he's standing," Sean has said. "Shoot low. His chest is deep. Take that two-pop and hammer him in the bottom third. Softs first, follow immediately with the solids. Just quartered straight on, clobber him point of the shoulder; if he turns to go, slam him up the rear. But whatever, keep the first one there and low."

I was talking to myself, what must be done. Remembering the else, if it was not.

"He was standing in his blood, waiting . . . " Samuel had said, of the badly shot Masailand bull that almost killed him. I needed to do this well.

Tedious minutes, avoiding the elephants, without the necessity of shooting one, but now we had made the slope of the intervening ridge. Then up and over it, to the gully beneath the bulls. The grass was taller and noisier than I expected. My shirt was soaked with nervous sweat, my eyes tearing from the salt, my ears thrumming with the heated rush of my blood. On we tipped, mincing our way, flinching at any tic.

Sean had chosen a big rock, on the hillside in line with the bulls, as a landmark. But now that we were closing, we could not find it. We were flying on gut instinct. Down now, crawling. Had to be close. One sparse bush to another.

On his knees, Sean cautiously lifted his eyes above the grass. Immediately, he dropped, turning his head under his near shoulder, mouthing to me, and pointing.

"They're bedded, just above us. Forty yards."

I wiped the sweat off my hands, reseated them on the big double. Thumb on the safety. Ahead and just above was one small bush. We wiggled our way there. Only 25 yards now, to the near bull, the one we would challenge.

I have always nurtured respect for any wild thing I have dared. This time the more. But I was talking to myself again, cruelly, as I had never for so long as I have hunted. Hardening myself. There would be no quarter. I had Sean, I had the Holland, and I had my wit. I, no one else, would die here. I would kill this black son-of-a-bitch and be done of the need.

Sean picked up a couple of small stones. "Up on your knees . . . get ready," he mimed, "it'll likely be straight on."

# AFRICA

I was on one knee, blood-hot, nervous and wet. But the big Holland came up and settled in. It weighed ten pounds plus and the sights came in as faithfully as the Rock of Gibraltar. Just as Fate tossed us a crumb.

Down the hill lumbered a sixth bull, prodding the bedded five. In groans and grunts, all lurched immediately up, ready, stiffening for a fight. Six huge bulls, 20 yards off the muzzle. I don't know that I felt anything at that point; impulse took the wheel.

The greatest of them, the bull we would have, had jerked hard to his feet – broadside. Huge, threatening and black.

"Now!" Sean urged.

The grass was too damn high, his lower chest obscured. I traced his shoulder, held lower than I could see. Funniest thing, one of the awesomest calibers in the world, and I have no consciousness of recoil or report. The Holland popped and the thud of the first big bullet slammed him hard through the shoulders.

He hunched – *whoomph* – went down. In periphery, three of the other bulls whirled, glowering, face on. In my vaguest senses, Sean was up now too, with the Dakota.

The bloodied bull was fighting to get up, grunting, lurching along on his knees. I dodged sideways for a better angle. He wobbled, spun, facing away. Up the rear, something said. My finger found the second trigger. The big gun popped again, and the bull slumped, thudded again into the ground, dust boiling.

I jacked the spents, thumped in two solids. The other bulls, thank God, had retreated midst the furor.

My bull lay on his side, heaving, running red blood blackening onto the sand. Still he fought to face me, his spine smashed above his tail. His heavy horns slammed the ground, as again and again he threw his massive head, trying to rise. It was then that remorse fought through the steel shell of my resolve, and I began to become more of myself again.

"Between the shoulders," Sean said. This time I felt the stiff thump of the rifle.

Suddenly it was over. Abruptly, it was done. Gradually swelled the dawning thought. I had done this thing, done it well.

I stood over the fallen buffalo. Already the *ndege*, the vultures, were arriving, wheeling the sky. In addition to the fresh tear of the bullets, the bull had an ugly, maggoty and horribly reeking gore wound in his neck. Should he have known we were there, he would have had reason to be surly and bad.

It was then that the trembles took hold. I ran hot and cold. Sweat poured. I tried to take pictures, and for the longest time, couldn't.

Butchering a buffalo is largely a matter of parting him in halves, rolling the ends apart. Samuel cut free the great heart of him. It was most as big as my head. He held it aloft, the sacramental essence of a daunting foe, the fresh, thick blood pouring down his forearms.

"Mbogo," he said in respect, once more for eternity.

A man lives 65 years, comes 8,000 miles, to find more than he has ever known that he is mortal. A buffalo calf is born, avoids the lions, survives 15 rains, grows old and gnarly, hard, wise and ill. Then, in the wish of a lifetime and the quick of a moment, destiny brings them together. One dies and one walks away. It is never certain which it will be. And whatever the conclusion, there looms the most mystifying question of all: When was their meeting decided? Yesterday, in the moment itself, or long, long ago?

Sean and I sat long by the campfire that last night by the Luwegu. We had spent the last three days of safari just wandering around Africa, warding off hippo, stopping with the boys for bush lunches of grilled buffalo loin by the water, walking across long grassy ridges under the scented, scarlet canopy of the mahogany trees. Hacking open the fruit of the baobab and sucking it like tangerine. Looking across green hills to the horizons, knowing there are places here still, so inaccessible they have not been visited, likely, since the time of Selous. Wondering with a hunter's heart – my Lord – what treasures of game must lurk there?

Over the river was a sheen of silver, born of the growing moon. Stars glinted like diamonds in a black-and-buttermilk sky. A lovely thing, it was, to ruminate before the flicker of the fire, safely past the dangers of the day. To absorb like a warm and soothing liniment the touch and sights and sounds of a broad African night. Listening . . . feeling . . . waiting – all around, the African evening orchestra. Waxing . . . waning . . . until, finally, distantly, it comes . . . *ughoommm, ughoommm* . . . the hunting chant of the lions.

A lovely thing, to think that yesterday you killed a buffalo, and a night ago you ate his heart – became one with him – and that tomorrow – the rest of your tomorrows – you could know a thing of yourself you could not before.

# KOPJES &
# SHALLOW GRAVES

*Hunting in a land both harsh and beautiful, for beasts worthy of
boyhood fantasies and grown-up obsessions.*

*By Rick Leonardi*

on't miss the drawings."
We walk a narrow, shaded path between
rock walls stretching upward on either side,
a welcoming shelter from the African sun.
Jan is pointing to what appear to be random
marks on a vertical slab, but looking closely
we realize with a tickling of the spine these
are not stray scratches but carefully etched
images from a time long past. Hoofprints and animal shapes prowl on
the granite, an unmistakable celebration of the artist's passion for one
thing . . . the hunt.

We touch the drawings gently, as if our fingers might erase what
thousands of years have left unscathed, and silently affirm that yes, we
too, are hunters.

# AFRICA

As the kudu bull ushers his harem of cows up the mountain, L'wyk leans close to me, restraint showing in his face, and says, "There are kudu we call 'last day bulls,' smaller than we hoped for, but time is running out. That one going up the ridge is a 'first day bull,' at least 52, maybe 53 inches."

I know I have disappointed him. I am looking for a kudu whose horns flare, however slightly, into that marvelous third curl, but their length is of no importance to me. This one, though beautiful, does not fit the bill and I decline the shot. My PH swiftly enters the middle stages of despair, for already I have passed on gemsbok and zebra, but this is our first morning of nine and time is on our side. Why rush?

In Africa for my third and likely last time, still not recovered from the miracle of a first trip, then a second, I will savor this one, going slowly, allowing events to unfold on their own. I returned from my first hunt a deep and unimpeachable resource on all things African: culture, languages, politics and of course, game. That I knew virtually nothing about the continent was brought solidly home on the occasion of my second trip, for so much was different, not having changed, but culturally, geographically, permanently different. This time I am a blank slate – a strip of undeveloped film ready to absorb and preserve another unique collection of marvelous images.

Namibia is at once harsh and beautiful, her rock-studded mountains, the color of a lion's coat, flanking broad plains of brittle grass, parched and dusty riverbeds coursing through lush savannahs of acacia and mopane. Though English is the official language, the lingua franca is Afrikaans, while myriad tribal tongues weave through this rich cultural blend in clicking accompaniment. It is peaceful and productive here, and game is everywhere.

My eldest son, Mike, and I are hunting with Jan and Mariesje duPlessis of Sebra Hunting Adventures in the Kunene region of northwest Namibia. This vast property is sectioned by low, smooth wire to limit the freedom of the cattle, but the wild animals are unrestricted, jumping gracefully over or slipping under the fences. The elephants, on their annual visits from the Namib, merely plow through.

Eventually a very good springbok, his horns hooking back instead of toward one another, finds too much distraction within his coterie of females. The stalk is simple and the shot close. The long hairs along his backbone rise up to expose their ivory undersides, a mating display almost as lovely in death as in life. L'wyk's frustration abates.

Zebra prove more difficult. Hunting is spot and stalk; the spotting from the vehicle or from kopjes rising randomly up from the plains as if the child of a giant built castles each day at recess. I do not understand kopjes. Great piles of rocks varying in size from breadbox to boxcar, they are said to be remnants of massive, ancient blocks of granite that, over the millennia, have crumbled and broken. This does not explain how great, big rocks were left scattered about in the first place. They serve beautifully, however, as vantages from which to spot and shoot game.

After seeing several more good kudu over the following days, we finally discover a handsome bull whose ivory tips flirt with the third curl I find so appealing. High atop a rocky hill, he stands in the shadow of an acacia, peering down at us in lordly fashion while L'wyk judges his horns and I range him at 215 yards. With L'wyk's blessing and a solid rest, I take the front-on shot and we hear the bullet strike. When the bull disappears over the top, we hustle around to the back of the mountain in hopes of catching him coming down, or better, finding him lying there. He is nowhere to be seen, nor can we spot the first sign of blood. Unable to locate the tree under which the kudu was standing, L'wyk decides to return to where I'd taken the shot and direct Mateus and me.

As luck would have it, he jumps the bull not 20 yards below the top of the mountain where it has lain down and allowed us to walk past as we climbed. I hear two quick shots and, after a minute, a muffled third one, the finisher. I am sick, convinced I have done this badly.

As it turns out, I have not. We discover my bullet has struck him right of center, gone through the ribs and into the chest cavity. That is why he laid down so soon, and didn't run but walked when L'wyk got him up. Left alone, he would have died there peacefully and quickly, but in Africa there is no waiting.

Perhaps the abundance of scavengers lends a sense of urgency to following up a wounded animal. What is important, ultimately, is that we settled him in a timely fashion. His horns do exhibit the beginning of a third curl, and they are beautiful.

I run my hands over the graceful spirals, touch the white chevrons on his face, and marvel at his size and musculature. A beast worthy of boyhood fantasies and grown-up obsession, he is likely the last of his kind I will ever take, but no sadness seeps from this realization, for I know the gods of the hunt have treated me like a favored child.

# AFRICA

Mike and Jan, meanwhile, hunting a pasture-like plain on another section of the property, also find a good kudu bull as they drive along. Abandoning the UniMag, they mount a stalk but the kudu is onto them and fades into the trees. Within a few miles they spot a second, bigger bull not 50 yards from the road and, hardly daring to look at him, drive on till they can pull around behind a kopje. Climbing quickly, Jan peeks over the top and motions for Mike to come up beside him. The bull is at 100 yards now, quartering away, and Mike is surprised to discover his hands are shaking. Steeling his nerves, he takes the shot and as the beast runs, shoots again.

The first shot is perfect, the second less so. As they approach him, Jan says in his quiet way, "Mike, you have killed a magnificent kudu." And, he has. The horns, at a majestic 58 inches, are high, wide, and glorious, and Mike is calmly euphoric, a trait he has perfected through the years.

T he days pass and Mike takes a fine springbok with L'wyk, while I chase zebra with Jan. We are hunting Hartmann's mountain zebra, without the shadow stripes, drawn to steep and rocky places, skittish as a hen in a fox pen. Jan and I spot a herd coming down the mountain in the late afternoon, seeking water and grass in the lower elevations. We stalk closer but they drift into a cleft between two hills and disappear. Another stalk on a second group ends as they spot us and, departing from the routine, move up the slope and out of play.

As we walk back to the truck, a sinister reality of Africa rears up, literally, and shows its ugly head. Jan steps over a rock and barely avoids treading on a horned adder, a thoroughly lethal snake that's coiled, cocked and loaded. Small and mottled the adder blends perfectly with the rocks and sand.

Taking great care Jan pins it with his shooting sticks, picks it up, and with a twig extends its wicked, curling fangs. Having given no thought to snakes before now, I consider the sobering implications of being bitten so far from camp and suffering a wild ride in the stiffly sprung UniMag while the poison explores my bloodstream. And on arriving at the house, what then? Henceforth, I will spend more time looking at the ground and not following Jan like a simpleton, secure in my faith he will protect me.

With our time half gone, L'wyk is called away unexpectedly, leaving Mike and me to hunt with Jan. What could be better? We welcome this chance to hunt together, having done so for most of Mike's 34 years, and our first day out sharply focuses the relationship between a father and his grown son.

We are on the gemsbok flats, a lush valley rimmed by mountains and interrupted by kopjes, looking for a harlequin-faced bull with long, thick horns. Intent on spending the entire day afield, we bring some of the cook's delicious sandwiches, and enjoy lunch and a nap in the welcome shade of a chunk of granite, beneath which happen to be the smoking fresh tracks of a leopard.

A nap has been a non-negotiable element of each day, and watching Jan sink into a semi-coma under that rock, I realize why. Mike, whose slumber is fitful because of my snoring, bumps me rudely seeking peace, and now we are both awake. He wonders aloud what would be the consequences if the Uni refused to start, given we are many, many miles from home base. I respond with an old man's bravado: "We would have to walk out . . . separate the men from the boys."

Mike considers this a moment and smiling, replies, "We would bury you in a shallow grave. Jan and I would soon conclude you were not going to make it and stop sharing the water with you."

A physician, Mike slips easily into his own style of triage.

Although we see many gemsbok, none are worthy of a stalk and happily, the big truck does crank, so we ride off toward the hills to find a zebra for me.

We post on a low ridge opposite the mountain on which we'd spotted the herd earlier, intent on intercepting them as they come down. The three of us wait beneath a leafless mushara tree where Mike falls immediately asleep, and Jan, a fancier of Mauser actions, disassembles the bolt of my Beretta, then shows me how.

The day is magnificent, as each has been in turn, and across the narrow valley the mountain rises, green and gold and gray. Turtle doves call out their dulcet messages of romance, and the air begins to cool. The shadows lengthen, the light grows softer, and I am enveloped in the sensory symphony that is Africa.

Finally, Jan hears the zebras coming down but cannot see them. Being essentially deaf from long abuse of my ear drums, I take his word they are approaching, and eventually they strike the valley floor and turn toward the fertile plains where they spend their evenings. We follow on a parallel course, Jan leading and pausing occasionally to glass while Mike films the stalk.

For more than an hour, during which I never glimpse the animals, we slip silently, bent low, through very thick mopane and acacia. Then, without warning, Jan sets the sticks, and pointing to a rare opening a hundred yards downhill, whispers, "Two kudu bulls will pass through that clearing, and after them will come the zebra. The first will be the matriarch who has a young foal. We will not shoot her. The second will be the foal. Shoot the third one."

Kudu bulls? Where the hell did they come from?

This is most exciting, this spotting and stalking afoot. The adrenaline rush is indescribable, threatening at times to blow the top off the kettle. I will sit again, I know, on deer stands enduring hours of frozen boredom or sleeping amidst the mosquitoes while God knows what passes by, but there is nothing like a stalk to cleanse a hunter's mind and free his spirit from the clutter of civilization.

The kudu bulls, both young, move through the clearing, but after a few minutes it's apparent the zebra have changed their itinerary. Jan raises his glasses and whispers casually, "They are coming up the ridge, right to us."

Now, even I can hear soft equine noises and the occasional clunk of hoof on rock while the tension mounts and Mike, looking over the camera, films the back of my head. The matriarch comes to a narrow opening not 30 yards away, stops and looks straight at us. Screened only by the purest African air, we dare not breathe or blink until, finally, she angles up the hill followed by the foal, obviously small, sweet and beautiful.

I whisper to Jan that I am going to shoot the next one. The third animal comes to the gap, presents its shoulder as a gift, and at the shot, falls immediately.

Offering his hand, Jan smiles and says, "You know you've killed two, don't you?"

I think he is joking, but he isn't. Two zebra lie there, the stallion I shot and a mare that was apparently on his offside, unseen by any of us until they fell. I am nonplussed and dismayed, but there is nothing to be done about it. I have two zebra rugs coming and I will never forget how I came to have them.

I cannot ignore the performance of the bullet. The 225-grain Speer Trophy Bonded Bear Claw from a Federal .338 factory load passed through the shoulders of the stallion, broke the neck of the female, and then spent itself somewhere on the mountainside. Both animals fell at the shot, mortally wounded.

A blend of melancholy and excitement, our last day is dedicated to finding a good gemsbok bull for Mike. We have seen, without exaggeration, at least a hundred, many long-horned and beautiful, but the stalks have failed because of bad wind, bad terrain or bad luck. We will give it our all today.

Checking a waterhole, we crouch low in single file like an otherworldly six-legged beast, finally hiding behind a tree to glass. There are several gemsbok scattered nearby, one of which spots us and approaches, his curiosity bringing him within bow range. No shooters in the offing, we retreat to the UniMag and drive to a series of kopjes where we will stalk in connect-the-dots fashion, using the rocks for cover and elevation. As it turns out, connecting is not necessary.

We climb the first kopje, and there at 200-plus is a terrific gemsbok bull. Mike rests his .375 on a chunk of granite, and I watch through binoculars as he takes the shot. The bull is instantly in high gear, and when I hear Jan say, "Shoot him again," I consider this a kindness, having no faith the first shot has connected. The second try is spectacular, rolling the animal in full stride, and I must restrain myself from whooping like a race fan.

We have finished our hunt on a high note and now look forward, with mixed emotions, to going home. While eager to see our families, we are faced with the resumption of our former lives, a less delicious prospect to be sure than another ten days of watching the sun turn the plains to gold, waking each morning knowing there will be nothing today but the hunt. In truth, we can think of little else but returning to the wild places where the wind sweeps hot and clean down the mountains, the dry river channels ripple with the tracks of wild game, and the people are as exotic and enduring as the animals we seek.

While we leave no images etched in stone, the passion we share with those hunters of a thousand years ago has not cooled. Nor will it ever.

# THE OTHER SIDE
# OF THE DREAM

*Truth, physics and T.S. Eliot in the African bush . . .*

**Story by Robert Parvin Williams**

*Through the unknown, remembered gate*
*When the last of earth left to discover*
*Is that which was the beginning.*
    – T. S. Eliot, Little Gidding

The sun was setting behind the dangling bait, a shoulder from the zebra Webster had killed two days before. Forty yards away, Webster watched through a peephole in the grass blind as the last crimson streaks silhouetted the vertical line of the bait and the longer horizontal line of the limb from which it hung. They made a skewed black cross precisely in line with the place the sun had buried itself. *Like Stonehenge*, Webster thought. The sun over the heelstone at the solstice. Or like mistletoe. We hang a sacrifice from the sacred tree and await the spotted god. The image made him chuckle inside, but only inside, and the outside part of him stayed still and silent as the sunset.

# AFRICA

When the light had gone and the leopard had not appeared, he and Christopher listened to the night sounds until the hunting car came for them.

"It was a big track," Christopher said again as they drove to camp. "An old tom. We'll try him again in the morning. You were steady in the blind? You could make the shot?"

"It was fine. I was thinking again about the zebra, though."

"You don't want to do that. Just think about the leopard, the angle he'll be standing at, where you want to put the shot."

"I know. The blind is so quiet I think it makes the ringing louder, so I start to replay the zebra, that's all."

"Ears still ringing, eh?" Christopher downshifted, snorted, grinned. "Not to worry. Leopards have nice spots to aim at – much better than stripes, you know."

For Webster, hot showers spawned ideas in odd shapes that wandered the mental landscape almost, but not quite, randomly. Inevitably, if the shower lasted long enough, one of the odd shapes would tumble exactly right into the jigsaw hole that was the problem he had been worrying about. Now, hot water drizzled from the bucket hanging from the tree above the canvas tent. A lantern hissed nearby. Somewhere on the hill a baboon screeched obscenities – a leopard perhaps, just beginning his evening hunt. Maybe the big one we're after. How big?

The water drummed against his head and the odd shapes began to tumble. Irresistible force, immovable skull, bits of Africa sluicing down, the bucket growing lighter, pulling less against the rope, over the branch, down to the tree, vectors up and down, the forces proportionate. Of course. The drumming slowed to a trickle. The shower had lasted exactly long enough.

The night chill raised goosebumps as Webster hurried to dress. A big moon, not quite full, cast soft shadows along the path to the evening fire. Christopher was waiting, his cigar lit, a beer mug on the table beside him.

"You really ought to use your flashlight, Webster. Puff adders, scorpions, safari ants . . . "

"Oh, right. Sorry. Puff adders. I was thinking about the leopard problem you were talking about. How to measure one in the bush. You want to weigh it, but there's never a scale, right?"

"Right. You can't just use feet and inches because people cheat. I've known professionals to cut the spine from inside just to stretch a decent cat into someone's eight-foot monster. You weigh them if you can, which isn't often. Usually you have to skin them before you can get to a scale. So you end up with these stories of two-hundred-pound leopards, and maybe some of them are true."

Footsteps approached in the darkness. Seth, the camp's headwaiter, materialized Jeeves-like in the firelight, bearing a frosted mug of beer on a silver tray.

"Asante, Seth."

"Karibu."

Webster took a long pull on the beer, and with a happy little grunt began the delicate ritual of cutting and lighting his cigar. He liked this, the small ceremony among the other small ceremonies of camp, surrounded by wildness and distance. "I think you can make a scale on the spot with a stick and some rope. Accurate to within a couple of pounds."

"Mmmph. Sounds like something from the Boy Scouts. Got your leopard scale merit badge, did you?"

"When I was a kid, my dad had this book from when his dad was a kid. *Two Little Savages*. It was about a couple of boys camping out in Canada playing Indians. One of them was good at math and he used geometry to calculate the height of a tree without having to measure it."

"There was a large Canadian leopard in the tree, I take it?"

"Well, there was a lynx, but that was in another part of the story. And you can go to hell. But there's a connection: the kid was using proportionate triangles. If you have two of them and you know the size of one, you can calculate the size of the other one, right?"

"Mmmph."

"Well, you can. So I was looking at the shower bucket on the rope hanging over the limb, and it made me think about how you could use proportions to weigh a leopard. You balance the leopard and something else from a stick, and the proportion between the lengths of stick on each side of the balance point is the same as the proportion between their weights. You with me?"

"Yes, actually, I am. It may be the beer. So if you know the weight of one side, you can measure each side of the stick and calculate the proportionate weight of the leopard on the other side."

"Right."

"Not bad. But what do you use for the counterweight?"

"Well, it could be anything, really, as long as you can weigh it later. Even a person."

"We can try it. You'd better keep your weight up if we're going to balance you against our big friend in the morning. Seth says dinner is ready. Shall we eat?"

But after dinner, alone in his tent with the sounds in his head, the zebra rises like a specter. His shot has gone badly. He knows it. Ears ringing, eyes following the zebra's distant galloping form, his mind fixes on the moment just before the shot, the irretrievable moment. I should have held it, backed off when it moved. The images roll like frames in a slow film, the moment when the gunsight holds the quartering shoulder, and the next when it creeps right, wavering across rippling stripes into gut as the picture breaks up with the gun's recoil. And now the zebra has disappeared over the hill and the last of its dust billows in the same wind that mutes the sound of the approaching hunting car, its own dust enveloping him as it pulls up, black hands clinging to the rollbar and the voices, "*Piga! Piga!*"

*Yes, piga I know. Hit. But not well.*

Christopher climbs from behind the wheel and stands on the running board. "He's hit, but a bit far back I would say."

"Yes. What do we do now?"

"We'll see if we can catch him up."

They trot quickly across the short grass where the zebra had fed, then more slowly into thornbush, eyes straining to see through the rough scrub. A flash of black and white ahead; the zebra is moving at a trot across an opening.

Webster finds the zebra in the scope and swings ahead. OK, how far do you lead one as it breaks into a full gallop . . . lead it, lead it . . . trying not to jerk the shots but each time knowing he has missed until there is only empty shimmering bush and the magazine is empty. The ringing in his left ear now is a sound he has never heard, a relentless howl on a single pitch.

"Nothing, Christopher. Absolutely nothing."

"No. I didn't hear any of them hit. He's gone into the thick stuff. We'll have to get the car."

"The car? Is that all right?"

"He's hit. We have to follow him, of course. I don't think we'll be able to see without the car."

They retrace their steps and Webster climbs with the gunbearers onto the bench behind the rollbar. The car grinds and smashes across scrub and heads into trees, plowing through eight-foot stalks of grass whose seeds explode like tiny grapeshot into his eyes. Too late the gunbearers signal to duck behind the cab when they hit the grass; Webster's eyes are already streaming tears, the seeds gritty and burning as he blinks furiously to see.

The zebra is well ahead. They glimpse it briefly as it crests a hill or weaves between trees, still moving easily and yielding nothing to its pain. It could be mistaken for unwounded, whole, except in the fact that it can be seen at all.

The jolting twists through high brush change Webster's sense of time and distance. He cannot say how long or far they have traveled, and if they have somehow circled to the place they began, it is still new to him. There is only the present, only this place. The chase is simply now, the zebra and car suspended at opposite ends of a single floating frame, connected only to each other and indifferent to the rest. His eyes are reduced to a stinging blur and the howl in his left ear is hammering his head. He could be swimming through the kind of deep-water dream that haunts the edges of sleep, the nightmare pursuit that is not any city's legacy but the collective memory of the species from a time when all, and in this same terrain, were perpetually hunting and hunted. The grinding gears and crackling brush are the sounds of hell.

Abruptly the car stops. The zebra is just visible as it stands on the edge of a wooded ravine. If it moves farther into the trees, the car will not be able to follow. Webster jumps down and is engulfed by grass and thornbush. The car is the only spot high

147

enough to see over the thick bush, and even so when he climbs back up he can see only patches of striped hide that are nearly indistinguishable from trees and shadows. He struggles for a moment with a lifetime's disdain, hating the car with a detached and furious clarity. So that's the price. That there isn't a choice. Our only chance now.

He wipes his eyes quickly and steadies the rifle on the rollbar, finding the shoulder in tangled thicket. He doesn't hear the shot, but sees the explosion of bark and the whirling stripes heading into the trees and without thinking, almost without moving, and still adrift in time he works the bolt and finds the centerline of the neck and the zebra is tumbling and down before the ejected cartridge has stopped rattling on the floorboards.

"*Piga! Piga mzuri!*" and they are slapping him on the back and scrambling down from the car. He sits a moment, breathing, resting the rifle on his knees, staring into the middle distance. The sound in his head has not changed and he knows the sound will be there a long time, perhaps always. The images will hang there, too, as a moment hangs always in its place in time. That, too, is the price.

Christopher is looking up at him. "Nice shot, that last one. I thought we'd lost him. Shall we go take a look?"

"All right. Let's go take a look."

H ello?"

Webster's head jerked on the pillow. Half-gagged in the middle of a snore he struggled choking to the surface, which was the dark tent and a repeated "Hello?" in the particular East African inflection that announces the arrival of morning tea.

"Oh, hello Jonas. Come in. Habari za asabui," because he was working on his Swahili and because the words gave him something to focus on to replace the dream.

"*Mzuri*," came the invariable response, a formula restoring order. Webster groped for the flashlight and took the mug from the proffered tray. The steam warmed the tip of his nose and the tea lit a warm trail inside him, pushing the dream aside.

Jonas watched for a moment, murmured "*mzuri*" softly again

and began rustling among the things on the washstand. He set a fresh washcloth and towel beside the ewer of hot water, put the soap beside them, and padded back out into the darkness.

"*Asante*," Webster called after him. "*Asante sana.*"

Webster dressed quickly under the covers, washed his face at the washstand, fumbled with the toothpaste and his flashlight and stumbled out of the tent into starlight and a setting silver moon. Christopher was waiting in the dining tent.

"You slept well?"

"Oh, yes," and it might have been true, after all; perhaps the dream had lasted only a minute.

"Good. Be sure to eat well this morning. Maybe some porridge with your eggs? Had a client out last year got so anxious he couldn't eat. Big tom came in to the tree on cue, all very nice, right? Walked past the blind, client's belly rumbled. Might as well have cranked a chainsaw. Leopard jumped like we'd pinched his arse, landed somewhere in the middle of next month. Never saw him again. Have some more porridge and then we'll go."

They drove quickly for the first mile or two. The headlights picked out the bright red eyes of bush babies and once the sloped form of a hyena as it crossed the track. Christopher slowed as they approached the blind, the sound of downshifting gears stirring Webster's memory, although it took a moment to identify it with the zebra.

No. Not that. Think about the shoulder, the spot just behind the shoulder. Don't think about any of it, anyway . . . and they were there, slipping out quietly and into the blind, resting the guns in their corners, settling back on the canvas camp chairs as the vehicle eased away.

For a moment his mind was empty and all he knew was the night air pinch on his face, the weightlessness of starlight. To be the beginning, he thought. Not just at the beginning, but of it. This place. This time. Now. Maybe that's the other side of the dream.

Christopher was leaning back in his chair. The starlight washed his face into a pale blank, with shadows for eyes. Webster imagined their faces floating side by side in the gloaming: twin shadowed moons in a grass-walled night, peering through holes into another world. He lost himself for a moment in the thought, and it was the sudden tensing in Christopher's neck and shoulders rather than the sound itself that recalled him.

The sound came again, closer: the deep, two-note ripsaw *huh-uh-huh-uh* of a big leopard staking his claim. Then silence.

Webster thought he could feel Christopher's muscles vibrating against the night, or perhaps it was the tension in his own spine and the strain of listening and trying to remember to breathe. Then without warning it was next to him, a faint rustling of grass and the light patter of soft pads on sand beside the blind, then silence again.

A minute passed, then another. A sudden scuffling at the tree made Webster start, then relax in warm relief. The leopard was in the tree. He hadn't left after all, but had been sitting under the bait having a look. It would be all right.

Webster was adrift in time again. For 30 minutes, or it could have been hours, the leopard fed. Each stage had a distinctive sound: the crackling and crash as the leopard tore the protective branches off the meat, the scratch of claws on bark as it gripped the tree with one paw and ripped meat with the other, the wet crunching as it chewed. Soon it would finish, and unless dawn hurried, the leopard would leave before there was light enough to shoot.

Christopher had been watching with binoculars and now motioned Webster to open his peephole and get his rifle ready. Slowly, still reminding himself to breathe, Webster moved the barrel through the hole and rested his elbows on his knees. Through the scope the leopard looked faintly pink in the early light.

Webster looked at Christopher hunched against the blind with binoculars braced against the frame. Christopher turned, grinned and gave a quick thumbs-up and wiggled his trigger finger to signal the shot. Webster leaned into the rifle and found the spot just behind the shoulder when the leopard turned abruptly, and looked left and right. Oh no, he's going to bolt. Webster found the near shoulder – the forward angle this time – and squeezed.

He wasn't prepared for the flash, a momentary image of the big cat's silhouette flying backwards in a flashbulb halo, a leopard supernova, followed by darkness and the sound of dead weight hitting the ground. Then it was still in the blind. The pinkness overhead seemed to light another place entirely. A fragment of a poem played in Webster's memory:

*After the kingfisher's wing*
*Has answered light to light, and is silent, the light is still*
*At the still point of the turning world and time began to move again.*

# SHADOWS
## ON THE HILLS

*The great bull stood in the ghostly shadows like the wispy smoke from a distant fire.*

*By Mike Gaddis*

One day, I want to shoot a buffalo. With paces between us, facing his dare. I want to know for once before I die, even if on the day I die, the tremble of doubt and the taste of fear. It is only just, before all I have hunted. Perhaps, also, a *chui*, a lovely, spotted tom of maybe seven feet. No longer, I think, elephant or lion or rhino.

But before them all has persisted a lifelong yearning for the ghostliest of the antelope. For surely as the Fabled Five portray the ferocity of Africa, the kudu perfects its grace.

"You must be ready," Garry Kelly said to me Britishly on the forenight of our safari, before the flickering pitfire of the *boma*, over a dinner of nyala filet, cinnamon butternut and a toast of Hamilton Russell pinot. "Where we will hunt it must be thick, for on the edge of it is where the biggest bulls will be.

"Should I say 'Shoot!' you must do it quickly. They will not wait."

# AFRICA

So opened an odyssey, a journey that had bridged 9,000 miles, 59 years, and the arc of a dream, to spend itself in the most spellbinding six days of my life. And I could not believe, believe that I was finally here, except for the evening sky. Vast and dark, much as Montana or Dakota, but deeper – so deep you could look beyond a million stars and find the enchantment that could only be Africa. Until I lay in the shallow hours of the morning, wondering at the impala rams, randy and roaring with rut. Until I listened to the rhythmic, fluid words of a black man, and they were Zulu.

I t is chilly this first morning. The sun struggles to chin the gray-blue humps of the Drakenberg foothills. It is May, the African autumn. Behind the south wind, a cold front will swell.
"Opposite you chaps," Garry observes.

You must think in opposites here. Not right, but left. Not of the North Star, but the Southern Cross. English, yes, but Afrikaans, the brogue of the Isles, Zulu, isiXhosa, the Bantu songs of the natives, as well. You must catch the sway of the land.

Close around is the bush, an ever-more mix of acacia and grassland. Eleven species of acacia stipple the panicum grasses, from four-foot scrub to robust trees. And halfway between, the canopy of the silverleafs, the bellies of their foliage the inspiration for their name, creating at a distance the illusion of a blossoming. Sometimes the collaboration is hardly more than a screen, through which you can readily spy the form and shadow of game. Again it's so thick and thorny as to be hardly penetrable, dark and deep, where the buffalo will wait to return your pain. Occasionally, towering haughtily above its homebred neighbors, grows a eucalyptus tree, a pine, a blue gum, that immigrated west with an Aussie settler.

We cruise slowly, searching. An ostrich darts into the path, effortlessly outstrides the Cruiser. Francolin clatter airborne. Zebra whirl and run. A gather of warthogs scatters, high-tailing it for cover. The Cruiser wallows abruptly in and out of one of their rooted-out holes, as unpredictably the neck of a giraffe ladders its way into the tallest trees. At every turn there is adventure.

The bush opens to a grassy veld – the scene as beautiful as the word, against the purple backdrop of the mountains – as an oryx skittishly retreats. Near its center, wildebeest race senseless circles in the lemon light of the waking sun.

Again the bush swallows us, and suddenly, not 60 yards off our trail, is my first kudu bull. He looms the color of the wispy smoke that rises from a damp fire. Stock-still he stands, half-hidden, and I find him by the flare of his great bellows-like ears. Afterward emerge the tall, thin legs, the white pickets of his flanks, the victory mark of his forehead, the twirl and gather of his horns. He is utterly erect and regal, and I have forgotten I am there to shoot.

"Young," Garry decides fortunately. Mid-40s, not the 50-inch plus majesty we have set our hat for. The bull nervously evaporates. "He'll be a good one in a couple of years – has that very deep spiral."

He smiles, knows I was shaken. Again. The afternoon before, barely after we arrived, there had been a good warthog. I had the rifle on him, longer than I should, and he had escaped into the grass.

"It's nothing," he had told me quietly, "you must shoot only when you're comfortable. I know the passion." My respect for him had soared.

Enoch, our Zulu tracker, has stopped the truck and Garry beckons me off. Ahead, through the shadowy bush, is the sunlit sprawl of a vast open plain. Enoch leads the stalk, Garry, myself and Todd Roberts, our cameraman, behind, single file – dodging the crack of a stick, the telling scrape of the thorns. Several hundred yards later we pause, squatting in a huddle and glassing a trio of blesbok, while Enoch and Kelly whisper together in native tongue their measure.

Garry motions me up.

"The one in the middle," he instructs, and in a rush I am facing the first shot of Africa. It's the sheer spell of the place I suppose. I've hunted as long as I've lived and I'm shaky as a pre-election promise. The buck faces us. I can see the bles, his white blaze, brilliantly through the scope. "Wait," Gary says softly, "wait until he turns."

I'm trying to talk myself down, and for the first time in my life I can't. Garry has to know. Still, he whispers "Now, take him!" for the buck has turned broadside and his hide burns mahogany-red in the sun, like the heart of the tree, against the tawny yellow sprawl of the veld and the blue of the mountains. I'm still fighting the rifle when it goes off. Knees buckle on both ends, as the buck drops in a *whumph*.

# AFRICA

**M**inutes later I kneel, to touch my first African animal. At the skinning shed, Enoch cuts out the blesbok's paunch, empties its sour green contents on the ground, and slices from the stomach wall a sliver, which he divides equally between the two of us. For among the Zulu, there is a ritual of safari, a tradition of time, earth and eternity. The proposition of your first kill, that by eating this portion of the animal you do it honor, become forever a part of it and what it has consumed, and thereby a part of the earth itself.

"Well done," Garry offers. Not so well, the shooting. I must do better.

In the afternoon, as the shadows spend their secrets on the backsides of the hills, an opportunity at a tremendous impala ram runs barren. Fate hands us another. A good gemsbok stands grandly under an acacia tree, distantly across the veld. Too open, the terrain, for a stalk. We back away, to the Crusier.

"When I say jump, jump," my PH urges. "Jump!" I cradle the rifle as we pile out, slump flat into the dust as Enoch pulls on with the truck. Crawling on our elbows, we close. The apprehension is electric, even at a couple hundred yards, but the gemsbok is not yet disturbed.

"Tight, against me," Garry hisses, jamming up the sticks. "Take him." We sit Indian-legged, and I'm trembling again as I hastily frame the target, forcing my attention away from the spectacular saber horns, which jut head to haunch.

We walk to him in the glow of sunset – even as far across the red-orange plain there are graphite sketches of scattered, feeding animals – and my spirit is as mellow as the light. I'm warm with the hunt, lost once more with how, finally, this can be. But there waits the gemsbok, big and chalk-gray as dirt, maned jet-black, the stunning throw of its horns better than a yard, and in the ceremonial markings of its face the imagery of Africa.

At the lodge, Rob Fancher and Steve Scott are flush with their own hunt. Rob fronts the U.S. operations of Swarovski, the renowned Austrian optics builder, and Steve, who heads WEI Productions, produces the Safari Hunter's Journal, a popular spot for *The Outdoor Channel*. Todd and Steve, along with pastels artist Natalie Caproni, are here to film a show. Both Rob and Steve are accomplished, world-traveled sportsmen. While we're here, Steve will celebrate his 100th night in Africa, and Rob will spin a hundred tales.

Garry Kelly and Bonwa Phala Safaris are a story to themselves.

In 1820, amid the tribal unrest of Mfecane, a daring young Irishman named William Edward O'Kelly forged his way into the African bush, the first man to settle Swaziland. Behind him came sons and grandsons, inheriting his love of the land and the wilds. Among them, perhaps Garreth Cullen Kelly embraced it fondest, especially the passion for hunting. It would become the grail of his life, after his father sent him to work with Norman Dean, of Zululand Safaris, who pioneered professional hunting in South Africa. At 19, he was taking clients out for rhino. Five years later he was on his own. Today, he's a large man, dapper and dashing at 50 – with three fine sons as well, Richard, Sean and Cullen, brother Brian, a cadre of top PHs, and the finest of Zulu trackers – 31 years in the business, with hunting concessions to dream about.

*Bonwa Phala*, Zulu for "where the impala drink," is 18,000 acres of South African highveld southeast of Johannesburg, near Warmbaths. It's home base for Kelly, offering distinguished, modern lodging or tent camping, carving out well the niche between old Africa and new, wild Africa and the Africa of amenities western clients have come to expect. The lodge, attended graciously by Vicky Merrett and her staff, rambles under a thatched roof through dining room, veranda and lounge, into the traditional *boma*. Neighboring chalets serve genially as living quarters.

A showplace of private game ranching, the property nurtures a plenitude of plains and bush animals, dangerous game including gold-class rhino and buffalo. From the lodge, it's a handy distance to the expansive, free-range of Borokalolo National Park, for exceptional waterbuck, kudu, sable, eland, impala and warthog. And the Mkuze Game Reserve, only one of three parks in Africa providing free-range white rhino, with the world's best nyala to boot. Or down to the Eastern cape for great mountain reedbuck, east cape kudu, springbok and cape bushbuck. Plus outstanding private ranch affiliations, like Boschveld, with its tremendous kudu.

It is on Bonwa Phala the second morning we're thwarted once more at impala, by a "go-away" bird, a gray lourie, and his incessant *waahhec, waahhec*. The African paradigm of a jaybird.

"Would that burrd 'ave gone any longer, I wou'd 'ave shot 'im," Garry fusses.

157

# AFRICA

Mid-morning we climb into a *machan*, above a waterhole. In a tomita tree. Garry stabs the bark with his knife and we watch the milky, poisonous sap rise and bead. Around us is the whooping chuckle of the doves. Impala, warthog, zebra, nyala and kudu come and leave. None, quite, to shoot. But on the way to camp, I have leveled the rifle. Two kudu bulls linger momentarily at the edge of the taller acacias. Heart thudding, I have the shoulder of the larger. Again, Kelly shakes his head. Relief and regret. Mid-40s, but oh so handsome.

It's cottage pie for lunch, fruit, fresh lemonade and a short nap, then Boschveld. "I anticipate your kudu this afternoon," Garry says.

Little more than an hour later, two kudu cows have crossed from the bush into a pasture. I lean into the rifle on the sticks. We have stalked the 600 yards here, are waiting for the great bull, which hopefully will follow. A young one emerges point-blank, blows, turns and bounds quickly away. There is another, a big one, far across the pasture. Too far. They are moving. We can hear others . . . when a warthog steps into the path 80 yards out, then another and another. I pay them little attention.

Garry nudges me urgently. Whispers "Do you want this pig? He's a very nice pig."

"No . . . kudu," I return tersely.

"Look at him," he insists. The boar has seen us now, is trotting away. I see through the scope two great tusks, one either side of his bobbling rump. My heart set for kudu, I watch him on, afraid a shot will bugger our chances.

"Too late, now," Garry laments. The kudu does not come.

Others do, between four and dark, after the field hands leave the pastures. A dozen bulls, maybe 15. Time and again I'm down on the rifle, as Garry sighs. Until the sun incinerated and there were only the faint, smoldering pink and purple vapors of it above the smoky clouds, and we spotted him, in the company of two cows.

"That's a good bull," Garry said. "If we can close enough I want you to take him."

We could not, and he spooked, ghosting back into the bush.

"Should have shot the bloody damn hog," Kelly said in the pregnant black journey back to camp.

I hurried off to retire, after dinner. I've traveled a bit now, hunted and fished a fair part of the world. Everywhere, every evening – I've wished the night away – longing for the morrow, that the hunt might begin anew. Never as in Africa. In Africa, I prayed, and my last prayer was for first light.

When it comes, there's a hippo standing on a rock island in the Lake of the Stone Wall Dam, a bulbous cow with twin calves. Dots of white egrets blotch the dark rocks. Anhingas crowd between. Along the shore, waterbuck flee. A massive white rhino does not. Sable, zebra and wildebeest watch from the bush. All morning, a plethora of plains and lowland game have mingled with exotic bird life. The Borokalolo. But not my kudu and I am anxious for Boschveld again this afternoon.

Soup and salad and Dutch granola for lunch, an impatient doze, and we're off. Five young bulls the first half-hour bolster our confidence, but prime time, when the great ones should be moving, there is nothing. Once more the sun expires, as we slip gingerly along the path to the watertank where yesterday we saw the big bull and his cows. He is not there.

Rob is waiting. Wearily, I shake my head. We celebrate instead his very fine warthog, and Natalie's wildebeest. Time wears on. Tomorrow is the fourth day. What will it bring?

My impala ram, it happens. After we have ridden all morning for kudu. From the *machan* in the tomita tree, at the waterhole. He is a grand and sleek old fellow past breeding height, seven or eight years mature, with thick bases and lovely lyrical horns.

"Well done, my man," Garry said. And it had been this time. We talked of rifles at noon. Garry showed us his working guns. A pre-64 Winchester, in .458, and a custom .375. The .458 is worn white. The tales it could tell. The one I want most to see and touch, the big Webley & Scott double, hunts with a friend.

Kelly speaks of buffalo, in the seconds between destiny and death. "Shoot him in the face, turn his head, he'll go that way. Not in the chest. It won't stop him."

Of elephant. "So massive. They knot your stomach from the beginning. You never know what they will do.

"The kudu just hide," he jokes.

159

# AFRICA

Prophetically, for another afternoon at Boschveld leaves us more desperate. There was another hog, suddenly. "Shoot him," Garry said, but he disappeared into the yellow grass. Garry waved it off with the toss of a hand. "Well, you've already turned down the world's record." There were only two kudu, as others barked their disgust from the bush. Without warning, Enoch jammed the truck to a halt, rolled out, grappled for the *panga*. A deft chop. A puff adder.

"Bloody damn snakes," Garry mutters.

A big kudu bull crosses in the headlights as we wind our way out. The ride back to camp is quiet.

"It serves nobody's justice to shoot an inferior kudu," Garry said to me at dinner. "We'll stay at it. We will find him. Tomorrow morning we will hunt the thick places here. We must cover much ground."

Once again, he has my respect. And complete accord. But I cannot avoid the shiver of uneasiness that effervesces and retreats, as secretly as the kudu themselves.

For now I knew. They would emerge, the greatest bulls, at the deep of dusk, as if they were born of the air. A loose suggestion of molecules, that had come together in a moment, and could vaporize as quickly as it collected. A presence, a force of indefinite shape and mass, where before there was nothing. So that you wondered with yourself if even it was there. Except that you felt it oddly to the soul, as you had the ghost stories of your childhood. They came as quietly as the darkness itself, and moved so naturally with the night that they seemed not to move at all, but drift, to appear and reappear, just here and later – you thought – there. And when so often they vanished, after you had hoped, tried and failed, it was as though the very core of you had left with them.

On Bonwa Phala the fifth morning, we hope, try, and fail. Only one bull, bedded, with broken horns. With the afternoon comes another good warthog, in a scatter of sows and young. I would have shot him except he eluded ultimately the attempts of our boys to drive him by. It is at the edge of dark, that pandemonium erupts. A bull and a cow whirl and bolt. I jerk and swing, find the blade of his shoulder. Garry is hesitating and I'm beginning the squeeze. "No," he says, "not quite. Just."

Five minutes later, there's no question. Our man from Boschveld stoops and points. Enoch is motioning also, with a cautious finger, across the cab of the Cruiser. Abruptly he is there – 70 yards deep – the bull we have wanted. With a blur of cows and a younger male. He has seen us, has turned and is drifting away.

"He's big. Shoot," Garry is pressing, "if you can get a shot at him, shoot!"

I have pieces of him through the scope, through the dense and dusky bush, desperately searching for a hole. I can't find it, only the obscure shape and travel of him, cows milling between. He's huge and I'm dying. If I shoot, it's only that, just shooting. He's faded now, farther into the bush. We scramble left, trying to find him again.

Frantically, Garry anew, "In the middle, do you have him?"

"Yes," for a moment, amidst the tangled confusion of the smaller bull and the cows, and then they are indistinguishable. When they part, he is gone.

Steve and Todd depart with morning for another location. Todd has followed me patiently with the camera. "I know you needed the kudu," I told them. "Luck of the thing," Steve said, "not for you to feel bad, but there's a place near here kudu abound. We took Natalie there and got a fifty-three-inch bull in one afternoon."

I nod.

Kudu medallions adorn the dinner menu. Salvation is the flawlessness of Amarula créme liqueur, done neatly.

Not much between us through the morning. Sean simply accompanied Garry to the Cruiser come time to go. Enoch paused, lifted his eyes – in his gaze was resolve and camaraderie. Our diligence would not falter this last afternoon.

Thirty minutes into the hunt, Enoch has eased the truck to a stop. There's a young warthog at the edge of the bush, by the path, 600 yards ahead.

I recognize the place even as Garry speaks. "We saw the big boar here the second afternoon, he may be with them."

Enoch kills the engine. No words are spoken; it is understood. We will proceed afoot. This time I will concede.

Our stalk is meticulous. We're standing stone-stiff now, the three of us pasted almost as one. The rifle is on the sticks. Thirty yards away in the high, golden grass are two pigs, now another and another. Then a sow. She has affixed us permanently, it seems, with her glare. I dread the instant she will snort and run and the moment will shatter like glass. But finally she is satisfied, falls back to rooting. Garry resumes his search for the boar. I catch the hump of a heavy body, moving from the bush. Gently I nudge and point.

"Him?" I whisper.

"Yes," he affirms.

The hog advances, slowly through the tall yellow thatch grass, and I am following him with the rifle, waiting for a spot. He reaches the place of the sow, a slight opening. I have only his head, for a second – the ivory either side to his ears – as he too finds us, for we are so close, and turns instantly back. But he is only wary, merely walking away. The grass parts to his shoulder, finally, and I squeeze.

The world is mad with hogs. Hogs here, there, everywhere, in a wild dash for the bush. In the tall grass I have lost the boar completely. Reflexively I jack the bolt back, slam in another cartridge, jerk one to the other – hoping not to find him. Then Garry is hop-skipping by me, stopping a short distance away, his face a caricature of disbelief.

"You missed the bloody damn pig," he stammers.

"What?"

"You missed the pig," he declares, laughing.

I notice his covetous glance at the Ruger Safari Grade rifle. He has hungered after it from the time I arrived.

"You and your shit rifle," he says.

I don't know whether to laugh or cry.

Then we make our way out, the grass parts again, and there is my pig.

My eyes jump to Garry. He's down laughing. "I ought to shoot you, you bloody Irish b-------."

I can't get over the tusks. It's a hell of a pig.

"He'll go high in both books," Garry remarks. "Well done, my friend."

I'm on the rifle one last time at kudu; Garry, Sean and Enoch are up with the glasses. Searching – all of us – in the final dusky moments for the bull pray be with the cows that have crossed ahead. He is not.

Dusk dies and night is born.

"Did you get the kudu?" Vicky asked earnestly of me at the lodge.

"No – no kudu," I replied.

She waited a moment. "Perhaps he is your spirit animal, and you are not meant to kill him," she said in a soft and bloody-beautiful British/Africaans' accent.

Perhaps. Perhaps I have wanted him too much. From the first word – the last book – there has been Africa. And after Africa – kudu.

There are times when life bestows even the most magnificent of its creatures almost capriciously. It has never been that way for me. For that, I have learned to be thankful.

I was proud of my pig. He seemed as meant to be as the kudu did not.

So wends the timeless enigma of the hunt, even in Africa.

# GHOST IN THE DUST

*Just getting to the land of these giants is difficult . . . and then comes the real challenge.*

*By David Cabela*

ey are zee ghosts in zee dust cloud. When you first see zem, you do not know if you did. Zen, zey are gone."

Bent to one knee, Pierre Guerrini examined a Lord Derby eland track on the dry savanna trail. "Zey are zee stuff of legend."

Lord Derby eland. The name itself is aristocratic, and for good reason – the Lord Derby hunt is considered by many well-traveled sportsmen as one of the best outdoor adventures in all of Africa.

I felt that nervous burn of adrenaline riding my breath.

"How fresh?" I asked.

"Garga say zey are two day old. We move on."

I nodded and followed Garga and Simon, our Douru trackers back to the truck.

Garga's skills were honed through years of studied practice. His deep, weathered eyes held the wisdom of many hunting seasons, including a few before the western adventurer brought his money and big bore rifles on such a regular basis.

At times, hours went by when I saw zero sign of any animal. Skepticism wriggled its ugly head when that happened, yet without fail, Garga and Simon always led us to our quarry.

"You must forgive my English, David," Pierre said. "It is not very good. I may have to repeat many times."

"I'll tell you one thing," I said.

"What is zat?"

"Your English is a lot better than my French."

A moment later Garga and Simon started chatting. From the back, Pierre tapped the roof of the truck. That was the driver's instruction to stop. More tracks. One day old. Half an hour later we found tracks crossing the road from the night before. They could be anywhere by now. We pressed on.

"We will do good, no?"

I shrugged.

"Do not worry. We may not get your eland today. But we will find him. It took your fahzer eight days zee last time he is here. But we did get his eland."

An ex-fighter pilot, Pierre never lacked confidence. He had a long promising career ahead of him had he chosen to stay in the military. Instead, he left the French Air Force to become an apprentice hunter in Cameroon.

"I tell you, David. It is not long before I zink maybe I make big mistake. Zee life of apprentice is not as glamorous as it may sound. My fahzer was contractor in Chad and I was wiz him until I turn ten. He send me back to France, but it is Africa I love. When my apprenticeship is over, zis concession become available. I am in right place at right time. It is one of zee great concessions in all of Cameroon. I have done all I can to make it zee best."

When we next stopped the truck, Garga, Simon and Wadjiri, the water-bearer and a fine tracker himself, started a lively discussion. Pierre listened. He turned toward me. "Come, get your rifle. We go by foot. Zees are only few hours old. We follow."

A screen of dust blowing in from the Sahara hazed the sun, but the morning temperature approached 100 degrees. The heat pressed down on our shoulders all day long. Wadjiri carried a cooler of water on his back during hours of long hiking. He was a hard, young man.

Sweat burned my eyes, while my ankles twisted with every step on crusted mounds formed by worms during the rainy season. A tsetse fly stuck my shoulder blade like a poison-tipped dart. All of these things were toying with my conviction. Was I tough enough? If Wadjiri could carry over five gallons, I could surely continue on with a seven-pound rifle.

"Shh." Simon held up his hand.

A low deep grunt, then another. From where? Simon and I pointed south. Garga pointed at the tracks going north. No one uttered a word.

Glancing at Simon, I pointed south, hoping for corroboration. Simon half-nodded, only a hint of conviction in his eyes. Holding his hand rigid, Garga shoved his fingertips north. Tracks rarely lie.

Another grunt.

We all froze. It sounded close – and south.

Wadjiri slipped up beside Pierre, pressing his shoulder into the Frenchman's. He pointed to the treeline – to the north.

"Ooh." Pierre's binoculars shot to his eyes. "Zer zey are."

A cream-colored shadow vanished into the forest, like something out of a dream. Had I seen an eland or had I imagined it.

"Oh, man. Big eland. We will shoot zat eland. Zer are many."

Where?

"Zat one is forty-six – zer is forty-seven – forty-five. Oh, zat one is big."

"Where are they?" I whispered.

"Zey are gone now."

"Did they see us?"

"No, just moved into forest. Ready? We must go now, David. Zey are moving."

Falling in step behind Garga, I expected a short stalk. On eland? Not a chance.

When I was younger, trying to communicate with my parents was futile. I had no idea what they were thinking. They sure couldn't read my mind. Talking is never really part of the deal, is it? When I was younger, I sometimes allowed such matters to trouble me. I was even more naïve than I am now. When I was younger, I failed to see how my parents, my mother and father, loved me beyond limits. They tried to share themselves the best that parents know how.

# AFRICA

It was on the trail of a Lord Derby eland when I realized there was a part of my father I understood completely. I understood what pushed him to force that one last step toward a black-necked ghost with spiral horns.

What makes this giant antelope so special? Foremost is the challenge, first in getting to Central Africa and then trying to find these wary animals in a land where temperatures blister above 110 degrees in the middle of winter. Eight hours a day hiking over worm-hole crusted ground for a week only to have the first eland you see bolt for another country is enough to make you question your toughness.

When we first saw them in the treeline they had been less than 500 yards away. Two hours later I began to doubt that I'd even seen them. Maybe they were ghosts after all. That's when Garga stopped.

Pierre snapped his binoculars to his eyes, then barked an order to Garga.

"Come, let us go. We must try to go ahead of zem. Hurry. Stay just behind. Keep up. Right here." He pointed at his heel.

Nodding, I jumped in step trying to suppress a cough – damn dust from the desert. Setting fires every chance we got didn't help much either – damn smoke. Somehow, through the light haze of dust and smoke and the sweat stinging my eyes, I caught a glimpse. Fleeting . . . vague . . . real. Maybe.

"Come, David." Pierre pulled on my sleeve, and then pushed me toward a tree.

"Zey come. Watch zat opening in zee trees, zer. You see it?"

"Got it."

"Be ready."

In a herd of around 50, getting the right bull to enter one of the few, small shooting lanes through the brush is like rolling the bones at a craps table. You really need that ten, but odds are it'll be a seven. A shooting lane full of grass and branches was the best we had. I'd have to pick my shot carefully. Problem is, eland never stop moving. They wander constantly, as if they have a purpose. What? I can't say. To figure out that purpose – vexing, at best.

"Not zat one. Forty-six. Female. Female. No. Forty-seven . . . not bad. Not zee one. He will not come here. We go now. Come quickly."

Garga raced off. Pierre and I followed, keeping up as best we could. After almost an hour of alternating between running and a half-jog, I had to put a stop to it. Pierre must have sensed it.

"We will rest," he said, his breathing not nearly as heavy as my own. "I zink we are close. But you can not shoot if you can not breaze."

I nodded, sucking in air like a 50-year-old chain-smoker doing up-downs with the high-school football team.

Pierre slapped my shoulder.

"You know, David. Your fahzer's last hunt is just like zis. Only he did it for eight days straight."

Eight days. That alone made me respect his toughness. But it wasn't on the hunting trail when I learned to admire it. It was when he almost died.

You see, less than two years prior, hunting in a remote region in Ethiopia, he was attacked by a bursting ulcer. It severed an artery. By the time they got him to the hospital, he'd lost nearly 80 percent of his blood supply. There was no hope, they said. Say your goodbyes.

After six months in various hospitals, much of that time in an induced coma, he learned to walk again for the third time in his life (he had polio has a boy). Tough by any measure. Tough beyond any measure of my endurance.

Dad relearned to walk, and then accompanied his family to Cameroon to hunt a legendary antelope. He wanted each of his five sons to experience what he believes is one of the top hunts in all of Africa. My four brothers already understood what drove him to pursue this noble beast. And though my father did not walk beside me, we shared something that day all fathers and sons should share. Something beyond explanation. Suddenly, pressing further wasn't so hard.

L et's go," I said.

"Garga say zey are many more in herd. He say zee bull travel in middle. We must intercept zem. Garga, he zink like eland. You will see."

So, with my feet heavy as watermelons, we stepped away from the tracks we'd been following for hours. Garga hadn't steered us wrong yet. Still, it took a good deal of confidence to walk away from a perfectly good giant eland track. We ran through half-burned waist-high grass, dodged termite mounds, and sucked in a swarm of mopane flies before catching up to the herd again.

"He is zer," Pierre whispered as we huddled around an acacia. "Stay in zat shooting lane. He is zee forz one in line. He is coming. He is coming. Be ready. Stay on zee spot. Tell me what you see."

"I don't see him yet."

"He is coming. Here he comes. Be ready. Oh no – he turned around zat tree. Sheet. We must go."

Rushing to get in front of them, we bumped into a straggling group of females.

"She's staring right at us," I said.

"Zat bull zer is not bad." Pierre pointed out a bull moving across an open field. "It is not him, but get on him anyway. Wait. Zey are watching. Don't move. Wait. Okay, get on him now."

He set up the shooting sticks in front of me. "Stop. Don't move."

The cow turned and ran, taking every other eland with her. We were after them like a pack of wild dogs. Just as they started to calm, we bumped a small herd of kob right into the eland. They were gone.

"Oh, hell." Pierre stood staring into the dust. He spoke to Garga for a few minutes. "Garga, he zink we can get back on zee track and catch up to zem again."

"How long before we catch up to them?"

"Hour. Maybe longer. Wadjiri is coming wiz water. It is hot, but we are not in zee hot part of day yet. We will drink. Zen we go get you eland."

Pierre smiled as he shook my shoulder. It was 110 degrees.

Garga was back on the track like we'd never lost it. He worked the spoor deftly, with the care of a predator whose life not only depended on it, but one who enjoyed it. Sweat dripping from my brow, I slapped at the most vile creature I've ever encountered. After whacking another tsetse fly only to see it buzz off unscathed, I tried to concentrate on Garga's eyes, tried to see what he saw. Every now and again, somewhere under a layer of leaves in the savanna woodland, I thought I might see a track – only it rarely seemed to be traveling the same direction as us bipedal predators. If it wasn't for those loathsome bugs, I might be able to concentrate.

I nearly ran into the back of Pierre while studying what I believed to be an eland bull track.

"Zey are moving zrough zee opening in zee trees. Do you see?"

"Got em."

"Look in your scope. Tell me what you see."

"Females. Four."

"Okay. None of zose. Zee bulls zey are coming. Okay. Not zat one. Zat's not him. Okay. Zis one. Do you see him . . . just behind zee female?"

"I got him."

"Zat's him. Shoot zat one."

As we approached camp that afternoon, our driver, Blaise, began blaring the horn while Garga, Wadjiri and Simon started singing, celebrating our success. I only understood one word – yamousa – eland.

Everyone piled out of the main lodge to meet us. Dad stood out in front of them all, a knowing smile on his face. He knew the Lord Derby. He knew that when you follow a giant eland track you are committing to a trek that will last hours. You are chasing an antelope that can travel in herds numbering in the hundreds and elude your pursuits as if they are little more than a dream. A dream you know you've had many times, but can't quite remember. But when you finally spot that first eland bull, like a cream-colored shadow, it is unforgettable. Then, through the dust cloud, you see him clearly. Only one word suits – regal.

# THE PRIDE OF MALONGA

*Nine hot, grueling days had come and gone – hanging and checking baits, sitting for long, sleepless hours on crudely built platforms of sticks and straw . . . waiting and listening and hoping. And finally, in the murky halflight just before dark, he was there.*

*By Lloyd Newberry*

T he grating bark of a baboon shattered the afternoon quiet and sent adrenaline coursing through my body. I rolled over slowly in our tree blind and glanced at Arthur, who nodded at me ever so slightly. I slid the rifle through an opening in the straw and peered down the barrel at the zebra hindquarter 80 yards away. We still had an hour before dark. Questions and uncertainties raced through my mind. Something had alarmed the baboon. Was it the big Malonga lion that we'd been hunting for the past eight days? And if it was him, would he come before scope-light waned or make his approach in the safety of darkness as he'd always done before? Was my 12-year quest to kill a lion finally coming to an end? I heard dry leaves crunching in the thick riverine growth. Something was coming our way.

# AFRICA

I had booked my first African safari in 1985, primarily for buffalo and plains game in Botswana where I'd taken several excellent trophies. But the animal that impressed me most was a huge male lion that we'd observed briefly at its kill. Just before disappearing in the tall grass, the big cat had stopped and looked back at me, and for a brief moment all that was Africa was embodied in that stare and frozen in my memory.

I hunted a variety of game throughout the world over the next seven years, but I never stopped thinking about that lion. Then in 1992 I traveled to Zimbabwe, where I killed a beautiful leopard and had several close encounters with lions, but never a clear shot. From our blind we had listened to them ripping and tearing flesh through the long African night, but they always left before daylight.

All I could think about was going back and trying again. It eventually became an obsession, and I spent a great deal of time researching my next safari. Of particular interest was the Lower Lupande Game Management Area, where Alex Walker and Safari Expeditions Zambia conduct safaris. Bordering the Luangwa River opposite of South Luangwa National Park, the Lower Lupande is known for large herds of buffalo, which in this area are the principal prey of lions.

At the 1997 Safari Club International convention I visited with Arthur Taylor, a well-known buffalo and lion guide who had once worked for Cotton Gordon. According to Arthur, their camps on the Lower Lupande had enjoyed 100 percent success on lion over the past six years. If I was willing to work hard, he said, I'd get a lion.

August 19th found us landing at the tiny Mfuwe Airport in the Rift Valley of northeastern Zambia where we were met by Arthur and another long-time PH, Zane Langman. Our party consisted of my wife, Martha, who would not dream of letting me go to Africa without her, my son, Wyck; his fiancée, Sherri; my attorney, Lloyd Murray; and his son, L.D.

On the two-hour ride to camp, Arthur talked excitedly about a big male lion that roamed the Malonga River drainage. He'd never seen the lion, though it was a familiar sight to members of the Akunda tribe. On several occasions Arthur had found the cat's long mane hairs lodged in the flesh of his kills and in several baits.

John Knowles, PH at the buffalo camp just north of us, had reported a deep-throated male roaring late into the night not far from where Arthur had last found a kill. He was convinced it was the Malonga lion. We would need to hang our baits quickly, so the next morning we shot an old, heavily scarred hippo and spent most of the day butchering and hanging quarters of the two-and-one-half ton animal.

Though exhausted from the heat and hard work, we didn't sleep much the first two nights. Our camp was situated along the Luangwa River and a wide pool that contained some 80 hippos. The cantankerous old bulls grunted and fought all night, and their flatulence sounded like partially submerged exhaust fans. Hyenas, attracted by the sweet smells of the skinning camp, howled and chortled while baboons cussed at a leopard slipping through moonlit shadows. Worse yet was a visit from an old bull elephant who plunged right through the camp's grass boma to dine on the seed pods of our acacia trees. The bull's constant munching and rumbling stomach combined with the other sounds to make sleep difficult.

But not even a lack of sleep could dampen our excitement when, early on our third morning we discovered that lions had fed on one of the baits. We quickly went about the task of constructing a *machan* high in a sausage tree. The floor was crisscrossed with small saplings and covered with a thick layer of straw. We decided to spend the night on the platform, hoping the lions would feed on the bait, then hang around till dawn. I was actually looking forward to catching up on my sleep in the tree, which was miles from the noisy hippos and marauding elephant. But Africa had other ideas.

Shortly after dark, a drop of moisture splattered onto my face. My first thought was that it came from one of the numerous fruit bats feeding on the tree's blossoms. I soon realized that it was nectar dripping from the big crimson flowers, and they continued to hit me no matter where I moved on the platform.

We had tied the bait about seven feet off the ground, within easy grasp of lions but too high for hyenas. It wasn't long before a chorus of hyenas had gathered around the bait, howling in frustration at the ripe-smelling meat just beyond their reach. Their wailing cries were joined by the barking of bushbucks and baboons moving through the dark shadows around our blind. I finally dozed off, only to be abruptly awakened by the sound of snapping limbs. Once again wide awake, I listened to a herd of elephants munching their way through the blackness. I might have dozed off, but only for a few seconds.

# AFRICA

No lions came, so at daybreak we set out to check our other "speculation" baits, as Arthur called them. One bait in an adjacent river drainage had been visited by lions, though all we found were the short mane hairs of an immature male. Regardless, we constructed a ground blind on an adjacent hillside in the hope of seeing the lion and determining his size.

Arthur, photographer Rob Austin, Wyck and I entered the blind an hour before dark, determined to spend the night if necessary. We had just settled in when, to our amazement, a handsome, long-tailed leopard strolled up to the bait. One shot from Wyck's 7mm Magnum found us breaking out the cameras and congratulating him on his fantastic good luck. A big celebration followed that night in camp; our safari was off to a great start.

For the next five days we continued to check the baits and search for lion kills, while taking a variety of record-book trophies, among them grysbuck, impala, kudu, waterbuck and even a 13-foot crocodile.

The young male lion was still feeding where Wyck had killed his leopard, but hyenas were the only visitors at other baits. Each night we could hear the loud coughing roar of what we thought was the Malonga lion. Scouts from several villages told us the big male roared nightly, and for several evenings his lionesses had terrorized hunters in a buffalo camp, striding boldly right through the middle of the compound.

On the ninth morning of our hunt, we waved goodbye to Wyck and Sherry who had to return home. I had hoped to take a lion before they left so they could share in the experience, but now I was beginning to question my chances of ever getting one. We had discovered two of the pride's kills – a full-grown hippo and an old buffalo bull, but the male never fed during the day. Nor had it touched any of our baits. It was certainly following its reputation of being smart, elusive and totally nocturnal.

Later that morning Arthur decided to hang a zebra hindquarter at the foot of the Muchinga escarpment, where dense growth along the Malonga River provided sanctuary and security for the lions. It was here earlier in the hunting season that Arthur and a client had driven right up to the Malonga lionesses. The fierce animals had refused to retreat from their position, even when a shot was fired in the air. Little did Arthur know that this dangerous situation would be repeated during our hunt.

We stopped by camp for supplies, then set out for the escarpment, dragging a piece of rotten meat behind the Landcruiser to leave a scent trail. The drive to the Malonga drainage was relaxing and scenic. Brilliantly marked carmine bee-eaters hovered over the red and yellow blooms of sausage and acacia trees, while giraffes and puku antelope gave us sleepy, if not disinterested, stares from the khaki-colored brush.

We arrived early in the afternoon at the base of the escarpment, where to our delight we discovered fresh lion tracks, including those of a big male. We hung the zebra hindquarter and prepared our blind about 20 feet up in a sausage tree. Arthur instructed the head tracker and driver to park the vehicle a mile away and wait until black dark. If they did not hear a shot, they were to drive back to camp, then return for us just after sunrise.

The thought of another sleepless night in another tree was not appealing, but the fresh sign was encouraging. Maybe our luck would finally change.

Arthur, Rob and I climbed onto the platform and made ourselves as comfortable as possible. We had an hour before dark, and I had just begun writing in my diary when a baboon barked.

Suddenly, the tawny form of a lioness emerged from the underbrush. Cautiously she padded over to the bait, then rose on her rear legs and grasped the zebra hindquarter with massive paws. The sound of snapping bones and tearing flesh brought two other females, and soon their snarls and low growls filled the air.

The females had been feeding for about ten minutes when we heard a deep, resonate *uurrunnghh unngh unngh*. The long, low roar reverberated through the foothills of the escarpment as though it was coming from everywhere yet nowhere. I could feel it as well as hear it, almost as if the earth itself was moaning from the heat of day and the drought of winter. We knew immediately that it was the Malonga lion.

The females melted back into the dense undergrowth and everything became graveyard quiet. For 15 minutes I stared down the barrel of my rifle as the bushveld grew darker and darker. The sun doesn't set in Africa; it gets close to the horizon and then drops from sight and the world becomes pitch black. I peered through my scope to see if I still had enough shooting light and noticed movement off to the left of the bait. And just that quickly he was there, standing broadside, surveying the scene in front of him. There was no question as to what manner of animal filled my scope; even the murky halflight could not diminish his massive profile.

I never hesitated. The crosshairs settled on his shoulder and at the impact of the bullet, he slumped forward, then instantly regained his footing and raced off into the brush.

Arthur grabbed me and began slapping me on the back. "Great shot! He's dead for sure!" But I wasn't that certain, because he'd bounded away so quickly.

"You two wait here while I fetch the Landcruiser," Arthur said, as he climbed down the tree. Thirty minutes later he pulled up next to the tree so Rob and I could climb down into the roofless vehicle. Rob took the wheel, while Arthur and I stood, rifles at the ready. As we neared the spot where the lion had disappeared, three pairs of bright yellow eyes glared in the headlights.

The lionesses were lying directly behind the body of the lifeless male, and as we edged to within ten yards, they crouched low in the grass, snarling fiercely and lashing their tails violently from side to side. They were not about to retreat – in fact, I feared they would leap onto the vehicle and into our laps at any moment.

"Shoot into the air," Arthur shouted. "Scream and beat on the bonnet!"

We fired off two rounds and the trackers joined in the commotion, beating empty coke bottles on the fenders. The noise finally unnerved the lions enough that they began crawling backwards into the brush, giving ground inch by inch. When they were about 20 yards away, Arthur and I used one hand to help the trackers load the dead male, while keeping our rifles pointed toward the yellow-green eyes. As soon as the lion was pulled aboard, we sped away, not stopping until we had put a considerable distance between us and the savage animals.

Suddenly everyone was talking excitedly and shaking hands. Someone dragged out the chop boxes and passed around the beer, and our trackers began their victory chant. As we drew near to camp, local villagers ran out to jump on the vehicle, eager to share in the free beer and jubilation.

The celebration picked up back at camp, where the lion was placed under the lights so everyone could see his massive body. Lions in the thick brush of Zambia do not grow the long manes typical of open-country cats, but what they lack in mane length, they make up for in body size. My lion measured almost ten feet and weighed upwards of 500 pounds.

As I stroked his thick, reddish-blond mane, I found myself awed at his size. Arthur bent over to shake my hand. "I knew he was a huge lion, definitely the largest of the year. He will go well up in the record book."

That was nice, but it really didn't matter. What counted most was that I had finally fulfilled my dream, and I'd done it after a long and extremely difficult hunt.

# FATED A DREAMER

*Long had he dreamed of hunting Cape buffalo,*
*but never did he even dare to dream this big.*

*by Dwight Van Brunt*

I never earned anything but an A grade on a school assignment, at least until discovering girls sometime early in my teens. That streak was almost broken in sixth grade when I did a report for science class. We were given the option of writing about any animal and I picked Cape buffalo. I wrote the paper, complete with the Latin name, ballistics table and a shot placement diagram for extra credit. Even had quotes – including one by Robert Ruark recounting how a wounded buffalo had chased some unfortunate up a tree and then licked the bottom of his feet bloody with a wood-rasp tongue. I cited the source in proper footnote form. Knowing my teacher, Mr. Jerry Wainscott, to be a fellow hunter, I turned the paper in early so he could enjoy it at his leisure.

That son-of-a-gun gave me a "C." He said I made up the quote – even called me out in front of the whole class and accused me of being lazy. That night, jaw locked in an underbite from all the mad, I searched the house, but the magazine had probably gone off with the trash.

# AFRICA

Determined to set things right, I stood hard against Wainscott's desk the next morning and bitterly argued the injustice, then later read the paper aloud without changes. He finally told me to let it go, or my first "C" would become my first "D." Having none of it, I stormed the principal's office at recess, scheduled an appointment for the next morning, and was there waiting when Mr. Robert W. Rumsey arrived.

An imposing man, Rumsey motioned me in, closed the door and waved to a chair standing sentinel before his equally imposing desk. While hanging his coat on a hook, he asked me what was on my mind, and when he turned, he seemed surprised I was still standing.

"Sir, I wrote a paper on Cape buffalo and Robert Ruark does not lie," I blurted in summation.

Rumsey looked at me in silence longer than I would have liked, then pointed to the chair again. I took the hint. "Explain," he ordered.

I responded in some detail. After I finished, Rumsey thought for a long moment, no doubt contemplating the wrong of it all, then asked how much I knew about hunting.

"I don't know, sir, but hunting is all that I think and dream about."

Rumsey stood, walked to a closet and hauled out a long wooden case. He laid it on a table, opened the lid and motioned me over.

"What do you know about this rifle?" he asked with seemingly genuine curiosity. The slight softening of his tone was appreciated, and the Winchester logo on the upper lid gave me a place to start.

"That's a Winchester .22, probably a Model 52 but maybe a 75," I managed. "First of either one I 've seen for real. It's for shooting targets, not hunting. Too heavy to carry for very long."

Rumsey pondered the response, then went back to the closet, removed a leather shooting coat and let me try it on, hauling down the straps as much as he could around my scrawny frame. He explained its purpose, then turned the conversation to bird hunting and asked about my father's bird dogs. After freeing me from the coat and putting the rifle away, he scribbled something down on a piece of paper, folded it, and pressed it into my hand.

"Give that to your teacher, and thank you for coming in for a visit."

Wainscott was at his desk. I waited for eye contact, then pressed the note into his hand. He read it, then read it again after giving me a stinkeye. Crumbling the paper, he pitched it in the garbage and reached for his grade book.

"You can go now," was all he managed. I went, too, because I had read the note over his shoulder and could not keep down a smile. It said: "Give the boy an A, Jerry. I read that Ruark article last week."

Y first chance to hunt buffalo came more than 30 years after that unforgettable day in 6th grade. It was on a combo with plains game in Zimbabwe. Nothing worked out. Still, I had managed to hunt them.

Hoping for another chance at buffalo and reasoning that my children really did not need a college education to make their way in the world, I ordered a Rigby double in .500 Nitro Express. It was a long year before the rifle was finished, but it was worth the wait. Stocked in exhibition English walnut and scroll-engraved with gold accents by Lisa Tomlin, it is as close to perfection as I will ever hold. Through express sights and off the sticks, alternating 570-grain Woodleigh softs and solids loaded by Superior Ammunition form a cluster at 50 yards that I can cover with a tennis ball.

I love Africa, and manage to find my way there almost every year to hunt a wonderful property in the northeast corner of Namibia called Eden. Jamy Traut is the PH in charge thereabouts. Our friendship has grown to the point I consider him family, and the success of Eden has permitted expansion of his hunting territory to include a vast concession in nearby Bushmanland as well as sporadic opportunities in and around the fabled Caprivi Strip. While Eden holds no dangerous game, it teems with plains animals like kudu, eland, waterbuck and sable. I have taken great trophies there, and even managed to be in camp when opportunity knocked for problem elephant and cattle-killing leopard and lion. Without fail, however, I would ask about buffalo.

Arranging a buffalo hunt in Namibia is difficult compared to most countries in southern Africa. When the country became independent, the new government was rightly concerned about making sure its people had jobs, and more importantly, enough to eat.

One of the early goals was to develop cattle ranches, but there was a problem: The buffalo in some of the earmarked areas were carriers of both TB and hoof-and-mouth disease. That prevented beef exports, something that would hamstring the industry, so drastic action was taken. A fence spanning the northeast corner of the country was built, isolating the buffalo in and around the Caprivi. Buffalo south of the fence were exterminated, and a fledgling cattle industry took hold. Buffalo herds in the Caprivi were spared, as was an isolated population in Waterburg National Park.

In 1996 the government decided that an additional population of buffalo was both valuable and desirable, so they purchased a farm in-holding in the vast Nyae Nyae Conservancy, surrounded it with a game-proof fence, trapped some migrating buffalo nearby and released them inside after testing for disease. The original 26 buffalo have since grown nearly tenfold, and what is now called the Buffalo Quarantine Area has expanded to 34 square miles.

Far from a park by any definition, the area is off-limits to anyone other than a few W.W.F. workers and Park Warden Dries Alberts, who has watched over the area since 1997. Dries is also a licensed PH, so it was inevitable he would cross paths with Jamy Traut.

Knowing how much I wanted to hunt buffalo, Jamy had been looking for a way to take me to the Caprivi for several years, but the concession holders had little trouble keeping a waiting list of their own clients for the limited permits. There was one other possibility. In 1999 Dries had determined there was a surplus of old bulls, each long past breeding age and likely to soon die naturally. The meat and the trophy fees would go to the villagers.

That first hunt was successful and a total of six bulls have been taken since. Notably, these bulls were big, with an average spread of over 42 inches. Jamy and I talked in detail about this opportunity several times, mostly because of my concerns regarding fair chase. Finally, after hearing stories from other hunters who had been there, and after looking at the country for myself, I decided to give it a try. Two permits came available, one for me and the other for my son, Ross, who had just turned 21.

O n a cool morning in July, Ross and I along with my wife Kellie, and daughter, Keni, drove through the Quarantine Area gate, where we were all swept back in time to primitive Africa. Other than a few tiny roads that permitted maintenance of scattered waterholes, there was nothing but bushveld – thick, thorny brush with occasional patches of grass tall enough to hide a full-grown buffalo.

We were eager to get started, so after a fast lunch we were off to a waterhole where Dries had found some promising tracks at first light. Four very long and hot hours later, one of the trackers came upon a pile of dung warm to his touch. Dries whispered that the buffalo were up and feeding, and that the slight breeze was running in our favor.

The trackers spread out, moving slowly, trying to separate the bulls from the thick brush. Suddenly the breeze twisted and we heard the bulls running. We found some shade and waited, hoping they would not go far. There was enough light left for one more try and before long we caught the bulls feeding in a tight cluster, indistinct black masses beyond a screen of thorns.

I followed Jamy and Dries, first crouching and then crawling until we closed to within 30 yards. Then the real work began, sorting one from another and judging horns. I made no effort to follow the whispered conversation in Afrikaans, but it was clear from their excited jabberings that several of the animals were big.

There was a small opening between us and the bulls, wide enough to allow a shot. We watched as several moved through, then one decided to bed down. He was initially facing broadside, showing the deep curl of his horns. When he turned, we could see his boss was solid, the hallmark of an old bull, and that his horns hooked out eight inches or so past his ears.

Dries had said earlier that these bulls measured about 32 inches across the ears, meaning this bull was in the high 40s.

Jamy motioned me up. Whispering, he made sure we were both looking at the same bull, then indicated that I should take him when he stood. "Soft, then solid," he said. "We must move slightly forward to clear his shoulder."

We crawled some more until things looked good, close enough that I could see a circular chip in the top of the bull's horns. Rifle ready, I slowly came up to a kneel. I thought we had him until the breeze hit me in the back of the neck again.

"He's standing," Jamy hissed, but there was no shot. The bull lunged forward, his shoulder hidden, put some of the other bulls between us and thundered off. "Sorry about that," Jamy said, watching the bulls disappear.

I was anything but sorry. One more day would not matter.

At daylight we were tracking a group of bulls we hoped were the ones from the evening before. The sign was hours old, so we were all surprised when one of the trackers quickly ducked down and pointed. Nine buffalo were lined out, meandering in our direction.

I followed Dries and Jamy forward, crawling again, until we found a good spot. The bulls kept coming, including one old warrior with a boss that stood above his head like a German army helmet. They got our wind at 15 yards and thundered off.

Dries chuckled at my surprise that we did not take one. "I don't care how long it takes," he said. "I want to get that big one we stalked yesterday."

We backtracked, picked up the original trail again and learned we had come upon the bulls by accident. The ones we were originally following had angled away in another direction.

It was late in the afternoon and miles away when we caught up to the bulls. Naude' Alberts, a master guide at Eden and distant cousin to Dries, located them after climbing high into a tree on a whim. After picking some landmarks, we moved in and then ducked downwind, hoping they would come to us and that the big bull from the day before would be among them. It almost didn't happen and probably shouldn't have by rights. We were looking in one direction and they appeared from another.

There were three, then five and then seven, spread more or less in single file. Dries and Jamy worked their binoculars to size them up. As before, the bulls moved through the only shooting lane we had until one cut our tracks and alerted. He turned back, head high, and snorted. The other bulls stopped like they had hit a wall, changed direction, then slowly passed back through the opening no more than 20 yards away. All we could do was watch them go, so close I could see their noses reading the air.

At the very moment I decided there would be no shot, Dries said "That's the big one. Take him." He did not need to say it twice.

I triggered the soft in my right barrel, hitting him hard in the shoulder. The bull's nose dropped nearly to the ground. He bucked high and hard, almost turning over on himself. I pulled the rifle down out of recoil, swept back to his shoulder and followed with the solid from my left barrel as he disappeared into the churning dust.

Ross was alongside, rifle raised. I told him to cover, ejected the empties in an arch between us and reloaded quickly with a pair of solids from my belt. I brought the rifle back up and pasted the bead on a bull standing near the opening where I had shot.

"That's not your buffalo, but watch him. He's looking for a fight," Dries said quietly. We stayed put until he moved off several minutes later.

"The shots were good, Dad," Ross offered with confidence.

Jamy crept around Dries, .458 at high port, and asked how I felt about the shots. I told him I felt good, but after waiting five more minutes and not hearing a death bellow, he asked again. I gave the same answer with less certainty, and just then we heard the bulls running in the distance.

Fearing the worst, we carefully picked a path to the spot where the bull had been standing at the shot. As we got close, I was more than a little surprised to see Naude', my wife and three trackers standing casually in the open. Kellie was pumping her fist up in celebration, then yelled out, "That is the most incredible thing I've ever seen!"

I thought she had gone crazy from the heat, but a few steps later we found all five of them standing over my bull. Both shots had passed through the shoulders and the solid had severed the spine, driving him straight into the ground. I recognized the chip in his horn.

We knew the bull was big, but none of us were willing to believe what we had until we fashioned a square at camp and checked him with a steel tape. Buffalo are ranked by spread, and the Namibian national record is 48$^1$/$_2$ inches. My bull spanned well over 51.

The next morning we went to another waterhole, searching for an old and generally solitary bull Dries hoped to find for Ross. A bachelor band had been there so we took the track. We eventually found the bulls, then later another bunch, but the right one was not among them. Ross took it in stride, losing himself in the hunt and savoring each approach. He joked with everyone when we stopped to take on water, assuring them this was the time of his life and that there was no need to rush. He was still smiling when we drove into camp long after dark.

Dries was confident that we would find the right track the next day, so I guess we were not surprised when he did. "It's him for sure," Dries said. "This bull is so old he drags his feet."

He might have been old but he could walk, and it took almost seven hours to catch him. We managed to get inside 30 yards without blowing him out. Ross was ready for the shot, but passed when we discovered one of the horns was broken at the bottom of the curl.

We were driving to another waterhole late that afternoon when Dries spotted several bulls in the distance. One was outstanding, horns stretching well beyond his ears. This time there was no question. Rifles were loaded and we moved to cut them off. It took most of an hour to get in front of the bulls. As we did, the big one appeared from cover, broadside, much closer than we expected.

Dries whispered something to Ross and the double thundered. The bull stumbled, swapped ends and disappeared. We waited five minutes and then a couple more for good measure, listening for the death bellow. It never came, so we edged forward to pick up the track, our heads on swivels.

Ross' bull had fallen on the other side of a little knob, and we walked right up on him. He lurched to his feet, but Ross was ready. He hit him with a solid and immediately followed with another, and the bull collapsed without taking another step.

Ross' bull was virtually a twin to mine; well over 48 inches wide, the seventh largest ever taken in Namibia. Long had I dreamed of hunting Cape buffalo, but never did I even dare to dream this big.

# THE WITCH DOCTOR

*For ten long nights they'd waited patiently, not daring to move, enduring the cold and close encounters with elephants and other marauders. Now, with his safari coming to a close, would he finally get his chance . . . or would the huge leopard once again work his black magic?*

*By Dr. William M. Flock*

here is a saying in Africa that you hunt an elephant with your legs, a buffalo with your guts, a lion with your heart and a leopard with your brain. Kevin Robertson, in his book, *The Perfect Shot*, describes leopard hunting as a game of chess in which the hunter and his PH match wits and wills with an extremely competent adversary.

The object is to get this shy and secretive animal to do something predictable – namely, come to your bait and present you with a reasonable shot. Therein lies my problem: on my two previous leopard hunts, my team was unable to outwit this cunning beast. However, when my wife Sue negotiated this safari with Huntley Ferreira, managing director of Huntley Ferreira Safaris, I felt confident I would take a leopard. Part of the negotiations was that I could not come home until I got my leopard. Huntley accepted the challenge and said he could make it happen on a 14-day hunt in his Botswana concession.

Huntley had employed, as our team leader, Botswana PH Colin Kirkham, a specialist in leopard hunts. The third member of our team was Jerry, our tracker, skinner and, most importantly, resident expert on

189

animal behavior in the Tuli block. From the first morning, it was evident that Colin and Huntley were clearly challenged by these cats and worked with an intensity I had not seen in many professional hunters.

Since the leopard is nocturnal, our hunt was centered around the blind where we had to create and maintain an environment that would not be detected by the cat's excellent night vision, his keen sense of smell or his hearing. The rules in the blind were very strict: no talking, no moving, no loud chewing, in short – no activity!

My rifle would be pointed at the bait, and I would set back from the opening until Huntley firmly grasped my shoulder, signaling me to move into position and shoot. Every hunt has obstacles that challenge the hunter. On this hunt it was to remain motionless for hours in the cold desert night, while remaining able and ready to make that once-in-a-lifetime shot.

As for our bodily functions, I was allowed to use a bottle. The first night I had a standard plastic bottle that proved difficult to say the least. The remaining nights I carried an adequate supply of wide-mouth bottles.

Ideally, a series of nighttime hunts should begin with the full moon, which provides sufficient shooting light from dusk till dawn. This was certainly true for my hunt. The bright full moon came up as the sun set, but with each passing day it rose later and later, and I would experience the total blackness of an African night. It's a darkness buffered by millions of stars no longer visible in our light-contaminated Northern skies.

Sitting in a blind motionless for long hours and staying awake was difficult. Since this was my hunt, I did not rely on my professional hunters to stay awake, even though I knew they would. As has been described by other leopard hunters, "it was like sitting in a dark closet," yet the rustling noises and strange cries outside the blind provided a new dimension to "closet sitting."

Was that noise a mamba looking for warmth? Or was it a leopard? Or hyenas? In the morning Colin would say, "Did you hear that hyena just outside the blind?" The most disturbing occurrence was to doze off and then in the absolute darkness not being able to tell if my eyes were open or closed.

To make sure we could always see the bait, a light was rigged in the tree and connected to a rheostat so the beam's intensity could be slowly increased without alarming the leopard. At the same time, I would illuminate the crosshairs of my Burris scope. I experienced this exciting action many times, only to be disappointed by one of the numerous critters that prowled the night.

On those long, cold nights I sat in a plastic chair dressed in my lightweight safari clothing, but wishing I'd brought my cold-weather gear. After the first night we added several heavy woolen blankets, which helped stave off the cold.

My rifle was positioned so it protruded slightly from the blind. This was both good and bad. The good was being able to lean forward and quickly settle into my gun. The bad was the rifle further restricted my ability to move. I found some relief after placing a large rock in front of my chair from which I could raise or lower my legs.

L eopards lead solitary lives and try to avoid conflict with other cats. When a tom enters an overlapping territory of another male or when he approaches the bait, he often issues a low growl. I'd heard this raspy, saw-cut-like growl many times as the cats came to our baits. I don't know what effect it had on nearby leopards, but it made my hair stand on end.

A mature tom patrols a territory of about 25 square miles, returning to his starting point every six to eight days unless he finds a female who happens to be in the mood for love. Mature females can breed up to three times a year. Colin estimated that eight to ten females called our hunting block home and that the territories of three or four mature toms overlapped the area. Males live 14 to 16 years. Both of the cats we were targeting were mature and extremely wary.

The territories of the two toms overlapped at our first creek bait. One came from the east and the other from the west. To my surprise, Jerry said they often fed on the bait the same nights. The last time they ate was six days before my hunt began. Jerry expected them back about three days into my hunt. On prior safaris, I'd spent more than half of my time waiting for the first cat to come to bait. This hunt was already building with excitement and anticipation.

After the cat that I called Tom East had outwitted us for the second time, Jerry started calling him The Witch Doctor. In his 20-plus years on the Tuli block, Jerry had come to know these secretive cats – their habits and where most of them denned. He'd occasionally seen a few of these nocturnal killers in the daylight.

The Witch Doctor, Jerry said, lived on a high rock ridge five kilometers to the east. Jerry and the other PHs had hunted the big tom a number of times. Colin and Huntley described him as "a no-neck rugby player" when they first saw him three years ago.

# AFRICA

On that hunt, Huntley and his elderly client were checking baits when they saw a huge leopard. Huntley quickly said, "Use my shoulder as a rest and shoot." As Huntley watched the end of the barrel, it slowly rotated in a small circle, then a larger and larger circle, then suddenly went up and backwards. His hunter had suffered a heart attack. Now Huntley was back to challenge The Witch Doctor one more time.

June 1st was the start of my 14-day hunt. The brisk, cold wind reminded me that it was the beginning of winter here in Botswana. We were checking baits hung prior to my arrival and found fresh tracks, but no hits. I shot an impala to freshen one of the baits and we retired for the morning.

Our daily routine was coffee and toast at 6 a.m., then into the safari truck by 6:30 for the very cold ride to the baits. We would check them, add fresh meat if necessary, then develop a plan for the night's vigil. We'd return for lunch between 11:30 and noon, then head back out by 1:30 to scout or build new blinds. On nights when we sat over a bait, we'd eat at 4 p.m. and arrive in the blind about an hour later.

Over the course of my hunt I shot five impalas, the leopard's meal of choice in this area. Stalking and shooting these wary antelope was a nice bonus. Going into the final days of my safari, I'd taken nine shots and had seven kills, but the most important shot of my life was yet to come.

On day two the first creekbed bait had been hit. We checked the others, and I shot a porcupine en route plus an impala to refresh the north bait.

We were in the blind at 5 p.m. and two hours later I encountered my first honey badger. This tough wolverine-like animal harassed us the entire hunt, coming to our baits night after night. Huntley didn't believe the leopard would come after the badgers were on the bait, so we left the blind at 8:00.

The next morning we found tracks of a very large leopard. The Witch Doctor was back, just as Jerry had predicted, eight days after his last visit.

The next evening the moon was full and rose at dusk, providing us with constant shooting light. At 1 a.m. Huntley whispered that a leopard was hanging on the back side of the impala but told me not to shoot because it was too small. Intently I studied the bait through my scope but only a long tail was visible.

An hour later Huntley suddenly squeezed my shoulder. I could feel his excitement as I shifted into the scope, knowing that a good leopard had appeared. I studied the bait and strained harder and harder to locate the cat. My field of view covered the bait and the surrounding tree limbs. But Huntley was looking at the base of the tree where a huge "no-neck cat" was looking wishfully up at a free meal. Apparently, the tom was too old to climb.

Meanwhile, I never moved from the scope, believing the leopard was somewhere in the tree. After what seemed forever, a very disappointed Huntley said, "He's gone. Why didn't you shoot . . . he was a monster."

"I couldn't see him! Where was he?"

"Under the tree sitting broadside," said my frustrated PH.

I had not heard Huntley whisper, "He's on the ground."

Was this confusion or just bad luck? Or was The Witch Doctor working his magic?

Saturday evening we returned to the blind, hoping The Witch Doctor would return. Leopards came from all directions. I could hear their growls, some very close to the blind. I was pumped with adrenaline, certain that at any moment a big leopard would be on the bait. The wind continued to swirl and the night became quite cold. All told, four leopards – three young toms or females as well as a small male – had come to the bait that evening.

Sunday and Monday were uneventful, but Tuesday morning, as we approached the middle creek bait, we saw that the impala was gone. A leopard had chewed through the impala's neck and dragged it off. The drag-marks were so fresh that ants that had been plowed over were still wiggling.

Colin whispered, "Get ready to shoot; he's just ahead of us." We tracked the leopard across a dry mopane flat, down and across a dry streambed. As we entered the bush on the other side we could smell the bait. We expected to see the leopard at any second, but he had abandoned his free meal without even a growl.

That afternoon we wired the bait to a tree, built a blind and returned by 5 p.m. Hours later, in the extreme darkness, a leopard growled from just behind us. The wind was swirling but we hoped for the best. At 7:30 we heard the dry mopane leaves rustle as the predator moved slowly toward the bait. In the tense moments that followed I got the shakes so badly I had to put the rifle down. With great effort I stopped shaking and continued to listen as more leaves were slowly turned over. At last we heard the bait being pulled and chewed. Was this finally my leopard?

Huntley squeezed my shoulder, the signal to illuminate the scope's crosshairs and get ready to shoot. As the light slowly increased I saw the critter that had driven me to the shakes standing over the bait looking directly at us. It was a very large, very ugly, bush pig. So much for the leopard! We left the blind realizing we had been busted again by the swirling wind.

On day five we checked our first creek bait – no action. Neither The Witch Doctor nor the Big Tom from the West had returned. At the second site we hung fresh meat and built a new blind. We returned to the blind around 5 that night. In the inky darkness a deep, raspy growl erupted behind our blind. The leopard had returned, winded us, growled and continued growling as he moved away. We were busted again by the swirling wind.

While walking back to the truck we discovered a fresh drag across the road. The next morning Colin followed the drag to a young impala carcass. We were excited about this gift from the leopard and built a blind to wait for his return. That night the wind swirled constantly, ending all hopes for an encounter.

The pace of the hunt suddenly quickened on the ninth morning. At the first creek bait we had tracks from the large Tom of the West who had not returned to this portion of his territory for eight days Like the Witch Doctor had done the Friday before, he'd studied the bait from below and had not attempted to climb up the tree. Colin and Huntley decided that a vertical branch on the tree prohibited the big cats from getting to the bait and that a new site and fresh bait were needed. The trophy warthog I'd shot the day before would be perfect. We placed it where the cat could easily take it from the ground and constructed a new blind, our fifth.

We entered the new blind at 4:30. The moon had been rising later and later each night, and so the first four hours of our vigil were in complete darkness. To monitor any activity around the bait, Colin had hung a motion sensor. The slightest movement would trigger a red light on our remote. In the cold dark night, it was a wonderful, warm feeling to see that red light suddenly glowing and know something was out there! Colin would turn up the rheostat and I'd illuminate my crosshairs, holding my breath as the light slowly intensified.

That night the light flickered many times and each time I was filled with anticipation and excitement. But time after time the warm glow of the sensor light revealed honey badgers, sometimes as many as four at a time. When the badgers weren't around, the night air was so still you could almost feel the quietness sitting on your shoulders.

Finally, at 3 a.m., on what had become a very cold winter night, we stumbled away from the blind on stiff legs that had not moved more than six inches in the last ten hours. We decided we would sleep four hours and return that morning to check the bait and our other hot bait about five kilometers to the north.

Saturday morning, the tenth day of my hunt, we checked our bait and found that a tom had followed one of our stomach drags to the warthog. Apparently, he'd arrived a few hours after we had left the blind, rested under the bait while swishing his tail (sand marks), and enjoyed an early morning breakfast of fresh warthog. This was not the western tom whose tracks had caused us to set up this new bait. It was The Witch Doctor who was back after a seven-day hiatus!

Despite missing him by an hour, Colin and I were in good spirits and extremely optimistic. Since the cat had eaten very little and appeared to be comfortable with the bait site, Colin believed he would return that night. I was now counting the hours till I met the Witch Doctor for the fourth time.

However, before our next meeting we had a few improvements to make. First, adjust the motion sensor. Slipping across the soft sand and with no tree to climb, the old boy would come in very stealthily. Second, our rheostat-controlled light was not bright enough and would force us to use the spotlight for the final shot. We had a very long cable that had to be causing resistance, so we shortened it. Sure enough, the light intensity doubled, making the need for the spotlight and a quick shot unnecessary. One more strike against The Witch Doctor.

At 2 a.m. on Sunday morning, we'd been in the blind ten and one-half hours and the cold winter air had settled over us, chilling me to the bone. During the previous eight nights, the wind had constantly swirled, alerting any approaching leopard. But tonight it was constant, blowing gently from the bait to our blind. The waning moon was directly overhead, finally breaking the absolute blackness that had covered us for five hours. Stiff and tired, I was wondering if I could make the remaining four hours to daylight, but I knew I must. My hopes of meeting The Witch Doctor were waning just like the moon as I had only two more nights to hunt.

Earlier, around ten, it appeared that The Witch Doctor was working his magic again. Not fifty yards from the blind, the pitch-black night was pierced by a hair-raising scream. I could feel Colin quickly move out of the blind only to return moments later and say, "Get ready to move. If

# AFRICA

I say 'go', leave your rifle and run." Only once before during a hunt had my PH given me such an ominous warning.

Colin left the blind again, this time with a light. After some time he returned without a word.

The next morning he explained that the piercing scream was an elephant hitting the high-voltage fence placed there to keep them out of the Tuli block. He had been worried that the huge animal might break through the fence, for on the other side a line of 40 elephants was slowly moving our way and would soon wind us. Since our blind was only a few yards off the fence, if the lone elephant moved to our side, he might run right through our blind when the herd spooked. Fortunately, it never happened.

At times the African nights are surprisingly quiet – so quiet that all you hear is a slight ringing in your ears. However, in this extreme quiet, the deadly game of life and death is continually being carried out. The night-stalkers – lions, leopards, hyenas and jackals – silently search out their next meal while their prey – impalas, kudus, wildebeests and other grazers – stand close to each other for warmth and safety. Each night the silent game of life and death is replayed over and over again.

Nature, however, handicaps the predators by employing many eyes and ears to warn of their approach. Monkeys and baboons go crazy when they see the predators, as do the francolin and Go-Away birds. Other prey animals, such as the kudu and impala, protect themselves by loud barks.

At 2 a.m. on our tenth night of hunting, Colin heard some monkeys cry out as The Witch Doctor started his nightly quest for food. A short time later we heard several kudu cows bark an excited warning as the leopard approached their waterhole. The Witch Doctor was on the move.

Thirty minutes later Colin squeezed my arm hard and I saw the warm glow of the motion sensor light click on and off. I moved into the scope as I had done numerous times before, illuminated the crosshairs and thought, Could this be the leopard? Could it be? Could it be?

As the light slowly intensified, I focused on the large warthog carcass. It was gone! I was confused for in its place was a creamy-tan spotted blanket. It was the leopard! His huge body was covering the entire warthog!

The big cat was stretched upward across the carcass with his back to me, and with his front legs, neck and head fully extended. As Colin had said when he saw him under the bait ten days before, he "looked like a rugby player with no neck."

I was surprisingly calm as I moved my crosshairs two-thirds of the way up his backbone, squeezed the trigger, saw the creamy blanket fall from my scope and remain motionless beneath the bait. All this in less than 30 seconds.

Colin said, "Reload," but I already had. For the next five minutes we intently watched the motionless form. Colin called Jerry to bring the truck and then proceeded to carry out the rest of his proven leopard drill. I got into the cab and he climbed into the back with a flashlight taped to the barrel of his 12-gauge shotgun. As the truck drew closer, Jerry announced "The leopard's dead!"

Later Jerry confirmed that it was indeed The Witch Doctor. The big leopard weighed 200 pounds and was 8½ feet long, with a 40-inch "bubba" size belly and a 22½-inch neck. His skull measurement would earn him the number 29 spot in SCI's record book. Though fat, the leopard was in the last quarter of his life, somewhere between 12 and 15 years old. His teeth were badly worn and his left incisor was broken. Colin had observed earlier that the leopard seemed to pull at the meat rather than chew, and that because of his worn teeth he was probably taking kills from the numerous females that lived in his territory. No wonder he wouldn't climb the bait tree.

My 270-grain Remington soft point had hit the spine just below the front shoulders, traveled along the backbone for at least a foot, then lodged in the middle of his throat just under the skin. I had expected a large exit wound because the soft points had opened up quickly on the impalas. In choosing this bullet, I'd taken Kevin Robertson's advice in *The Perfect Shot*: "It's better to have a hole in the leopard hide than a hole in yours."

At last, my boyhood dream had been fulfilled, thanks to the undying support of my wife Sue and my expert leopard team.

# BLAME IT ON RUARK

*"You kill an elephant with your legs;
you only execute him with the rifle."– Tony Sanchez Arino*

By Patrick Meitin

I t starts badly. No, that's not exactly right. It starts with celebration, hope. It starts just after my friend, Alfredo Julian, sends a 1,100-grain arrow into the elephant's armpit from his 93-pound bow. It appears to have worked. We're congratulating each other, that jolly backslapping and handshaking following triumph. The black trackers, Max and Patrick, show sugar-cube teeth, adding to the quiet festivities. Everyone believes we've pulled it off. We're all in agreement in that regard. Outwardly the arrow was placed perfectly, penetration seemingly ample.

All believe Alfredo has killed the great jumbo with his bow.

Two hours later we know it has only been an illusion. The arrow has centered a two-by-four rib. The required penetration had not materialized.

The bull is only wounded.

Alfredo's disappointment is palpable. Still, I can only guess what he's thinking, feeling. After several hours of tracking, it becomes apparent the PHs are no longer working in Alfredo's best interests. Alfredo stays with our group for ten miles, but the despair of an unlucky hit, disgust that the PHs seem more interested in killing the jumbo themselves than earning him another shot, make it easy to think about dropping out, especially when the numbing fatigue we all feel takes hold.

The jumbo has to be finished. He could very well savage the next native he encounters. There are obvious ethical issues. And there's the money. When hunting in Africa, if you draw blood, you pay, even if the animal will survive. That's fully understood.

These are details you ruminate fully only after the fact. At that moment my feelings are ambiguous, yet ultimately clear. Only because of Alfredo's extreme generosity do I share his experience, but then, I have a rifle in hand and I am hunting elephant. That's what really matters at that very moment. I can't help it, but like the PHs I would like to be in on the finish. My feelings are quite clear in that respect.

We'll track Alfredo's wounded bull two days, dog his telltale spoor through 37 miles of clutching thorn and bush. We'll follow the palm-sized delta imprint created by his right-rear pad, as clear as an endorsement on a signed bank draft. We'll push the twisting trail across red, boot-sucking sand, through oppressive midday heat following an ear-biting morning chill. I'll feel the burn of sweat in my eyes and scabbed tick bites, taste the salt on my chapped lips. All of this lies before us. It's our obligation to the jumbo; but we also do it for ourselves.

That first day we drain every water bottle by noon after seven nonstop hours of tracking. We've invested 17 miles of trailing by the time we come to the road. Gary, the towering and powerful PH, a white Zimbabwean with yellow lion's eyes, offers an out, hoping to unburden himself of excess baggage.

"We'll likely not see water in five or six hours' time," he says in UK-English. "There's no roads where these blokes are headed, and no turning back."

He's the local muscle, very much in charge. There's also the South African, Abrie, the booking agent for this safari, another powerful man. Already it's obvious the Zimbabwean loaths him for reasons other than inexperience.

Everyone is thirsty, fatigued, but Alfredo works under the added burden of hopelessness and disgust. Abrie, who is obviously suffering, considers dropping out, but his ego will not allow it. He must continue.

The two trackers have no choice in the matter.

Gary eyes me. "I'm good," I say. I'll only drop out at gun-point.

In *Horn of the Hunter*, Robert Ruark shouted, "God damn Ernest Hemingway!"while vaulting to his feet to charge into a milling herd of cape buffalo with PH Harry Selby. It was through Hemingway that Ruark conceived of hunting Africa, and buffalo, even while brusquely admitting they frightened him witless. It was through Ruark's work, then – Papa's as well – that I ached to hunt Africa in general, elephant more pointedly. It remained a dream well out of reach, a dream as unlikely as a winning lottery ticket.

Still, Africa haunts me. It has nearly claimed me on several occasions. It has provided my most poignant memories. Africa runs in my blood. I will return the moment finances permit, assuring a continued deficit of retirement funds.

God damn Robert Ruark.

In Zimbabwe, President Mugabe has single-handedly scuttled the nation's economy. There's no fuel to pump water in the forest concession we hunt. Gary's forced to trek to Botswana to secure what's needed, returning with armed guards to deter high-jacking.

Five miles into the first day's trailing, the wounded bull and his *askari* burst from thick brush, towering suddenly at 20 meters. The trackers, others in the procession, scurry in retreat. I clamber recklessly forward, not wanting to miss any part of it. Shots are fired into swallowing bush. There's much cussing, PHs sprinting through ripping thorn, seeking another opportunity.

Stopping short, Gary heeds us to cover our ears, spitting acrid curses, hip-shooting his .416 Rigby into the ground. This only adds to my confusion. Only much later do I learn his rifle had failed to fire when the elephant turned toward us. Abrie had fired two hasty shots, hitting nothing. Gary is looking him over closely. Harsh words are exchanged, accusations hurled between them, the tension thick and tangible.

We travel fast, pushing through mopane and thorn at a ground-gobbling pace. We've covered 17 GPS miles since morning. The heat is intense and in time the others bow out. Gary commandeers the assistant's glossy rifle. I'm handed the battered and questionable Rigby. I'm shocked that I'm not simply ordered to join the others.

The water's gone. It's just past noon.

# AFRICA

The pace is brisk, moving out onto mopane flats bisected by thick thornbelts. Tongue clucks or finger snaps bring the procession to abrupt halts. The one who's spotted a suspicious shadow or tree trunk points. Everyone probes with binoculars. Often it's the binocular-less trackers pointing; more often the South African. He's too much on edge, yet every false start must be taken seriously. A charge is believed imminent.

Gary gestures abruptly and through glass I see something, which resolves into a swinging elephant trunk, the whole of him suddenly plain. His sheer dimensions make it unfathomable that he can be so close yet so invisible. There's much maneuvering to inspect ivory and make sure he's the correct jumbo of the pair. But there's too much deliberation. Gary nods affirmative just as the bull vanishes into the thorn, like smoke before wind and just as silently. Those carrying rifles shimmy forward in crouching gestures, but the bull no longer exists. There's only the tracks that once again must be followed.

The *askari* tows the wounded bull across the loose, red sand through the day. The sun smites hammer-like, our concentration forced and heavy. The trackers are tired, losing the track intermittently, ranging. The trail crosses and is crossed by elephants of all dimensions along the way, which makes tracking all the more difficult. Ultimately, we relocate the bull's trail, his distinctive rear pad condemning him.

At sunset we enter an old burn, only game trails allowing painless passage. The trackers squat suddenly, hearing something. Gary drops to his knees, then his belly, peering through glass, looking for elephant hide.

I find a piece of the bull through binoculars, using a different gap than Gary is privy to. I stare at length before most of the jumbo materializes; again that dumbfounding and inconceivable juxtaposition of bulk and camouflage. He's only 15 meters away. I watch his head as I inch ahead on elbows and toes, the heavy rifle in my crooked arms. I find tusks and know he's the one. I'm as certain about this as I've ever been about anything. The bull releases a barrage of thumping dung and I cluck for Gary's attention. I nod emphatically.

He mouths silently, "It is him?" I bob my head briskly.

"You are quite sure?" he asks, breathed only. I nod more enthusiastically. He does nothing. Shooting the wrong jumbo would pose a ticklish situation.

"I can kill him," I whisper.

"You are not to shoot!" Gary hisses, worry written plainly in his lion's eyes. Who am I but a client? I take a deep breath. The bull vanishes.

202

The tracks tell the tale. It was him, alright.

The sun descends and it turns suddenly cold. It comes to me abruptly that we've described a tremendous circle, are nearing the day's beginning point, and water. I've been completely turned around for quite some time. It makes perfect sense the bulls would gravitate to this place in this drought.

The first stars show as we reach the small waterhole, where Abrie and the trackers slump to the ground in exhaustion. With black night the bulls come. Gary and I slip within 30 meters, shining my diminutive AA flashlight into their faces from across the pond. This induces much ear-flapping, grumbling. The light delivers no details. We cannot be sure which of the bulls is the one wounded. Gary orders a retreat.

We start a fire as other elephants crowd the nearby water. The Cruiser arrives two hours later.

As convoluted as the trail proved on the previous day, it's laser-straight this morning, approaching the sanctuary of a national park the elephants presumably know nothing of. We're a long procession again – two trackers, Gary, Abrie, the assistant Bootie, Alfredo and myself – crossing a flat valley, climbing higher hillocks, entering more jungly burns. From rises we spot distant, grotesque, high-voltage lines marking the park boundary, startlingly out of place in this seeming wilderness.

The jumbos' trail begins to weave, turning away from the park abruptly, but still uncomfortably close to a boundary that will end it outright. The sun has begun to carry perceivable weight, but the trail has not warmed. All anticipate the worst, legs joint-sore and muscle-achy from yesterday's march of 20-some GPS miles, the additional ten we've invested today.

Mopane bees, fly-like and unstinging, find us. They create a tremendous distraction, exploring ears and noses, droning, erasing any audible edge. I remember when we approached three bulls several days before, their tusks ultimately deemed unworthy, and how the bees arrived and quickly became more unbearable the closer we moved to the musky jumbos. Today this doesn't seem to correlate.

It's just after noon when the bulls appear unexpectedly, 80 meters distant, unaware. They're under a single acacia, standing head to rump in stingy shade, tails twitching, huge ears fanning, heads hung in sleep. A momentary vantage reveals them, but the bush closes as we advance.

# AFRICA

The trackers spoor while we hold rifles across our chests. The bees are intense. The battered Rigby slips in my sweaty hands.

Now within 50 meters there's the matter of determining the correct gentleman. We edge closer, in single steps. Soon I see the distinctive chip missing from the closer bull's right ivory. Gary recognizes a pattern in the bull's corrugated hide. After much discussion Gary has agreed to take Alfredo in for another bow-shot.

While they angle in to address the wind, Abrie and I move to another flank, hoping to cut off an escape. We can see Gary and Alfredo clearly, moving in two- and three-meter snatches, watching, stepping around grass, leaves. They're alarmingly close. All of us want badly to settle the matter quickly. Gary leads, Max beside him tipping ash from a plastic soft drink bottle. I see Max tip more ash. He knows before any of us.

The sleeping bull's head lifts abruptly, snaking trunk reaching, ears pinned. There's a piercing squeal and he charges. I see Gary shoulder the .458 Lott, hear the shattering explosion. The jumbo spins, barreling right to left. I run forward, bringing the massive rifle to shoulder as he crashes side-on. I'm tightening the trigger when Abrie's head suddenly appears before my muzzle. I let off the trigger a moment before it certainly would have gone off.

Abrie's rifle belches but the bull continues, crashing out of sight, making good time. I move left in a hundred-meter sprint, losing track of the others, of the second bull. The wounded bull clears brush, a tank on legs, turning slightly as the Rigby's express sights swing with his ear. The .416 rocks me. I grab for the bolt as the mighty bull crumples, dropping from sight.

We converge on the pole-axed bull, shouting nonsensical curses to dissuade the *askari* who seems inclined to stay. He faces us and rocks side to side while flapping tent-like ears. Gary fires into the sand beside him to dissuade any heroic notions. He retreats and is abruptly swallowed by impenetrable brush. We all rush the fallen bull, Gary yelling "Clear!" and shooting him between the shoulder blades. We wait a few seconds, then Gary stalks forward to poke the haunting eye. There's a sudden release of tension.

I've been close to wild elephants on several safaris, but admit having never noticed much in the way of detail; the wire hair, the weed-trimmer tail-strands, the horny feet. I walk around him like a used car, inspecting every part of him. It's a major exploration. I climb on him like a mound of fill dirt.

My desire to shoot an elephant is old enough that its beginnings remain fuzzy. I understood from its conception that doing so would likely illicit tears, even sobbing. Oddly, I feel no such inclination today, only relief to end two long days of suffering by all involved. I'm awed by his supernatural tenacity, the sheer size of him, by a continent and countryside vast and wild enough to support him, but his death fails to sadden me.

Back in camp, heaping loads of elephant meat arrive aboard a flatbed trailer hauled by a throbbing, dilapidated tractor. I've a cold Zambezi beer in hand, a stiff, new elephant-hair bangle on my wrist that Patrick had quickly crafted me. I'm puffing a good Cuban cigar. Gary stirs across the licking thorn-wood fire, the Southern Cross swinging high, jackals screaming, hyenas giggling, rutting impalas roaring lion-like.

"Some of that meat'll arrive as biltong two-hundred kilometers from here," he says, his eyes shinning in the flickering flame. "Every scrap'll be consumed."

In its most basic terms, then, the death of an elephant represents perhaps two tons of meat to feed a hungry nation coming apart at the seams, being slowly nibbled away by ax and snare. But it also represents hard currency to keep water pumps thumping, poacher patrols employed. I find myself praying, as I did only the year before bowhunting cape buffalo 50 miles from here, that Zimbabwe can hang on, can be saved from itself, that the game which makes it such a paradise will continue to be protected.

I ponder these thoughts during a long minute of silence, suddenly understanding my earlier feelings, my feelings following the death of a single elephant.

# THE ROAD TO KAMANJAB

*The boy is 12 and coming-of-age, not quite man,
not quite child. We celebrate his first steps on the road
to manhood with a hunting adventure in Africa.*

By G. Duncan Grant

Trekking for miles over a dry, gently rolling landscape, the road to Kamanjab flows past sprawling cattle ranches, tiny villages, shanty towns and the graveyards of pioneers who began settling this land in the 1600s. Under a cloudless sky it bridges the banks of rock-strewn riverbeds where water courses only a few times each year. The road curves gently between towering, rust-colored mountains that puncture the sage-green, semi-desert floor, then rise thousands of feet and cast miles-long shadows in these months of winter.

The road is in surprisingly great shape – wide, relatively smooth, well-maintained and in places spear-straight. Modern automobiles speed along its length, leaving fat tire tracks in its sandy surface and a fine coat of dust on the fences and brush. Squinting from air-conditioned, leather-upholstered compartments, passengers might wonder how the first settlers survived even one summer in a land so harsh. But riders in the slower, donkey-powered carts already know. At their peaceful pace they can see in the road the countless prints of wild animals: kudu, gemsbok, springbok, duiker, elephant, impala, zebra and hundreds more. Wildlife

# AFRICA

is everywhere. Open your eyes a little wider and you begin to see it too. A hundred yards or so back from the bordering cattle fences, cleverly camouflaged bodies browse the bush with wary eyes. Here one, there two, over there, twenty-something. This is the road to Kamanjab. This is Namibia.

For me, the road to Africa began a long time ago. Maybe it was in a dream 40-something years back when, after a day of quail hunting with my dad and while under the spell of Ruark or Roosevelt or Courtenay Selous, I fell asleep by counting kudu. Perhaps it was 24 years ago when we first imagined, then launched *Sporting Classics* magazine, that Africa became an honest-to-God attainable destination rather than just the textbook starting point of our evolutionary beginnings, and my own hunting fantasies. Certainly, the road began 12 years ago when my son, George, was born. I knew I wanted him to understand that hunting is much more than just a sport. What better place to teach him than Africa?

Many American kids (many adults too) have no idea that they live on a golf course, an environment just as plastic as Disney World or Hollywood. Ask most children where their meat comes from and they'll tell you the name of a grocery store. Soft isn't the word for them. They can play ultra-complex video games, but "survival of the fittest" is a term they don't really comprehend. Most have no concept of what a real bullet can do. In their video game world, you can always add a few more lives. I wanted something more for my son.

I wanted George to understand why I think hunting is important, why I'm mystified by it, fascinated by it. Hunting may have contributed to our learning to stand upright. Some scientists believe eating animal protein gave us the luxury of more time to develop other skills, thereby increasing the size of our brains. It is certain that for much of our existence we have used what we learned from hunting to feed, clothe, protect ourselves and defend our families. We chose leaders based on their hunting skills. Made better weapons and tools. Created wealth. Hunting is a lot more important than the size of a trophy, and it deserves more respect than it's given by today's anti-hunting crowd. I believe it is ingrained in our DNA. You are either predator or prey.

So George and I have put ourselves on the road to Kamanjab, seeking to experience the same closeness our ancestors must have felt, and used to conquer the millennia. Like them, we want to follow the tracks.

Watch the animals and learn from them. Take the lives of just a few of the plentiful ones. Taste the meat. And bring home samples of skin, horn and bone to remember it all by – our version of the Lascaux cave paintings. There are risks: While Namibia is one of Africa's most stable, safe, friendly and democratic countries, there are animals out here that will eat you, namely lions, leopards and hyenas. But there are other rewards as well: In some places there's not a golf course for 500 miles.

Outfitter Jim McCarthy has booked us with Trophy Trackings Hunting Safari, owned by Danie (pronounced Donny) Jansen van Vuuren and his wife, Carina, two of the finest people you are ever likely to meet. Our plane lands first in Johannesburg, then on to Windhoek, Namibia's capital. Danie is waiting. He is young, 25. Don't let that fool you. His great-great-grandfathers are buried here. He knows exactly what he is doing.

Danie takes us four hours north on excellent paved roads to the tiny hamlet of Outjo. Another hour on a gravel road and it is pitch-dark when we reach his 12,000-acre ranch. It lies near his father's. Both are tucked back off the main road between Kamanjab and Fransfontein. We are jackal-tired from the long flights and the drive. So the guest rooms in his ranch home are inviting – very nice – comfortable beds, tiled floors and your own private bath with walk-in shower. No tents this trip.

The first morning is beautiful, cool with a slight breeze. We sight in our rifles, then hunt Texas-style, spotting animals from a bed-mounted seat atop a seemingly indestructible Toyota pickup. Our driver is Tegone Kampala, and he can spot animals like a hawk. Danie's' exceptional abilities are evident from the start. He sees a tiny speck at 800 yards, right through the mopane and acacia, and determines if it's a male, the size of its horns. Then, he raises his binoculars to see what else might be hiding near it.

Within an hour Danie spots a very nice 14-inch springbok. *Time for the first test*, my thought comes fast.

I turn to George and whisper, "Son, would you like to kill a springbok?"

His eyes and face are suddenly filled with hesitation. Then I remember: Back at the ranch, just hours before, using big soda bottles, he'd helped Carina feed milk to an orphaned pair. And the biggest thing he's killed so far is a dove. Don't want to hurry this, I'm thinking. It has to be his choice.

Reading his face, I confirm my suspicion, "You sure?"

He nods. So I kill it with a head-on shot that is a bit too high.

"Dad, you got him! Congratulations!" He is as happy as I am. I'm relieved. Maybe he was just reluctant to shoot first. We all shake hands and pose for photographs before loading the springbok on the truck.

We return to the house for lunch, then head out to another section of the ranch, passing through a half-dozen cattle gates, following the donkey cart roads. We see hundreds and hundreds of animals, antelope to zebra. As we approach they lunge through or leap over the low fences, bounding away into the bush. In a sandy pan we find the sun-bleached bones of an elephant. George is spellbound by the size of the skull.

It is mid-afternoon and warming. The bakkie engine strains as we climb an impossibly steep hillside. Suddenly Danie taps lightly on the roof, signaling Tegone to stop. He stands and peers intensely at a hill some 300 yards away. Mopane and acacia block my view. I can't see a thing.

"*Tegone, kom terug!* Gemsbok. BIG gemsbok!" Danie whispers, and the Toyota reverses a few feet. He glasses the area then glides quietly over the side of the truck, motioning for me to put a round in the chamber and follow. Tegone kills the engine.

"Wot grains, in de chambear, you got?" Danie's whispered English is blurred by his native Afrikaans.

"One-eightys," I reply softly, wondering why he'd ask.

"Gute," he says, nodding. With that, he and I move out single-file toward the hill.

We stalk 200 yards through thorn-armored bush to the shade of an old acacia. Danie stops and glasses. I do the same. My Leicas bring the magnificent head and top portion of the incredibly beautiful animal into ultra-sharp view. Long spike-like horns sweep up and back, forming a V-shape high above a masked face. The animal's chest is obscured by brush.

Danie quickly sets up the rifle pod. Through the scope I can see only the very top of the shoulder. *Take your time*, I caution myself, trying to calm my heart from the stalk and the excitement.

The gemsbok had been eating grass, but now raises its head and still chewing, eyes us with mistrust. Remembering my first shot was too high, I am lowering the crosshairs when the animal suddenly backs away from the low bush, and luckily for me, into an opening. The crosshairs find the target and I squeeze the trigger.

As we approach Danie cautions, "Day're b'very danecherous, eef vuneded. Ve vait."

But the .30-06 Remington Premier Safari Grade bullet has done its duty and we spend the next half-hour loading the 600-pound gemsbok into the Toyota. After hunting for another hour, we return to the ranch.

Like most boys would be, George is fascinated with the butchering process, quietly studying the men as they cut, slice and pull, noting the smells, examining the organs and intestines with a stick, then watching as they salt the skins.

About dark, while Carina prepares our supper and seasons the meat from my gemsbok, we deliver the remainder to families of various helpers living in the deeper recesses of the ranch. George's job is to hand the heavy packages to children sent out to retrieve them. It is a good trade: They are extremely happy to get the meat. He learns how much of the world lives.

Danie cooks on an outdoor grill that consists of an elevated concrete-and-stone platform with a metal grate. Dry wood is stored in open compartments underneath. The fire is built, then the coals are shoveled as-needed into the cooking section.

We eat at a candle-lit table under the stars. The gemsbok fillets are slightly sweet, with a texture like beef, but very tender. A red wine compliments the steaks. Fried cheese with berry sauce, red cabbage with apples and fried potatoes are followed by a desert of creme caramel.

George eats two plates-full and, still tired from the previous day's flight, asks to be excused. But first he comes over and gives me his traditional good-night hug. I'm wondering how much longer that's going to last, when he says the magic words: "Dad, do you think I could shoot something tomorrow?"

"Sure son," I say teasing, "I'm certain Mister Danie can find something a boy like you would be worthy of . . . maybe a warthog? I can see Danie and Carina smiling from across the table. George, already lost in thoughts of tomorrow, heads off to bed.

After we clear the table, I walk back outside to contemplate our first day of hunting on the Dark Continent. A full moon has risen and is illuminating the nighttime landscape and, strangely, me. I make two of those startling discoveries that occur every so often in one's life: In Africa the moon is not a disk. Rather, it is an eerie, three-dimensional sphere. With no lights and little water vapor to pollute the view, you can plainly see its surface curve. Here, the moon is a real world, distant . . . yet close. It hovers above the mountains like some giant, cratered, off-white ball, casting a cool glow on the wonders of this water-starved land. As I walk back to our room, I now understand why people worshiped it. I can see why it effects the tides. As I crawl beneath thick blankets, a realization sinks in: Only a handful of days in my life will ever match this one. So even before I doze off I am aware: Some of my dreams have already come true.

After a breakfast of juice, cereal, eggs and biltong, sunrise finds us bumping along in the *bakkie*. George is smiling his best green-eyed, freckle-faced smile. A cool breeze flows over us and I'm thinking that it will be hard to beat yesterday. We ride for an hour or so, up rocky hills, down ravines, across large open grasslands and through thickly wooded areas. A black eagle rides the thermals of the warming terrain. To get a better view, but keeping an eye out for leopards, we climb a kopje and spook a troop of nearly 50 baboons that continue to bark at us from half-a-mile away. George soaks it all up. And Danie is steadily heaping lessons on him: animal names and habits, tracks, droppings, gun safety, plants, local customs, the list is endless. Danie is going to make a great father.

On a tarp in a sandy, dry creekbed shaded by huge Anna trees, we eat a lunch of spingbok sandwiches, baked tomatoes and fruit, then take naps. While everyone sleeps I watch three kudu cows and a medium-sized bull cross upwind of us not a hundred yards away. As I doze off, I am thinking about Namibia's incredible quantity and variety of game and wondering why most hunters still venture to East Africa.

Tires spinning, we pull out of the sandy, tree-lined riverine to continue our hunt. Rare black-faced impala, warthogs, steenbok and dik-dik scramble out of our way. A caracal eyes us, then disappears. Two huge secretary birds, looking dinosaur-like, cross behind the Toyota. The sun begins to sink.

Moving higher, we hunt the drier, red-soiled vlakte – the open plains surrounding the kopjes. Sure enough, late that afternoon we disturb the dinner plans of my dream kudu. He high-tails it to our left, putting a looming kopje between us. We climb out of the truck and, nearly running, cover the 200 yards to the huge mound of granite rocks. George follows Danie and I up the treacherous slope. When we reach the top, the bull is still moving to the left. He sees us and turns back to the right and down, his horns a roller coaster ride of looping curves. Danie's excitement is infectious as he assembles the shooting sticks. Carrying rifle and camera bag I am too winded from the climb and when I fire downhill the bullet passes cleanly over the top of him. It's my third big game miss in 44 years of hunting. I watch in slack-jawed disbelief as my magnificent spiral-horned dream bounds over the top of the adjoining hill. Disappointed, I sit down on a desk-sized boulder to catch my breath and contemplate my mistake.

"Dad, you missed!"

I didn't even look up. "Guess, I'm not Annie Oakley, huh?"

While he may not be a math scholar, and has never heard of Annie Oakley, the boy is perceptive and quickly realizes that he has unnecessarily stepped on the old man's already bleeding ego. So he sits down next to me and puts his arm on my shoulder.

"It's okay dad. You'll get the next one."

As the sun sinks beneath the mountains behind us, the hills in front gradually turning to orange, then crimson, then purple, I remind myself of why I am here. Sitting there with my son, on a big rock in Namibia, watching the sandy road to Kamanjab curve away in the distance, I am thankful, despite my miss. Very thankful.

We get up late. Today we drive back south, first to Windhoek for some shopping, then on to Carina's father's ranch an hour or so east of the city. On the way in, much of our trip up had been cloaked in darkness so now we get to see some of the country we missed. George is astonished by the native women carrying gigantic bundles balanced on their heads, something I had seen growing up in the South as a kid. They walk with a slow, assured rhythm that seems to define Africa.

Carina's parent's home is magnificent. Polished granite tile floors and walls. Animal skin rugs. Private rooms and baths. A full-sized swimming pool in the living room. Handsome trophies along one wall. Huge, ornate, hand-carved bar. It also has the standard outdoor grill, but this one is made of granite. The whole outdoor dining area is covered by a beautiful African-style thatched roof with recessed lighting. Guess I'll have to let the boy get dirty camping when we get home.

It is the perfect morning. We are hunting from a classic, zebra-striped, 1949 Land Rover, driven by long-time ranch hand Sampie Hoaseb. Sitting up high on the bed-mounted seat, cold air stinging our faces, we hunker down in our warm coats. George, stuffed with a huge breakfast of eggs, ham and bacon, is comfortably wedged between Danie and me. A smiling Danie slaps the bleary-eyed boy on the knee and blurts loudly, "George! You vready to kill undt impala?"

# AFRICA

Eyes wide with surprise, George answers, "Sure, Mister Danie. Where?" Danie nods in the direction of a grassy meadow a quarter-mile away. "Perhops dere, along doze trees." He says something to Sampie and the Rover turns into the wispy, khaki-colored grass. We've only gone a couple of hundred yards when Sampie cuts the engine. Danie glasses the treeline and motions George and I over the side. We follow, stalking from bush to bush.

Another hundred yards and we can see the herd of impala looking nervous against an acacia green background. As Danie hurriedly sets up the shooting sticks, he whispers, "De beeg won on de lef!"

George struggles to get the big male in his scope, but the rest is a bit too high. The animals grow increasingly agitated as Danie adjusts the sticks. George takes aim just as the herd begins to move. I can hear my own heart pounding. Time slows to a crawl.

Unconsciously, my eyes move from the herd to the muzzle of my son's Model 64 Winchester .30-30, a rifle that seems to have been designed to fit the boy's small frame. I follow the barrel down to the action, where I see his finger gently squeezing the trigger. His right eye is focused intently through the scope, forever connecting him to this animal. My mind somehow erases the sound of the gunshot, but through the tall grass I watch the big male fall.

It was a decent lung shot. We have to track the animal for a half-mile, but even that is part of a lesson I enjoy watching my son learn. Sometimes animals don't die easily. He needs to know that. Down on their knees, Danie and Sampie show George what to look for as they track the dying animal. His young eyes easily spot the blood trail in the tall grass. When we finally find the impala, Danie smears some of its blood on George's forehead and nose. He never flinches. His first step into the real world, I think, then silently I say a little prayer.

Later in the evening, while we dine on his impala, George still wears its blood on his face like a red Boy Scout merit badge. It occurs to me that, come fall and school, he'll probably have the best summer vacation story in his class.

So did I get my kudu? Yes I did, the very next day. No, he won't show up in Namibia's record books like the 72-inch trophy killed in May 2001, or even match the 58-inch animal that I missed. He is a beautiful silver medal kudu, nonetheless, and he will take the prime spot above my fireplace.

But he will never be the most important animal of the trip. That distinction will always go to the impala.

Six months later, as I am finishing this story, Danie and Carina are expecting their own child. The photographs I took on our safari show a much younger looking George. At thirteen, he is changing rapidly and has grown at least four inches. A few more years and he'll be off to college... a few more, with a family of his own. Thinking about the passage of time reminds me of the second of my discoveries: You remember, that night of the full moon . . . at Danie's ranch . . . near the road to Kamanjab:

In Africa, the Milky Way is not a candy bar. Here, you can clearly see our galaxy attaching us to other stars and planets and moons, too numerous to count, too far away to reach, too different to comprehend. The African sky is a place where you can view the universe . . . not to understand it, but to understand your place in it.

# THE GAME OF KINGS

*If you probe the dark thickets and brushy hillsides of
Zululand, you'll eventually encounter the 'great shaggy form'
of a bull nyala. And like legendary hunters and early Zulu
kings, you will come to revere this elusive animal as the most
beautiful of all African antelope.*

*By Ron Spomer*

Life is extraordinary in Africa. On my first trip to the
continent I watched elephants browsing in fields at the
edge of towns and Merc-powered bass boats roaring
down the Zambezi River past natives in dugout canoes.
On my second trip I ate nyala antelope before I even
hunted it.

"Mmmm. The ostrich is good. Very tasty."

"Try this hartebeest. Excellent. Mmm. Excellent."

"Actually I like the nyala best. Yes, that and the kudu. Here comes the
man with the spear. Oh waiter, is that nyala? More of that please. Don?
David? Care for any?"

Our server lowered the tip of a long, willow-leaf-spear – skewered
through the center of a nyala haunch – onto our table, raised a big cutting
knife, and sliced a medium-rare slab of flame-roasted meat deftly onto
my plate. Don Terrell eyed it and said, "Yes, I believe I will have a bit
more of that, too." David Brashear declined, his mouth full of ostrich.

Ah, Africa. Where else can you dine at an all-you-can-eat restaurant
with the *hutzpah* to call itself The Carnivore and to serve a dozen

varieties of wild game roasted over an open-pit fire on Masai spears? And just 40 minutes from the Johannesburg International Airport. From its walkway bridge over a babbling brook to its zebra-hide upholstery. The Carnivore was the perfect introduction to our South African hunting trip. And my trophy nyala was a fitting conclusion.

Don Terrell, who books wingshooting travel adventures on three continents through Wings, Inc. initiated the trip as an experiment in African bird hunting. He, David and I spent a delightful ten days alternately pass-shooting waterfowl, jump-shooting guineas and francolin, and game-viewing in Hluhluwe/Umfolozi wildlife parks, all the while enjoying the bed-and-breakfast hospitality of Professional Hunter Rick Lemmer and his associate Adelle Van Niekerk at Heartease Farm in the shadow of the snow-capped Drakensburg Mountains. Hunting birds and photographing wildlife are two wonderful ways to pass the time while waiting for the chance to hunt African big game. My chance came during our last three days when Don and David flew to Victoria Falls for a scenic tour.

"Bye! Take lots of pictures. Don't drown. See you at the airport." And Rick, Adelle and I were off for the nyala range in northern Zululand.

Not so renowned as the kudu nor so coveted as the sable, the nyala is, nonetheless, one of the most elusive, striking antelope in all of Africa. It was royal game in the days of the great Zulu kings. Confined to a rather limited range in northeastern South Africa, eastern Zimbabwe, Malawi and Mozambique, nyala are lovers of dark thickets, wooded lowlands near water, and brushy slopes interspersed with grassy openings. A bull's spiraling, lyre-shaped horns suggest bushbuck, bongo, sitatunga and kudu. Indeed, it's a cousin to all these *Tragelaphus* genus members – the spiral-horned antelopes.

A slate-gray, mature male nyala falls between the bushbuck and greater kudu in size – about 250 pounds – but where it differs markedly is in its shaggy coat. A ventral fringe of long, charcoal-gray hairs drapes from chin to belly. Up top, a crest of white hairs runs from skull to rump, blending into a bushy black-and-white tail and feathered haunches reminiscent of an English setter's. Nyala bulls flare these hairs during dominance displays to increase their apparent size as much as 40 percent. They're as fooled by cosmetic puffery as humans for, according to researchers who study such things, the biggest *looking* bull always wins. This reduces fighting which, considering their sharp, 24- to 33-inch horns, could be deadly. Why risk it when a bit of ostentatious display settles the argument?

As luck would have it, Rick and I actually witnessed such a display. We were sitting on a steep slope above a highland tributary of the Black Umfolozi River near dusk, glassing adjacent slopes for mountain reedbuck when a nyala bull stepped into a grassy opening below. Judging horn length is difficult from above, but Rick assured me this was a young animal, still showing some of the red coat of adolescence and with horns less than 24 inches long. Nevertheless, it was courting a cow that appeared to be in estrus. She was a fetching little thing about three feet high at the shoulder and a third smaller than the male. Her chestnut hide almost glowed in the sunset light, vertical white stripes melting down her sides like vanilla ice cream down a cone.

We weren't surprised when a bigger bull stepped out of some trees and walked stiff-legged toward the couple. He approached like an arthritic old man with agonizingly slow steps. The smaller bull lowered its head, arched its back and flared it hairs. The big guy turned broadside, matched and then exceeded this display, his long tail arching over his rump and flaring magnificently as he froze in all his splendor. Slowly, ever so slowly the smaller bull deflated and inched away to join two other bulls at the edge of the trees.

There was no way to approach the animals unseen, so we continued watching, eventually spotting another bull and four bright cows slightly above them, a herd of impala silhouetted on a ridge even higher, and a band of six mountain reedbuck on the grassy slope before dusk closed the show.

That we had witnessed so many nyala and such intimate behavior would scarcely have been believed by turn-of-the-century African hunters who found the species exceedingly rare and confined to dense jungle lowlands in Amatongaland – today's Mozambique and extreme northeast Zululand.

Frederick Selous wrote in his 1908 *African Natures Notes and Reminiscences* that the "inyala is perhaps at once the most beautiful and the least known [antelope] to naturalists and sportsmen." Late in his career the great African hunter/naturalist made a special trip from Pretoria to the Maputo River just to secure the species for two museums and his own collection. He complained of having to hunt "bent nearly double" while creeping along hippo tunnels through thick thornbush where he found his quarry exceedingly shy. However, Selous also noted the virtual absence of all other wild game from rhinos to lions, owing to constant persecution by native Amatonga hunters. He credits the nyala's survival to their jungle haunts and secretive habits, brought about, no doubt, by excessive hunting pressure.

In contrast, Rick and I found nyala quite common in the mountains of Hluhluwe/Umfolozi National Park and 60 miles northwest in the Vryheid district where we hunted. At both places we spotted single bulls and small bands of cows and young bulls in grassy meadows and open woods, beside palm-lined rivers, and in thorn-scrub both mornings and evenings. I suspect, like most game when unharrassed, nayla are not so nocturnal nor secretive as generally supposed. *The Safari Companion*, a field guide to African mammals, describes the species as feeding in grassland mornings and evenings, retiring to deep cover during hot, midday hours, resting in light shade in the open on cool winter days, which was how we found them.

There! Nyala bull," Rick said as he simultaneously jerked the hand brake and opened the door of his Land Rover just minutes into our first day's hunt. We were passing through dense brush in late afternoon near the edge of open grassland – just what the book predicted.

I slipped out my door, took the rifle from the rack, and padded quietly into the brush behind Rick. As if hunting whitetails back home, we stepped once, looked twice, trying to glimpse the beast that had melted into cover. I'd seen only his dark side and the base of his horns an instant before he'd turned away.

"How big was he?" I whispered. "Should I shoot if I see him?"

"Yes. No. I mean he's close. Twenty-eight inches I think. But I need a better look at the bugger. Be ready."

Step, look. Step. The air is calm. Quiet. A few birds twitter. The ground is dry, dusty, the vegetation already weary from the start of the annual drought. There are cloven hoof-prints in the dirt, some smaller than a whitetail's, some as large as a big buck's. Duiker and nyala. Then there is the sound of something rushing through the brush: hoof-beats. Rick runs forward. I follow. We break out above a brushy draw and see nothing.

"Ah, he turned up that *donga*. If he'd gone out the far side, we'd have had a good look at him. A good shot." We gaze across a broad, grassy flat far below and spot a cow and two calves.

Ours was a fast start, but not unprecedented. Selous, guided by the son of an Amatonga chief who warned that nyala were "very cunning and difficult to get sight of," came upon a female an hour from the headman's kraal. Selous toppled her with his first shot, then was astonished to see her place taken by the "great black shaggy form" of a bull. Quickly reloading his break-action single shot, he fired and felled the male.

While I couldn't duplicate Selous' feat with nyala, I nearly matched it with mountain reedbuck, nxala to the Zulus. This small cousin of the common reedbuck is adapted to survive on high-fiber, low-protein grass unpalatable to most other species. It ranges discontinuously in mountains above 4,000 feet from South Africa to Ethiopia. One of Rick's Zulu trackers, Hlaba, spotted my buck at dawn within a quarter-mile of where we'd seen the small herd the night before. It was emerging from a brushy *donga* and starting up a dry mountain slope dotted with aloe plants ablaze in red flowers.

Leaving the trackers behind, Rick and I slipped behind screening trees, hurried to the *donga*, belly-crawled out the far side, and relocated the ram walking uphill. Rick got his binocular on him immediately. "He's a good one. Really good. Seven inches or more. Take him."

The ram had stopped and was looking back over its rump when I found it in the scope, which I'd had time to crank up to 8X. Though less than 200 yards away, the 70-pound antelope was a small target, but I was prone with the rifle held reassuringly steady. At the shot the first mountain reedbuck ram I ever saw toppled. Selous didn't have all the luck in Africa.

As is the case on most African hunts, one's principal game isn't one's only game. The diversity of species makes any safari potentially a mixed-bag hunt. On this short adventure we were primed for gray duiker, red duiker, impala and blesbok in addition to nyala. Gray duiker were common. We glassed several of these petite *impunzi*, as Hlaba called them in his native tongue, including two good bucks that looked to go over four inches, but we were unable to clear a shot.

Several herds of impala, called *rooibok* by the Africaaner, offered stalking opportunities. We tried for a long-horned ram on a grassy mountain top where a deeply eroded donga provided good stalking cover. While Rick sat well back behind a bush, occasionally waving his hand to hold the herd ram's attention, I slipped within 150 yards, crawled over the bank and dropped the sentinel with a shot through the chest.

# AFRICA

In addition to nyala, I was quite interested in hunting blesbok, a migratory grazer and great runner closely allied to topis and often compared to North America's pronghorn in choice of habitat, herding and flashing a white rump in alarm. Blesbok once swarmed across southern African by the tens of thousands. Being an open-country beast, it was hunted mercilessly by pioneer ranchers and farmers for meat, hides and as grazing competitors with cattle. Like the American bison, it was rescued from the brink of extinction by ranchers and now thrives in thousands of private herds. As such, hunting conditions are a bit contrived, but stalking the herds and selecting a big male from the bunch at least provides a taste of what must have been.

We found a bunch of 40 roaming a broad, grassy plateau and crawled toward them. Over the grass we could see black horn-tips, then brown heads and white foreheads. But before we could clear the roll of ground for a shot, two-score pairs of horns raised to face us like a phalanx of spears. Then just as quickly the spears turned and we heard the pummeling of hooves. On our second stalk I sat up to clear a shot, but could not identify a good bull before the herd again fled. Blesbok cows wear horns, too, but the bull's are heavier at the base. On our third stalk we got lucky and located a splendid set of heavy horns on the right edge of the troop. Definitely a bull and in the clear. One 180-grain Speer Grand Slam bullet ended his run.

Near the scene of this hunt, Hlaba showed us a large boulder sprouting from the grass like the top of a giant mushroom. The granite surface was marred by numerous deep grooves and an obvious blackened fire pit. The charcoal was the recent leavings of stock boys watching cattle. The grooves, said Hlaba, had been cut 200 years earlier by Zulu warriors sharpening their *assegais* while standing watch over the broad Umfolozi hills stretching to the southeast where Shaka's Royal Kraal lay some 30 miles distant. According to legend and much historical fact, these hills once ran red with the blood of Shaka's victims.

One afternoon Rick and I hunted down off the mountain toward our stone-and-thatch camp, hoping to catch a big nyala in the brushy draws leading to the river or perhaps in the grassy river valley itself at dusk. Like Selous we hunched and crept down tunnels through a jungle of thorns, yellow wood, stinkwood and mountain cabbage trees, but our tunnels had been made by cattle, a sad commentary on the loss of wild Africa. Still, there appeared to be sufficient cover and plenty of game tracks, yet we found but one nyala cow and two duiker on a distant slope. Rick blamed our poor luck on the weather – heavily overcast and threatening rain. Indeed, it thundered and rained that evening as we sat around the fire beside our *rondavaals*.

After all our sightings, still-hunts and stalks, the taking of my nyala, as is often the case, was anticlimactic. We spotted it resting in a thicket no more than 80 yards away. I almost didn't want to shoot. But then I remembered Selous and his first easy bull.

"As the report of the rifle sounded, he plunged madly forward, and was instantly lost to sight in the thick scrub. But I felt sure he carried death with him; and so it proved, for we found him lying dead not twenty yards from where he had stood when the bullet struck him . . . Thus to secure a very handsome . . . inyala . . . after little more than an hour's search was indeed a most glorious and exceptional piece of good fortune, which, however, has been balanced by many and many a day that I can remember of unrequited labour in search of game."

Amen, brother Selous. Amen.

# OBSESSION in BLACK

*The most coveted of Africa's so-called "glamor" species, the sable is a living masterpiece, unsurpassed for his regal beauty and elegant bearing. And if your passion is to hunt him at his biggest and best, then western Zambia is the place. But look out for the lions.*

*By Chuck Wechsler*

I n the parched soils of the Zambian winter you will find their heart-shaped tracks, wending through the gentle woodlands, circumscribing a muddy waterhole, then meandering on to be lost over a blackened plain where swirling dust-devils whip columns of ash into the African air. And if you follow their tracks long enough, if you are patient and resolute and perhaps lucky enough, you will eventually see them: satiny black and rich mahogany, heads with distinctive white slashes, and wonderful, long and sweeping horns. And finally, when you gaze upon the bull you want – the trophy you have hoped for, longed for all these many months – it will seem as if the world has suddenly stopped.

# AFRICA

My world had stood still only an instant before, but suddenly things were happening at dizzying speed. At the crack of my rifle, the big sable bull had wheeled around and, laying his scimitar horns back across his massive shoulders, raced across the burned meadow and into a nearby woodland.

With Chole, our keen-eyed tracker in the lead, professional hunter Zane Langman and I began following the sable's tracks, scanning the dry ground for any indication of a hit. As we walked, concern mounting with every step, I reviewed the moments leading up to the shot. The bull had been standing about 100 yards away, most of his ebony form visible through the thornbush. I had knelt down and, sighting through a clear gap in the brush, pulled off what I felt to be a steady shot. The sable, however, had showed no signs of being hit, nor had we heard the slap of the bullet.

A half-hour later, with a blood-red African sun poised on the horizon, Zane called off the search, and we trudged back to the Land-Cruiser for the long drive to camp.

"Your bullet may have clipped some brush but I didn't hear it ricochet," he said. "I'm afraid it was a case of too much adrenaline. I've had hunters miss a leopard only 25 yards away. In all the excitement, your mind can play tricks on you. You think your aim is dead-on the shoulder, when you are actually just seeing the animal's body in the scope."

Our nightly session around the campfire proved quieter than usual, especially compared to the previous evening. The day before, our second at Bilili Springs Hunting Area in western Zambia, I had taken a Defassa waterbuck with 27½-inch horns, good enough for what may be fifth position in the Safari Club International record book. The stalk had been challenging and had culminated in a well-placed, one-shot kill. That evening, Zane and John Kabemba, managing director of United Safaris Zambia Limited, along with hunting partner Doug Truslow of South Carolina and Minnesota wildlife artist Ron Van Gilder, who joined our August safari to take reference photographs, had helped me celebrate an unforgettable day of hunting.

But now, staring into the murky Ninzhila River, listening to the grunting of hippos somewhere downstream, I found myself brooding over my errant shot. To make matters worse, Zane had estimated the sable's horns at 46 to 48 inches, an outstanding trophy. But I had blown it. As of tomorrow, it would be Doug's turn in our two-on-one hunt, and with only six days remaining, I would probably not get another chance.

My obsession to hunt sable antelope had begun two years earlier on a safari in neighboring Zimbabwe. While tracking a herd of Cape buffalo, we had seen a small group of sable led by a beautiful, inky-black bull. The safari operator had already filled his quota on sable, so all we could do was watch as the bull guided his harem through a distant stand of mopane. Although we enjoyed a successful hunt for buffalo and plains game, I came away from that safari determined to make a return trip, primarily for sable.

Of the 70 or so species of African antelope, the sable is unsurpassed for its regal beauty. In *African Hunter*, S. Newton Da Silva writes: "He carries himself with a dignity so studied it approaches pomposity; he seems always to be posing rather than standing, strutting rather than walking. He is, in a word, a masterpiece – one of the aesthetic high points that nature attained in the evolution of the species."

Standing over four feet at the shoulder and weighing up to 500 pounds, a mature bull (four years or older) is glossy black from head to tail, accented by patches of rich chestnut at the base of each ear and a snow-white belly. An erect, heavy mane runs from the base of his shoulders to his head, where streaks of white flow along the entire length of his muzzle. The female has these same harlequin markings on her head, though her body is reddish-brown overall.

Three races of sable are found in Africa. The smallest, both in body size and horn, occurs only in the Shimba Hills country of Kenya. The subspecies with the longest horns is the royal, or giant, sable which lives in a small area of north-central Angola. There are plenty of hunters who would trade every head in their trophy room for a chance to break Count de Yebes longstanding record: a tremendous, 65-inch royal sable taken in 1949. They may never get the chance, however, because the royal sable may already be extinct, another victim of Angola's long and bloody war.

Today, only the typical race of sable is hunted, and Zambia has the finest bulls, some with horns up to 50 inches. Sable are also taken in Zimbabwe, Botswanna and Mozambique, but seldom do their horns exceed the 43-inch mark. Still, to most African hunters, any sable above 38 inches is respectable.

# AFRICA

In Zambia, sable are most common in grassy woodlands of Brachystegia, called *miombo*, a widespread genus of broad-leaved, deciduous trees that provide both food and cover. The animals live in herds of 10 to 30, each dominated by a master bull. The biggest bulls, however, are usually outcasts – older animals driven off by the younger, stronger herd bull – which remain in close proximity to the herd. The bull I had missed was obviously one of these loners.

It is a rare occurrence to encounter one of the old patriarchs, and rarer yet to see a second, but that's exactly what happened just two days later. At sunrise and less than an hour out of camp, we happened upon a magnificent bull sable walking across an open meadow. Keeping a large baobab tree between them and the bull, Zane and Doug quickly closed to within 50 yards. One shot from Doug's .375 and he had taken the trophy of a lifetime.

Even Zane, who has been guiding hunters in Zambia for ten years, was surprised by the sable's horns. Measuring $46^2/8$ and $47^2/8$ inches with 10 and $9^6/8$ bases, they totaled $113^2/8$ points, which according to Zane's calculations, will place the animal in SCI's top 50. (Months later we would learn that Doug's sable was the second largest in Zambia in '89.)

**B**ilili Springs may be the best place in Africa to hunt trophy sable. The hunting unit lies along the southeast corner of Kafue National Park, which at 14,000 square miles, is one of the largest game sanctuaries in all of Africa. The area is mostly open woodland of mopane and Brachystegia, broken by long stretches of level plains, or grassveld. By March, the tail end of the African summer, the plains are covered with grasses as tall as a house. From April to August, the winter season, natives burn off these wild pastures, generating lush new growth that attracts animals like sable and waterbuck.

Elk-like in shape and posture, the waterbuck is particularly captivating with its pitchfork horns, and a coarse, shaggy coat that seems out of place for an equatorial mammal. Zambia has two species of waterbuck: common and Defassa. The former is larger in size (up to 600 pounds), and has longer horns and a distinctive white circle on its rump. The Defassa is more numerous, slightly more grayish overall, and has a white patch on its rear.

Like Doug's sable, my waterbuck was a chance encounter. We had seen dozens of bulls, including several with sizeable horns. But each time Zane barely gave the animal a second glance – that is, until he saw the huge bull I took on our first morning.

We also had permits for hartebeest and blue wildebeest, the latter an ungainly, unpredictable creature that one early explorer described as "designed by committee and assembled from spare parts," and what another referred to as "the four Marx brothers stuffed into the same costume." They were close to the truth.

Late one afternoon we stalked a small herd of wildebeest on the open plain, but they saw us and broke into a wild gallop, as if terrified by our intrusion. After running nearly a quarter-mile, they abruptly switched direction and came racing toward us, their long black tails streaming behind, their hooves kicking up a great cloud of dust. Then, just as suddenly, they stopped less than 200 yards away, and several males began fighting and bellowing loudly, carrying on as if we didn't exist.

A bird-watcher's paradise, Kafue National Park is home to some 400 different species. One day we stopped for lunch in a riverine forest where dozens of colorful birds darted through the canopy overhead: red-billed firefinches, violet-eared waxbills and a Ross's lourie with its deep-violet body and crimson crest. As we ate, a lone wattled crane – about the size of our American whooper, but more elegant with its tuxedo-like plumage and red-and-white wattles – drifted slowly overhead.

Francolin and guineafowl were everywhere, and each day we devoted an hour or two to hunting ("chasing" is a better word) the skittish birds. Francolin and guineas break into a hard run the moment they sense danger. The only way to get a shot is to leap from the truck and run after them. Then, as soon as they flush, you have to slide to a stop, pick out a bird and throw a shot in its direction, all in one motion. Great fun, but it didn't put much meat on the table.

Whether hunting, photographing or just enjoying the sights and sounds of Africa, we found ourselves fascinated by Zane's knowledge of everything around us. Someone once said that a professional hunter spends only ten percent of his time actually hunting and 90 percent entertaining clients. If that's the case, Zane must be one of the best professional hunters in Africa, for he is never without

# AFRICA

an intriguing story or personal experience, rattling off interesting tidbits about the flora and fauna as a ticker tape covers the action on Wall Street. One moment you are learning about a tree with sap so deadly that just a few drops on a poacher's arrow will kill a bull elephant. A few minutes later you find yourself immersed in a detailed recounting of African's violent tribal wars.

Our evening campfire sessions were especially engrossing, the topics ranging from politics to poaching. After a deliciously hot shower from 50-gallon drums suspended above our huts, and dressed in freshly washed and pressed clothes, we would meet at the campfire to relive the day. Drinks in hand, we would sit beneath a brilliant Milky Way, listening to the sounds of the African night – the chugging of green swamp frogs, the distant hooting of a fish owl – and watching the fishermen poling slowly upriver, their narrow dugout canoes filled with bream, catfish and tilapia.

Not all of our evenings were so relaxed.

For the American sportsmen, Africa is still a place of adventure, fraught with all sorts of perils and dangers, from malaria and poisonous snakes to animals that would just as soon crunch your bones as those of a gazelle.

On our first evening in camp we had been greeted by Patrick, game officer for the southeast sector of Kafue Park. Jabbering excitedly in a mixture of broken English and his native tongue, he explained that a pair of lions had been terrorizing the skinners and that, on the previous evening, the male had chased one of the natives up a tree.

Our compound, located about 50 yards from the skinning area, consisted of grass huts surrounded by a six-foot-high thatch wall. Problem was, the entrance to the compound did not have a gate.

Dead tired after our long drive from the capitol city of Lusaka, we quickly unpacked and climbed into bed, but not before I wedged the thatch door tightly into the entrance of our hut. I knew it wouldn't stop a hungry lion, but anything trying to enter would make enough noise to wake me up. My gun stood loaded with arm's reach. That night passed without incident.

It was on our third night that the lions made their move. Shortly after

230

sunset the male walked brazenly past the terrified skinners and into the meat hut where he began chewing on one hindquarter of my waterbuck. Their shouts brought Zane, who drove the truck right up to the doorway of the shack, pinning the lion inside. Seeing no way out, the angry cat burst through the thatch wall as easily as a football player glides through a paper homecoming banner.

Zane picked us up and we loaded the half-eaten hindquarter onto the truck, then took it to a tree about a half-mile from camp. After hanging the meat just out of reach, Zane declared: "That ought to keep them occupied for awhile." It did, for one night.

Two evenings later the lions returned just after sunset. The skinners threw sticks and rocks at the cats, who simply ignored the missiles while they dined on a zebra carcass. Once again we used the truck to scare them away and once again Zane declared our lion problems were over. Wrong again, and this time the aggressive lions didn't wait as long.

Around 2 a.m. the male returned, walking boldly into the compound, past our sleeping huts, and into the kitchen area. There, acting more like a black bear in a northwoods fishing camp, he began ransacking cartons of eggs and other foodstuffs until his nocturnal prowling awakened the camp and he was frightened away, plunging through a thatch wall and into the surrounding darkness.

After reading *The Man-eaters of Tsavo* and other African classics, I had developed a healthy respect for the King of Beasts and found myself sleeping lightly. The lions' antics, however, illicited different reactions from my companions. Zane, who has been hunting Africa's dangerous game virtually all of his 55 years, almost seemed to enjoy their visits, referring to them as "big kitty-cats just looking for an easy meal." Van Gilder, always the stoic, just smiled and mused: "If they're gonna eat you, there's probably not much you can do about it." Truslow was quick to rib me about keeping a loaded gun by my bed. But once back in the states, he admitted that he had devised his own emergency plan. If a lion entered his hut, he would clutch the cot and mattress to his chest with one hand and roll onto the floor, thereby protecting his tender vitals from the big cat. At the same time, he would reach under his pillow with his other hand, grab his hunting knife, and deliver a killing blow. Sure . . .

# AFRICA

Over the first six days we took several other good trophies, including two impala, a zebra stallion and a warthog. Doug was particularly interested in shooting a Cape buffalo, and we spent many hours in search of the animals. On several occasions we came close, our nostrils greeted by the familiar barnyard smell, but each time the wary animals managed to avoid us.

The only buffalo we did see was a dead one, felled by a poacher's bullet. Each day we saw evidence of poaching, mostly wire snares set around the few remaining waterholes and makeshift camps where the natives had skinned their game. One afternoon we came upon a zebra mare caught in a drag-snare. In her efforts to struggle free, she had prematurely expelled her foal, its tiny white-and-black body still enveloped in the birth sac. Taking care to avoid the mare's sharp teeth and hooves, Chole managed to chop the wire that encircled her hock, and the zebra limped away. Two days later we saw her back with the herd, still limping slightly, but on the road to recovery.

One finds it difficult to criticize villagers who rely on wild game for sustenance. But most of the poaching can be traced to greed – renegade types employed by corrupt officials who indiscriminately kill everything from duiker to elephants, male and female alike. The Zambian government is attempting to crack down on poachers by establishing Village Scouts in all of its 32 game management areas and by returning hunting revenues to local villagers. Hopefully, it is not a case of too little too late.

It was early on our last full day of hunting, while driving to a broad plain where we had seen buffalo sign on the previous evening, that Chole and I spotted the sable herd almost simultaneously. One good bull and at least 20 cows and yearlings stared back at us from deep within the Brachystygia, their black-and-brown bodies glistening in the dappled light. A quick tap on the roof of the Land-Cruiser brought the vehicle to a grinding stop, which set the entire herd in motion.

Staring through his binoculars Zane announced: "That's a splendid bull. Let's go!"

Soon we were walking single-file through the woodland, Chole, Patrick and Zane hunched over, reading the tracks in the sandy soil. After nearly a mile, Chole dropped to one knee and, peering through the trees and tall grass, pointed out the switching tail of a sable. Zane and I edged forward, alternately scrambling bent-over and crawling until we got within 150 yards of the herd. But try as we might we could not locate the bull. Suddenly, a dozen heads lifted almost in unison and turned to stare at us. Spooked, the animals galloped off into the bush.

We caught up to the herd a half-hour later. Once again, Zane and I had to crawl into position, the dry, razor-sharp grasses cutting our knees and forearms. This time we spotted the bull grazing beneath an open canopy of flat-topped acacias. But just as I raised my rifle, several zebra that had gone unnoticed off to our right began running toward the sable. In seconds panic gripped the animals and they were gone.

Tracking was easier for the next hour, but once we rediscovered the mixed herd, stalking became more difficult with so many eyes and ears on alert. Yet another long, stealthy crawl brought Zane and me to within 150 yards of the bull, his deep-chested body and saber-like horns barely visible from behind a tree. One step in either direction and I would have my shot. Just then, more bad luck! From off to our left came a small group of eland, barging directly into the sable. Though not alarmed by our presence, the sable decided to tag along with their larger cousins and off they went, the eland, sable and zebra in one large, integrated group.

Turning to Doug, my frustration growing by leaps and bounds, I asked, "So what's next? A herd of elephants?"

"Just be happy they aren't lions," he laughed.

Another hour passed before we regained the herd. By this time the African sun was burning hotter, the ubiquitous tsetses biting more aggressively. Fortunately, the zebras had slipped off to one side and the eland had gone their own way, leaving the sable scattered over an open woodland with sparse, waist-high grass. Zane and I began our fourth stalk, which after several minutes of crawling, brought us to within 40 yards of a cow seemingly asleep in the grass. But try as we might, we couldn't locate the bull. Finally, after watching and waiting for what seemed an eternity, we decided to stand up, hoping that I could get a quick shot when the bull scrambled to his feet. But unbeknownst to us, he had moved to the point position in the herd and was nearly 200 yards away when we saw his dark form knifing through the trees.

# AFRICA

"Shoot," Zane hissed.

The roar of my rifle sent the entire herd careening through the trees and the bull along with them, obviously unhurt.

Traipsing back to the vehicle, my knees and arms cut and bleeding, my throat raspy from the heat and dust and excitement, I resigned myself to the fact that taking a sable was not meant to be. I had had my chances; the hunt had been thrilling and memorable, but there would be no sable for my trophy room, at least not from this safari.

To my professional hunter, however, the game was just getting interesting. Zane Langman is a man of boundless energy and never-ending enthusiasm. Discouraged? The word is not in his vocabulary. Disappointment? There is no such thing, as long as there's light left in the day.

"Don't give up yet," he smiled, patting my shoulder. "We've had a bit of bad luck this morning. Things will swing our way."

Now approaching mid-afternoon, we drove back to the road to see if my shot had spooked the sable out of the area. After circling the woodland and not finding any fresh tracks, Zane headed toward the far western end and one of the few waterholes in the area.

"Sable drink twice or even three times on normal days," he explained on the way. "These guys have had a pretty rough morning with a lot of running. They must be getting thirsty by now."

After breaking for lunch and quenching our own thirst, we resumed the search. We had walked less than a quarter-mile when we saw the sable resting with the same herd of zebra.

Zane and I started our fifth and final stalk, eventually crawling within 75 yards of two zebra and three sable cows who lolled contentedly at the edge of an expansive plain. The bull was nowhere in sight, so we sat down to wait him out. After nearly an hour, with the afternoon sun slipping toward the horizon, Zane decided that we couldn't wait any longer, so we tried the same technique as before: standing ever-so-slowly so we would not spook the entire herd.

Finally, a break! As we stood, several cows saw our movement, but instead of running off, merely walked out of the trees and onto the grassveld. One by one, over a dozen cows and young bulls got to their feet and joined the procession.

Suddenly, there he was – beautiful satiny black, his long, exquisitely arced horns shining in the African sun – and once again my world stood still.

My arms felt numb after so many hours of strenuous crawling, and I had trouble holding my rifle steady. The 300-grain bullet struck well above the shoulder where there would be little bleeding. But luck was with us and instead of ducking back into the timber, the bull trotted onto the plain, hurt and confused, struggling to keep up with his herd. One more shot and the day-long chase was over, my magnificent obsession along with it.

From far across the plain came the shrill barking of zebra, while closer by, a dust-devil whirled and played beneath a multitude of cotton clouds. My world had reawakened.

# TO SHOOT
# AN ELEPHANT

*Pulling the trigger on 10,000 pounds of bone-crushing death is an awesome challenge. Full of courage or scared to your soul, you'd better do it right. Your life depends on it.*

*By Art Carter*

Young men unthinkingly take chances by driving fast cars and chasing fast women because they believe they are immortal, that they will never die. More mature men choose to openly embrace danger because they know they are not and most surely will.

Hunting an animal that can kill you as easily as swatting a fly really doesn't make much sense on a purely intellectual basis. It is more on emotional or philosophical terms that men pursue close encounters with death. To place oneself in harm's way, to stalk mere yards or even feet away from a quick and horrible demise by way of fang and claw attached to 500 pounds of angry feline; wickedly hooked horns driven by nearly a ton of vindictive rage; or six-foot spears of ivory tusk jutting from 10,000 pounds of cunning, crushing death is for some an inevitable culmination of a hunting life's dreams.

# AFRICA

To take rifle in hand and face magnificent beasts honed by eons of evolution, to best not only those animals on their own terms and ground, but to conquer one's personal frailties and fears, is not a decision to be taken lightly. Nor is it for everyone. It is, however, a chance to walk on the razor edge of what makes us hunters.

The new-penny-copper glow of daybreak over the Okavango Delta was still just a hint in the east as cape turtle doves, red-billed francolins and fork-tailed drongos erupted into their morning chorus around our tent. I had been awake for at least two hours anyway. My time had come to experience a hunter's life to it's fullest, to put myself in the path of the largest land animal on Earth. I was wide awake. Even at 52 and a hunter for more than 40 of those years, I was still unable to believe it. I was an elephant hunter.

Butch Searcy, builder of high-quality double rifles in Boron, California, was beginning to stir in the other bunk. He and I had met at a sports show several years ago and soon became friends. If I were to shoot an elephant, I wanted it to be up-close with one of Butch's doubles. Two years previously I had traded several of my bolt-actions for one of his accurate creations in the traditional .470 Nitro Express caliber. It was through our friendship and Butch's close relationship with professional hunter Johan Calitz that we were now ensconced in Johan's Ivory Camp in the middle of northern Botswana.

Johan owns one of the largest and best-run safari operations in all of Africa, with nine different camps. A tough, likable and infinitely honest man of Afrikanner descent, he is undoubtedly the most knowledgeable PH I've ever known. After a week of hunting with him and standing together, shoulder-to-shoulder in thigh-deep water, the long grass three feet above our heads, as we sorted out a wounded and very angry Cape buffalo, I now had grown to consider Johan as a valued and trusted friend.

Going on this trip had been a unique decision, unlike any I'd ever faced in my outdoor experience – to resolve in my own mind if I even wanted to hunt an elephant. I had never given it serious consideration until I met Butch and Johan. But when one of Johan's clients cancelled unexpectedly, the opportunity became a reality.

My quandary wasn't that I thought elephant hunting was wrong or immoral. Those are the overly emotional sentiments of the uniformed. When I told a friend's wife at dinner one night that I was going elephant hunting, she reacted indignantly, "Why would you want to shoot an elephant? Do they still let people do that?"

I explained that elephants are thriving in countries where sport hunting is an effective management tool, the best means of keeping their numbers in line with their habitat. Because a large portion of the monies spent on government licenses and trophy fees are funneled directly into the African communities where the elephants are shot, local residents benefit from new medical clinics, schools, medicine and other services. These monies also pay for anti-poaching measures, further ensuring the safety of the herds. The elephants win and poachers, the real culprits in the depravation of elephant numbers, lose.

When Botswana reopened elephant hunting in 1996 after a ten-year hiatus, there were about 80,000 in the country. Now, estimates range from 120,000-150,000. This year about 150 trophy bulls were killed – only one in a thousand. Taking one old bull, past his breeding prime, can ultimately save the lives of a hundred. Or a thousand. In addition, all of the meat is used by the locals. Nothing goes to waste.

But was it for me? Over the years several PHs had told me that unequivocally, the African elephant was the grandest game of all. When I asked Johan, his answer was immediate. "Cape buffalo are fun to fool around with but elephant hunting is the ultimate. That's because they are the biggest, the most intimidating, the smartest and most cunning and the most dangerous and hard to stop when wounded." That was enough for me.

Botswana, one of the least populated countries in the world, is an outstanding safari destination. The southwestern third of the country is covered by the vast Kalahari Desert, and to the northeast, the Chobe area ranges from thornbush to mopane forest. Both have excellent hunting, but Botswana's crown jewel is the Okavango Delta, a wilderness covering more than 7,000 square miles.

Bordered by the Kalahari, the Okavango is a spectacular oasis of flooded grasslands, serpentine waterways and islands. Created by the Okavango River and its many tributaries, the crystal-clear water of the delta creates one of the most verdant areas on the planet. Its wildlife dazzles the visitor's imagination with more than 160 species of mammals and a staggering 400 different varieties of birds.

After breakfast each morning Johan, Butch and I boarded an aluminum boat with Olly and Dan, our Tswana trackers, and Active the local community's game scout. Beginning in the morning when the air was cool and a light jacket felt good and throughout the sun-baked days, we motored the endless channels of the delta. Other days we bounced across huge tracks of countryside in the Land Cruiser. More miles of shoe-leather were expended following dusty elephant tracks and wading waist-deep water filled with saber-sharp marsh grass.

For seven days we hunted hard for the right trophy bull. In the mornings we looked for plains game and buffalo, but as the sun became hotter toward noon, we searched for the elephants that came to the main river channels to drink a portion of the 30 gallons of water they require each day.

And indeed, we saw elephants. Many elephants. At least 20 to 30 bulls every day though none possessed the 60 pounds of ivory per side that is the benchmark for Johan's clients. Something in the mid-50s was starting to look good.

The huge bull, one of the largest elephants in Botswana, was in the beginning of his last decade of life. Having lived through 52 rainy and dry seasons, he had trekked great distances, migrating not only across much of the northern third of Botswana but also hundreds of miles in Zambia, Namibia and Zimbabwe. He had grown wise. He knew where the sweet grasses and tasty tree limbs grew, where he could find water even during the dry times. In his earlier years, during his musth periods when breeding dominated his mind, he had known where to find the cow herds.

The old bull had returned to his favorite palm plantation on a large island. He was there to gorge on the delicious nuts that fell at his feet when he used his massive head or his thick, heavy tusks to shake the palm trees. Water to drink and mud to roll in were both nearby. His comrade, a mature but much younger bull, would keep him company and help watch for any signs of danger.

I n the afternoon of our fifth day we thought we had found our elephant. Olly, Dan and Active spotted him in a herd of nine bulls at least a half-mile inland from the river. We beached the boat, and the trackers ran ahead to judge the big bull. Soon they were back, describing his long, beautiful ivory. From their description of more than 40 inches outside the lip and medium-heavy thickness, Johan thought the tusks would go in the high 50s, perhaps crowding 60 pounds per side. We immediately began our stalk. Evidently the elephants had already watered and were heading back into the bush to resume their 20 hours of feeding for the day.

Nearly an hour later we were close enough to hear them popping tree limbs as they fed. The one we wanted was right in the middle of the group, but as we crossed an opening a young bull spotted us, threw his ears out and raised his trunk. We froze. In a few moments he seemed to calm down, and when the elephants began traveling again we closed the gap.

Stalking to within 60 yards of where they would all come out into an open plain, I readied myself for the shot. Johan and Butch would back me up. A bull walked out into the open. Not our guy. Then another and another. In single file, eight bulls strolled by, but not the one we wanted. When they were out of sight, we doubled back but found nothing. The big bull had vanished. He had probably sensed something was wrong when the younger elephant raised his ears and trunk and had simply walked away. We never saw him again.

Two days later we drove to an immense palm plantation an hour and a half from camp that Johan knew to be a favorite feeding ground for elephants. With more and more bulls showing up each day in their spring migration from the Chobe area, we might get lucky.

On the way we spotted a large bull just emerging from the trees to water at a pan. He had short, thick ivory but moved back into the bush at the sight of the truck. We jumped out and quickly closed to only 25 yards downwind of him. As the big bull walked into a clearing, we could see that he had one tusk of about 55 pounds, but the other side was badly broken. We reluctantly decided he wasn't for us.

There were many elephants in the palms, their huge, gray shapes dotting the scene as they feasted on the golf ball-sized palm nuts. They had already destroyed at least a thousand acres of 30- to 50-foot mopane trees nearby, uprooting the trunks to reach the few juicy twigs at their tops.

# AFRICA

We saw nothing with heavy ivory, although we looked over a middle-aged bull with extremely long but thin tusks. As we glassed him, a youngster about 15 years old screamed indignantly at our intrusion, mock-charging to within 25 yards and flapping his ears. He stopped, then glared wildly at us before taking off at a fast lope, trumpeting all the way.

Then, after sighting more than two dozen elephants, we noticed a large bull far off from the others. As we approached to within a couple of hundred yards he moved deeper into the forest, but as he turned sideways, I got a glimpse of his tusks. They were thicker by far than any we had seen. I knew he was the one we had been looking for. Johan and the trackers agreed, and quietly motioned for us to ready our rifles.

As I buckled on my heavy cartridge belt and dropped two .470 solids into the chambers, I began to feel a tremendous pressure in my mind and indeed, within my soul, to do well. This couldn't really be happening. I was going to shoot an elephant. I took a deep, mind-clearing breath as we walked toward where we had last seen the bull.

T*he old bull lost sight of his younger companion, his second set of eyes, who always traveled with him. No matter, his own senses had never let him down. But he didn't know there was a small, frail being, a man the same age as him, only a few hundred yards away. The man and several other humans were looking for him. Over the years the old matriarch of his herd had trained him to run away when he smelled such beings, that they were as much a part of the food chain, as much a part of the law of survival of the fittest, as the lion and buffalo. But no such dangerous stench reached the old elephant and besides, he had eating on his mind. There was much more food to consume this day and the nuts of the tall trees were very good.*

W hen the .470s clunked into the chambers of my rifle and we started out after the big bull, the same feeling hit me as when I had hunted buffalo earlier in the week and had approached close to other elephants. But it was a completely different sensation from anything I had felt on past hunts for deer, elk or plains game. Not only was there excitement, but also extreme apprehension.

We stalked closer and closer to the bull, which was ghosting though the forest only 35 yards away. Johan motioned for me to step up even with him and get ready to shoot. The bull's tusks were heavy and long, one broken off just a few inches at its blunt tip. Easily weighing more than five tons, the elephant was as big as a house. A very large, powerful, intimidating house.

The bull suddenly stopped in a small clearing and looked our way. His tiny amber eyes seemed to recognize that something was wrong with the landscape. His giant head, ten feet above us, turned in our direction; huge ears fanned out, straining for sound. His massive trunk, framed by tusks as big around as my leg, raised in defiance of any potential danger. The feeling in my gut and the taste in my mouth had a new flavor – the flavor of fear. The fear of the unknown. Of what was going to happen when I pulled the trigger. I raised the rifle and pushed off the safety.

"Wait until he turns," Johan whispered. "Wait. Wait."

The great head began to turn away. Hot, nervous, scalding sweat ran down my face and into my eyes. I began to take up the slack in the trigger.

H*e sensed rather than saw the forms to his left. The huge bull swung his head around to get a better look. Though his eyesight had never been that keen and was certainly not as good as it once was, the small and vaguely familiar shapes, both black and white, were very still. They didn't seem, in their insignificant smallness, to pose any danger. Neither could he smell anything out of the ordinary.*

*As he turned to leave, the old bull saw a flash erupt from one of the tiny forms and he stumbled, stunned. There was little pain, but now he realized they were a threat and fury engulfed him. Eyes blazing, he shook his head and flared his ears in anger as he took a step forward to crush out their very existence.*

T he big rifle kicked hard into my shoulder but I never felt it. The bead of the front sight had been right where I thought it was supposed to be for a well-placed shot. Microseconds later, as the rifle returned from recoil to rest on the target, my brain screamed that something was wrong. Very wrong! He hadn't fallen!

# AFRICA

It took only a couple of seconds before my second bullet and one from Johan's rifle were on their way. But it was long enough for me to see the unmistakable look in the bull's eyes, to fully comprehend that the first shot had had little effect other than to enrage the huge animal. It merely set into motion his intent to kill what had stung him. It was now either him or us.

When the second shots hit, the bull fell in a cloud of dust, but Johan grabbed me by the shoulder, quickly pulling me to the side of the elephant.

"He could still get up," he near-shouted into my ear. "Give him another shot for insurance." I pressed the trigger, the rifle roared one last time and everything was still.

In awe, I stepped over and touched the bull's immense body, felt the roughness of his wrinkled skin and admired the beauty of his tusks. With congratulatory handshakes all around and my pulse inching down closer to normal, I propped my rifle on a thornbush. Not a little shaken, a spate of emotion washed over me, and I felt like laughing and crying and running away, all at the same time. I am not ashamed to admit that I then experienced the most overwhelming sense of hunter's remorse I have ever felt. Not wanting to talk to my companions or even face them for a bit, I wondered if these feelings represented some weakness I had never discovered in myself before. I walked around the clearing for some time while trying to cope with the enormity of what I had done.

After nearly half-an-hour of basically circling the fallen giant, I finally came to the realization that shooting this elephant was simply part of the chain of life, where death of some form is inevitable. That it had been at my hands was only a detail in the great scheme of things and for this elephant, this "grand old man" as Johan so eloquently described him, to be immortalized in photographs and words was perhaps better than his starving to death in just a few short years, a shell of his former strength.

The bull was beyond my wildest dreams. I had told Johan at the beginning of the safari that I tended to be a lucky hunter, but none of us had ever thought that we would find such an elephant. His right tusk, measuring 19 inches around at the lip and well over six feet long on the curve, weighed 74 pounds. The thicker-yet left tusk, even with eight inches or so broken off, still weighed 73 pounds and would have topped 80 had it been whole. The bull will probably rank in the top five taken in Botswana in 2000 and was one of the largest killed in Africa last season.

His ivory tusks, with their creamy, glowing whiteness and intricate patterns of surface cracks from decades of wear, along with the character of the broken tip, perhaps shattered decades ago – to my eyes, were beautiful beyond describing. They will forever be a magnificent reminder of the grandest hunt of my life.

# RETURN to MASWA

*Tracking a wounded buffalo in thick cover is not for the faint at heart.*

## By Robert Parvin Williams

U ntil this safari, I had always hunted Maswa in the dry season. I knew it only as a sere hell of thorns and rocks, the riverbeds dry and bleached, the horizon broken by dark, cloud-bound mountains, dormant volcanoes that retained an air of latent violence.

Now, in November, the first rains have fallen and Maswa has become an Eden. There is water in the rivers and the plains are new-green and sprinkled with flowers. Impala, wildebeest and zebra parade their young. And still the old volcanoes brood. Just across the Serengeti Plain in Olduvai Gorge, the rains wash ancient bones from ancient ash. Some of those bones are human, or nearly so, and some are of a breed of huge-horned buffalo, now extinct, perhaps ancestors to the big cape buffalo for which I've come to Maswa again and again.

Always, in Maswa, there is a sense of returning to a beginning. Despite the new colors and life in the November landscape, I'm pleased to find no change in the primeval menace of the place or of the buffalo themselves.

The last time professional hunter Ian Batchelor and I hunted Maswa together, we shot an old bull late in the afternoon and had to follow it into thick bush as the sun set. The bull had been hit in the heart, but still had a lot of fight when we caught up with him. Shooting a charging buffalo in a thicket lit largely by muzzle-flash is exciting, but better avoided.

On this hunt we're hoping to find an old bull with well-worn horns on which to try a new rifle – a .500 Nitro Express double rifle by Merkel that seems just the thing for big bulls in tight places. The cartridge itself is impressive: half-an-inch wide, three inches long, firing a 570-grain bullet, it is considerably stouter than the .416 Rigby I usually like for buffalo. The Merkel had shot well during a year of stalking deer, armadillo and the occasional tin can – so well, in fact, that I meant to try barking squirrels with the big bullets, but never quite got around to it.

In keeping with the traditional double rifle strategy, I load a soft-point bullet in the right barrel and a solid in the left. I've always used only solids on buffalo in the past, but this seems like a good opportunity to give softs a try. This decision turns out to have some interesting consequences.

The rains have brought more buffalo into Maswa than I've ever seen anywhere. In one day we count a thousand before we tire of counting. Most are in herds, which we avoid. The herd bulls, while often sporting impressive horns, are too often still of breeding age. One doesn't shoot them. Moreover, the sheer number of eyes in a herd of a hundred buffalo can make close stalking remarkably difficult.

One technique does seem to work pretty well. Ian has brought a couple of black umbrellas that allow us to approach buffalo even in open country if we're careful to stay behind the round, black shields. The theory is that the buffalo think we're ostriches, but it may be enough that round black blobs simply don't look like humans or lions, the only animals buffalo need to worry about. It's hard to keep an umbrella open as we move through thick bush, but collapsing it slightly as we squeeze between trees seems to work as long as we don't get snagged on thorns.

The best bulls we see are always alone or in small bachelor groups, almost always in thick bush near rivers where they can water and lie up during the heat of the day. This makes the hunting tricky: if we simply follow tracks into thickets, which Ian and I dearly love to do, we may well stumble into a bedded bull so close that a charge is inevitable. That's not only a little unhealthy, but it's more difficult to be selective about what we shoot. We've killed enough good bulls together to have gotten past caring about an extra inch or two in trophy size, but we really would like to find a bull that's old and full of character, if we can. So instead of just following tracks, we drive and walk slowly through likely areas, trying to see bulls before they see us.

T hree days into the hunt we get lucky. After lunch we return to a stretch of thornbush along the Semu River where we had jumped some bulls earlier in the day. Starting well downwind of the area, we walk for only a few minutes before Mathias, our tracker, spots buffalo ahead. Ian can see two bulls through his binoculars, one of which looks very old. The bulls are feeding among some acacia trees on the other side of an open patch. We break out an umbrella, line up behind it and slowly stalk toward the bulls. They spot us and watch curiously, then begin to move away. We wait until they start to feed again, then move closer.

After an hour we reach the trees and can use the cover to gain ground. After another hour we're within 50 yards of the nearer bull, and even without binoculars I can see the sharp bones of his hips and the smooth white sweep of his boss and horns. He's without question a very old bull; not as big as some we've seen, but very nice. I step outside of the umbrella, the bull turns to face us, and I put the Merkel on the sticks.

The light is beginning to fade and the bull's lower half is obscured by brush, but he appears to be facing us directly or at a slight quartering angle. I squeeze off a shot from the right barrel – the soft-point bullet – at the center of his forequarters in line with where his heart should be. The bull reacts, hunching with the impact, wheeling and running straight away, dragging his right foreleg. I try a second shot offhand through a gap in the trees, but it feels like a miss.

Ian, Mathias and Samira, our game scout, move quickly to the blood trail as I reload. Everyone has spotted the broken shoulder, but no one is quite certain of the bull's angle at the time of the shot. Ian is concerned that the bull was facing directly, not quartering, in which case a broken right shoulder would signal a shot well to the left of the vital organs.

It's rapidly getting darker. We press the follow-up as quickly as the light allows. Mathias and Samira pick out droplets of blood on stems of grass while Ian and I watch the trail ahead. Each time the trail approaches a clump of brush or a termite mound we give it a wide berth, well aware that earlier in the season one of Ian's colleagues had been badly hurt by a wounded bull that ambushed him from behind a termite mound and took several more bullets before disappearing into the bush.

We cover several hundred yards before Ian calls a halt. "It's just too dark, Bob. I hate to leave him, but we'll have to wait until morning."

He's right, of course. The trackers can't see the blood and we can't tell shadows from buffalo.

That night I sleep badly, rethinking the shot, wanting the bull not to be hurt, hoping to find it dead just beyond where we stopped for the night, wondering if we'll find it before the lions and hyenas do.

In the morning we reach the blood trail at first light. We find where the bull stopped running and waited next to a termite mound, leaving a puddle of blood, then turned and walked toward the river. We lose the trail for an hour in the tracks of a small herd that crossed the trail during the night, then pick it up again as it moves into dense growth along the river.

The tension mounts quickly in this terrain and I find myself wiping first one palm then the other. I shake out my arms and hands to relieve the ache from holding the rifle constantly at the ready. Visibility shrinks to a few yards, sometimes a few feet. If we find the bull waiting for us in here, he'll have an overwhelming advantage.

The riverbed drops sheer in front of us. Ian and I take turns covering each other and the trackers as we climb down, across and up the other side. The trail turns briefly into a narrow tunnel through thick brush, then to our relief breaks out into more open scrub. The tracking becomes very difficult on the dry soil, the trail consisting only of tiny spots of dried blood that the sun is rapidly fading.

At last, under the wide branches of a low bush, we find what we had hoped we wouldn't find: a matted, blood-soaked patch of dirt where the bull had lain down during the night, and more importantly, from which it later arose. Properly shot buffalo do not get back up once they've gone down like that. Something has gone badly wrong.

"He's only got a broken shoulder," Ian says bitterly. "Thanks a lot, Bob."

I can't blame him. He has a wife and young son, and this is starting to look ugly. What I can't understand, though, is how a straightforward shot I could make in my sleep could have gone so far astray. If the bull's only injury is to his shoulder, I reason, he must have been standing straight on and the shot must have hit nearly a foot wide. Had the bull been quartering at all, a broken shoulder should have put the bullet into the vitals. But I have to forget all that for now and concentrate instead on every bush and shadow. Somewhere ahead is an angry bull with a wound that won't slow him much at all.

Somewhat grimly we carry on. The trail re-crosses the river and we find another spot where the bull has lain for a while, then the trail doubles back and leaves the river to cross a wide floodplain. The sun bakes our backs as we approach a wooded hill. It's almost noon. We've been tracking for five hours and at least that many miles.

As we move into the trees, Mathias spots a low black mass in the shadows ahead. We move closer from tree to tree and see a sleeping buffalo, then another, but neither is our bull. Perhaps he has joined these and is bedded nearby? Ian searches with his binoculars and spots a third buffalo facing away on the other side of a deadfall. From the whitened curve of the right horn, Ian thinks it's our bull, but we can't see well enough to be sure.

Suddenly, as if it senses us, the bull begins to stand.

"That's him! Come on!" and Ian sprints toward an opening. I follow and the bull starts to turn, his bad leg giving him a pronounced wobble. Ian reaches the opening first and fires into the bull's neck. The bull rolls and I hit him in the chest as he goes over. He lies still, his eyes glazed.

I turn quickly to check on the other bulls, but they've gone the other way. We move slowly behind the downed bull and twitch his tail. No reaction. We touch his eye. Again nothing.

Then we grin a little and shake hands and take a drink of water. Mathias heads back to get the vehicle and Samira rests on a fallen tree while Ian and I inspect the holes from our bullets and admire the old bull.

My first shot yesterday had indeed broken his right shoulder, but at a quartering angle, not from the front. There's something odd about that. That shot should have hit the heart and lungs and killed the bull quickly.

We're standing by the horns, talking, when the bull snorts and shakes his head to rise. I shoot him as fast as I've ever shot anything, down between the shoulders and into the chest at a range of maybe three feet, and he goes down for good.

Ian and I look at each other. "Not one of the easy ones, was it?"

"No."

Samira is looking at us and the bull, shaking his head.

When the vehicle finds us an hour later, we skin out the carcass and start to get answers to some of our questions. My first bullet, a soft-point, hit the shoulder in line with the heart, but never even made it through the ribs. Instead, it shed its jacket when it hit the shoulder joint and blew into fragments, most of which were lodged against the fifth and sixth ribs. My second shot, taken as he bolted, appears to have missed completely. Ian's shot, a soft-point from his .500 Jeffery, hit the bull squarely in the neck and was stopped by the massive knob of bone at the base of the skull. The impact knocked the bull out cold, but that's all it did. A perfect shot, but the bullet simply didn't penetrate far enough to be fatal.

My third and fourth shots, both solids, performed correctly. The third centered the heart and would soon have finished the bull. The last was only necessary because the bull regained consciousness and presumably smelled and heard us a few feet away.

Over sundowners that evening we talk about what conclusions, if any, we should draw from all of this. No more soft-point bullets on buffalo? Hard to say. Soft-points have certainly killed a lot of buffalo.

I look around at the old volcanoes crouched on the horizon and the deceptively tranquil November costume Maswa has assumed, and sense a certain smugness in the atmosphere. Almost got us this time. For me, next time it's going to be solids.

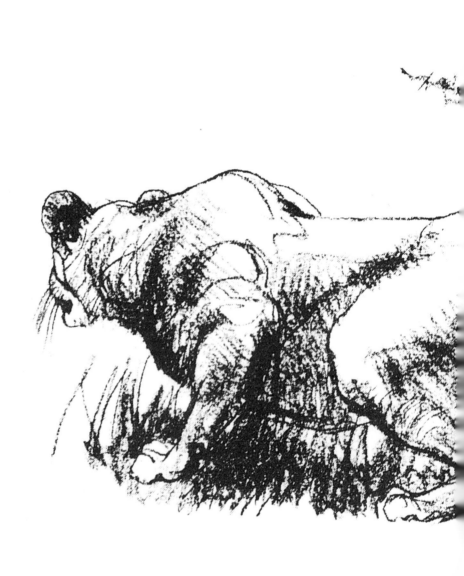

# FACING DEATH

# KILLING A
# LION WITH A KNIFE

*Beginning around the turn of the 20th century, Harry Wolhuter served 44 years as a ranger in South Africa's Kruger National Park. His accomplishments were legion; his life a legend. What follows is first a selection from the Foreword to Wolhuter's memoirs, written by J. Stevenson-Hamilton, another late warden at Kruger National Park, followed by Wolhuter's amazing escape from a pair of hungry lions.*

*By Harry Wolhuter*

W hen, in July 1902, I made my debut in the Low-Veld as warden of the newly reproclaimed Sabi Game Reserve, I naturally looked round anxiously for someone of local experience who might serve me as guide, philosopher and friend.

Every "old hand" whom I approached said the same thing, "Try and get hold of Harry Wolhuter; he knows the country better than anyone else."

When at last I was successful in making contact with him, I found that Wolhuter's appearance and manner justified his reputation. Tall, spare but powerfully built; purposeful, for all his quiet voice and unassuming manner, he seemed emblematical of the best type of pioneer hunter.

All the years of close companionship and friendship that have since passed, I have never ceased to regard the day of that first meeting as a red letter one in my life. I suppose there can be few if any men in Africa possessing a deeper knowledge and wider experience of bush lore in all its phases and in his prime, Harry Wolhuter held all the qualities requisite to give effect to that knowledge and experience; a powerful frame, an iron constitution; cool courage and quiet determination.

# AFRICA

His unique exploit in killing, single-handed, and armed only with a knife, a full-grown male lion which had seized him, and was carrying him off, was in itself a feat rendering superfluous any further tributes to his rare courage and coolness; but it is worth remarking that in the many hazards – happily all safely surmounted – which he has since incurred in the course of his duties, his nerve has shown itself to be just as calm and steady as it was when he underwent that terrible experience.

Unfortunately, he never fully got over the injuries he then received. Nevertheless, right up to the date of his retirement in 1946, he was still taking chances with lions, and only a year or two before, he had even dispatched a badly injured one with a knife, "to save a cartridge!" – J. Stevenson-Hamilton.

On August, 1903, I was returning from one of my usual patrols on the Olifants. On the second day after leaving camp my objective was a certain waterhole en route, at which I intended spending the night, but when we reached it, we found that the pool was dry. It was now about 4 p.m., and the only thing to be done was to push on to the next waterhole which was about twelve miles distant. Accompanying me were three police boys driving the donkeys which carried all my possessions, and three dogs; the latter all rough "Boer" dogs, very good on lions. I instructed the boys that I would ride ahead along the path to the next waterhole and they were to follow. I then started to go ahead along the trail, and of the dogs, "Bull" escorted me; the bitch "Fly" and a mongrel-terrier remaining with the boys.

Although it became dusk very soon I continued to ride along the path – as I had often travelled that route by night during the Boer War to avoid the heat of the summer sun. I gave no thought to lions, as I had never before encountered these animals in those parts. Most of the herbage had been recently burnt off, but here and there a patch of long grass remained. While riding through one of these isolated patches, I heard two animals jump up in the grass in front of me.

It was by now too dark to see, but I imagined that the animals in question were a pair of reedbuck, as this had always been a favorite locality for these antelope. I expected them to run across the path and disappear; but instead, and to my surprise, I heard a running rustle in the grass approaching me.

I was still riding quietly along when two forms loomed up within three or four yards, and these I now recognized as two lions, and their behavior was such that I had little doubt but that their intentions were to attack my horse. Although, of course, I had my rifle (without which I never moved in the veld), there was no time to shoot, and as I hastily pulled my horse around, I dug the spurs into his flanks in a frantic effort to urge him to his best speed to get away in time; but the approaching lion was already too close, and before the horse could get into its stride I felt a terrific impact behind me as the lion alighted on the horse's hindquarters.

What happened next, of course, occupied only a few seconds, but I vividly recall the unpleasant sensation of expecting the crunch of the lion's jaws in my person. However, the terrified horse was bucking and plunging so violently that the lion was unable to maintain its hold, but it managed to knock me out of the saddle.

Fortune is apt to act freakishly at all times, and it may seem a strange thing to suggest that it was fortunate for myself that I happened to fall almost on top of the second lion as he was running round in front of my horse, to get hold of it by the head. Had I fallen otherwise, however, it is probable that the lion would have grasped me by the head, and then this would assuredly never have been written! Actually, the eager brute gripped my right shoulder between its jaws and started to drag me away, and as it did so, I could hear the clatter of my horse's hooves over the stony ground as it raced away with the first lion in hot pursuit; itself in turn being chased by my dog, "Bull."

Meanwhile, the lion continued dragging me towards the neighboring Metsimetsi Spruit. I was dragged along on my back, being held by the right shoulder, and as the lion was walking over me his claws would sometimes rip wounds in my arms. I was wearing a pair of spurs with strong leather straps, and these acted as brakes, scoring deep furrows in the ground over which we travelled. When the "brakes" acted too efficiently, the lion would give an impatient jerk of his great head, which added excruciating pain to my shoulder, already deeply lacerated by the powerful teeth.

I certainly was in a position to disagree emphatically with Dr. Livingstone's theory, based on his own personal experience, that the resulting shock from the bite of a large carnivorous animal so numbs the nerves that it deadens all pain; for, in my own case, I was conscious of great physical agony; and in addition to this was the mental agony as to what the lion would presently do with me; whether he would kill me first or proceed to dine off me while I was still alive!

Of course, in those first few moments I was convinced that it was all over with me and that I had reached the end of my earthly career.

But then, as our painful progress still continued, it suddenly struck me that I might still have my sheath knife! I always carried this attached to my belt on the right side. Unfortunately, the knife did not fit too tightly in its sheath, and on two previous occasions when I had had a spill from my horse while galloping after game during the Boer War, it had fallen out. It seemed almost too much to expect that it could still be safely there after the recent rough episodes.

It took me some time to work my left hand round my back as the lion was dragging me over the ground, but eventually I reached the sheath, and, to my indescribable joy, the knife was still there! I secured it, and wondered where best first to stab the lion. It flashed through my mind that, many years ago, I had read in a magazine or newspaper that if you hit a cat on the nose he must sneeze before doing anything. This particular theory is, of course, incorrect; but at the time I seriously entertained the idea of attempting it, though on second thought I dismissed the notion, deciding that in any case he would just sneeze and pick me up again – this time perhaps in a more vital spot!

I decided finally to stick my knife into his heart, and so I began to feel very cautiously for his shoulder. The task was a difficult and complicated one because, gripped as I was, high up on the right shoulder, my head was pressed right up against the lion's mane, which exuded a strong lion smell (incidentally, he was purring very loudly, something after the fashion of a cat – only on a far louder scale – perhaps in pleasant anticipation of the meal he intended to have) and this necessitated my reaching with my left hand holding the knife across his chest so as to gain access to his left shoulder. Any bungling, in this manoeuvre, would arouse the lion, with instantly fatal results to myself!

However, I managed it successfully, and knowing where his heart was located, I struck him twice, in quick succession, with two back-handed strokes behind the left shoulder. The lion let out a furious roar, and I desperately struck him again; this time upwards into his throat. I think this third thrust severed the jugular vein, as the blood spurted out in a stream all over me. The lion released his hold and slunk off into the darkness. Later I measured the distance, and found that he had dragged me 60 yards. Incidentally, it transpired later that both first thrusts had reached the heart.

T he scene, could anyone have witnessed it, must have been eerie in the extreme as, in the darkness, I staggered to my feet, not realizing how seriously I had wounded the lion whose long-drawn moans resounded nearby. I thought first to frighten him off with the human voice and shouted after him all the names I could think of, couched in the most lurid language. Suddenly I remembered the other lion that had chased my horse. It was more likely that it would fail to catch the horse, once the latter was at a full gallop, and then, what was more probable, it would return to its mate, and find me there, quite unarmed except for my knife – as of course my rifle had been flung into the long grass when I fell off my horse.

At first I thought of setting the grass alight to keep away the second lion; and, getting the match-box from my pocket, I gripped it in my teeth, as of course my right arm was quite useless, not only on account of the wound from the lion's teeth in my shoulder, but also because its claws had torn out some of the tendons about my wrist. I struck a match and put it to the grass, but as there was by now a heavy dew, the grass would not burn – fortunately, of course, as it turned out, else my rifle would have been burnt.

My next idea was to climb into a tree and thus to place myself beyond the lion's reach. There were several trees in the vicinity, but they all had long stems, and with my one arm I was unable to climb them. Presently, however, I located one with a fork near the ground, and after a great deal of trouble I managed to climb into it, reaching a bough some twelve feet from the ground, in which I sat.

I was now commencing to feel very shaky indeed, both as a result of the shock I had sustained, and loss of blood; and what clothes I had left covering me were saturated with blood, both my own and that of the lion, and the effect of the cold night air on the damp clothing considerably added to my discomfort, while my shoulder was still bleeding badly, I realized that I might faint from loss of blood, and fall off the bough on which I was sitting, so I removed my belt and somehow strapped myself to the tree. My thirst was terrible; and I would have offered much for a cup of water. One consoling reflection was that I knew my boys would find me as I was not far from the path.

Meanwhile, I could still occasionally hear the lion I had stabbed grunting and groaning in the darkness, somewhere close by; and presently, resounding eerily over the night air, I heard the long-drawn guttural death-rattle in his throat – and felt a trifle better then as I knew that I had killed him. My satisfaction was short-lived, however, as very soon afterwards approaching rustles in the grass heralded the arrival of the second lion, which as I had surmised, had failed to catch my horse. I heard it approach the spot where I had got to my feet and from there, following my blood-spoor all the time, it advanced to the tree in which I sat.

Arriving at the base of the tree, it reared up against the trunk and seemed to be about to try to climb it. I was overcome with horror at this turn of affairs, as it appeared as if I had got away from one lion, only to be caught by the other. The tree which harbored me was quite easy to climb (had it not been so, I could never have worked my way up to my perch), and most certainly for a determined, hungry lion! In despair I shouted down at the straining brute, whose upward-turned eyes I could momentarily glimpse reflected in the starlight, and this seemed to cause him to hesitate.

Fortunately, just then my faithful dog "Bull" appeared on the scene. Never was I more grateful at the arrival of man or beast! He had evidently discovered that I was no longer on the horse, and was missing, and had come back to find me. I called to him, and encouraged him to go for the lion, which he did in right good heart, barking furiously at it and so distracting its attention that it made a short rush at the plucky dog, who managed to keep his distance.

And so this dreadful night passed on. The lion would leave the tree and I could hear him rustling about in the grass, and then he would return, and the faithful "Bull" would rush at him barking, and chase him off, and so on. Finally he seemed to lie up somewhere in the neighboring bush.

Some considerable time later, perhaps an hour, I heard a most welcome sound: the clatter of tin dishes rattling in a hamper on the head of one of my boys who was at last approaching along the path. In the stillness of the night, one can hear the least sound quite a long way off in the veld. I shouted to him to beware as there was a lion somewhere near.

He asked me what he ought to do and I told him to climb into a tree. I heard a rattling crash, and he dropped the hamper, and then silence for a while. I then asked him if he was up a tree, and whether it was a big one: to which he replied that it was not a tall tree, but that he had no wish to come down and search for a better one as he could already hear the lion rustling in the grass near him! He informed me that the other boys were not so far behind, and I then told him all that had happened – a recital of events, which, to judge by the tone of his comments, did little to reassure him of the pleasantness of his present situation!

After a time, which seemed ages, we heard the little pack of donkeys approaching along the path, and I shouted instructions to the boys to halt where they were, as there was a lion in the grass quite near, and to fire off a few shots to scare him. This they did, then as they approached to the tree in which I sat, I told them first of all to make a good fire, which did not take long to flare up, as some form of protection in case the lion returned; and then they assisted me down from the tree. It was a painful and laborious business, as I was very stiff and sore from my wounds, and I found the descent very much harder than the ascent.

The first question I asked my boys was whether they had any water in the calabash, which they always carried with them. They replied that it was empty, and so the only thing for us to do was to set out for the next waterhole, which was about six miles farther ahead. Before leaving, they searched unsuccessfully for my rifle in the long grass. To arm myself I took one of the boys' *assegais*, and then, with the donkeys, we set forth.

Before leaving the place we took some firebrands from the fire and threw them into the veld in the direction where the lion had disappeared; nonetheless, he followed us for a long way, and we could hear him now this side of the path, now that; but we had three dogs with us now, and they barked at him, successfully keeping him off.

At last we came to one of my old pickets of the Steinacker days where the huts were still standing. Here, formerly, there had always been a large pool of water, so I sent two of the boys with the canvas nosebag, which was the only utensil we took for carrying water. My disappointment can be measured when they returned to report that the pool was dry, for you must remember that not a drop had passed my lips since the previous day.

I said that I must have water, or I would die, and told them to take a candle from among my baggage, place it in a broken bottle and with this rough lantern to go and search for water. They were two good natives, and off they set once more. They seemed to be away for hours, but when they did finally return, they had the nosebag half full of muddy fluid; and this they set on the ground in front of me. It was pretty filthy-looking stuff; still it was water; and I knelt down beside it and drank until I could drink no more – leaving just a little with which they could wash my wounds. They proved to be too awkward and clumsy over the latter job, however, and after a few minutes I could bear it no longer, and ordered the boys to desist. Actually the wounds received no dressing of any kind (I could not see the largest wound, which was on my back) until I reached Komatipoort – four days later!

# AFRICA

I then told the boys to unroll the blankets so that I could lie down. My arm was so painful that I instructed them to strap it to one of the poles in the roof of the hut, thinking thereby to ease the pain, but it did no good, and afterwards I had it undone again. I need hardly add that there was no sleep for me that night, and next morning I was in a raging fever; and though I had walked six miles on the previous evening, I was now unable to walk – or even stand.

We remained in the camp that day and I sent the boys back to skin the dead lion. I instructed them to return to the tree in which they had found me, follow my blood-spoor for a short distance when they came to the place where I had stabbed the lion, and then to follow its blood-spoor for a short distance when they would find its carcass. I could observe that they were a bit dubious about the reality of my having actually killed the lion (though they had politely refrained from hinting their skepticism) as it was an unheard of thing for a man to kill a lion with a knife.

All my orders were obeyed, and in due course they returned with the skin, skull, and some of the meat, and the heart to show me where I had pierced it with the knife. They also brought with them my horse, which had later returned to the scene of the accident. It is strange that the horse should have returned, after the terrible fright it had sustained, but I put this down to the companionship between horse and man in the veld. The bridle was broken, but the saddle was intact; in fact, I am using the same saddle today, forty years later! The boys brought the horse to the door of my hut where I crawled to see him. He was badly clawed on the hindquarters, and we rubbed a little salt into the wound (I should have done the same to mine at the time) and this certainly seemed to stop septic poisoning setting in as a result of the lion's claws. The horse recovered completely, but, though it was a valuable animal – being salted – and a good shooting horse, he was of no further use to me afterwards as he remained so nervous that the sight of a mere buck in the veld was sufficient to make him attempt to bolt. I was obliged therefore, to part with him – much to my regret.

My boys told me that the best treatment for the wounds caused by the lion was to bathe them in the soup formed as a result of boiling its skull, but I remarked that though this treatment might prove effective with natives, it would not be suitable for a white man.

I knew that there were some native kraals not more than four miles away, so sent one boy off to commandeer assistance in order that I could be carried by *machila*, in relays of four bearers, to Komatipoort. Having collected the necessary number of natives, I instructed them how to make the *machila* with blankets, and early in the morning we set out on a five days march to Komati.

My wounds now became septic, I had fever, and was in great pain. I could, of course, eat nothing and took only water, which I consumed in great quantities: two of the natives being occupied solely in carrying it in calabashes, which they replenished whenever we passed any. By the time we finally reached Komatipoort my arm and shoulder were swollen to enormous size, and were smelling so badly that I had to lie with my face turned the other way.

On my arrival at Komati, Dr. Greeves attended me, but he had no morphia to deaden the pain which by now was excruciating. Next day my friend W. Dickson accompanied me by train to Barberton Hospital, where I received every care and attention.

I remained on my back for many weeks, and at one period the doctor despaired of my life. Once again, however, a sound constitution saw me through, and although I have never since had the full use of my right arm, I consider myself exceedingly fortunate in not having lost it altogether. As it is, I can still, with difficulty, lift it high enough to pull the trigger! After some months I was able to return to M'timba to continue my duties. I once again began to hunt lions; and as I had an old score to wipe out, I think I did so with interest! The chief souvenirs of my grim adventure, the skin of the lion, skull, and the knife concerned (the latter has never been used since) are preserved in my house, and they have all been photographed many times.

The faithful and plucky dog "Bull," who played a great part in preventing the other lion from climbing the tree and pulling me down, was eventually killed in combat with a baboon, though the baboon also died as a result of the fight. The old bitch "Fly," after presenting me with several good litters of puppies, was finally killed by a leopard. Each of them, in common with many other unrecorded dogs and horses – faithful and staunch companions of the men in the veld – played their part in the achievement of the present-day world famous Kruger National Park, and all of them deserve their small tribute.

*Wolhuter's saga is reprinted courtesy of Jim Rikhoff, publisher of Amwell Press, which published the story in its 1990 book,* Cats! Tales of Hunting Cheetah, Lion, Leopard, Cougar, Tiger & Jaguar.

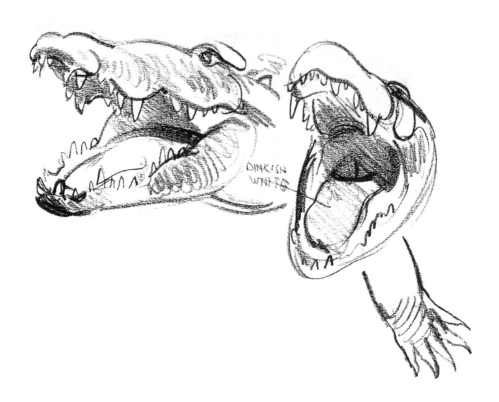

# ATTACKED
## BY A CROCODILE

*Africa's greatest storyteller recalls the life-and-death struggle
of four men against a giant crocodile.*

*By Peter Capstick*

The rasping metallic whine of Christmas beetles saturated the hot, still air at midday of November 21st, 1976, the shrill sound blending with the oily, watery roll at the head of the pool of the Sabi River in South Africa's Kruger National Park. The smoke of barbecue fires paled the lances of sunlight through the riverine bush as the chatter of relaxed Park staff paused to hear the thump and roar of an approaching ranger's bush vehicle. In a swirl of hanging red dust, rangers Tom Yssel and Louis Olivier got out and walked over to the party, which included the families of Park helicopter pilots Hans Kolver and Dickie Kaiser. They had been studying for an exam they had to take the next day, but the summer scorch of the Lowveld changed their minds and they decided to join their friends for an easy afternoon. *That* it would not be.

Frans Laubscher, the Kruger's chief engineer, was also there, fishing across the river from a wide stone outcrop while his wife and family got the low coals ready for *boerewors* sausages and beef. Tom and Louis decided to wade out and see how he was doing while the food was grilling, and as they splashed through the shallows at the side of the pool, it suddenly came to Tom that he had forgotten to strap on his constant companion, a Ruger .357 revolver. Curiously, Louis had also forgotten his sheath knife. A deadly mistake on both parts . . .

At a shout that *skoff* was ready, Frans reeled in and came over to the two rangers. Louis led the way back, followed by Tom and Frans, still fussing with his fishing rod. Pausing, Louis let Tom pass him and waited for Frans to come up. As Louis opened his mouth to speak, there was a depth charge of bursting water, a dull flash of something gigantic and a searing scream from Tom froze the area into shock.

*Damnit*, thought Louis, *Tom shouldn't play the bloody fool like that!* Only Tom wasn't kidding. He had been grabbed by 16 feet of crocodile, his lower right leg crushed between the thick, rounded teeth. A low, bloody wake spread as the onlookers gasped in terror, the huge croc effortlessly swimming into the deeper water of the pool with Tom as helpless as a rag doll.

Perhaps it was Tom's face that prompted Louis; that look of utter agony and death that still haunts him. Louis' brain shifted into that frozen, savage clarity of combat and he threw himself in a half-dive straight at the giant croc. Pushing below it, he tried to grasp it around the body, but it was far too large. Finding the bottom under his feet, he struggled to slow it, as it swam with the inexorable power of its 2,000 pounds. His bare feet bloodied by the sharp river rocks, he surfaced, and in the second he drew in a sweet, new gasp of air, he saw that the croc had moved his terrible bite up to Tom's thigh.

Tom Yssel was wrapped around the croc's head, clinging with every reserve of his strength to prevent the croc from ripping off his leg. Despite his agony, he reflexively gulped air every time his head was clear of the surface. Beneath him, at the croc's belly, Louis had grabbed a rear leg in a desperate bid to keep the killer from reaching deep water. Incredibly, with the raw power of desperation, Louis managed to change the angle of the huge eating machine a few degrees towards a sand bar and away from the dark depths of the pool. Almost certainly, this success prevented Tom's being drowned immediately.

In the oxygen-starved brain of Louis Olivier, there suddenly bloomed the realization that there was a small knife in his rear pants pocket. Holding the now thrashing, lashing croc with one hand, he managed to get it free and opened the 2½-inch blade with his teeth! Pressing it against the croc's stomach, he tried to "zip it open." As he tried to shove the steel in, there was a small *twink!* and the blade broke off at the handle.

Berserk with fear, anger and frustration, Olivier actually then pulled himself onto the croc's back and attacked it with his bare fists, smashing away until his knuckles and hands were a mass of raw flesh from the armored head and back. Still punching with all his strength, Louis Olivier and his best friend disappeared under the surface as the croc submerged.

In the mad thrashing and twisting, Louis lost his grip. A thump from the giant's tail knocked him over and over, finally reaching the surface as he almost passed out. When he cleared his vision he was astonished to see Hans Kolver on top of the croc, swinging insanely with his fists at the croc's head.

Hans, who could see only the croc with his jaws set on Tom, had known that Tom was beyond help. Yet, he couldn't let him die without knowing that his friends had tried to help. He jumped straight for the animal's head! Incredibly, Tom was still conscious and had the presence of mind to scream to Hans, "Go for the goddam eyes!" Hans did. So large was the head that Tom had been unable to reach them himself.

With a savage tear, Hans dug at the slit-pupils and knew he was getting the reptile's attention. It exploded in a flurry of agony, shaking Tom above the water like a heron with a small fish in its bill. Even the horrified families on the bank heard the loud, soggy *snap!* as Tom's thigh was broken. The croc then slid below the surface again, but by now, Louis was back in the battle.

Somehow Louis Olivier got under the croc's head and, with a huge burst of adrenalin, forced it and Tom's mangled body clear of the water. Tom even had a chance to take another breath and croak his thanks through his agony.

Louis was at this point incoherent with rage, actually believing that he could kill the crocodile with his own hands, and this an animal that can and has dragged full-grown rhinos inexorably to a watery death. He tried to grab it in a bear hug again, but it was far too large. Grabbing a hind leg, he tried to drag it to the bank, but the irresistible smash of the great tail knocked him almost senseless yards away.

While all this was going on, Hans was still thumping the skull and trying to rip the eyes out. He was hurting the croc, too, as it flipped and reared each time the finger dug deep. Had Tom not been so tightly wrapped around the snout, his leg would have certainly been torn off.

Louis, half-dazed, realized that he was no match for the croc barehanded. A weapon! Where? He staggered out of the pool and made it to his car. A chill hit him as he realized that he had not brought his knife nor had Tom thought to strap on the .357 Magnum. Forgetting that any cookout is stiff with butcher knives, he weaved back to the bank and jumped in empty-handed!

Somehow, the croc had surfaced beneath an overhanging tree at the pool's edge and Tom had grabbed the branches in a death grip. To everybody's increasing horror, the croc was now holding him clamped across the stomach, the terrible wound pumping blood in a swirling cloud that billowed downstream. As Tom hung between the jaws and the branches, Hans strained with all his might to keep the huge, tooth-studded head up. Tom, almost dead from shock and loss of blood muttered that he would see Hans "on the other side." Hans snapped at him to quit that kind of talk, but Tom could not have had much hope. Nearly 15 minutes had gone by since he was attacked.

# AFRICA

Back at the scene, Louis scrambled up the bank, grabbed a stout branch and dangled his legs in front of Tom, yelling for him to grab on. With the help of Dickie Kaiser, who was now thoroughly involved, Louis had Kaiser hold him under the arms as they tried to literally rip Tom free from the jaws of the croc, which may have been partially blinded by now. With each tug, the terrible teeth tore deeper into Tom's midriff.

Something seemed to give and the men on the bank thought they might be winning. But, it was Hans, back underneath the croc, killing himself trying to lift it. Of course, it was not possible and the croc began to gain, the branches being torn through Louis' bleeding hands as he and Dickie were inexorably drawn down the bank.

Dickie Kaiser's wife, Corrie, ran up with a small one-handed gardening shovel and put it into Louis' hand. He slipped into the river next to the croc's head and tried a slash at the eyes. But, Hans thought he was passing it to him and stuck out his hand. The tool flipped off his knuckles and sand to the bottom of the pool.

The battle for Tom Yssel's life continued. The croc would not let him go nor would Tom's friends give him up. They tried everything, including suffocation by sticking fingers into the creature's nostrils, but it was hopeless. Even worse, the croc, with frightening speed would sometimes release Tom and slash at one of them, only to again grab Tom before he could be pulled free. Each new bite opened huge wounds and tatters of intestines fluttered in the pink current. Tom Yssel was dying in a hurry.

Knowing that Tom was almost gone, the others decided on one more attack on the croc's eyes. As Tom tensed for the awful shaking of the croc's head, there was a lighting surge of power and teeth as the croc released Yssel and lunged at Hans! By reflex, he crossed his arms before his chest, but the croc snapped down on his wrist, crushing it like dry spaghetti. As Hans turned away, he was then caught by the upper arm, tearing off much of his bicep. The front teeth held him as surely as they had Tom.

Next to Hans, Tom was chest-deep in the bloody water, balanced on one leg and trying to keep his insides from becoming his outsides. Hyped on adrenalin, he desperately wanted to help Hans, but thought better of it when he noticed with no small interest that one of his feet was facing backwards! Realizing that the stream of blood downstream would likely bring reinforcements for the croc, he started for the bank.

Hans had, probably more by good luck than design, managed to get a firm thumb grip on the croc's eye socket. This enabled him to turn with the spinning animal as it tried to tear his arm off. As he struggled, Corrie Kaiser arrived again, this time with more substantial armaments in the form of a butcher knife. Louis Olivier got hold of it and waded over to Hans and the croc. Carefully, he felt for the eye not containing Hans' thumb and with all his strength shoved the steel up to the hilt. The croc quivered, released Hans and sculled off to deep water.

Chest deep in bloody water, the three men realized that a mass attack could happen any second. Hans, despite his own terrible bites, almost literally threw Tom up the bank into the hands of Louis and the rest of the party. He then took what he called "the longest walk of my life" – about 20 yards through the gore-stained water to where he could climb to safety.

Louis, at this point, was overcome with anger. Incredibly, he waded back into the river with the butcher knife, the blade bent into a U from impact with the croc's skull, and stood screaming for the croc to dare come and get him. Happily, there were no takers. After a few moments, he almost collapsed and waded back to shore to help load up Tom Yssel for his trip to the stitchery.

T om's right thigh bone was completely bitten in half and he drifted between life and death for many weeks at Nelspruit Hospital, where he had been flown by helicopter. He was so weak, in fact, that the doctors dared not take off his leg. Most of his wounds became terribly infected from the croc's teeth, but thanks to then-new miracle drugs, when I spoke with him at Pretoriuskop, his park headquarters last July, he was in fine fettle despite an obvious limp.

The croc fared not so well and was executed the next day by a ranger. He was five meters long, which makes about 16½ feet. This is a lot of crocodile, especially if it is biting you.

Both Louis Olivier and Hans Kolver were later awarded the Volraad Woltemade decoration, the highest civilian award for valor in South Africa, equivalent to Britain's George Medal.

I can think of only one comment to reference this heroic and grisly tale, and it was made by PH Gordon Cundill after we were charged by a bull hippo: "Africa's a great place," said he, sliding the safety back on his .375 H & H, "but don't made any mistakes . . ."

# LEOPARD IN OUR LAP

*The Kalahari is one of the most hostile places on earth, where water is so scarce that predators rely on fluids of their prey to survive. It's also known for unusually aggressive leopards that are prone to attack . . .*

*By Thomas P. Aplin*

W hen our family of five set out on our hunting safari in Africa, we were prepared for a great adventure. Although we knew Africa could be a dangerous place, we weren't too apprehensive because we felt secure in the hands of our two professional hunter guides. Besides, Mom, Dad and I had been on safari before, and we thought we knew what was in store for us.

We had come to Botswana to experience some of the last truly wild regions of Africa, and to hunt leopard, a prize that eluded us on our earlier safari. Mom, my 23-year-old sister Jennifer and 19-year-old brother Reese were here to witness the spectacle of beautiful landscapes, wild animals and the excitement of the chase. Dad and I would do the hunting, while the rest of the family observed from a safe distance. At least that was the plan.

# AFRICA

The Kalahari Desert is one of the least hospitable places on earth. The vast bush country is not typical desert – there are plenty of trees and hiding places – but no permanent water. The numerous dry lake beds, or pans, contain water only during the rainy season, so the hardy carnivores of the desert rely on the fluids of their prey to survive. It is a difficult life, and the leopards that live there are unusually aggressive. We had been told that Kalahari leopards sometimes charge the hunter – a thrill that shouldn't be missed.

The Kalahari is also unique because it's one of the only places in Africa where leopards can be tracked on foot. The typical method is to place a bait high in a tree, then wait silently in a blind, sometimes for hours, hoping a leopard will appear. But the sandy soil and sparse undergrowth in the Kalahari makes tracking possible, which appealed to us because it promised an active hunt. The trackers were native bushmen who could trail a leopard for hours, without food or water, never losing their way in the wilderness.

Our plan was to set out in different directions each day. Dad's professional hunter was Jeff Rann, an American who learned to hunt in Africa as a boy. Jeff has hunted in Botswana extensively and is one of the best in the business. My PH, Peter Hepburn, has lived in Africa all his life, and his understated manner and British accent evoke memories of those great hunters of the past. We had hired Chip Payne, a videographer already stationed in Botswana, to film our safari. But when we arrived in camp after two long days of travel, we learned that Chip had recently broken his hand and that his cast made it impossible for him to operate his camera. It appeared that our memories of the trip would not be captured on film.

We had barely settled into camp the first evening when Jeff and Dad found a fresh leopard kill. Since it was nearly dusk, we decided to return early the next morning, hoping to pick up a fresh track. Since we had only one leopard tag between us, I decided to join Dad on the leopard hunt. Even though I wouldn't be stalking the animal myself, I didn't want to miss out on the excitement. After an anxious night's sleep, our entire entourage set off in the Land Cruisers on a crisp, cloudless, winter morning.

Less than an hour into the hunt, the haunting eyes of a half-eaten springbok peered at us from the fork of a tree some 20 feet off the ground. Leopard kills are almost always found high up in trees, hidden from marauding hyenas and the ever-present vultures. We felt lucky.

This leopard had returned to feed during the night. Hopefully, with a full belly, it had not gone far. Though leopards like to find a shady place to rest during the heat of the day, we knew the cat would sense our presence long before we saw it and would be on the move. A leopard's stamina is not great, so if pressed hard enough, we should eventually overtake him.

The morning gave way to afternoon and the desert air grew hot. I removed my hunting jacket, exposing bare arms. Though I didn't pay attention at the time, Reese did not remove his jacket. Our Land Cruiser was open in the back, and Reese and I sat on a bench behind the cab, surrounded by a steel roll bar. Chip and two of the trackers kept us company. My rifle, a pre-1964 Model 70, was secured by bungee cords on the gun rack in front of us, its scope covered to protect it from the thick Kalahari dust. I did not plan on firing my rifle that day, but as a precaution, I kept it fully loaded with four bullets, one in the chamber.

As the day wore on, I marveled at the beauty and abundance of wildlife in this parched land. Small herds of kudu, hartebeest and gemsbok were common. Occasionally little bat-eared foxes, always traveling in pairs, would flee at the sound of our vehicles, their large ears giving away their identity even from a distance. We stumbled upon an African wild cat, no larger than a house tabby and similar in appearance – an odd sight so far from civilization. We had no time for photographs, though, stopping only when the trackers needed to confer about the leopard's direction.

Finally, in the middle of the afternoon the trackers got excited. The distance between the pug marks revealed the leopard was running – it was close. I immediately felt my throat go dry and my stomach turn. Reese and I looked at each other and smiled, anticipating the excitement that was to begin. Jeff ordered the trackers onto the trucks so we could move quickly. We couldn't afford to let the leopard increase the distance between us.

Hearing a commotion from the trackers, I saw a blurred form dart between bushes off to our right about a hundred yards. The drivers veered in that direction and we reached a spot where we thought the animal had gone. It seemed to have vanished. Then, without warning, the leopard appeared only 20 yards from our truck. Had I been the shooter, I could have taken it at that moment, but this was Dad's trophy and I wasn't about to spoil his hunt. Besides, shooting from a vehicle is hardly sporting.

Jeff ordered my driver to stay put, so he and Dad could pursue the leopard on foot. Recognizing that too many people in close proximity to a dangerous animal presented an unreasonable risk, Mom and Jennifer were ushered into the cab of our truck. Reese and I remained in the back with Chip and two of the trackers. Peter, meanwhile, volunteered to accompany Jeff and Dad and to operate the video camera. We were determined to get this hunt on film, with or without Chip. I was the only one in our truck with experience in handling a rifle.

Dad and Jeff angled away from us in the direction the trackers thought the leopard had gone. Suddenly, I noticed movement in the bushes to my right and I heard Chip's startled cry, "The leopard's charging! You're gonna have to shoot him!"

*This couldn't be happening*, I thought. The trackers are never wrong, and they were following the leopard in the opposite direction. I tried to discern reality from reason, but sure enough, the leopard was bolting straight for us less than 50 yards away. The determined yellow eyes seemed as big as saucers and they were fixed directly on me! Surely this leopard, angry as it was, would not challenge a truck full of people. Yet here it came, without breaking stride, and I knew that I had better do something – *fast*.

I grabbed my rifle out of the rack, ripped off the scope cover and raised the gun to my shoulder. I peered through the scope to find the leopard, which by this time had closed to within ten yards, but saw nothing. The scope, set to magnify an object by seven times, was totally useless on a moving target at such close range. An open sight would have allowed me to fix on the animal. Instead, with the scope in the way, I could not tell where it was. At the last moment, I held the rifle away from my body and opened both eyes as if firing a shotgun. The leopard was charging right at me, only a split-second away from springing onto the truck. I fired, but nothing happened. I thought I had missed.

In an instant the leopard was upon me. It jumped over the roll bar and onto the bench that I had occupied moments earlier. I was now standing along the side of the truck, and Reese huddled under the bench, desperately trying to stay away from danger. I glimpsed one of the trackers vaulting over the cab and onto the hood. At that moment I was alone, facing 200 pounds of terror bent on making me pay for invading its turf.

I had no opportunity to eject the spent shell or to chamber another round. The rifle was the only thing keeping the leopard from tearing me to pieces, so I thrust the barrel forward and watched it enter the leopard's mouth. Had there been a cartridge in the chamber, it would have been all over. But with one swipe of its big paw, the leopard sent my rifle flying toward the back of the truck.

Now totally defenseless and with only inches separating us, I instinctively barrel-rolled off the side of the truck, right over Reese, and onto the ground. In one motion, I scurried underneath the vehicle, arms draped over my head.

I was praying that the leopard would leap off the truck and scamper away into the bush. Instead, it ran smack into Reese, who had nowhere to go. The big cat pounced, sinking its teeth deep into Reese's arm, while trying to grab his neck with both paws so it could disembowel him with its hind claws, as is the leopard's custom. Mom and Jennifer watched helplessly, horrorstricken, through the rear window.

For what seemed like an eternity, I lay underneath the truck, blind to what was happening to my brother, hoping only that Dad and Jeff had heard the commotion and could reach us in time. I heard noises, but they were muted underneath the truck. Mercifully, I finally heard the gunshot I had been waiting for. Then, after a short silence, another shot. Still, I had no idea what was happening and remained motionless.

Suddenly, I was confronted by a new threat as dangerous as the leopard. Our driver had started the engine. "Oh my God," I thought, as I stared at the rear axle, inches from my face. "I just survived a leopard attack, but now I'm about to be decapitated by the truck!"

I sensed that the driver was going to pull forward, but there was no time to roll out from underneath. I was trapped. Somehow I managed to squirm down into the sandy soil. As the truck passed over me, I felt the axle scrape against my scalp. Thankfully, I was still in one piece, but my refuge was gone, and I had no idea what had become of the leopard. I instinctively began to run, but as I scanned the area for a tree to climb, I heard Dad's voice calling out to me, "Tom, are you alright?" I stopped, looking over my shoulder and saw the leopard lying still on the ground, 20 yards away.

Just then Chip called out, "We have a problem over here." Reese was bent over at the waist, motionless. There was no obvious sign of injury, but his heavy jacket was shredded. When we removed the jacket, we saw his gaping wounds. Bite marks the size of quarters exposed the raw flesh in his arm. The leopard's claws had opened deep, nasty cuts on his knee, hand and neck. Reese needed medical attention, and fast. After applying a tourniquet and securing him in the cab for the long trek back to camp, we were finally able to discuss what had happened.

# AFRICA

Neither Jeff nor Dad had shot the leopard as I had assumed. Chip had watched the attack from his vantage point in the rear of the truck, trying to keep out of harm's way. When my rifle landed at his feet, he grabbed it clumsily with his one good hand and somehow expelled the fired cartridge. From only a few feet away, he watched Reese and the leopard tangle. Reese was literally hanging off the side of the truck, punching the leopard frantically with his free fist as it gnawed on his other arm. It was a desperate struggle, one that Chip knew Reese couldn't win. Chip inched toward them, and when it appeared that Reese and the cat had separated for an instant, he fired. The bullet missed, gouging a big chunk of metal out of the roll bar. A ricocheting bullet could easily have killed anyone in proximity, but luck was with us, and it landed harmlessly. Chip fired a second shot, dispatching the cat. When the leopard dropped to the ground, the driver started the engine to try to get away, not knowing whether the leopard would recover or that I was underneath the truck. Chip, broken hand and all, had saved the day.

I felt terrible. I could have prevented the whole thing if only I had killed the leopard when it charged. How could I have missed at such point-blank range? I cursed the damn scope.

After examining the dead leopard, Jeff walked over to me and said, "You know, you probably saved your brother's life."

I thought it was a bad joke, but then Jeff showed me the bullet hole in the leopard's broken paw, which Jeff said had prevented the cat from getting a stranglehold on Reese. If that paw had not been broken by my shot, Jeff assured me, the leopard could have easily delivered a fatal bite to Reese's neck.

*How ironic*, I thought, *a broken hand had hindered the leopard, but not Chip*. I was glad it wasn't the other way around. I felt a little better, but Reese wasn't out of the woods yet.

Reese never said a word the whole way back to camp, and we feared that he was in shock. We also worried that he might bleed to death or that infection could set in. The victims of leopard maulings often succumb to infection caused by bacteria in the decaying flesh within the claws.

We arrived in camp just before dusk, too late to summon a plane from Maun, the nearest town. A small plane could land on the dry *pan* adjacent to camp, but only during daylight. Reese was going to have to make it through the night.

We carried Reese to the dining table where we treated his wounds. Jeff dipped Q-tip swabs in alcohol and plunged them into Reese's arm. Though he was obviously in a lot of pain, Reese didn't utter a sound, except to ask the trackers to bring the dead leopard into the dining tent so he could see his foe, face to face. I knew at that moment that my little brother had grown up on that makeshift operating table deep in the Kalahari.

At dawn the next morning a small plane arrived with Maun's only doctor. Reese and my parents were whisked away to a hospital in Johannesburg, the nearest treatment center. We learned by radio that night that the prognosis was good and that the doctors expected to release Reese from the hospital after only a few days. What a relief. It mattered little that we would have to return home, aborting our month-long safari after only a few days.

Upon release from the hospital, though, Reese surprised us all by announcing that he wanted to stay and finish the safari. "We came to Africa with a purpose," he said, and "I'm not about to let a small setback like this spoil our trip."

We remained on safari for three more weeks, and Dad and I collected all of the trophies we wanted. The most important one, though, didn't belong to either of us, but to Reese, who now proudly displays the leopard for all to see.

# FACING DEATH

*A professional hunter relives two harrowing encounters with Africa's most dangerous game.*

By Vic Gebhardt

*For all professional hunters in Africa, it's only a matter of time before they come face to face with death, whether in the form of a charging lion or a spitting cobra. After many years of guiding in five African countries, I've certainly had my share of run-ins with dangerous animals. Following are two harrowing encounters, one that I dealt with firsthand and another told to me by one of Botswana's most able trackers.*

aving just enjoyed a week's break with my family in Gaborone, the capital of Botswana, I found myself safely strapped into a light aircraft as it took off from Maun airport and headed toward my luxury safari camp deep in the Okavango Delta.

Below me stretched a blanket of semi-desert, but as the Cessna buzzed through the air, casting a shadow on the ground that looked like a toy plane, the landscape began to change. Soon, isolated tufts of green emerged and the soil, no longer baked into cement, formed into patterns of dusty paths etched out by generations of herds, all leading to mysterious destinations in the distance. And then came the palm trees – tall, thin and seemingly out-of-place in this African environment, yet the living symbol of the delta.

# AFRICA

The pilot pointed to a herd of elephants moving through ribbons of green vegetation – lush reeds and soft rushes lining a maze of ever-widening streams. Soon the water was deep and wide, dark and unfathomable, arranged in winding coils that looked as if they'd been painted on the ground with black oil.

As the water began to dominate the landscape, the animals became more visible. Lechwe, with their ragged red coats, stood knee-deep in the marshes, grazing uninterestedly and ignoring our intrusion, while small clouds of plovers flitted around their feet, seizing bugs disturbed by the herd's movement. I could barely make out the outline of a hippo wallowing in the murky depths of a large pool, its tiny ears protruding above the surface.

The plane began its descent and minutes later we were bouncing down the secluded dirt airstrip. The passenger hatch opened with a creak, and I climbed stiffly from the aircraft. The white heat reflecting from the airstrip hit me in the face, and a cloud of dust disturbed by our landing swirled around us. It was hard to breathe, but I was glad to get this piece of Africa in my lungs, on my skin and in my hair.

There was a faint, musky smell of wilderness in the air, reminding me that I had arrived in the very heart of the Okavango, far from the restrictions and familiarities of civilization. Having accepted this onslaught of heat and dust, I listened to the combined chatter of a thousand tiny birds in a nearby tree and the intermittent screeching of cicadas, altogether an appropriate soundtrack for this African wilderness.

I stood back, staggered by the overwhelming embrace of nature on my senses. The dust, the heat, the smell, the sounds – this was Africa's welcome.

Members of my staff were at the airstrip to welcome me and soon I was escorted back to my "manager's hut" on the outskirts of our camp. A few days later, after readjusting to the trials and tribulations of running a luxury safari camp in the African bush, I was confronted by another unique challenge.

On December 2, 2000, I was informed by one of my bush rangers that he'd encountered a wounded buffalo that had somehow survived a ferocious attack from a pride of lions. How the buffalo had managed to escape was unclear, though once I witnessed a huge bull jump into a river with three lions clinging to its back. The buffalo managed to swim into deeper water, where the lions broke off their attack. Perhaps this buffalo had done the same.

Accompanied by two of my guides, I drove into the bush with our 4x4 vehicle and found the buffalo standing in the shade of a large tree. It had cuts and scratches across the entire length of its back and some of the deeper lacerations were covered with flies and obviously becoming infected.

I immediately radioed the Department of Wildlife in Maun and requested they send someone to put the poor animal out of its misery. They radioed back a few hours later, informing me their entire staff was on Christmas holiday and that as long as I held a Professional Guides license, I should handle the situation as I saw fit.

While I was weighing my chances of successfully disposing of the dangerous animal, the buffalo disappeared and for the next two days, peace and quiet reigned.

Then, early on December 5 another staff member brought me the disheartening news that the wounded buffalo had almost killed a child. To make matters worse, it was now terrorizing all the other villagers. I was also informed that many of my staffers were reluctant to venture into camp until something was done about the situation.

I had no other choice but to deal with the buffalo – and quickly – before someone was killed. I sent out several of my rangers and they followed the bull's tracks to where they found it resting on a small island in the middle of the river.

The only firearm I had in camp was an old .30-06, which was used to discourage troops of marauding baboons. It certainly was not enough gun to bring down a large buffalo, that when injured, is one of the world's most dangerous animals.

Realizing I had no other option, I inspected and loaded the rifle with five rounds of ammunition and then asked for a volunteer to pole my *mokoro* (dugout canoe) across the river to where the buffalo was hiding. As if by some miracle, all my staff suddenly developed some form of ailment or disability, which ruled them out for any physical exertion. Finally, after I had threatened to go alone, my maintenance foreman, KT, who was an accomplished *mokoro* poler, reluctantly volunteered to take me across to the island.

# AFRICA

**B**efore long we had approached to within a hundred yards of the island. I stood up in the precariously unstable craft and shielded my eyes against the glare of the bright sunlight as I scanned the island for any sign of the buffalo. As the canoe drifted silently through the long grass near shore, I suddenly noticed the huge animal lying in a small clearing. He was staring directly at us.

With adrenalin rushing through my veins, I slowly reached down and retrieved the rifle from the bottom of the boat and loaded it. With my heart in my throat, I raised the rifle, aimed at the buffalo's chest and squeezed the trigger.

The recoil almost toppled me out of the boat, but with practiced skill, KT was able to stabilize us. Looking back at the buffalo, I saw to my amazement that it had jumped up and was charging straight toward us. The bullet, which had crashed into its broad chest, seemingly had no effect.

Less than 20 yards away, the buffalo suddenly changed direction and turned broadside to race along the shore. Somehow, by pure instinctive reflex, I managed to reload the rifle, and aiming for a spot just behind the shoulder, I fired again.

The fast-moving beast dropped its head, and enveloped in a small geyser of water, sand, mud and grass, somersaulted through the air and came crashing down with a loud thud. At that moment I was shivering from head to foot, and as I turned to look at my assistant, I was greeted by a mouth frozen in a silent scream and eyes as big as saucers.

As the dust settled, I asked KT if he thought the buffalo was dead or just shamming death. He replied that he did not know and quite frankly, did not care. All he wanted to do was get the hell out of there and return to camp.

I explained that we had to make sure he was dead and the only way to do that was to get closer. KT looked at me as if I was completely mad. He informed me that I could do whatever I wished, but that there was no way he was going anywhere near the beast.

After considerable coaxing, KT did agree to maneuver the boat closer so I could wade ashore and somehow establish whether the buffalo was dead. I stepped from the *mokoro* and cautiously approached the buffalo, the rifle in one hand and the long boat pole in the other. Seeing how I was struggling to carry both implements, KT's pride got the better of him and he reluctantly came to my aid.

I asked him to prod the buffalo with the pole while I stood ready with the rifle. Shaking nervously, he extended his arm and the long pole to its maximum and with his body turned toward the waiting boat, he closed his eyes, uttered a silent prayer and gave the buffalo a light prod . . . then a second, harder push. Feeling a little braver, I hurled a large clod of earth at the buffalo's head. The animal remained motionless. Cautiously I walked around to the front of the bull and after looking closely for any signs of life, I announced to my brave assistant that this buffalo would never again terrorize the villagers.

With a sigh of relief I reached for my mobile radio, contacted our camp, and asked them to notify the villagers that there was now an ample supply of fresh meat. I then turned to KT, gave him a big hug, and thanked him for his most valuable help. We returned to a hero's welcome at camp, and within a few hours, everyone in the village was enjoying delicious buffalo steaks.

When slaughtering the animal, the villagers found that my second bullet had passed right through the buffalo's heart. A bloody good shot, I claimed. A bloody lucky shot, claimed the villagers.

A while later, as I reflected on what could have happened if the buffalo had continued its charge, an involuntary shudder went through my body, and I reached for a bottle of spirits to calm my nerves. It was then that my mind drifted back to a previous incident that had almost cost the life of one of my senior rangers.

✿    ✿    ✿

Two years previously, Amos, one of Botswana's most experienced trackers, had survived a horrific attack by a wounded lion. Prior to joining our safari company, Amos had been the chief tracker for a well-known professional hunter in the Okavango. Only after much pleading and persuasion on my part did he agree to relate his terrifying, if not miraculous, escape from the jaws of death.

It was late afternoon, deep in the African bush when Amos and his tracking partner, Sanga, learned that a visiting hunter had wounded a large male lion. The animal had disappeared into dense patch of bush, and despite a long and cautious search by the PH and the trackers, it remained at large. Since the light was falling rapidly, they decided to resume their search at first light the next day.

Shortly after daybreak Amos and his fellow trackers were driven to where they'd last seen the lion, and soon found where the big cat had spent a very uncomfortable night. The grass and shrubs in the area were flattened and blood was everywhere.

# AFRICA

At this point everyone's nerves were as taut as a bow-string, knowing the lion might charge from its hiding place at any second. Amos and the other tracker kept their eyes glued to the ground, looking for any telltale signs of the lion's movements.

The PH and his client walked slightly behind and on either side of the trackers as they slipped into the thick undergrowth. As they entered a small clearing, both trackers stopped dead in their tracks as a big Egyptian cobra raised its deadly hooded head and challenged them to take a step closer. After a few minutes in this threatening pose, the reptile lost interest and slithered away into a thicket.

For many African people, seeing a deadly snake is a bad omen, and one can only imagine the turmoil that was raging in Amos' head. He knew that it was his duty to follow the lion, but after encountering the cobra, he knew that doing so was to defy the gods.

Reluctantly, and with a heavy heart, Amos continued the pursuit. After several minutes he stopped, and with a shaking finger pointed toward a dense portion of the bush ahead. It was then that everyone saw the two amber eyes, narrowed to thin slits of sheer hatred.

With a roar that made the earth tremble, the huge killing machine charged from cover toward the trackers. Both hunters fired almost simultaneously, but the lion kept coming, knocking one of them to the ground as he charged past.

Suddenly there was a loud scream of agony, and they all turned to see the lion savagely clawing Amos, with his powerful jaws clamped onto the tracker's skull. The PH rushed forward and was about to fire into the lion's head when the enraged beast jumped off Amos and disappeared into the bush.

At that point Amos was lying motionless, face down in the sand, and when his colleagues turned him over, they were shocked to see that the top part of his head was badly torn and completely covered in blood. Fortunately, he soon regained consciousness, and after receiving emergency first aid treatment, Amos was rushed to a nearby landing strip where a light aircraft, which had been summoned by radio, flew him to the Maun hospital.

The hunters then had the unenviable task of returning to the scene and making sure the severely wounded lion was put out of its misery. They followed fresh blood spoor in the safari vehicle until Sanga, the other tracker, spotted the animal lying in the thick grass. As the two hunters stood to get a clear shot, the lion came charging toward them.

Two more shots were fired, but still it came. With its last remaining ounce of energy, the lion tried to jump onto the hood of the vehicle. Another bullet at point-blank range knocked the animal off the hood, and as it turned to run, another shot finally killed it.

Altogether, the lion had absorbed ten bullets from high-powered rifles before succumbing. It was one cat that had certainly used up all of its nine lives. On close examination, the hunters found that one of the earlier bullets had shattered the lion's lower jaw. This explained why it did not crush Amos' skull when it had his head in its powerful jaws.

Amos spent almost four weeks in the hospital and eventually made a full recovery from his gruesome wounds, though the emotional and psychological scars of his terrifying ordeal remain with him to this day.

# CONGO BONGO

*Charged by elephants, buffalo and hippo. Imperiled by snakes,
crocs, pitfalls, cannibals and trigger-happy rebels –
all in oppressive jungle heat. The amazing story
of the single-most difficult hunt ever made.*

*By Ken Kirkeby*

**M**ost of us are familiar with the name Jack Atcheson. His company, Jack Atcheson & Sons, has served as consultant and booking agent to more than 15,000 sportsmen worldwide. With a lifelong dedication to hunting that borders on fanaticism, Jack has pursued big game in some of the most remote corners of the earth. Many of his adventures have been truly remarkable, but the one he calls his wildest ever was his five-week safari for bongo and elephant in 1971.

Formerly the Belgian Congo, Zaire is one of Africa's largest countries, about one-fourth the size of the U.S. Back then, it would have been an understatement to say conditions in the central African nation were primitive. Even now, with new roads and oil exploration, many areas remain as they have for the past 200 years. During Jack's trip, the Congo was still in the wake of a bloody civil war. Leftover landmines dotted the roads, tribal fighting continued, and deep in the bush, many natives practiced cannibalism.

# AFRICA

Jack and fellow hunter Larry Hammer were met in Asiro by safari operator Arnold Callins, a former mercenary who a few years earlier had been wounded by four arrows and left for dead. Since the weather was hot and dry, Jack and Larry agreed to hunt elephants and buffalo while waiting for rain to improve tracking conditions. Bongo, their interpreter explained, are impossible to track in the dense forest except when the ground is damp.

They were also told that some excellent elephants had been taken by earlier clients, but to find a really big tusker, the safari would have to venture deep into largely unexplored forest along the border of the Central African Republic.

Crossing the Uele River on a pontoon raft of old canoes, the group arrived at a mission called Anvo, where 20 nuns and 24 priests had been hacked to death by local chieftains four years earlier.

One of the survivors, a Catholic nun, described the horrifying incident and pointed out a few nearby men who had participated in the slaughter. The nun explained the men had only been acting on orders from the witch doctor and doing what seemed right to them. She assured the hunters that everything was quiet now, but from that day on Jack always kept his rifle loaded.

The next day the group visited Chief Suffa, who had actually helped stop the Anvo massacre. Hoping to get his permission to hunt, they found the chief holding court in a thatched hut, surrounded by nervous natives and the newest of his 15 wives. The chief was busy settling some squabbles and meting out punishments to thieves. After obtaining his approval, Jack's group elected to depart before the sentences were administered (one man was scheduled to lose a hand for stealing).

In the weeks to come, the Americans would be continually amazed at how each village would already be anticipating their arrival. This was due to the system of drum communication between settlements. Wherever they traveled they could usually hear drums beating in the distance, day and night.

The only water available to the safari was in creeks, and while it appeared clear, it had to be boiled and purified. Dereck McCloud, Jack's PH, refused to drink boiled water and soon became ill (after the safari, doctors discovered the man's intestines were riddled with parasitic worms). Dereck's illness would result in Jack hunting alone much of the time, with only a tracker or two to assist him.

The group soon arrived at their hunting camp, a site Jack remembers as one of the most beautiful he'd ever seen. The spot had been swept clean to deny cover to poisonous snakes and biting insects. While there were few mosquitoes, the hunters did encounter army ants, sometimes in columns ten feet wide. Large bats and snakes were also numerous; one native tried to sell the hunters a 28-foot python skin.

The trackers chose to hunt dense, streamside thickets where elephants and buffalo had ample amounts of food and cover. A number of women and children who had ventured too close to the rivers had turned up missing, so the men were constantly on the lookout for crocs and hippos.

This was uncharted wilderness – definitely not a good place to become sick or injured. There was no plane to call in and no radio to call on. The camp did have a snakebite kit, but if someone was struck, they would have to positively identify the reptile so the correct antidote – and the antidote for the antidote, if needed – could be administered. Jack and Larry agreed that if bitten, they would most likely die, so wherever they went they tried to follow in the footsteps of a tracker.

Although the trackers and local tribesmen appeared friendly, many still ate human flesh. Chief Suffa had joked that white flesh was probably as relished by local tribesmen as it would be to crocodiles. While everyone was laughing at the chief's comment, Jack casually buttoned up his shirt to hide his pale skin.

The men observed a variety of monkeys and smaller animals, but the natives had decimated the game close by the settlements. The group did find tracks of elephant and buffalo, but other big game was scarce, so they decided to venture farther afield.

The hunters visited another village to obtain permission and to hire guides, and after Jack took several Polaroid snapshots of the chief and his wife, everything was set. Once again pictures proved better than money.

The new area was just as thickly vegetated, but now the group had to watch out for game pits, each lined with sharp bamboo spikes. The trackers soon found fresh elephant sign leading into thick, jungle bottoms where the men followed tunnel-like runways formed by elephants and hippos. Tracks were everywhere, but the going was incredibly dangerous. In this dense growth they could not detect the big animals until they had virtually stumbled onto them. What made matters worse is that many of the elephants had been wounded in the past by muskets and arrows, and once they detected a human, they were more apt to charge than run away.

Hoping to drive a herd of elephants toward Larry, Jack and his PH were edging quietly through the bush when they heard deep stomach rumblings. A bull elephant stood less than ten feet ahead, testing the air with his trunk, his ears fanned. Suddenly, there was a great crashing as 30 or 40 of the huge animals stampeded away.

The tracker explained that the nearest bull's tusks were not very large, so they elected to follow a herd of red buffalo that had ran off with the elephants. The men trailed the buffalo, eventually catching up to them in heavy brush. Jack hit a good bull with his .458 Winchester, but was forced to abandon the blood trail at dark. The next day a tracker found the bull, completely devoured by hyenas and vultures. With no concept of trophy value, he had not bothered to recover the horns!

In the days to come new trackers and porters replaced those from other villages. Each native wore only a breechcloth made from pounded tree bark and carried several spears. All had elaborate tribal marks cut into their faces and bodies, and their teeth were filed to point. Some had never seen a white man.

Near the same area, Jack picked up the tracks of a large elephant and followed him into a dark creek bottom. A strange snake slid through the water only inches from Jack's leg. Drenched from the heat and humidity, his clothes clung to him and he drank continually, doubling the number of Halazone pills each time he filled his canteen with the yellowish water. Dereck's fever persisted, forcing the group to stop and rest often. The going was slow. The men had to place their feet carefully, stepping around or through a maze of long, clinging vines.

Jack's tracker stopped to squat and listen. In sign language he warned of many elephants only 25 feet away. At that instant a wall of small trees began snapping in front of them as the entire herd bore down on the hunters. Dereck and Jack dropped to the ground as the animals thundered past. The charge was over in seconds; luckily, none of the elephants stopped to look for the hunters. As he rose to his feet Jack heard laughter and looked up to see his tracker waving from the safety of a 30-foot tree.

The hunters were also subjected to attacks by much smaller adversaries. Jack had heard stories of army ants eating livestock and even people, and one night he was awakened by a stream of ants crawling over his face and all across the tent floor. On another occasion, while reaching for his waterbag just outside the tent flap, he stepped barefoot into the middle of a column of army ants. The pain from their bites was excruciating.

The PHs suggested another area, so they visited yet another chief who after receiving gifts and having his picture taken, allowed them to hunt where no white men had ever been. Jack hired 20 porters for the 40-mile hike and promised each of them plenty of meat, including elephant meat and intestines, which the natives ate raw.

With no maps to guide them, the hunters thought their position to be in one of the drainages of the Gwanie River. Although they primarily wanted to hunt elephants and bongo, Jack and Larry had to spend more and more time hunting whatever they could find for camp meat. They killed buffalo, waterbuck, warthogs and even a large hippo that charged to within five feet of Jack and Dereck before they stopped him with a volley of well-placed shots. Larry, meanwhile, had to kill a cow elephant that charged him in the thick brush.

Now with enough meat, the Americans had to deal with a new problem. Some of the porters wanted to bring the meat back to their villages to sell. Jack and the PHs insisted they stay and dry it into strips, called biltong. Through the night the Africans talked loudly and looked at the Americans with contempt. Jack slept with his back against a large tree and kept his rifle close. By morning five natives had left, taking much of the meat with them.

The days grew hotter, with the temperature climbing to 120 degrees. Still, they managed to cover about ten miles a day, stopping occasionally to sip water directly from elephant tracks. There were puff adders and other poisonous snakes along the way and crocodiles lurked at every waterhole. While crossing a narrow stream, Larry fell into a deep hole and disappeared from sight. The trackers thought he had been grabbed by a croc, but in seconds Larry popped to the surface and sputtering loudly, quickly swam to shore.

The rains finally arrived, making it easier to track bongo, but worrying the PHs that they would be unable to get the vehicles out. The decision was to made relocate once again. After several days of driving, without a map and in a truck with no brakes, the group reached Dungu where they were able to purchase badly needed supplies from a store owned by Greek merchants.

Here, too, the hunters found grim reminders of the savagery gripping the war-torn country. Just below the bridge into town they noticed several rows of freshly dug graves. An interpreter explained that the makeshift cemetery contained the bodies of 20 nurses who had been gang-raped and slain by rebel soldiers. Some of the same men who had raped the women had helped to bury them – or so they were told.

Two hours farther along brought them to the tiny village of Duro, where they stopped to repair the truck's brakes. The next day, after a late start, the safari set out on a rough, rain-soaked road and it was after midnight before they crossed the Nyeka River and reached their bongo camp.

Though it hadn't been used in a year, the camp was in surprisingly good condition and in a lovely setting. Still, the interpreters continually warned the Americans about hostile natives and to "sleep light." Jack slept on the ground in a corner of the tent with his rifle and pack full of escape gear. Larry was equally watchful, and several times they woke to see a man standing outside their tent or staring at them from behind a tree.

Other problems plagued the safari. The trackers often lied about seeing bongo or tracks simply for the Americans' reward money. Jack suggested he hunt alone, with one good tracker. When he visited the local chief and met Bittee, he knew he had found his man. Friendly and powerfully built, the native had filed teeth and Jack was to learn later that Bittee had consumed human flesh on many occasions. Though he could not speak English, Bittee made himself understood through pantomime, often playing the role of the bongo. One fact was crystal clear, however; Bittee could track an ant across solid rock.

Jack and Bittee hunted the first few days without seeing anything. They followed countless tracks, but each time the bongo would disappear like ghosts. They made a number of game drives, but the animals would circle soundlessly behind them and escape. Once again the hunting was dangerous – snakes and capture pits were everywhere. Witch doctors would confront them and interrogate the trackers, and Jack had to use extreme care not to offend them, as doing so could be fatal.

The brush was thick, the strangulating air hot and humid. The bongo led the men into low, almost impenetrable jungle, where they would soon lose the trail. What made their pursuit even more difficult was Bittee's fear of getting too close to a bongo. The Azande people believe that the animals climb trees and then drop down onto their pursuers, impaling them with their horns. They also believe that bongo meat should never be touched or eaten because it carries leprosy and an evil animal known to pursue and rape women.

Once, while following the tracks of a big bull through a tangled creek bottom, Jack noticed an odd-looking stick only inches from his face. Bittee motioned him to slip off to the side and it was then Jack realized that the twig was actually a highly venomous stick snake.

On their fifth day of tracking bongo, the hunters were edging through the dense undergrowth when suddenly Jack felt a strange sensation, as if being watched. Through his binoculars he saw an eye, a bit of ear and some horn about 30 feet ahead. Jack pointed his rifle at where he thought the shoulder would be and fired a 500-grain solid from his .458. Hit, the bongo raced off through the forest. Jack fired again, with the bullet smashing into a small tree. The animal turned and ran toward the men. At 15 feet, Jack shot a third time and the bongo crashed to the jungle floor. It was a cow, but with exceptionally massive horns and what Jack still calls his greatest trophy ever.

Although the pressure was finally off to kill a bongo, Jack and his companions could not really relax or let down their guard around the natives. While returning to their hut, Larry reported that one of the crew had been strung up and beaten with sticks. They investigated the situation, but were warned by the interpreter not to get involved. The next day they were told the man had died, though they never saw his body. Jack still wonders if he was eaten by his killers.

Jack continued to hunt bongo, right up to the last afternoon of the safari when he shot a bull only 20 feet away. The 500-grain bullet cut a noticeable tunnel through the leaves and branches, hitting the bull between the eyes. The bull had a much larger body than the cow Jack had killed, but its horns were somewhat smaller.

Now that their safari had come to a close, the Americans faced another series of difficult and frustrating moments in their attempts to get out of the country.

After a dangerous incident with some armed and drunken boatmen, the group arrived in Isiro to find their plane seats had been commandeered by the military. Most of the soldiers occupying the town carried automatic weapons and appeared to be drunk. Arnold Callins had already had several run-ins with the military and he was inclined to drive their gear and trophies to Kenya. However, he was hesitant to take Jack and Larry as the trip might involve shooting it out with local factions at the border. A Greek merchant put the hunters in touch with a man who operated a river boat traveling to and from Kinshasa. Problem was, the trip would take 35 days through malaria-infested jungles.

Refusing to spend another month in the country, Jack and Larry pooled their money, a total of $4,000, and bribed the airport manager to get on the plane, leaving their trophies with a Greek merchant. (Their trophies arrived in the U.S. about a year later.)

After landing in Kisangani, Jack was able to find an American "representative" of sorts, a Peace Corps hippie who was distributing communist literature. Reluctantly, the man helped the Americans arrange a flight to Kinshasa, the capital city. Hours later, en route to a hotel in the Kinshasa, the driver told the Americans to remain in their rooms because some rebels were scheduled to be executed that day. Sure enough, they were.

The next morning Jack and Larry were able to catch a flight to Spain, though their problems were still not over. Somewhere over North Africa the aircraft made an unscheduled landing at a remote airstrip where all male passengers were thoroughly searched at gunpoint. Finding nothing, the police officer apologized, shook hands with each passenger, then passed around free Cokes. Jack and Larry reboarded and were relieved to finally land in Madrid.

Although Jack Atcheson would continue to make exploratory hunting trips around the globe, he remembers his Congo hunt as far-and-away his most difficult and dangerous adventure. For 36 days he hunted hard, enduring insufferable conditions, to take one of the world's great trophies. And, in Jack's words, he had seen the end of ancient Africa.

*The complete story of Jack Atcheson's bongo safari has been published in* Hunting Adventures Worldwide, *in which the author relives more than 25 expeditions around the world, including Jack O'Connor's last hunt, for Montana whitetails in 1977.*

# GORED!

*It's the African hunter's worst nightmare:*
*A misfire or dud in the middle of an animal's charge.*

*By Peter Capstick*

*In* The Last Ivory Hunter, *Peter Capstick documents the fascinating adventures of Walter Walker Johnson, perhaps the last commercial hunter of elephants, and certainly, one of the greatest living legends in all of Africa. The following includes most of the chapter entitled "Gored," in which Johnson shares his most harrowing encounters with Cape buffalo.*

The buff, an extremely dangerous animal that is mighty hard to kill straight off, is the only one of the Big Five that actually got Wally in all his hunting life. That's if you blackball the Gaboon viper from the Big Five club (elephant, buff, lion, leopard, rhino . . . the classic man-killers).

Wally has no idea exactly how many buffalo he has shot, but he knows that he killed a great many more buffalo that he did elephant. With some thirteen-hundred bulls to his credit, that would mean something like two thousand buff, what with meat hunting for the mine staff and actual safari work. Now, with so much exposure for so long to such dangerous animals, the odds are outstanding that the pro hunter will eventually get caught.

Wally was – and here's how he remembered it.

# AFRICA

A pretty terrible incident occurred once with some Shangaans who were in the habit of distilling a real stump-blower called *nipa*, which was made from sugar cane: whew! It would really pick you up and feed you to its young! I was out hunting with an American doctor at the time when I got word that one of these Shangaans had been badly gored in the groin by a buffalo. It had come to eat the sugar cane, as buff often did. I asked the doctor if we could try and help the victim, who was in a nearby village headed up by Chief Kanjaan. The doctor readily agreed and we headed straight for the village, together with the messenger who had brought the news.

We reached the village. There was no electricity, and it was already dusk. By the light of my flashlight, the doctor examined the poor guy; he had one hell of a hole in his guts and was in terrible pain. We got one of my gas lamps off the car and the doctor did what he could. He organized hot water and sewed the man up, putting a drain in the wound. He instructed the chief as to what the womenfolk had to do if the man was to have any chance at all of surviving. After powerful shots of this and that and a painkiller that knocked the man right out, we left. The doc confided in me that if ever he had seen a goner, that man was it. Hell, I personally had seen what looked like part of his stomach hanging out of a huge hole in his lower chest!

Well, ten days later this man walked into my camp from his village a few miles away! He told me that he felt just fine, had taken out the stitches and the drain himself, and was completely okay. He thanked us, the doctor in particular, and went on his way to get more cane to brew up more hooch.

The doctor couldn't believe his eyes. "My colleagues back home will never believe this one," he said. "Never!"

While in the area of Chief Kanjaan, I got word on a different occasion of a very bad bull buff near his village that had already killed several people. It may have been the one that gored the man we had fixed up some time before, but I could not be certain. Well, this big bull used to hang out in the long stuff along the riverbank. Chieft Kanjaan himself – not an underling – came to me to ask that I cancel this buff's career, as it was really becoming a menace to his people.

The chief came with us when we went after it, through grass that was easily 15 feet high. I took the hunting vehicle, as I wasn't about to get stuck into a rogue on its turf if I could possibly help it. After a while, we heard what seemed to be the sound of the buff running away, and so I tried to catch up.

Unfortunately, I did.

This thing was huge! It swung around and charged the car, hitting it with a tooth-grinding slam. The client got a shot into it, but I knew I had to put it down before it disappeared, wounded, back into the bundu. I did this and the bull collapsed. But that son-of-a-bitch had hit that car with such force, it had actually lifted the front end well off the ground, meaning that I had something of a patch job before we could get out of there. Anyway, Chief Kanjaan was delighted and I could always count on his cooperation whenever I was in his area and needed any sort of help or advice.

I always loved hunting buffalo and enjoyed taking out Walter, Jr., in the mid-1950s. He was at boarding school in Umtali, Rhodesia, at the time, just across the border from our home at Vila de Manica. He used to bring some of his chums from school if they had a long weekend, and I daresay the kids had the time of their lives in the bush.

One of these youngsters had a little .22 Hornet, which only fired a 45-grain bullet but at decent velocities. Most Americans I had out thought that it was even too light for woodchucks or groundhogs. Well, I reckoned the kid could take a duiker or a steinbuck with that gun, so I told him to bring it along. We all went on a real 'picnic safari' to Moribane, the closest good hunting area to home.

Once there, we settled in and soon ran into a big herd of buffalo. I took Walter, Jr. on a one-hour stalk with his .30-06. I was carrying a .375 with 300-grain bullets. We found a pretty good one and I dropped it, but the whole damned herd started running in our direction; they hadn't caught the wind and were confused by the location of the shot.

Lord above, but the kid with the .22 Hornet took a shot at a buff and astounded the lot of us when it fell stone-dead! He'd hit it, whether by accident or design, right behind the ear, flattening it. Well, maybe it was just a lucky shot, but this story shows how dangerous even a tiny gun can be. Remember, Karamojo Bell killed buff with hyped-up .22s.

On another 'picnic safari' down at Moribane, I took my wife, Lilly, my son and daughter, as well as another family friend and her two children. The kids were keen to take a couple of antelope for *biltong*, dried meat, to eat back at school. I knew the area very well and we camped by a murky water hole about 25 by 30 yards across. Elephant had been drinking there and had really stirred it up. I decided we needed some meat and went out to swat a buffalo, taking Walter, Jr. with me as well as two of his school pals. I nailed one with the .375 and we had to go back to the car to bring in the meat.

Now this was a very hot day and the kids all wanted a swim in this water. In the meanwhile, my men were cutting up the buff on a big canvas sheet, which became so bloody that they soaked it in the water overnight. At dawn, the damn thing was gone! We couldn't figure out who in hell had taken it so we shrugged our shoulders as there was no spoor. When we returned from hunting at around eleven that morning, my wife showed me a huge croc she'd shot just after we'd left. Lilly had used the spare .30-06. It was tremendous. Obviously, this was where the tarpaulin had gone. I should have known better.

That night I plugged a big spotlight into the cigar lighter and picked out the eyes, glowing ruby red in the water, of a least 15 big crocs. My God, but we had been lucky. You can bet that nobody else went swimming in that waterhole afterward.

Like all the dangerous species, there are hundreds of personal stories I could tell you about buffalo; but there is one story in particular that I most definitely will never forget. It sticks in my mind as if it happened yesterday. One of the buggers, in fact, got stuck into me. Literally.

I had two Americans with their wives out to hunt in Mozambique. One of the men was named Gerry Knight, to whom I owe my life. His companion, who may be equally culpable for my survival, was a veterinarian, Al Plechner. The entire party was from the Los Angeles area.

We were out one day early in the safari, and found a very good buff in a herd. One of the men hit it, and the buff went off on its own. Although it was losing a lot of blood, we followed it for over an hour into some of Capstick's famous long grass.

At 20 yards, it jumped up, half invisible. I yelled for the men to fire and both did, as the animal began an immediate charge. I also shot. Now dream of this: One man's magazine floor-plate sprang open, dumping all his cartridges over his shoes, and the other guy had a lock-tight jam! I shot twice more but the buff never faltered, even though I could see my bullets were going into the right spot.

The bull chose me as a target. In an instant, it was on top of me. I stuck the muzzle of my rifle in the crease between the horns and pulled the trigger. Nothing happened!

The next I knew, I was upside down, with my rifle spinning away from the impact. Then, somehow, I was under his damned great belly. I managed to crawl out, as this thing was pretty sick – or should have been – and found myself, through some reflex action, landing on top of its bloody back!

I can clearly remember looking over his horns and seeing my clients and trackers white with fear. One of the trackers had a spare .458 Winchester Magnum and I knew it was stroked with solid 500-grain bullets. One of the clients was shouting for the black with the rifle to shoot. Instantly, I realized that the solid would go right through the buffalo and kill me in the process.

"For God's sake, don't shoot!" I screamed over and over.

But Gerry Knight grabbed the rifle from the man and shot anyway. Rapture of raptures, he hit it in the spine and killed it instantly. The bullet did pass through the bull, missing me by inches. I was able to pull myself off, as everybody else was more in shock than I was.

At that point, I didn't know the extent of my injuries, except that my leg felt odd. I looked down and damned near passed out. There was nothing in my thigh but raw meat with blood pouring over it. It was a hole I could have actually stuck my fist through!

I said, 'Oh hell,' and quickly sat down as the men got their act together and came over to help. They saw what had happened and did what they could for me. We put a tourniquet on the leg and tied it up, slowing down the terrific bleeding. Gerry Knight, the man who shot the buff out from under me, managed to get me on his back. We headed for the car, which was a good hour away at a brisk walk without the impediment of having to carry me. From there, it was another two hours back to camp. By the greatest luck, the buff had missed the femoral artery by a fraction of an inch, or I might have been a goner right there.

Hell, I was incredibly fortunate that Gerry had been able to kill the buff, as it surely would have gored and maybe stomped me again. I really owe my life to Gerry. He was a brave man and was practically on top of that buffalo when he shot and killed it.

Anyway, by the time we got back to the vehicle, I was really in severe pain, as the shock of the wound had worn off. The horn had gone through the back of my left leg and come out the front of the thigh. Gerry or Al drove the vehicle back to camp and I faithfully promise you that every bump was perfect agony.

It happened to be a Sunday, and as soon as we got to camp, they put me to bed and did all they could for me. The veterinarian had some *muti* with me and poured some stuff into the hole to try and stop infection. It largely poured out the far side. I was in such pain that I drank half a bottle of Scotch but certainly didn't get any sleep that night.

The next morning, one of the men figured out the radio and got in a charter that flew me to Umtali, Rhodesia. There, the doctors stitched and patched like on a quilting bee and I lay there for 12 days.

I was an idiot and left too early, despite protests by the doctors. It was early in the safari, and I felt that I had a responsibility to give my clients a good hunt. Anyway, I got back to camp and took them out after elephant, not a good choice at that stage, as it entailed so much walking. I had more stitches than a damned parachute and was still weak from loss of blood. Nevertheless, I went back.

So, off we went for a tusker, my leg heavily bandaged. But after a mile or so, the fool thing tore loose and I could feel the meat squishing in my leg against the bandages as the blood began to seep through. I wanted to go on despite this, but Gerry Knight saw my agony.

"Hell, no," he said. "That's it. You must go back to the hospital and get retacked!"

I took his advice and went back until the leg had healed up a bit. When I got out, a tight bandage helped a great deal. Nonetheless, it was many, many months before I could walk properly again, and I was damned lucky at that.

Gerry Knight, who was an amateur gunsmith, had a look at my rifle, recovered after the goring, and went over it thoroughly to determine why it didn't fire when I stuck it in the buff's face and was backpedaling as it poured down on me. Gerry thoroughly cleaned it and found it quite dirty. The primer of the cartridge was indeed dented, but the round did not go off. Who knows? It worked fine after that, but can you imagine the odds on a triple breakdown of rifles during a buffalo charge? Impossible.

But it happened. Africa.

I t was the only time I ever really got nailed, despite many very close incidents. That scar has been a reminder ever since that, in the African hunting situation, death is only a hair's breadth away.

After Gerry finished polishing up the rifle, I took that same lot of ammo and tried it out. It wouldn't fire, even through the primer was properly indented by the firing pin. Just old, perhaps. I never could figure it out, as the action and barrel were as clean as a mirror after Gerry had finished with them. Maybe just *kismet*. Why I never went into real shock with that goring, I just can't figure. Maybe I'm just an overboiled hyena!

# STAND AND FIGHT

*Moving like a ghost in the dense cover, the wounded lion waited for the moment when he would finally confront his tormentors.*

**Story by David K. Faust**

T here's your lion."

One hundred yards away the lion faced the men. The lay of the land and the high grass made it impossible to see any part of him other than his great head surrounded by a long, blond mane. The lion looked into the sun with heavily lidded and absolutely cold yellow eyes. The sun prevented him from seeing the men. His head moved up and down slightly as he panted. He was more menacing than beautiful.

In front of the lion and ten yards closer to the men, a lioness lay on her back with her legs extended upward, basking. To the lion's left, the hindquarters of another animal, the second female, was visible. Occasionally her tail, tipped with a dark tuft of hair, jerked spasmodically.

# AFRICA

J ack, the amateur hunter, and Wade, the professional, had followed the trio for hours. It had not been a challenging trail and Peter, tracker extraordinaire, had led at a fast walk. The lions were hunting a herd of buffalo and had stampeded their prey three times. They failed to kill and had continued their pursuit into the wind. They had no idea other hunters were about.

Jack stared at the lion. It was not his lion yet. Wade whispered into his ear again, "This is what you wanted . . . isn't it?"

Jack nodded. He vainly tried to control his pounding heart and his audible, gasping breath.

Wade spoke into Jack's ear. "We can crawl to that downed tree 25 yards ahead. Stay flat on your belly. If you let your ass get high, they'll see you. When we get to the tree, you'll go to the right. I'll be next to you on your left."

Wade eased into an absolutely flat position and began inching forward, silently pushing his rifle before him. Jack followed, keeping his face inches from the soles of Wade's boots. The PH stopped every few feet and turned his head to look at Peter. With an almost imperceptible nod Peter indicated the lion was unaware of their approach.

It took 15 minutes to cover the distance. Jack thought it had taken 15 hours. Wade stopped crawling when he reached the tree trunk. With his hand flat and an inch off the ground, he pointed to where Jack should go.

Wade murmured with unnatural dispassion, "Rest your rifle on the trunk . . . keep low . . . now look through your scope. Can you see him?" Jack nodded. "Is your field of fire clear?" Jack nodded again. "We'll wait until he stands up. Then you'll take him through the shoulders. You will not shoot until everything is perfect. You'll wait for that moment. Do you understand?"

J ack nodded and for the first time noticed sweat running down his face, stinging his eyes.

The men waited for more than an hour. They did not move. They did not talk. The sun grew more intense and the colors around them began to fade. The world seemed all black and white and gray.

Once in a while the lion would turn to look at his companions. He breathed through his mouth in characteristic lion fashion. Mostly he stared straight ahead with those merciless eyes. Jack thought the lion was staring at him and knew what was in his soul.

The lionesses got up. They had decided to move and wanted the male to join them. They greeted one another and licked each other's face. They paraded in front of the lion, who regarded them with disdain. Then the lionesses moved a few feet into the golden grass – and disappeared.

Wade leaned in, close to Jack's ear. "If the lion gets up quickly, he's gone. If you have a clear shot, put the bullet right under his chin. He's facing directly toward us. The bullet will go through his chest and all the way through him. If you have the shot, take it. Make it good."

Jack moved the crosshairs from between the lion's eyes to a point under his chin. The crosshairs were steady. Jack's index finger caressed the trigger. He did not anticipate the shot; the roar of the rifle came as a surprise. Jack expected the lion to collapse. Instead, he saw hindquarters as the lion wheeled into the grass. Then he heard Wade.

"I don't believe this. I thought he was facing us, but he wasn't. He was lying with his body to our right with his head turned to look our way. He's hit all right, but not badly. Not bad enough by far. How did the shot feel?"

"The crosshairs were right under his chin when the rifle went off."

Coldly, Wade said, "Well, I couldn't tell how much he was turned when he got hit. His mane was so long I could only see his face. I should never have let you take the shot until he stood up."

Later, Jack found that the bullet had penetrated the right shoulder and ranged along the rib cage without entering the chest. The lion experienced a painful wound, but no vital organs had been struck. Had the bullet hit two inches to Jack's right, one lung would have been destroyed and death would have been quick. But now they had a lion in the long grass with a painful, non-disabling injury.

Wade took command. "Peter, let's get on him. I want him before sunset . . . don't want to be in the grass with him in the dark. Be careful. We don't know where his lady friends are. They may take all this personally."

Then to Jack. "Make sure you have an expanding bullet up the pipe of that .375 and make sure the magazine's full. Don't get excited and put a bullet into Peter or me. Stay with me and keep your eyes up. Keep scanning. Peter will have his eyes down, watching the trail. It'll be you or me who sees him first."

Jack, sick to his core, said, "Wade, I'm sorry. I don't want anyone to get hurt."

Wade, disgusted, replied, "You talk like a little girl. Now pick up your balls. We have to organize this lion and we will organize him." Wade rechecked his rifle and was off, ten yards behind Peter. Jack hurried to join them.

The lion moved in a straight line to an area of heavy cover half a mile from where he was wounded. He traveled alone, to the hunters' relief, and just fast enough to stay ahead of them. He paused to watch his back trail before entering the heavy cover.

Peter saw him 50 yards away, snapped his fingers, and pointed. Wade and Jack threw up their rifles as the lion vanished into the dense bush. Just for an instant Jack saw those yellow eyes boring into him. Jack knew the lion was convinced he could take him. He was waiting for the right moment.

The heavy cover was circular in shape and 200 yards in diameter. The profusion of trees and bushes, all equipped with inch-long thorns, indicated that within this mini-jungle there was some source of water. This area, so unlike the surrounding grassland, was familiar to the lion. He had picked where he would stand and fight. He picked well.

Peter stopped at the edge of the cover. The three men came together and agreed on a simple plan. Peter would track the lion. Wade would keep his eyes up and scan ahead of them. Jack would stay immediately behind Wade and guard the rear. There was no predicting from which direction the charge would come. They knew one thing for sure. The lion would not leave this cover. When he was pushed enough he would come to them.

They entered the bush slowly. Everyone spent more time looking than moving. No one took a step without first studying precisely where he would put his foot. No one talked. No one took a deep breath – deep breathing compromises hearing.

Tracking a lion in heavy cover is more art than science. The pad of the lion does not sink into the earth like the hoof of a herbivore. There was never going to be the small telltale sound of rocks clicking off a hoof. He moves silently and without disrupting the soil.

Peter noticed an overturned pebble, a slightly bent blade of grass then an almost imperceptible indentation in the dirt made by one toe of the lion's foot. It was a painstaking process, and Peter was unerring.

Twice the men saw leaves parting as the big cat moved away from them. The lion was a ghost, a presence in the bush. He was always near but never visible.

For three hours the lion circled. Sunset was near, and still his tormentors would not let him rest. No matter where he moved they stayed with him. He always knew precisely where they were, and it seemed to him they were equally aware of his position. He was tired and thirsty and his shoulder hurt. He turned on his back trail and dropped flat to the ground, facing the sound of the men. His back feet sought purchase on the gravel soil so his charge would be as sudden and sure as a sprinter coming out of the blocks. His tail, lying straight out behind him, twitched slightly. His ears lay back against his skull. Nothing else moved. The cold eyes stared at the sound of the men. They were close.

There, ten yards away, a man came into view. He was looking down. The lion preferred his prey looking down when he charged.

A cough, not really a roar, escaped his throat as he took his first step. It was a quick sound, low and hoarse. It was not a loud sound, yet it dominated the environment and every living thing in it.

Jack had never heard that sound before, and, terrified, turned to find the source. Before Jack could complete his turn, Peter fell flat on the ground to open a shooting lane for Wade. The lion lost sight of his closest pursuer, but another was standing five yards behind where the first had vanished. The big cat instantly pivoted and turned his charge slightly to take the standing one.

Wade focused on the sound. His rifle came up before he saw the huge lion coming at him. The shot was instinctive. The bullet went through the lion's open mouth and destroyed his brain. He slid to a stop a yard from Wade's foot.

Jack never saw the lion before the shot. He had come too low and too fast. Jack had looked right over him. He knew with certainty that had he been alone, the lion would have killed him.

Jack had not broken and run, but this was not his lion. It was Wade's. Everyone knew this, though no one spoke of it.

Wade stared at the great head lying in front of him. He worked the bolt of the rifle and seated another round. Without taking his eyes off the lion he said to Jack, "Take a few steps so you can see him broadside. Then place one of those big bullets through his chest. I would prefer this gentleman not get up."

The rifle's report was strangely subdued. The lion's shoulder moved only slightly when the bullet struck.

Wade sat down with his legs crossed. Peter placed a hand on his shoulder and whispered something. They shook hands. As the hands clasped, Peter placed his left hand over Wade's right with great solemnity.

Jack understood something for the first time. The adrenaline rush, that fist-shaking excitement Americans so ardently seek, was not what he had come to find. He wanted to find the courage to do whatever needed to be done, and to do it coldly, unemotionally, efficiently. A man who meets any challenge with his best effort was superior to a thrill-seeker.

Wade looked up at Jack with a wan smile. "You stood in with me on a lion charge. Well done."

Jack, embarrassed, replied, "I stood there and completely missed seeing the lion. If I had been alone, the lion would have won."

"The lion does not win or lose," Wade said. "He will always be a lion. You went into his world and played according to his rules. Someday, when you look at the skin on the wall, you'll remember the lion and the charge and how you stood there. Visitors will look at the skin, and they will ooh and aah. But they can never understand."

Wade instructed Peter to get the truck and bring it as close as possible, then handed him his rifle. He did not want Peter unarmed in lion country. Jack and Wade would remain behind to protect the lion from hyenas.

Jack leaned his rifle on a bush and the two men sat there in the gathering dark, savoring each moment. The truck reached them a little after sunset. It came much too soon.

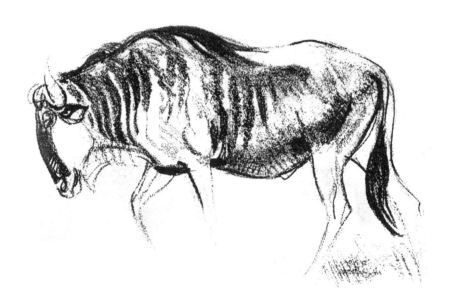

# BAD DAY IN THE BUSH

*When PH Johan Calitz found himself on the wrong end of a
wounded buff, he understood his chilling premonition.*

*By Mike Baker*

n the morning of September 30, 2001,
professional hunter Johan Calitz awoke with
a start. Outside his tent the quiet sounds of
a safari camp coming to life mixed with the
chatter of raucous francolins greeted the
sunrise. This is how Johan began most days,
his ears filled with the sounds of cooks and
trackers preparing for the hours ahead, with
birdsong and often, the last roars of lions just before sunrise.

This was normally when he felt most at ease, the sounds of the
African bush a tonic for the stresses of running large safari operations
in Botswana and Mozambique. But this morning Johan felt a sense of
dread so profound he was tempted to roll over and spend the day in
bed. A weight, a vague heaviness upon his chest, left him paralyzed
with apprehension.

Johan was accompanying an old friend and client on a safari in Tanzania,
and felt out of place in this somewhat ill-defined role. Johan was a safari
operator of note across the African continent, but here he was asked to

act as a "quasi observer" on someone else's hunting concession, deferring to a French PH with much less experience.

Johan Calitz is a man with admittedly strong views when it comes to hunting dangerous game. He shot his first cape buffalo at 14, and has spent a lifetime sharing his love of Africa with clients and friends. He brings an expertise to his job that recalls the professional hunters of time gone by – mechanic, cook, field surgeon and crack shot, with a 'bush sense' honed by the military and now by his Bushmen trackers.

He speaks of his time in the Bush Wars of Angola in only the vaguest of terms, generalities that let you know he'd like to move onto another subject. But if you have hunted with him, if you have shared a campfire and shown respect for the game and that land he so dearly loves, he will tell you the story of what happened that fateful Sunday in Tanzania, when against his better judgment, Johan pulled the covers off and climbed out of bed.

"I contemplated even being on the safari," he recalls. "What was difficult for me was figuring out what role I was to play. Would I play the role of companion? Would I be there to consult with my friend or the French professional hunter? Or would I be asked to sort out problems that I didn't start? In the end that's exactly how it happened. I wasn't consulted in which manner we were to hunt these beasts, but when there was trouble, I was invited to help sort it all out."

There already had been problems as the safari progressed – busted stalks and poor decisions, and the language barrier was proving difficult for the group. Neither Johan nor his friend spoke French, and the Frenchman spoke only the most basic English. The resulting confusion weighed upon Johan as he lay in bed on that beautiful Sunday morning feeling great unease and on the brink of staying in camp for the remainder of the trip.

The day began typically enough for a three-week safari. The group was making a circuit through the concession, checking leopard baits for any hits. One showed the signs of a very big tom from just hours before, and a blind was quickly fashioned from the surrounding flora for an evening hunt. They left the area and went to zero the gun at 50 yards – the distance from the blind to the tree where the bait was hung.

By now it was mid-morning, with camp still a good drive ahead, and Johan found himself holding his tongue as the young PH laid out his plans for the day. When Johan tells the story some five years later, he voices an opinion he reluctantly decided to keep silent that morning in Tanzania. One thing a professional hunter does not do is question another on how he conducts a safari, and Johan held to that code, despite the difference in opinion.

"I felt we should go back to camp. We should relax, get the client in a mental state where he was at ease and had confidence – that's what you do. You deal with the leopard, and the leopard alone. My fellow professional hunter was of the opinion that we should quickly head out and shoot something else as it was still early in the day. To me, that was not the greatest of ideas. Because if you end up wounding something and have to track it for a couple of hours . . . or if you shoot poorly, you might worry about your shooting and your mental state is not right. Then, you find yourself in the blind waiting for the leopard and you are doubting yourself . . . and a leopard blind is not a place for doubt."

That is the practical side of a professional hunter speaking – the voice of a man entrusted to plan and adjust to the ever-changing challenges and opportunities of safari in order to maximize success. But in that PH beats the heart of the hunter, and the decision to try for another animal struck a wrong chord with that side of Johan as well.

Safari is about the experience – whether you shoot a record-book animal or get the truck stuck in the mud for hours, you must look at it all as one great adventure. Too often collectors rush into camp with a list of animals and a tape measure in their pocket. They are in such a hurry to fill their tags they miss the best moments of a safari. A leopard is an animal to be savored. It is the preparation, the anticipation, and the very real danger of a leopard hunt that can wind a sportsman up in knots – and have him still basking in the afterglow of success days later.

T he sun was beating down on the alkali ground at midday. As the truck wound its way along a small river, the trackers watched for a nice spot for lunch or any animals that might have come down to drink. They talked quietly in the back of the Rover while Johan scanned the horizon. Everyone seemed to spot them at the same time.

Two old buffalo bulls stood in the shade of wild fig tree. They saw the truck but were reluctant to leave such a choice little bend in the river. They started with the look of passive hostility that only a cape buffalo can give; content to chew their cud if left alone. But one of the bulls was a good trophy, and the French PH waited until they were out of sight before killing the engine and preparing to try a stalk.

They moved through the cover into a position about a hundred yards from the buffalo. The equatorial sun is harsh at midday, and a cape buffalo in the shade of a tree is surprisingly difficult to make out even with binoculars. They could see the two bulls, but were unsure about which way they were facing, and once again the language barrier proved frustrating. After some time the French PH motioned to the tracker to set up the shooting sticks, trying to convey where he wanted the client to aim on the buffalo.

Johan kept back, letting the man do his job, but that sense of unease returned as he watched his friend and client draw a bead on the shapeless black form.

The blast of the .470 interrupted the peaceful river scene, and the two bulls turned and headed into even thicker cover on the river's edge. The hunters rushed to where the bulls had been standing and the debate began as to whether the shot had connected. At first it seemed like a clean miss. The trackers canvassed the area like detectives at a crime scene, finding no sign of blood. But as the group tried to determine what had happened, Johan's eyes were drawn down a narrow trail by the river. He walked about ten yards in and saw one of the worst things a cape buffalo hunter can see.

"I found a green leaf with stomach contents on it," he says, "They were mixed in with blood. Normally, that means trouble. The animal has been gut-shot; he is in quite a bit of pain, and the wound is not fatal – at least, not immediately. He's not going to die in the next hundred yards; he's going to die in the next couple of days, and it's going to be a very painful and unpleasant death. The ethical thing to do is to follow up that animal and to end his suffering – to make sure that what you've inflicted on him you can finish."

As they moved down the trail, the spoor became increasingly fresh. Finally, the group jumped the bull out of a thicket. They all took off in a full sprint, Johan stopping momentarily to try for a shot. As he did, the trackers and the PH passed by him, trying to close the distance. The PH attempted a shot as they moved in, but missed, and as John caught up with the group he saw the buffalo stop, turn and come straight for the young Frenchman.

Much has been written about the charge of a cape buffalo. If you hunt enough of them, it is an inevitability. But until that day comes, you'll always question how you would react when a one-ton buff is bearing down on you. Like a soldier heading into his first battle, you can prepare and practice for the situation, but until it occurs there will always be that uncertainty.

Johan has faced down several charging buffalo in his career, and he talks of the danger without dramatics or braggadocio. This is a man who has pondered his unique job hazards, and he speaks philosophically of what a buffalo charge means to the hunter.

"Nobody can prepare themselves for that moment. I've heard a lot of professional hunters and a lot of clients say "I wish that bastard would turn and charge.' And if it works out, great, it makes us feel better as men. Because in our eye we have withstood a challenge . . . we have overcome a fear in our lives that we don't deal with often. But when it goes wrong, it goes terribly wrong, and you say to yourself 'my God I'm in trouble. I'm in deep trouble, and I honestly don't know whether or not I'm going to make it.'"

For Johan Calitz, it was all about to go terribly wrong, and suddenly that great uneasiness he'd felt at daybreak was about to make complete sense.

I reached the French PH just before the buffalo did. But my movement caught the buffalo's eyes, and he changed his focus to me as he drew closer," Johan recalls. He shot his double, a .500 Nitro Express 3½, from the hip, but with no positive results. He then jumped out of the way, trying another shot from the hip, which he missed. The buffalo hit him and crushed his ankle with the first swipe, spinning Johan 180 degrees.

"I was still on my feet when he rushed again. I tried a futile block with my right arm, which he hooked and used to throw me up in the air. I landed and made eye contact with him, and every time our eyes would meet, he would just beat the living hell out of me. He put his horn into my upper leg, picked me up and threw me again, then he shoved his horn into my abdomen and threw me once more. Finally, I decided to play dead and see if he would leave me alone."

While Johan lay in the dirt, the PH, having fired his two barrels earlier, was forced to chase down the tracker carrying his shell belt. At the sight of the goring, the trackers had scattered in all directions, leaving Johan for dead and the French PH with an empty weapon. The client was still back down the trail, and Johan found himself alone with an animal in great pain, intent on doubling the agony towards his victim.

"The buffalo started pushing me around on the ground. He was looking for something – an obstacle, where he could crush me. And as he was pushing me, I felt he was talking to me. He made a low grunt, and I knew that it was 'that time' – and I started praying. And as he was pushing me, I heard a shot and then another and the buffalo raised his head for a moment and looked at me. Our eyes were only inches apart. That one bloody red, turned-up eye looked at me, and I've never seen so much hatred and pain and anger. But not a bit of fear. It was absolute anger. As he raised his head I turned and tried to get out from under him, and he collapsed on me and died, pinning me beneath him."

The French PH had chased down his tracker, returned with a loaded firearm and finished the buffalo. But Johan lay underneath a ton of animal, with several large open wounds, and the danger was far from over. The trackers attempted to roll the buffalo off Johan, over his shattered ankle, which made him almost pass out from the pain. He knew that remaining conscious was critical to getting out alive, and as he lay there bleeding and broken, Johan was forced to take charge of his own rescue.

"I was trying to communicate to the Frenchman to get a radio and get help but he didn't understand at first," he says. "Once he left for the truck I started to go through my wounds. Amazingly, I saw these huge open wounds, saw my stomach moving, but there was no blood – which to me was a miracle. It was a prayer being answered. I knew I could not survive a severed femoral artery. I did have a punctured lung, and this was my greatest immediate concern."

While the PH headed back to the truck to radio for help, Johan was forced to begin first aid alone. He signaled to the tracker to make a splint from some nearby trees for his leg, and then literally reinserted his bowels back into his abdomen. The pain was about to set in, and Johan lingered on the edge of consciousness in absolute misery.

It took 4½ hours to reach medical help. Johan credits a French physician with making good calls throughout the rescue. He eased his pain with massive amounts of morphine, and insisted Johan's arm was not to be amputated nor any blood transfusions to be given. These instructions to the Tanzanian hospital staff were the last thing Johan heard before he fell into unconsciousness.

A long hospital stay in South Africa was followed by more than a score of different surgeries. Over the past five years, Johan's pronounced limp continues to improve, and while pain is still a constant companion, he is starting to regain a sense of normalcy after that life-changing morning in Tanzania. To return to hunting dangerous game after such an event is a physical miracle, but it is the mental game Johan knew would be the real challenge. He is at peace with fate, and with Africa and the wild game he loves so much. But he still struggles with the failings of man, and never again will he put himself in a situation beyond his control.

"When I look back, I've made peace with that buffalo," he says. "It was almost expected in a career that spans more than three decades. I got away with many charging buffalo, and I stopped them. How can you expect an animal you hurt big time not to retaliate? All that buffalo did was to do what I would have done – give him my best – and that he most certainly did. If you ask me whether I am disappointed in human beings, yes I am. I would have loved someone to have helped fix me up and sort me out.

"I have to thank the French hunter for chasing down his tracker and shooting the buffalo off of me. But if you asked me, 'Would I hunt with him again?' I would say no. If you asked me, 'How would I deal with the next wounded buffalo?' I would approach it with a lot of respect, with a different mind, and with a lot of carefulness. And I will only deal with it when I'm in charge."

# ELEPHANT BY INCHES

*In their native tongue, the trackers challenged him to 'Dream your elephant,' but now, with the huge bull glaring down at him only 25 paces away, it could suddenly become the worst of nightmares.*

*By Chip Anderson*

f course, he knew we were there, but with his myopic vision, he was forced to rely on his acute sense of smell and his sharp hearing. We stared with breathless horror as, like some decapitated serpent, his trunk waved left and right over the top of the palms, desperately trying to catch our scent, his great bulk obscured by the thick African bush.

It was a game of nerve and patience, the three of us crouched with hardly a breath between us, not 12 yards from the bull, knee-deep in this lukewarm, somewhat rancid bit of swamp. Mosquitoes swarmed us, but no one dared slap. I remember wondering if, like sharks, crocodiles could smell blood in the water as my legs were bleeding quite freely from our last mad dash through the thorns and razor grass. With several tons of enraged elephant bringing up the rear with murderous enthusiasm, one doesn't take too much time to worry about the route of escape.

# AFRICA

Here I was on the seventh morning of a 14-day elephant hunt in Botswana's great Okavango Delta. Man! This morning had started bad and from the looks of things, it wasn't getting better any time soon.

It had been a week of fruitless tracking and disappointing marches over miles of thorn and scrub, covering the delta inch by bloody inch, long treks under a hot sun, the soft sand taking away one step for every two you take, evenings by the fire spent self-medicating, pouring perfectly good single-malt scotch over prolific thorn wounds on various body parts, although I assure you, I administered some internally.

Certainly elephants were present. Hell, we were constantly into them. In fact, running from irate cows and dodging small bulls anxious to prove their manhood became a daily exercise. We even had one chase our jeep for several miles.

The usual routine each day was a dawn patrol to the waterholes and favorite elephant paths, looking for a track that was something around 21 to 23 inches and with frontal depth. This could mean heavy ivory. So far, most large tracks had panned out well, proving to be very large bulls, but as luck would have it, after stalking as close as we could, the bull would reveal himself to be ivory poor or more often than not, he would have one tusk broken off.

Elephant hunting is certainly not for the unfit or unfaithful. I'm not sure who said it, although I believe it was Peter Capstick, "No one kills an elephant with a rifle; you kill them with your feet." Truer words were never spoken.

Just the day before we had trailed five bulls for at least eight to ten miles through some of the roughest country I had yet to see. It seemed like one or two should be carrying very good ivory. As the heat of the morning grew, they slowed down and we finally caught up with them about 11:30. Closing in to about some 30 yards or so, I was absolutely stunned by the view before me.

Here were five grand bulls. Three were wearing about 30 to 40 pounds, obvious *askari* types, but the remaining two had ivory in the 60- to 70-pound range. Here they were, all under one small grove of mopane bush and they were sound asleep – SNORING!

The breeze was dicey and changing constantly, not at all in our favor to approach for a shot at the largest of the five, and truth be told, there is no way I could bring myself to interrupt his dreams with 500 grains of alarm clock. Besides, we had another problem of imminent concern. In our excitement as we had closed in on this bunch, we had inadvertently worked our way almost on top of a herd of perhaps 200 cows and calves.

Matsumi, our tracker, climbed an anthill, where he explained with animated signals and frantic Setswanan that we needed to leave now, as quickly and quietly as possible. To fire a shot under these circumstances would be insanity. Someone would certainly be killed. Giving the group our best, we backed out, very, very carefully.

Around the campfire that night, Mike Murray, my professional hunter, suggested a break from chasing ivory since we were all a bit burned out physically after six days of this kind of stuff and a bit on edge after our past few exciting forays. Well, I had a buff license anyway, so it was settled. At dawn we would head out in the *makuros*, paddling deep into the marsh where thousands of small islands that make up the delta hold the biggest and baddest buffalo. Certainly, it would be easier than tracking elephant. Besides I was really having a craving for some more of that wonderful buffalo bone soup we had been dipping into all week.

N ext morning we had scouted a half-dozen islands about five miles out before we found the spoor of a large herd of buff in the tall grass. Beaching the *makuros*, I threw two soft-nose shells into my Wilkes .470, while Mike loaded his Brno Mauser .458. Soon we were creeping up the beachhead with Matsumi and Byeti in front, pointing as the tracks led deeper into the dark grass. It was like walking through a tunnel, except that I couldn't see the light at the other end. In fact, what was waiting at the other end was most likely a thousand pounds of sharp-horned bad attitude with nowhere to go except the way he came in, which was right where we were standing.

Moving at an agonizingly slow pace along the trail, Matsumi stopped occasionally to insert his finger into droppings; the warmer they were, the more excited he got. Obviously, we were getting close. We had only moved inland some hundred yards when both Byetei and Matsumi froze. They were definitely upset by something, pointing and whispering in an agitated manner. Mike and I moved up to investigate.

# AFRICA

Apparently we were not alone in this little piece of green hell – twin sets of spoor from two very large male lions were now on the same course, heading toward our buffalo. This was definitely not a good situation, particularly with the dodgy breeze and our limited visibility. A decision was made to give this up as a "bad deal." Besides, the buff were going to wind one of us and the ensuing stampede would be very scary indeed.

Back at the beach, as we lay in the morning sun, Mike climbed up the steep bank to glass the farther islands. Suddenly he shouting down to me, "Quick! Quick! Look!"

Pointing north out across the water, I fumbled to get my binoculars focused. Coming into my view were three large forms, floating like grey ships on an ochre ocean.

Elephants! I could see through my binoculars they were moving away, but as the middle bull walked, his head swung side to side and the sharp glint of long ivory played peek-a-boo with us.

Mike turned, his eyes wide with excitement, and said to me, 'If we want him," (Boy, did I want him!), "we have to go now. No boats, shed the packs, travel light." Matsumi would remain behind, our beacon in the dark, as it were. It was only 8:30, but with elephant you never know just when you'll catch up.

So Mike, Byeti and I hit the water. Waist deep and cold, I struggled with each step, mud sucking in my feet and requiring great effort to pull free, but even this couldn't dampen my enthusiasm. All I had ever dreamed of was somewhere across this water, mud and grass. Knowing this gave me some strength. My grail lay ahead.

We reached dry land after nearly a mile of slogging, leeches and all, and I must tell you that razor grass really does cut you to ribbons! Using the small cloth bag of campfire ash, we checked the breeze and crawled up through the mopane. This bit of ground was thick with scrub and of course, lots of thorn and more lion tracks (oh great!). The three bulls had moved off into the center of the thicket.

Circling to get the wind right, we approached the thickest part of the island, where their spoor seemed to lead. Frustrated after trying desperately to see our quarry in this dense bush, Mike shimmied up an anthill to look over the situation. Byeti and I remained quiet at its base.

After a minute or so Mike hissed down to us that the bulls had moved to the next island. At least, he could see the back end of one walking up the bank. It was exactly at that moment, out of the corner of my eye, that I caught a movement. Turning quickly, coming at full deadly speed, I saw a dark form, curiously silent. The only sounds were the swish of branches sweeping out of the elephant's way.

No time for any detailed explanations, I yelled to Mike, "We've got to get out of here!" He must have seen it, too, as he was already sliding down the anthill and all three of us ran through the bush, rolling downhill into the water, splashing downwind as fast as we could.

Obviously, this *askari* to the old bull had laid in wait while the other two bulls left the island ahead of us. And now he was intent upon eliminating the problem. One of the things that makes hunting elephants so fascinating is their incredible intelligence, the same quality that makes them dangerous.

So, there we were, frozen in the black water, with a very motivated bull elephant now hunting *us*. As I mentioned, this day had started bad and at the moment it didn't look like our odds were about to improve. Waiting for the big boy to lose interest seemed like hours, but even after that grey trunk and crown disappeared back into the palms, we weren't taking any chances and gave it about ten minutes before we dared to move.

His tracks revealed that he had set off to join his companions on the next island, confident, I'm sure, that he had discouraged us sufficiently.

As we tracked down to the swamp edge, I couldn't believe what lie ahead – at least 20 yards of very deep water. We couldn't wade or swim to the next island. I could not see how we could get there.

Quickly sizing up our predicament, Byeti started cutting papyrus and laying it across the shortest point between the two islands, laying the tall reeds into thick mats and forming a semblance of a bridge. His construction project was completed in about 20 minutes. Eying his contraption suspiciously, I felt there was no way I was going to get on that thing.

# AFRICA

Byeti rightfully crossed first, with Mike carefully belly-crawling from behind. I shook my head dubiously. Swallowing deeply, I slid my rifle forward and snaked my way onto the makeshift bridge. I really have to admit, at that moment I was at my physical and emotional end. I thought I was fit, but real ivory hunting separates the men from the boys.

Of course, the worst happened. About halfway across my legs plunged through the rickety contraption. Struggling against the cold current, I managed to keep my head and shoulders above water while holding my beautiful Wilkes rifle above my head. My leg muscles had seized up from calves to thighs – I literally could not move.

Mike crawled out as far as he could risk and was trying to encourage me.

I told him, "I can't go on. I don't care anymore. Let's just leave this elephant."

Meanwhile, through my pained haze, I could hear Byeti scolding me in Setswanan. He seemed very irritated, though I could hardly care at the moment.

Mike was saying, "You have to pull yourself out of there. There are big crocs! You must push your gun down and pull yourself out."

Right! I'm going to shove a $10,000 double rifle into this water? Forget it! Let the crocs eat me! What is Byeti yelling?

Mike translated his abuse for me, "He is saying, 'If you want to be like a woman, then you should stay at camp and cook. If you are a man, you will get out of there and kill this elephant.'"

Oh, God! I thought death by crocodile was one thing, but to be shamed by your tracker is another whole issue, and as reluctant as I was to do it, I pushed down on that beautiful stick of circassian and iron, filling its twin barrels with cold marsh water. *AAAUUGHH!* My legs wouldn't work, but my arms found the strength and inch by excruciating inch I dragged myself across the papyrus bridge.

While I lied on the bank, trying to work out my leg cramps and get some feeling back into my freezing body, Mike tested the wind and as usual it proved treacherous. Our best strategy was to circle the island low to the east, coming up ahead of the three bulls who would hopefully be feeding or napping in the heat of the day. The breeze shifted constantly as we hit the far eastern banks of the island, where we arrived at a monkey roost, a disgusting mess of feces and urine. *No elephant alive could scent us in here*, I thought.

Peering through the bush outside the roost, we could make out the three bulls, now feeding in heavy cover. Staying as low as possible on our stomachs, once again we did the army crawl, guns cradled in our forearms, moving only inches at a time, freezing in place whenever they lifted their heads. It took about 20 minutes to cover 50 yards. With sweat in our eyes and the ice pick bite of tetses to torture us, we continued to slip forward. I had come too far and been through too much to blow it now.

A t 25 paces from the huge animals, I slid the barrels of my .470 forward, crouching deeply to get an open shot through the brush.

"No," I heard Mike whisper.

I looked at him questioningly. "If you are to do this right, you must stand up and out from these bushes and face this elephant."

As tired as I was and eager to end this, I knew he was right. There would be shame to do otherwise. There is a mistaken impression by the non-hunting public that sport hunting is some kind of assertion of virility or will over nature. But the hunting of dangerous game is truly a test; not of you against the animal, but ultimately of you against yourself. To take a shot at my elephant like a sniper from the bushes, I would rob myself of all I had come here to find out.

So I gathered myself and stood. In that instant, I felt so small, somewhat akin to David confronting Goliath. There was a brief second of shock for both the bull and myself as our eyes met and each of us sized up the situation. I distinctly remember the cloud of dust billowing off his ears as he pumped them forward in threat and recognition. (*Would I be so bold and defiant when I finally confront the end?*) With the rear V and blade settled perfectly between his eyes on that second wrinkle down, I squeezed the trigger, sending 500 grains of metal and lead into his skull. The resounding boom erupted panic in the askaris and they crashed off violently in the opposite direction.

# AFRICA

The bull's head snapped back, hi trunk raised as he collapsed, first to his haunches, then to his side. The entire island seemed to shake. Byeti and Mike raced through the thorns to his rear, while I kept the rifle trained on the bull to administer the *estocade*.

Rushing toward the bull, I moved in much too close as he rocked forward in an attempt to rise. I was literally on top of him as he cleared the ground and tried to get his front feet under him. I fired my left barrel into where I believed his heart would be. Another bullet rocked him, but with little effect. Quickly reloading, I flanked him until I could level my sights past his ear.

Concentrating, holding steady as I could, I fired a perfect side brain shot. The bull crumpled as if pole-axed in a haze of brown dust, again shaking the earth beneath my feet.

We had spoken so many evenings around the fire about what the natives called "Dreaming your elephant," which until that moment I had mistakenly taken as literal. Some kind of local magic, juju, mojo or what have you. But in this instant, I suddenly knew what it meant. The experience, the miles, the emotions and yes, the dream – all had brought me to this point. It was as it should be. I had hunted hard and fairly and finished this labor honorably.

It took me a long time to compose myself. I sat near the bull's head, running my hands over and over his 60 pounds of cold, smooth tusk, not ashamed that I felt tears running down my cheek. The awesome responsibility of having reduced this great giant to so much inert flesh and ivory was coming home to sit deeply. My head was swimming with so many thoughts, and I couldn't help but remember what the great hunter Bror Blixen had said that "no man was worthy of killing an elephant." Of course, Blixen had killed many in his life and now I had done so myself.

Non-hunters may never understand how it is to pursue something that you love passionately and to be able, at the final moment, to take not only its life but the essence of its very soul, to possess it in some small way and cherish it, as you would a great gift. Those who never hunt ask why? Those who do never need to ask at all.

If there is a moral or metaphor here, it may be that the long days and hours in slow, agonizing pursuit of this glorious animal that now lies still before me, collecting flies and gathering tribesmen, looking not nearly so noble in death, makes me realize as I travel on in age and time that we are all heading in the same direction, getting there by inches.

# A LION'S FURY

*Tracking a wounded lion into thick bush becomes
a deadly game of high-stakes hide-and-seek.*

*By Joe Coogan*

We were camped on the edge of Pom Pom Lagoon in the game-filled Matsebe concession, located deep in northern Botswana's 4,000-square-mile Okavango Delta. Here, brush-covered islands, mopane sandveldt and vast floodplains supported large numbers of plains game and big herds of buffalo, primary prey of the area's magnificent lions.

The year was 1982, and Dave Harshbarger was on his first African safari with his good friend and California business associate, Steve Colwell. Accompanying the California hunting buddies were Soren Lindstrom and myself – Dave would be hunting with Soren, while Steve hunted with me. At the time, Soren and I worked for the Maun-based outfitter, Safari South, whose roster of respected professional hunters included Harry Selby, Tony Henley, Lionel Palmer, Simon Paul, Steve Liversedge and Dougie Wright.

# AFRICA

After careful consideration Dave and Steve had chosen Botswana for a three-week general bag safari because of the variety of terrain and the sheer abundance of game. Buffalo topped Dave and Steve's want-list, which also included kudu, warthog, zebra and gemsbok. Both of the Californians were keen wingshooters and they looked forward to sampling some of Botswana's excellent bird-hunting. Dave was especially interested in taking a big-maned lion.

About a week into the 21-day safari, Soren and Dave were cruising the islands and floodplains of the Okavango with lions in mind. It was late in the afternoon, and they were about to turn toward camp when they rounded a point of bush.

Lying on a termite mound was a big lion and four lionesses, all intent on watching a herd of wildebeest. At the sight of the vehicle, the lion stood up and trotted across the grassy plain toward an island of brush.

"He's a good one," Soren said, knowing if the lion ran, it would be a risky shot for his client. But Dave had proven to be a capable marksman, taking several head of game with single, well-placed bullets. Soren felt certain that Dave could do it, but they had to act quickly.

Dave jumped from the vehicle, brought up his rifle and found the lion clearly visible in the 3x9 variable scope. The lion stopped at 75 yards and looked back at the hunters. He then began to lope toward cover.

Swinging his .375 H&H rifle slightly ahead of the bounding cat, Dave felt confident with the sight picture and squeezed the trigger. The crack of the rifle-shot echoed across the plain, followed by the solid thump of the bullet. Before Dave could shoot again the lion had melted into the long grass.

"It sounded like a hit," Soren said, "but I can't be sure. I saw no reaction."

Dave got back in the vehicle, and the men drove to the where the lion had disappeared. With rifles in hand, the two hunters and their trackers climbed out to examine the tracks. Squinting against the glare of the sun, Soren studied the deep, dish-size depressions in the sand. Small splatters of blood confirmed a hit. But the sign was meager, suggesting the lion sustained a less-than-lethal wound. Even so, once an animal is wounded, particularly a dangerous one, it's up to the hunter to finish it, no matter how sticky the situation gets.

"Where do you think the lion was hit?" Soren asked Joseph, his head tracker.

"I don't know. He didn't jump or growl after the shot. It's not good," the tracker observed grimly.

Soren's grip tightened on his .458 double rifle at the thought of a wounded lion hiding in the thick bush only a few yards away. His thumb automatically felt for the safety catch, and he pushed it to the off position as he knelt down and peered into the shadows. He looked for a shape or movement in the dense undergrowth. He knew that tracking the lion across the sandy ground would be relatively easy, but he also knew that what lay at the end of the tracks would be nerve-wracking, gut-wrenching work.

The lion escaped into the thickest part of the island, heading straight into the setting sun. Soren explained that it would be almost suicidal to follow the cat into the thick tangle, particularly with the sun's bright glare in their eyes. They circled the island, checking for tracks, but found none.

"If the lion remains in this island of bush tonight, we'll find him tomorrow," Soren said, attempting to reassure Dave.

What Soren didn't say was that Dave might also get a chance to see firsthand why the Botswana lion's reputation is so fierce. Over the past 20 years the country has experienced more incidents of man-eating lions than any other African nation. Most of the attacks have occurred in game parks and reserves where wildlife is protected, but owing to constant presence of people, many animals, including lions, have shed their fear of man. Lions and hyenas are opportunists and occasionally regard people as prey. The parks and reserves are not fenced, and the big predators roam in and out of the areas freely.

Soren studied the surrounding bush to get a lay of the land before darkness finally veiled the African landscape. Switching on the Landcrusier's headlights, he turned the vehicle around and headed toward camp.

Earlier in the day Steve had taken a good buffalo and he was ready to celebrate his success when Soren and Dave rolled into camp. When they walked up to the campfire, their faces reflected a somber mood, which soon permeated the camp atmosphere.

Dinner was strangely quiet that evening. Dave couldn't erase from his thoughts the sight of the running lion and his shot at him before the cat disappeared into tall grass. After dinner we sat by the fire and discussed our strategy for finding the lion. It was a job that nobody liked, but Soren and I agreed that it would be best to team up. Both of us, along with our trackers, had followed wounded lions before, and we knew that when pressed, the lion would most likely come for us.

We also knew that tracking the wounded lion with more than two guns could complicate matters, sometimes tragically so. Fresh in our minds was the case of Henry Poolman, a professional hunter from Kenya who was accidentally shot and killed by a tracker when Poolman stepped between a charging lion and his client. I knew from a couple of my own close calls with charging lions that whatever happened, it would happen fast.

We decided to position Dave and Steve and my tracker Sanga in trees where they would have a degree of safety, but more importantly, the advantage of height would help them spot the lion if he moved from us and came in their direction. They might even get a shot at him. Meanwhile, Soren and I, accompanied by the other three trackers, would track the lion on foot. Our team included my number-one tracker, Galabone, (pronounced Ha-la-boney) and both of Soren's trackers, Joseph and Kelibile (pronounced Kill-a-bee-lee), all experienced and well familiar with dangers in the bush. We would leave after breakfast.

Arriving at the brush-choked island the next morning, Soren pointed to where the wounded lion had escaped. We circled the island to check again for his tracks and found none. We were pretty certain he was still hiding somewhere within the dense bush. At the opposite end of the island we positioned Dave, Steve and Sanga in trees that offered commanding views of the area.

I left my LandCruiser parked nearby and climbed into Soren's vehicle, then we drove about a half-mile back to the other end of the island. After discussing the situation with our trackers, it was agreed that Galabone and Joseph would work side-by-side, scanning the ground for tracks while Soren, Kelibile and I would keep watch for the lion in the bush ahead.

My custom bolt-action Mauser, chambered for .458 Win. Mag., was capable of dropping a charging elephant. It was fitted with express sights and stoked with factory Winchester loads pushing a 510-grain, soft-nosed bullet at slightly more than 2,000 feet-per-second. Together, our two .458 rifles could unleash more than five foot-tons of energy – a massive amount of knockdown power if directed to the right spot.

Taking up the lion's tracks locked us in a deadly game of hide-and-seek. We moved slowly and deliberately while Galabone and Joseph bird-dogged the tracks, while our eyes looked through, around, over and behind every bush, tree, termite mound and fallen log. It was tedious and tiresome work, without an ounce of joy to it. Inching forward on hands and knees, we wiped sweat from our eyes to peer into thick foliage that we parted with our rifle barrels. Tension gripped us like the clenches of a coiled snake, and each of us could hear the breathing of the others as we moved toward an invisible quarry. Like the silent support of a friend, my rifle's familiar feel was reassuring.

An hour of painstakingly slow progress brought us to an area where the grass was matted and spotted by dark, dry bloodstains. Here the lion had lain in four or five places during the night. Blood sign had decreased gradually, and there was little to suggest he was weakening from his wound. Tracking became more difficult with less blood to follow, and moving through thick bush we were often forced to split up and cast about to locate the tracks.

Spending an extended amount of time in a state of condition-red eventually took its toll. After three hours our concentration began to lag, and ironically, fatigue from stress triggered an impatience that actually caused us to quicken our pace. In a subconscious call for confrontation, we pushed forward, almost daring the lion to charge or run, or at least growl.

We were tired and frustrated, and our state of mind shouted for something to happen. But this would come at a cost – our actions unwittingly pushed the pendulum of advantage to the lion's side.

Lions are superb hunters who bring down large prey by instinctively knowing the best time to launch their attack. That same instinct works for them in defensive situations. Armed with large, bone-crushing teeth and claws that grab like steel hooks, the lion is one of the most formidable game animals on earth. Add to that mix a poorly placed shot, and you have all the ingredients for a disaster.

Our battle would begin at the lion's choosing – when we were least ready and our guard was down. While the rest of us looked for tracks on the ground, Kelibile spotted the lion first. The tracker, with a minimum of movement, quietly reached for my arm and pointed a stubby finger at the thick undergrowth

50 feet away. I followed the direction of his finger to see two yellow eyes blazing with anger.

The instant the lion locked eyes with us, he began lashing his tail, signaling his intention to charge. With the trackers behind us, Soren and I concentrated on the ball of fury in front. The lion's lip curled back, revealing long sharp teeth, and a deep angry growl ripped the still air.

The enraged lion charged in a quick rush, but somehow the world shifted into that slow-motion state that's often described by those in life-threatening situations. In two bounds he was only a few yards away. Soren, a fine shot and quick to reflex, fired first.

Staring in disbelief as the animal kept coming, I shot with the beast only a few feet off the end of my barrel. Slowed only slightly, he kept coming.

We were trapped in a living nightmare with a deadly lion, and it felt like we were defending our lives with cap guns. I remember thinking this monster must be bulletproof, and wondered how we'd end the madness before someone was bitten. I wasn't long to wonder.

The lion knocked Soren to the ground like a rag doll and ran over the top of him, brushing by me so close that I could have touched his back with my hand. Even if our shots had missed, I could only imagine that two rifle-blasts in his face must have shocked or confused the big cat, for by all rights he should have pressed his attack on Soren or me.

Before I fully registered what had just happened, a blood-chilling scream came from behind me, and I turned to look in horror at the lion's rear end as he began mauling one of the trackers. Hunched over his victim, he shook with the effort, much like a terrier shaking a rat. As I bolted a fresh round into my rifle, the screams from underneath the lion stopped as suddenly as they had started.

I could not shoot from where I stood, for fear of hitting whoever was under the lion, so I moved forward with the intention of placing the barrel in the lion's ear and blowing his head off. But before I had taken three steps, the lion abandoned his victim, moving directly away from me. I snapped off a shot at his rear end before he was swallowed by thick bush, and then ran to the tracker, fearing the worst.

The bloodied body was face down and lay motionless in the sand. The lion continued growling nearby, and Soren rushed up beside me to keep us covered in case the lion charged again. I carefully turned over the prostrate body, and winced in shock at the sight of Galabone's expressionless face. The top of his head was badly gashed, and blood from deep claw wounds seeped through his ripped and torn green overalls in several places.

When I felt for a pulse in Galabone's neck his eyelids began to flutter, and I silently thank God he was still alive. When the lion finally stopped growling, Soren knelt down to help me check Galabone's wounds to be sure there were no arteries severed or bones broken. Miraculously, everything seemed to be intact. Joseph and Kelibile materialized beside us and shuffled him over to my vehicle several hundred yards away.

Dave and Steve, surprised by the shots, were even more shocked by the screams and roars they'd heard. They had maintained their tree-borne vigilance until we shouted for them to climb down, and then had came running to look on in horror as we limped in with the bloodied tracker.

We immediately broke out the first aid kit, then set up the radio to call for a mercy flight. We irrigated Galabone's wounds with a syringe of strong antiseptic wash and got him to swallow a handful of painkillers and antibiotics. Still silent, he began shaking uncontrollably from shock and we wrapped him in a blanket. Within a couple of hours of our call for help, Galabone was picked up by an aircraft at a nearby bush airstrip and was under a doctor's care at the Maun Hospital.

We then requested that our safari headquarters in Maun leave the radio on with someone monitoring it, for we still had to deal with the wounded lion.

We now recognized that whatever the extent of the lion's wounds, they were only serving to anger him. Short of administering a paralyzing shot to the brain or spine, we were sure to face another furious charge.

We formed another plan and regrouped by putting Dave and me and the three trackers in the back of Soren's Landcruiser. Soren drove with Steve next to him, both cradling their rifles. Even though our nerves were frayed and raw, we headed back into the bush to face the lion once again. Soren pushed and crunched his Landcruiser through a thicket of bush, trees and vines to where we had last heard the lion. Dave and I held onto the lurching vehicle with one hand and our rifles with the other.

When we could go no farther with the vehicle, we began scanning the brush and soon spotted a patch of tawny hide about 20 yards away.

As we tried to make head from tail, the lion burst out of the bushes in a scene that's seared in my mind like a freeze-frame from a horror movie. His head was bloody, his mouth gaped open hideously, and his eyes bore straight through us. Dave fired just as the cat reached the front of the vehicle, and I fired a fraction of a second later.

Rearing up on his hind legs, the lion tried to claw his way onto the hood. Dave fired again and his bullet knocked the lion off the Land Cruiser. He was moving back into the brush when I fired a shot that dropped him. Dave shot again – the *ninth* round to be fired at the lion – and he finally lay still. He would not get up again.

Only after inspecting the lion were some of our questions answered. Upon his initial charge, one of our shots had ricocheted off a tooth and gone on to smash his lower jaw. The enamel on a lion's tooth is hard enough to deflect a bullet, even one with 5,000 foot-pounds of energy behind it. That's why shooting a lion in the head is considered a risky shot.

Galabone had survived the bite to his head because the lion's jaw had been shattered. When the cat tried to bite him, he only gashed the top of Galabone's scalp with his upper canines. It could also explain why the lion had left him so quickly.

When a lion attacks, he normally stays with his victim long enough to inflict serious injury or death. A wounded leopard, however, often dashes from person to person, biting as many as he can. Dazed, shocked and unable to bite properly, the lion left Galabone to seek the nearby security of the bush.

The tracker spent a little less than three weeks in the Maun hospital and we released without further complications. Later, he told me the lion knew that Galabone was the one pointing out the tracks and that's why he passed up Soren and me to attack him.

There is little love for lions among native Africans, who historically regard them as an evil menace. Plenty of superstition surrounds the big predators, and the safari crews always celebrated as if the devil himself had been killed whenever a lion was brought into camp. Some Kalahari bushmen believe that certain lions are capable of transforming themselves into human form. Those are the lions, they say, that you don't want to mess with.

Galabone rejoined Sanga and me on safari a month later and completed the rest of the hunting season with us, showing no hesitation to track up a lion on foot. But he did say that the next time we had a wounded lion in thick bush, he would let someone else point out the tracks.

# DEVILS & APE MEN

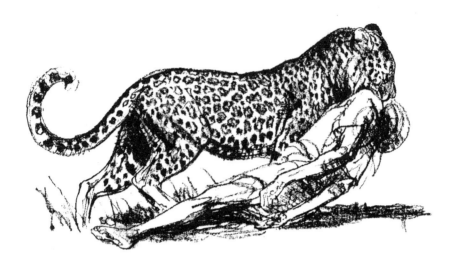

# DEVIL CAT

*African literature teems with accounts of strange phenomena –
and strangest of all are tales of witchwomen who have the power to
change themselves into wild and savage animals.*

*By Robert F. Jones*

W e had just finished a memorable safari in the Northern Frontier District of Kenya, one of which I had taken a very fine leopard in the eleventh hour of the final day. It was my first. A male, it pegged out at nearly eight feet from nose to tail tip, and we were celebrating the kill, relaxing at Bill Winter's home in Nanyuki before my imminent departure stateside. It was a Sunday afternoon, cool and cloudy on the slopes of Mount Kenya. We decided to run down to the Sportman's Arms for tea. A British regimental band held forth on the hotel grounds that lazy evening, and we took our tea on the veranda to the strains of "The Colonel Bogey March."

You know the tune, but if not, perhaps the words often sung to it will bring back the melody.

"It's horseshit – that makes the grass grow green . . ."

# AFRICA

I sang them *sotto voce* between sips of piping hot Darjeeling.

"Look at that old gent, Bwana," Bill whispered after swallowing a bite of lemon tart. He cast his eyes briefly to my left. Seated near us at a wickerwork garden table, one gouty foot propped on a chair as he beat time to the music, was a splendid wreck of a fellow, mottled of cheek but bright of eye, with a hoary set of sidewhiskers and a magnificent if somewhat drinksodden moustache. He sipped at a rust-colored gin and bitters, no ice.

"Sir George McArthur Ponsonby, V.C.," Bill said, "A grand old ruin, hey? But he was a dume in his day, a real bull. Won the Victoria Cross at Passchendaele in the Great War, marched on Waziristan with General Climo in 1919, exemplary Colonial service, both military and civilian, in Nyasaland, the Cameroons and Tanganyika, a veteran of safaris *mingi sana* – many, many great hunts – back in the days when the word meant something, when they went in on foot, with porters balancing the loads on their heads. He can tell you a tale or two, old Sir George. What say we ask him over for a drink and a bit of a chin-wag?"

We did, and in due course Bill told Sir George about my leopard.

"Wasn't by chance wearing gold ankle bracelets, was it?" Sir George asked when I finished my modest story. "Graven with mystical writing?"

"No, sir," I answered, puzzled. Bill was grinning behind his hand. "Should it have been?"

Sir George chuckled and assured me most definitely that it should not have been. Not if I valued my health and sanity.

Bill winked, then tugged his left earlobe, a signal advising me to activate the small tape recorder I carried, locked and loaded, in the breast pocket of my bush vest.

Sir George ordered another gin-and-bitters. When it arrived, he proceeded to relate a tale of his own concerning leopards, the tale of a strange and dreadful hunt. It had occurred nearly half a century earlier, in the same reaches of the NFD from which we had just returned. Some years ago, he began, in the early 1920s he and another Englishman were hunting along the Ewaso Nyiro River, slowly following its sinuous route through that great game country to where it hemorrhages finally, as so many African rivers do, into the sands of an ever-expanding desert, leaving only a fetid marsh to punctuate its finish. Here then is his tale, abridged only slightly so as not to offend what is blithely termed a "family" readership . . .

I n the course of our trek down the 'Washo' we happened upon a small *manyatta* – a village of shabby grass huts – on the edge of the Lorian Swamp, where that great blood-red river ends its career. The inhabitants, a degenerate breed of Marsh 'Dorobos, had never seen white men before. They fled weeping at the approach of our safari. Our porters, feeling superior to these rude savages, laughed long and hard at them, making jests in raucous Kiswahili that accused the poor savages of such bestial sins as snake worship and intimate congress with hyenas.

"The naked bums of these dusky Adams and Eves had no sooner vanished into the nettles than our lads began looting. We had already discovered, to our mutual dismay, that there was no controlling these boisterous hirelings once theft was in prospect, short of shooting a few of them. Twice thus far we'd been forced to do so, and both of us feared that yet another such episode would precipitate a full-scale mutiny. Our ammunition was running low. We might not be able to quell a concerted uprising without burning the rest of it, at which point our own lives would be forfeit. And even if we slew enough of the obstreperous rascals to bring the remainder to their senses, would the survivors fulfill their duties to us the rest of the way to the Coast, or decamp in the dark of moon with all they could pilfer?

"What to do, what to do . . . My companion must have perceived my indecision. He smiled coolly.

" 'Heigh ho,' said Rawley. "I don't know about you, Sir George, but I fear my heart's all a-twitter.'

"The ball was now clearly in my court."

" 'By my troth, I care not,' quoth I, with what I hoped was an insouciance equal to the moment. 'We owe God a swoon, and let it go which way it will, he who swoons this year is quit for the next.'

"Rawley punched me lightly on the shoulder. 'Pukka sabib,' said he.

"At that point, Kabiza, our burly headman, emerged from a squalid hut with a woman in tow. He crowed lustily. The other lads gathered round in eager anticipation. It was the old story. Nothing better enlivens a friendly afternoon of looting than a spot of jiggery-pokery! Though our gang would have been content with a withered old crone, this woman was young, nubile and to some tastes, I reckon, quite lovely to gaze upon.

"She had something of the look of a Somali about her, a tall, lissome, coffee-colored wench with the poignant overbite and wide-set, almond eyes peculiar to Hamitic women. The women you see in those ancient

Egyptian murals at the Victoria & Albert, you know, or among the Berbers and Tuaregs of contemporary Saharan Africa.

"Oddly enough, she didn't seem frightened, though she must have know how these sessions inevitably end. One of the bullies, his passion and interest spent, brains his sobbing victim with disdainful swing of his knob-kerri. Yet she stood there in the mud, the late, low sunlight mottling her golden skin, and smiled inscrutably into the distance.

"An innocent young savage, you ask?

"I wondered myself, even then. A brace of delicate, artfully wrought ornaments, forged from some precious metal, encircled her trim ankles, touches of a higher, perhaps forgotten culture. The anklets winked in the day's red decline. The girl's cat-like eyes impressed me as well, empty as they were of any recognizable human emotion. They had a classic, almost Pharaonic look to them, as if they had been carved from antediluvian amber and buried for centuries in some great king's tomb. Then she yawned, quite prettily it seemed to me, and turned to Kabiza with a playful smile.

"That worthy threw her to the ground, cast aside his *shuka*, the toga-like garb of the country, and with a low growl proceeded to cover her. The girl drew back her knees, whether in repulsion or acceptance of her fate, I know not. Kabiza's rowdy cohorts cheered. He thrust home . . .

"I averted my eyes in shame, then looked back suddenly as a hideous, soul-chilling cry split the air."

He paused to sip his gin-and-bitters.

"Who was it?" I asked.

"Kabiza, of course," he said, smiling wetly. "The headman's hips seemed to buck upward for an instant. He rolled to one side, on his back, his entrails spilled forth onto the mud in a welter of gore. His eyes bulged horribly, the scarred, ape-like face contorted in pain, his fingers clutching spasmodically at his innards as he tried vainly to replace them within his gaping abdomen. And Kabiza, of course, disemboweled, shuddered and died a few moments later."

Again Sir George paused for refreshment.

"And then?"

"The girl was gone!" Sir George said triumphantly. "We stood dumfounded. 'My God!' Rawley suddenly cried. 'Look, there!' He pointed toward a narrow alleyway that led between huts into the depths of the swamp. I saw the thing for only an instant – the sleek, sinuous form of a leopard, its hind paws and white-furred underbelly spattered with blood, disappearing swiftly into the man-high marsh grass. Or so it seemed.

"We sat long and late at the campfire that night. Rawley had broken out the medicinal brandy – Napoleon, 1813 if I'm not mistaken – and we slugged it back as if it were hock. Our rifles stood leaning against our camp chairs. The firelight played eerily on Rawley's manly features, aging him to a seemed simulacrum of himself, a feeble octogenarian if you will.

"Major Alistair Frederic Rawley-DePuis, D.S.O., V.C., late of Her Majesty's Coldstream Guards, was no stranger to the Arcana of the African bush. Seconded at his own request to the King's African Rifles at the end of the Boer War, he had battled Kikuyu, Turkana, Suk and Nandi spearmen from Kirinyaga to the Nyandarua, from Lake Rudolph to the Kisii Plateau. By his own modest count, he had slain full three score of more of these swarthy adversaries, all of them in single combat. 'It's amazing,' he told me once, a sweet smile playing about his lips, 'how easily a bayonet slips into a man, and how difficult it is to withdraw.'

"He had fatally pistoled a laibon of the Kavirondo nation at point-blank range during a nefarious native ambush, wrestled a *rungu* from a crazed Maasai moran and killed him with his own warclub, been hexed by a Turkana witch whose potion of spider venom and euphorbia sap had been slipped unbeknownst to him into his sundowner by a turncoat batman, survived countless life-threatening episodes of African mayhem and intrigue. After seventeen years of service on the Dark Continent, though, his good Dorsetshire common sense had been subtly altered. He had begun to believe in The Darkness.

" 'She's a Leopard Woman,' he said now. 'No doubt of it, Sir George.'

" 'Oh, I say, old son; I could not help but splutter. 'Isn't that putting, er . . . just a touch too much credence in the arcane?'

" 'Not at all, he replied. 'Though I've never come across it myself, the literature teems with eyewitness reports of such phenomena. Many of these African witchwomen have the power, one way or t'other, to change themselves at will into leopards or hyenas or aardwolves, even puff adders or mambas if they so choose, or so at least I've read. An old mess-mate of mine, Colonel Sidney Cartwright-Graham, reports witnessing just such a transmogrification in his book, *Nightdrums & Devilry in Danakil Land*. Chapter XIII, I believe. And Professor Woolworthy, the Cambridge myth wallah, devotes three whole chapters to the phenomenon, citing numerous examples in one or another of his swotty tomes – *Black Rites on the Blue Nile*, if I'm not mistaken.'

" 'But might there not be a simpler explanation?' I asked. 'The girl could have had a knife secreted about her person, and when Kabiza jumped aboard she gralloched him.'

" 'You saw the leopard as clearly as I,' Rawley replied. 'Where did it come from, and in broad daylight to boot?'

"He had a point, of course. Yet the eyes have a way of playing tricks on the forebrain, particularly at moments of stress, when confusion reigns and events transpire too swiftly. The African bush, as I'm sure you chaps are well aware, provides an all-too-fertile ground for the sensitive European imagination. Fantasy runs riot.

" 'Well, at least the incident seems to have put a quietus to the porters' mischief,' I said. 'I noticed them just now replacing their ill-gotten goods, all of them meek as lambs.'

"We decided to break camp at first light the following morning. The sooner we were clear of this unholy ground, the better. Another five days of long marches through the Hothori and Sabena deserts should find us on the verdant banks of the Tana River, where we could hire new porters and continue our hunt in a more leisurely fashion, downriver toward Lamu and the coast.

"The boys built a tall, strong *zareeba* of thornbush around the *manyatta*, fueled up their fires, and wrapped themselves uneasily in their blankets for the night. We too retired. About three hours later Rawley and I were awakened by screams and shouts. Snatching our rifles, we leaped out of the tent clad only in our *kikois*. Total confusion reigned. Finally we were able to learn that the leopardess had returned, grabbed Achmed, one of our likeliest lads, between her jaws, then quick as a wink bounded clean over the top of the *zareeba*, back into that awful darkness. We could hear the poor boy screaming and bewailing his fate, the sound fading slowly into the depths of the morass. Then through the dark came an audible crunch, followed by silence. Rawley and I sat up the rest of the night, our rifles across our knees, but she did not return. No, no . . .

"No, she saved that for the morrow."

Sir George finished his gin-and-bitters, ordered another from the comely Meru waitress hovering nearby with her tray, then continued.

"We were up before dawn, the boys gladly shouldering their heavy loads, our meager, dwindling supplies as well as an abundance of horns, hides and no small weight of ivory, for Rawley had slain a tembo whose tusks weighed more than 140 pounds each, and I one only marginally less toothy. Shunning a proper breakfast, we wolfed down a few pieces of biltong on the march.

"We gave the Lorian Swamp a wide berth as we skirted it, heading south by southeast for the Tana. Toward noon, just as we neared the end of the savannah, with the supposed safety of open desert visible dead ahead, the leopardess struck again. Creeping up through the tall grass, she nabbed the last porter in the long line. Nabbed him by the throat this time, so he could utter no more than a muffled shriek before she disappeared back into the waving grass, with him dangling crosswise in her jaws. Once more we were treated to the sound of The Queen of Darkness at table, harsh purrs of contentment emanating from her throughout her repast.

"We hurried on. Ironically enough, the Sabena Desert, one of the fiercest in the world, offered us our only hope of succor. Not even a spring hare could hide on its barren surface, much less a large, spotted cat, no matter how stealthy her approach. The pitiless sun, which dried us like so many pieces of that very biltong wherewith we had broken our fast, at the same time illumined everything under its gaze. We counted on it to highlight the leopardess, granting us at least enough law to get off a shot or two – from my 'best' gun, a .450 Rigby Nitro Express double rifle, or Rawley's .303 Lee-Enfield. Ah, but Old Sol let us down, that he did.

"At midafternoon she appeared out of nowhere – perhaps a small, unnoticed depression in the otherwise flat ground. She disemboweled two more porters with quick paw slashes, leaving her just time enough, before we came up, to peel away their faces with her remorseless jaws. This time we did not pause to bury the bodies.

"All day it went that way, and the next day, and the one after that. Our route across that ghastly wasteland was marked, and perhaps still is, with the bones of our dead. And with the loads they were carrying. Many fine trophies went to waste out there, eaten no doubt by jackals and hyenas.

"We tried, for the first few evenings, sitting up over the corpses of the newly slain in hopes of a shot at this demon leopardess. But she was too clever for us. While Rawley looked one way and I the other, she crept into camp unbeknownst and murdered a few more of our gibbering porters.

"Finally, Rawley had had enough. 'The next time she strikes,' said he, 'I'm going after her.'

" 'But man!' I remonstrated, 'that's just what she wants. She'll do for you, mark my words!' All the rational explanations I had held of Kabiza's death had long since evaporated in the desert's dry air, in the unmitigated terror of the awful, endless trek. 'She's uncanny,' I cried, 'unkillable, the Devil herself, incarnate!'

"He smiled, rather sadly, I thought. As if he were resigned.

" 'I cannot sit idly by for one more hour without doing something,' he calmly replied. He picked up his Lee-Enfield and checked its fittings, tightening an action screw here, a sling swivel there, then applying a thin coat of gun oil to the parts he felt required it. Lastly he scrutinized his soft-point bullets for deformities, to ensure against jams. It was a work-worn weapon, that Enfield. It had seen service in South Africa, France, India and Africa, from Cairo to Capetown. It had dispatched more big game and more enemies of the Crown than any other dozen of its kind. Now it would pit its pluck, its English mettle (if you'll pardon the pun) against the dark, daft power of the Supernatural . . .

"Just then came an all-too-familiar scream and gurgle, trailing off into the night. Without a moment's hesitation, Rawley plunged into the gloom."

Sir George stopped. The regimental band had packed up its instruments and long since departed. Night had fallen, and with it a sharp, bone-biting chill. The old gentleman peered about, then shivered.

"Perhaps we'd best resume our conversation at a later date," he said. "It's getting a bit parky for these old bones."

"No, no, Sir George!" I said, nearby babbling. "I'm leaving for America in the morning; don't know when I'll be back again. Why don't you come inside and join us for supper? Be our guest. It would give me great pleasure."

"Hmm," he said doubtfully, knowing full well that he had his hook planted in the corner of my mouth, through and through. The tippet would never part. "Perhaps just a small bite of something, a modest Ploughman's Lunch, no more, but in from the cold, at any rate."

It seemed to take forever, what with our moving inside, waiting for a table to be readied. Sir George making a long overdue visit to the loo, then ordering drinks and dinner. But finally he was settled.

"Where was I?"

"Rawley had just plunged . . ."

"Yes, yes – into the gloom. I sat there alone for a minute, maybe more. Then my suddenly aroused sense of shame at being thought a coward propelled me after him. I pushed through the *zareeba* into the chill desert night. Rawley was nowhere to be seen, not even as my eyes adjusted to the dark. Nor could I hear him. Or anything, for that matter, save some jackals yipping far away, off in the back of beyond. I walked cautiously forward, the loaded Rigby at high port arms, my thumb on the safety for a quick shot rather as if I were on a rough shoot for suddenly springing red partridge.

"Off to my left I could see the dark line of a *nullah* – a coulee or gulch, I believe you Yanks call it. Somehow I was instantly, perhaps instinctively, certain that the final act of this ghastly tragedy would unfold right there. I walked toward it with mounting trepidation. As I neared the edge, I heard a low whistle. It was Rawley, crouched in the ice of a boulder. I crouched low and made for him.

" 'She's down there,' he whispered. 'Eating our man, the good Baraka. You can hear her at it.' I listened. I could. 'But you must return to camp, Sir George. This is my job, by rights. I invited you on this safari, and thus I am in command here.'

" 'Tummyrot,' I answered. 'I outrank you ten ways from Sunday. The King says so. Now what shall we do?'

"His smile brightened the night. 'Good show,' he murmured. 'All you must do is cover for me. I will work my way down to that next boulder, from which I should be able to see her. When I shoot, you must be alert to movement in my direction. She may flee at the shot, if I miss her, even if I hit her for that matter. Or she will charge. And leopards, as you well know, especially supernatural ones, are chargers. Stop her if she comes for me. Understood?'

"I nodded, and Rawley began to inch his way down the steep wall of the *nullah*, taking infinite pains not to disturb a single one of the many small boulders and stones that littered its tilting surface. The rattle of even a pebble would set off the leopard's fuse, causing her to explode in one direction or another. What felt like hours ticked past, lifetimes – spots crawled before my eyes – but finally he was in place. He looked back up the slope at me, raised his thumb, then slowly raised the Enfield . . ."

At that moment a steward arrived at our table with Sir George's entrée. It was a smoking platter of langouste, flown up to Nanyuki at great expense from Malindi on the coast. With the lobster came a bowl of melted butter, a tray of capers and sliced lemon, a mammoth serving of rice, veggies and pickles and an iced magnum of champagne, Moet & Chandon "Dom Perignon," no less. Some Ploughman's Lunch. Bill and I were having bangers and mash.

"Enjoy," I said, with a touch of acerbity. "But please go on with your story. And don't hesitate to talk with your mouth full."

Sir George laughed.

"*Bang!*" he said.

"What?"

"*Bang!* Rawley fired at the leopard. I saw the long gout of flame from the Enfield's muzzle and perhaps it blinded me for an instant. All hell broke loose, as they say. A loud, high-pitched pantherine shriek. The clatter of violently disturbed rocks. A long swift dark shape momentarily eclipsed the stars above Rawley's boulder. Then his sudden, anguished cry of rage . . . All this in a heartbeat. The leopard had him, and he had her. I saw them for an instant, standing and swaying together like lovers, the leopard clutched in Rawley's strong embrace, her hind claws working at his abdomen. But of course I couldn't shoot for fear of hitting him. Then they toppled down into the *nullah*. I ran over to the edge and peered down, rifle at my shoulder.

"There she was – an elongate streak heading up the far side of the declivity. I swung with her and fired . . ."

The fork that Sir George had laden with lobster, rice and a tidbit of stewed tomato and held, poised at mouth-level, throughout this discourse, now disappeared into his maw. He chewed 30 times, maybe more, then finally swallowed. He muffled a belch behind his napkin.

"And . . . ?"

"Where was I . . . ?"

"The shot, you'd just fired the Rigby."

"Yes, a right and left, *bang-bang*, like two shots run together. The recoil and muzzle flash prevented me from seeing if either shot had told. I heard no scrabbling in the rocks, as from a moribund animal. Not a single cry from Rawley, not even a low moan. He was dead when I found him, poor chap. Disemboweled as completely as Kabiza. I dragged him back to camp by myself, the lads refusing to come beyond the *zareeba* until it became light. I sat by his body, waiting for dawn, thinking sad thoughts of the Empire, and of the men who built it. They were heroes, all of them. Where is their like today?"

"And the leopard?" What happened to her?"

"Never found her," Sir George said in a cryptic grin. "Pug marks galore down in the *nulla*, but no blood, no hair, no scuff marks on the bare rock. I did find something, though."

"What was it?"

"These," he said, reaching into the pocket of his frayed bush jacket. The wrinkled old paw, covered with liver spots, trembled, then unclenched, palm up. In Sir George's hands lay two well-worn golden anklets, graven with strange runes or cuneiforms. They looked ancient – far older even than this husk of a man who sat before me, smiling gently but quizzically into my soul.

Old beyond time itself . . .

"The lads and I found these on the dessicated body of an aged woman, who lay near a boulder at the top of the *nullah*. Just about in line with my shots. She had been there a long, long time, mummified by the sun and the hot, arid winds so that her corpse was light as a feather. God knows why the vultures and jackals hadn't found her, or at least the driver ants. Her leathery body was clad in skins, dry as parchment now."

"We sat in silence as Sir George finished his lobster. He stretched finally, yawned behind his hand, shot a cuff and looked at his wristwatch. It was a find old timepiece, perhaps a Patek Phillipe, but its leather hand had been mended near the buckle with duct tape.

"Well," he said, "you lads will have to finish the champers. No heeltaps, mind you! I'm afraid I must toddle off to slumberland. Young children and old men, they both require an early bedtime. You two young stalwarts will learn the truth of that maxim, all in the fullness of time." He rose and smiled down at us, leaning his dropsical belly against the chair top.

"Thank you for my supper," he said, "not to mention the liquid refreshment. And pleasant dreams, both of you."

Sir George's tale had made my own leopard, killed from a blind as most are nowadays, appear rather hum-drum. All I could remember of the hunt now was the interminable waiting, the insect bites, the yearning for a smoke, the leopard's sudden appearance, as if from thin air, and then the shot that killed him. He dropped without a sound, stone dead to one touch of the trigger, one soft-pointed nip from the .375 H&H Magnum. Talk about anticlimax. Rather like modern life, really: hurry up and wait, then wait some more. Just about the time you're totally bored, bang, it's over.

"What do you make of it?" I asked Bill when the old man was gone.

He laughed and shook his head.

This is Africa, Bwana," he said at last. "Anything can happen. But whatever the truth of the matter, it makes a nice bedtime story, doesn't it?"

# WILD!

*Just when you think a hunt couldn't possibly get more dangerous and exciting, something really wild comes along.*

**By Chris Storm as told to John Whinery**

T
he dogs barked. Then one appeared upside down above the shoulder-high grass, tossed into the air by the enraged buffalo. Next came another cur, flipped end over end.

The four mongrel dogs with all ribs showing belonged to the five pygmy trackers who, along with my French professional guide, Rudy Lubin, made up the team. We had followed buffalo tracks since early morning in the three-tier rainforest – a canopy 30 stories high over low trees and brushy, viny, thorny thickets. All of it under clouds hanging low in thick, moist air.

In Cameroon, we were one or two degrees north of the equator. I sweated profusely in the hot, wet place with sticking and scratching foliage so thick the pygmies used sharp machetes to clear the way. We had found the forest buffalo, which grow to 800 pounds, and are said to be as bad about charging as their Cape cousins.

A cleft in the forest canopy allowed the tall grass to grow where the mongrel dogs found the buffalo and attacked. Size differential made no difference. They knew their job and it meant food. There was no statuesque stand with tail-high point; these dogs would bite from all sides, holding for the hunter. We'd followed three buffs, and one remained as we came close to see it. Between its horns, on its forehead, a dog flailed the air. As the buffalo turned to face us, the dog fell off.

The pygmies ran. Rudy and I stood perfectly still as I slid the safety off. The buffalo glared. Body size and horn boss showed it to be a cow. A dog nipped at her heel. She turned, then backed away . . . from five yards. The jungle quickly hid us.

We stood, rifles leveled, for minutes . . . long minutes, listening. She didn't come. We didn't go for her. Although either sex was legal, we hadn't come to shoot a female.

While we walked out, tendrils of mist still hung in the morning sky. Then rain, too warm to refresh, fell steadily. Earlier, my glasses had fogged. Useless, I took them off and adjusted my scope to compensate. Somehow the dogs, all four of them, found us at the truck. They appeared beat-up. One limped, but none bled.

Following the pygmy trackers was a wonderful experience. They showed the very essence of the hunt, pure hunting – *primeval*. Our lead man would stop to listen with his left leg posed in the air. Focused! At first thought by white men to be subhuman, the small people have shown otherwise. They have become bilingual – French and their own language. They have a sense of humor and have superbly adapted to their difficult environment. Their curs, working close, are better trained than most of the dogs I've hunted with.

Probably unchanged since prehistory, the jungles of Cameroon are hard to believe. They both thrill and scare. Three- and four-foot-long monitor lizards dart through the canopies of gigantic trees anchored by barked roots that rise 20 feet above the forest floor. And the sea of leaves, through which we often moved, sharply shortened our view. Only our knowledge and gear evidenced civilization. In such a primordial place, one's survival instincts surface. The hunt here requires discipline and will. It's not for the faint-hearted.

A former logging camp now served us. We got there from town after eight hours on a single-track road – open in the river washes, otherwise walled by thicket and forest. Rough-cut planks on a pair of tree trunks laid across the streams supported the pickup, but two bridges looked so "iffy" we chose to walk across.

The morning after the dog-tumbling, we seven men plus dogs again rode the old Toyota pickup down narrow logging roads, sometimes just traces . . . the jungle too vast and too thick to hike. The pygmies' eyes didn't miss a track and when they judged it recent, we followed. We would hunt whatever animal had left fresh tracks. In the previous two weeks we'd found bongo, Peter's duiker, blue duiker, sitatunga and Red River hog, which looks like a cross between a feral pig and a javelina.

Soon we came upon fresh buffalo spoor so easy to read that even I could track them through the tall grass. There were several animals, one they judged huge – Cape buffalo size.

We followed along a river for about a mile, then the animals headed into the forest on a trail. Rudy walked ahead of me, our trackers to the side and ahead a bit. I remembered the experience Bill Matney, another hunter at the camp, had the day before when suddenly a buffalo appeared, coming on fast. The buff was young, he thought, but still big.

"I was totally surprised and transfixed, with my eyes and mind glued on him," Bill had related. "I didn't move. Instinctively, I held my rifle across in front of me. He ran over me. Then, after twenty yards or so, he decided the forest was the place to be and he ran back up the trail. I felt a fool; somehow I didn't get hurt, only scratches from the fall."

A hundred yards into the forest the tracks went left. We entered thick underbrush and I again offered my rifle to Dieudonné, the largest pygmy, to ease my travel, but he shook his head and said, "*Tien, Patrone. Il est pres d'ici.*" (Take it boss. He's quite near.) He pointed to mud scraped from an animal high on some sharp-edged elephant grass. Between my fingers it was almost liquid. We were not far behind.

Quietly as possible we worked our way through the forest for 15 minutes. The stillness was as immense as the trees. Then, a dog yipped, followed by a loud bark as the dogs closed in for another gang fight and tumble. Maybe not too smart, these mongrel dogs had much spirit of combat.

A buffalo made a loud, low grunt. The trackers urged me forward and I tried to ignore the thorns that stuck and the vines that held.

Just 15 or 20 yards ahead, the dogs and buffalo mixed it up. Barks, grunts and some yelps, which said the dogs were being hooked or hit. Another wild, close encounter. Rudy and I hurried – it was like running under water.

# AFRICA

A shrill scream stopped us. It came from our right. Total quiet followed for about five seconds. No one moved. Then, more angry, high-pitched screams from both our left and right.

Rudy turned. "Gorillas," he said.

To the screaming, the barking and buffalo grunting came the rapid *tat*, *tat, tat* of a big male's knuckles beating his chest. And he bellowed, deep and heavy. All of it was loud, close but hidden. The pygmies vanished. Rudy and I stood alone in the soggy forest, absorbing the powerful sounds of rage, fear and anger.

The buffalo had led us between a family group of gorillas and their peripherally stationed guard. Then, added to the ferocious noise came roars – abruptly beginning and ending, like a horn honking.

The enveloping leaves blocked our view – and theirs. Foliage hanging so still contrasted sharply with the cacophony of screams, grunts, roars, barks and chest poundings . . . stillness amidst chaos. Made it seem louder. Then, motion in the stillness, perhaps ten yards left, hip high. A blur of black arm, big nose and big eyes showed. It screamed. It feigned a charge – just a step or two – and was gone.

It wasn't terror or even fear that I felt. It was intense awareness. Every sense, every pore and nerve red-lined. I glanced questioningly at Rudy. He put his finger to his lips. Of course we'd not run. There was nothing for us to do. Too many animals, only two rifles. The sounds overwhelmed. I thought, *never again would I hear such a ruckus*. But I could also hear my heart pounding in my ears.

The fight seemed to be moving away to our left and as the distance grew, a little relaxation came. Then, one of the dogs let out a wild howl. It must have been grabbed, thrown or swatted hard by a gorilla. That may have motivated the other dogs to quit. One came to us and then two more seeking cover. We had hoped they would have brought in the big buffalo. But apparently he was gone and gorillas were not for dogs to fight.

Continuing their chest beating and their guttural screams, which reminded me of shouted obscenities, the gorillas slowly moved away. The danger passed. Our small friends reappeared and acted with bravado that those darned gorillas had ruined our hunt (their meat).

Walking out, I had mixed feelings: exhilaration from experiencing the primitive world, and sadness the hunt was over. I had no more time. But a trophy would not be needed for me to remember. That fierceness – so close! – will be in my memory as long as I have one.

There was no killing of buffalo, but the hunting, "the chase," was genuine, good and exciting beyond fantasy.

Now, remembering that those buffalo and the gorillas who saved them that day are still there, *wild*, in that fantastic, humid, dense rainforest gives pleasure . . . and perspective to my life.

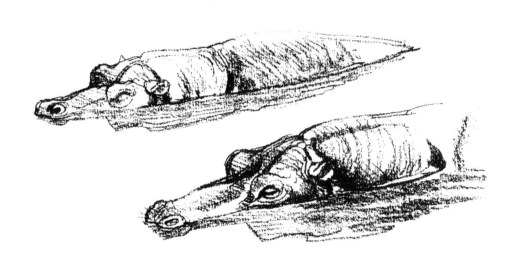

# MAMBA
## BY ANY OTHER NAME

*It happened so incredibly fast. The snake had bitten him before he could even think of reacting. And now he was alone, a wave of nausea wracking his entire body. He was going to die.*

*Story by John Levi Chilton*

It was toward the last of his safari that it happened. Having successfully collected nearly every big game animal that he had come for, Jackson Taylor set out one afternoon on foot from camp with Shabani, the tracker, looking for guineafowl. They had stumbled across one or two conveys of the crested variety, and he was having a grand time shooting at them and missing as they dodged between the dry tufts of grass and scrub, while Shabani, trotting along behind, shouted in Swahili for him to shoot again and again.

But the flocks of hustling guineas stayed wisely ahead, just out of range. When he slowed, they slowed; when, upon recovering his strength, he pushed forth with a sudden burst of speed, so did they. Only when he happened onto an unsuspecting flock did he manage to get one before they took to the air. And they had thundered up from the ground with the commotion of a flock of wild turkeys, eventually returning to the ground and to the use of their seemingly inexhaustible legs some hundred yards away. But the chasing was as much fun as the shooting, and so he had kept after them even when he knew the effort was futile.

In between flocks, he and Shabani would stop to catch their breaths and wipe the sweat from their brows. Inevitably, Shabani would commence with trying to get some point across, resorting at last to hand signals that were often as unsuccessful.

The sun was still high above the trees, mostly acacia and mopane, and the ground had become black with the charred remains of a sizable burn. Only the dry, head-high grass, runty bits of scrub, and any fallen trees or discarded limbs littering the ground had been burned. Healthy trees were left untouched, and new green shoots of grass poked up here and there like cat whiskers all across the burn.

"*Kanga upesi!*" Shabani said in gasps, as they came to a stop after another unproductive but invigorating chase. It was something about guineafowl, but Jackson wasn't sure what.

"*Upesi?*" Jackson asked huffing.

"*N'dio. Upesi mingi sana,*" he told him, his big yellow teeth showing as he grinned.

Jackson had to shrug.

"*Upesi. UPESI,*" Shabani said, as though repetition alone should make the meaning clear.

Finally Shabani gave up, resorting to the tried and true. "*Jua kali,*" he said; literally "Sharp sun," which Jackson had learned on his first day meant that it was very hot.

"*Jua kali!*" Jackson agreed strongly, wiping his forehead once more.

His shirt was soaked through at the neck and under the arms, and he could feel beads of sweat running down his back. But it was a pleasant, exhilarating feeling. And his head was swimming with the slight euphoria that comes from pushing oneself to exhaustion. If asked, he probably could not have thought of a happier, more exciting time in his life than right then.

After another minute's rest, they started on. Soon they came to a part of the river – the same narrow, smooth-flowing river that ran out in front of their camp – which now wound its way through large, flat-topped acacias and the beginnings of the wait-a-bit brush that grew here in clumps, but eventually grew very thick as it approached the rocky hills beyond. It was at the base of these hills that they had gotten a large male leopard. He and professional hunter Robin Smith.

It had come just at dusk to feed on an impala bait hung from the high, well silhouetted branch of an acacia. And Jackson's heart had charged into his throat when, sitting in the grass-thatched blind, he first heard the leopard's claws bite into the bark of the tree. Any distance between them shrank instantly to nothing when, at a nudge from Robin, he eased the barrel of his rifle into the tiny grass ring of a peephole and through the scope saw the spotted cat, crouched bigger than life on the limb above the bait, turn its head in their direction and cast its cold, green eyes on the blind.

It was like coming face to face with a killer in a dark alley. It didn't matter that the killer did not have a gun. The killer had claws that at a single swipe could disembowel him as handily as a surgeon's scalpel and jaws that could crush the vertebrae at the back of his neck.

Jackson had been quite ecstatic about killing it with one shot, for he had read many accounts of how easy they are to wound, and what a menace they are to follow up. That was three days ago.

Shabani grew watchful as they neared the river's edge. And Jackson, noticing, likewise peered as best he could into the shady clumps of brush along the bank. A shotgun was no match for an angry hippo or a rogue buffalo bull should one decide to explode out at them. Just five days before Jackson had seen – or rather *hadn't* seen – how well a wounded buffalo could hide himself in even the tiniest patch of scrub.

He and Robin Smith had just rounded one such clump, following ever-so-cautiously the generous blood trail the bull had left behind, their rifles clenched at port arms, their eyes darting searchingly about the brush, when a little less that ten short steps away there came an abrupt snort. And then the whole forest had seemed to explode at them. The wounded bull – appearing from nowhere – stormed out from behind a patch of thorn and plowed toward them with the thunder of a hundred charging horses, its heavy horns raised and ready to wage battle, its black mass billowing up behind.

Robin had hammered it in the shoulder before Jackson had even gotten his safety off. Yet, when after only a slight stumble the bull came on, now headlong, Jackson managed a shot into its neck. Then

Robin hit it in the nose with a .460 solid that dropped the bull in a cloud of dust almost at their feet.

Jackson was quite proud of himself, for he had not been fully certain how he would react under such a charge. You might promise yourself over and over again – even while calling the most horrifying scene to mind you can imagine – that when the moment comes you will stand your ground to the end, that even when it appears certain that you are going to be gored or mauled or trampled that you won't panic and throw down your gun and run, but you can't know for sure until you're put to the test.

Afterwards, after he had passed, Jackson Taylor felt invincible, as if there was nothing in this world he could not tackle. The world, along with any potential menaces it might possess, seemed such a peaceful, hospitable place.

He and Shabani were now working their way quietly along the riverbank. The brown, muddy water of the river was slipping past as opaque and thick-looking as milk chocolate. A loud splash came from somewhere downriver as an unseen hippo went crashing into the water. The uproar sent a family of baboons on the opposite bank scampering for the trees, hooting and hollering as they went. The biggest male sauntered slowly after them, glancing now and then over his shoulder and baring his teeth. Just then a grassy patch burst to life with the leaping forms of impalas; like sheep, they sprang into the air one after another, and the males – in a separate herd to themselves a hundred yards off – stuck their necks out long and low so the tips of their lyre-like horns scratched at their backs.

The river was slipping quietly along on their left. To their right, a lofty, flat-topped acacia towered up from the sandy soil, casting its shade in patches about them.

They had crept but little farther when it happened. Jackson only barely saw it coming of the corner of his eye. Perhaps because he had been expecting, if anything, something big, like a buffalo, that it took him so by surprise.

They were passing between the river and the acacia, scanning both shores for the fleet-footed guineas, when Jackson became suddenly aware of a thin, fast-wriggling movement on the shady ground beside him. But before he could think to run or jump or even to shoot – it happened so incredibly fast – the snake had raised its head and bitten him through the pants on his calf.

Shabani jumped quickly aside, exclaiming, as the blackish snake whipped past him and then slithered over the bank of the river and into the muddy water.

"*Christ!*" Jackson blurted, as the realization hit. And it hit him as solidly as a bat hits a home run ball.

Dropping hastily to his knee, he jerked his pants leg up to his calf. He saw at once the terrifying proof that the snake had indeed bitten him – two puncture marks were oozing droplets of fresh blood.

He looked hopefully to Shabani, who had squatted beside him and was probing the wound with his black fingers.

"What kind of snake. *Snake. SNAKE . . . What kind?*" he cried.

Shabani presently rattled on again, and he said something about camp and something about Robin and something about the river, but nothing Jackson could understand about a snake.

There were probably 500 different species of snake it could be, 80 percent of them deadly. He knew further that poisonous snakes typically come with one of two types of venom: that which poisons the blood and tissues, and that which attacks the nerves, causing paralysis and finally death from either suffocation or heart failure. The former is comprised of the puff adder and the boomslang; the latter, the cobra and the mamba, both green and black.

Jackson felt certain it wasn't a puff adder, as his tentboy had killed one in camp on the third day of safari, and he had studied it quite closely. They are a fat, sluggish-moving snake, with a spade-shaped head and reticulated markings. Nor was it a gaboon viper, another extremely deadly snake that he had seen inside a glass cage in the museum in Nairobi. The small plaque beneath the glass had explained that the viper is maliciously gifted with both types of venom, and the ability to inject one or the other, or both. This snake had no fan to its head, either, which ruled out a cobra. And it was too big for a boomslang. Which left only one snake that he could think of – that he did not want to think of because it was possibly the most deadly of all, and he pushed the thought quickly aside.

Shabani was still rattling away, though Jackson could make nothing of it. Well aware of the fact that to slow the spread of any venom he should move as little as possible, Jackson now pointed back the way they had come and directed Shabani: "Camp! Robin! Get Robin!" He stripped off his belt and tied it snugly about his lower thigh, then limped to the acacia and slumped down with his back against its base.

"Camp! Robin!" he cried again, for Shabani had made no move to go.

But Shabani was soon waving a hand at him and shaking his head, his face showing true concern.

"*Hapana, Bwana,*" he said. "*Mamba mto. Mamba hapa!*"

And at his words, Jackson felt instantly chilled all over, as if the temperature had fallen 50 degrees. The feeling intensified until it felt as if there were a thousand bugs beneath his skin, all crawling and scratching, trying to get out.

"*Mamba.*" Shabani insisted, pointing to the river where the snake had disappeared.

Then, recalling what Robin had told him earlier about the fatalist mind-set maintained by a good many Africans, it hit him why Shabani would not go. Shabani probably realized there was nothing he could do, and was telling him so. He should simply sit back and accept it.

"No!" Jackson roared. "Get Robin . . . *Robin!* Go!"

Shabani hesitated, looking a bit puzzled, and then motioned with his hand for Jackson to follow.

"No! Camp now!" Jackson pleaded angrily. By now he was almost ready to point the gun at Shabani to get him going. But after another minute's stare, Shabani reluctantly whirled and started at a fast trot in the direction of camp.

Jackson, now alone, laid his head back against the tree, briefly wincing his eyes. So that was it, then. His worst fear realized. A mamba. It was over. He registered with a terrifying shudder that he had somewhere between two and twenty-four hours left to live.

The overwhelming thought numbed him from head to toe. Then, as it hit him again, he felt a great, suffocating pressure bearing down upon him as though he were pinned beneath the crashing spill of some giant waterfall. A second later a wave of nausea wracked his body. What surprised him, when it ceased, was what popped into his mind first of the things he suddenly realized he would never again see. They came piling painfully into his mind like the cars of a runaway train.

Strangely enough, his first thought was of Max, the family golden retriever. Then came his wife and his kids and his mother and work, and the desperate, compelling notion that somehow he must speak to his wife before he went. He must. But God, what would he say? What could he say? . . . Perhaps the safari company could place a call to his home in Houston from Arusha and broadcast it over the radio back to camp . . . If he made it back to camp.

*He was going to die.*

The recurring thought numbed him again. Then it sent a ripple of tingles through his body. It seemed that his entire life, that everything he had ever said or done or experienced, had all been merely a hazy dream, and he was just now awakening these last few hours before he died.

It was as though he had been snapped strangely awake by a sense of total, horrifying awareness.

Everything appeared altogether different as he glanced around – it all seemed to be so startlingly in focus and in color. It was almost as if he had been suddenly, but ironically, blessed with a badly needed pair of eyeglasses, now, in his last hours. The leaves of the acacias were green as he had ever seen, their branches surprisingly intricate structures, their bark a complex fascination. The blue sky budding above the flat-topped trees and the few puffy whites pushing slowly overhead appeared alarmingly and strikingly real, as if all the thousands of skies and sunsets and panoramas he had seen in his lifetime, as he now recalled them, had been nothing more than a collection of lackluster imitations painted by some second-rate artist.

All around him the trees and bushes and the tufts of grass seemed curiously alive; they fairly swelled with life and previously unnoticed movements. He guessed he had been too closely and intimately involved with them before to notice. Or perhaps; it took his looking at them away from life, from near death, to see all this. The occasional bits of breeze made sounds in his ears as he had never heard. When he glanced down, his hands – how many times in his life had he seen his hands? – were a wonder to him. He discovered freckles he hadn't known were there, and creases in the palms, and the exact shape and color and textures of his fingernails as though they had all along belonged to someone else and were just now his. He noticed a faint scar at the base of his thumb he'd picked up in the third grade while play-wrestling one of his classmates, and had all but forgotten. A callus on his right middle finger from pushing a pencil at work. And the small veins and capillaries that wormed their way beneath his skin like . . . like little snakes.

*Jesus!*

Just then he felt a marked shortness of breath. *Was the poison taking effect already?* It seemed so quick. He forced a deep breath and briefly shut his eyes. It felt much harder to breathe than normal. He could feel the beads of sweat running to his forehead and neck, his heart knocking to get out of his chest, and he glanced down at the shotgun across his lap, which brought a haunting thought.

*Now we'll see if you put your money where your mouth is,* he thought.

Five years ago, Jackson had watched his father wither and die with cancer. Toward the end, when the medications seemed hardly to dent the pain at all, Jackson had promised himself that should he ever fall prey to some debilitating disease, he would, without question, opt for a quicker way out.

With this in mind, he pulled the shotgun around and laid it lengthwise between his legs so the barrel was pointed at his chest. But he would wait, he told himself, until the pain became unbearable. Then he would do it.

He found himself pondering, with a startlingly rush of fear, whether between the eyes or in the roof of the mouth would be best. If he were lucky, maybe he would simply slip unconscious first – before it got bad.

A second later, however, he was struck with an encouraging hope. The idea came into his head that he might beat it, that somehow he just might live.

But quickly striking down this wishful fancy was the recollection of something he had once seen on a television program about snakes. A mamba, angered by several villagers out hoeing in a field, had gone amuck and savagely struck 13 natives before one managed to chop off its head. Before the sun set the following day, all 13 had died.

Some had even made it into town for the antivenin. But antivenin, administered in even the slightest amount too little or too much, can be equally deadly.

There was also the amazing story, which might have brought a glimmer of hope if he had only recalled it a little sooner, about a mamba victim who had actually survived a bite, the only person known ever to have done so. It was the story of a game biologist who, after having been bitten while milking a mamba for its venom, saved his own life by sawing off his thumb with the dull blade of a pocket knife in what he later claimed took less than 15 seconds.

*Christ!* Jackson thought bitterly, You just slit your own throat. If you'd been thinking instead of so busily chasing him back to camp, you could have gotten Shabani to cut it off at the knee and he cursed himself while recalling how quickly and skillfully the tracker had dropped the hindquarters off the buffalo.

If he'd had a knife, he might even have tried it himself. But he doubted, as he thought it through, that he could have finished the job without passing out first. And, anyway, it was probably too late.

Jackson drew another deep breath. It felt extremely shallow, with even a spot of pain as he breathed in deeply. He glanced down at the shotgun in his lap. It looked as new to him as the hands that now held it. God, let him hurry!

It was perhaps half an hour later, though to Jackson it seemed a good bit longer than eternity, before he heard the sound of the Land Rover approaching from upriver. Finally, he caught glimpses of it as Robin came driving at top speed, weaving around the brush and trees and raising a large cloud of dust. He could see Shabani standing and hanging on in the back.

As the vehicle skidded to a stop in front of him, Robin smiled, and with a jubilant indifference and an expression quite unlike anything Jackson had expected, said, "Why, my good friend, you look as if you've just done battle with a buffalo – and lost."

Which stunned Jackson for a second. But then he blurted forth in a rush: "Have I a chance with the antivenin?"

"Antivenin?"

"Yes – For God's sake, hurry and let's try it."

But Robin just sat there. He wasn't looking at him with the expression of someone facing a man who was about to die. In fact, he was looking more like someone about to step down from the cab and join him for a cup of tea.

"You shan't be needing any of that, I'm afraid."

"Jesus! It won't work on mambas?"

The rather queer expression returned to his face.

"That wasn't a mamba," he said.

"It wasn't?"

"Good Heavens, no. If it had been, I'd be out a bloody bundle in trophy fees. Although I dare say I wouldn't mind keeping that handsome kudu of yours for myself. It would hang quite nicely on my porch at home."

"It wasn't a mamba?" Jackson repeated in disbelief.

"Not at all."

Still perplexed, Jackson glanced questioningly at Shabani, and said, "Well, then why the hell was he crying 'Mamba! Mamba!' then?"

After half-turning his head to make a quick exchange in Swahili, Robin grinned widely from behind the wheel, then fell at once to laughing. He carried on again in Swahili, and now Shabani was laughing.

"What? – What's so funny?" Jackson demanded. "What is it?"

"I – I'm sorry, Jackson," Robin said, trying to compose himself. "You poor, poor bugger . . ." and he broke into another laugh. "But you misunderstood him completely. Shabani wasn't telling you that you were bitten by a mamba. Christ! He was trying to tell you not to sit so close to the river because of the crocs . . . You poor chap; mamba in Swahili means crocodile. You're not going to die! That was just some rubbish water snake that got you. Shabani had quite a good look at it. They're completely harmless, I assure you."

It took a second for what Robin said to sink in. But when it did, it settled over him like a freshly heated blanket on a blustery cold day.

"Jesus!" Jackson exclaimed with a loud sigh. "Jesus f------ Christ!" he said, snapping onto his feet a second later, a new man. He stripped the belt from his throbbing thigh and, feeling the life flooding back into him, hobbled over to the car and rested against the side and with his fist pounded the sun-heated hood. Then he sucked in a deep, painless breath of air and sighed again.

And all the short drive back to camp, and throughout most of the rest of the trip, Jackson Taylor found himself studying his hands.

# AFRICA'S TERRIBLE TIGERS

*The fish with the chainsaw mouth.*

*By J. Douglas Johnson*

an, I'm really fishing now. Dedicated. Fixated. Eyes glued to the tip of my rod. Tim Hardin, my photographer/friend, watches the little screen on a Humminbird LC400. It reads forty feet. My bait is down there inches off the bottom – eight sardines on a 2/0 hook. Mark "Butch" Butcher, our professional guide, is at my elbow. "Any time now," he says quietly. I glance over just as confetti blips drift into the lower third of the scope.

Tim whispers, "They're comin'! A whole mess of 'em!"

The rod-tip twitches then plunges.

Butch yells, "Hit him!"

I'm on my feet and rear back. "One! Two! Three! Four! Five!"

Tim whoops, "Reel! Reel! Reel!"

I pump and crank. Butch shouts, "Keep tension on him!" "Reel! Reel!"

I strain to bring the fish up fast, before it snags the line on a limb. There's a forest of submerged trees down there. I can see shadows of leg-sized branches four feet below the boat.

# AFRICA

"Reel! Push the rod down! Keep him in the water!" (If he jumps he may spit the hook.) "Let him run! Tire him out. Easy. Bring him in closer. Let me get the net under him. One more pass . . . Got him!"

Everybody hollers! We do high fives and shout and laugh and everybody hammers me on my back, and I hammer everybody on the back. Even Alec Ncube, Butch's unflappable tracker, flashes a wide, ivory grin and laughs out loud. What a thrill! My eyes are misty. My hands shake. I gasp for breath. My knees are mushy. I've never been happier.

Photo op time! Tim fires up his Nikons. We chuckle and chortle and hold the fish high. We measure and weigh. He's my best tiger yet, a credible eight pounds, three ounces according to my digital scale.

What a kick! I've been working on this adventure for a long time, read and dreamed about tigerfish for years. There was an article in the IGFA's 1994 record book that supplied fishing tips and the scientific name, Hydrocybus vittatus, or "striped river dog." Other stories told me that world-record fish were caught in the Zambezi River and Lake Kariba. Somebody reeled in a 32-pounder.

One writer described tigers as "brutal, voracious, arm-wrenchers and bruisers." The have horrendous, chainsaw mouths, a streamlined tarpon-esque body, silver sides with blue-black racing strips and orange-tipped fins. And they are rare, found only in Africa, from the west across to the Nile and south to the Zaire, Zambezi and Limpopo river systems. They're members of the Characidae family which includes infamous toothy critters like the piranhas and payaras of South America. The species is so celebrated in Zimbabwe that its leaping likeness is pictured on the nation's two-dollar bill.

You can see why I got hung up on tussling with an African tiger. I needed to add it to my life list of catches. One morning I phoned Murray Stacey, then Marketing and Communications director of Sporting International in Houston. The company has strong sports connections all over Africa and one thing led to another.

On September 18, 1994, Tim and I headed for South Africa on USAfrica. (It's no longer flying, but it was a great airline while it lasted.) In Johannesburg we joined Air Zimbabwe, which whisked us north on a 1½-hour flight to Victoria Falls. Mark Butcher waited in the baggage area to claim us. He was one of four enterprising locals and wives, all in their mid-30s, who pooled resources to create a savvy operation for visiting sportsfolk. It's called Matupula Holdings.

One branch, Matupula Hunters, runs 24 safaris a year during the dry, cool months of May through August.

Butch said, "We're filling our slots every year. We can't do much more, so we're developing Matupula Safaris to specialize in fishing and photography trips from September through November. I want to show you all we have to offer."

Butch explained that we would travel in a rough triangle around the northwest corner of Zimbabwe. We'd go from Victoria Falls airport downriver 40 miles for a few days at Sadinda River Camp. From there we'd drive east about 130 miles to the town of Binga on Lake Kariba From Binga we'd go southwest 100 miles to huge Hwange (Wang-ee) National Park, and from Hwange we'd drive 120 miles northwest back to Victoria Falls to catch our plane for Johannesburg and home.

We loaded his Toyota Land Cruiser and set off to the river camp. After we settled in, we made a brief trip into Vic Falls to check out the shops and see the river gorge. It was a challenge for Tim to photograph. So huge! Awesome! Because of a five-year drought and the fact that it was the dry season, there was less water than we'd expected. That was good, really, because when the river is in spate, there is so much mist that photographs turn out to be big white blobs.

The next morning Murray Stacy from Sporting International showed up. He and his attractive wife, Charlyn, were touring camps in Zimbabwe, where his company has its main operation. What a pleasure to fish with Murray after all his help in getting us to Africa. Later, Butch's wife, Tracy, drove in. She is a statuesque woman of Yugoslavian ancestry with a mane of black hair, an effervescent personality and a bell-pealing laugh.

We congregated in the lounge with its bar, veranda and dining area. The A-frame ceiling was 25 feet high at its thatched apex. Below were shellacked, flat, fieldstone walls. Our view was of Chezia Pool, about 130 yards across with the hills of Zambia on the far bank. Each room had a large viewing platform with an outside stairway. At night the camp was lit by fluttering candles and kerosene lamps, reminiscent of "darkest Africa" in the movies.

The next morning we assaulted the river. There was no angling pressure; only people from the lodge fish this stretch. To get around they had an orange inflatable boat with a fiberglass hull for rigidity and a pontoon body for buoyancy. It had a 40-hp Mariner outboard on the back, and two anglers could cast out of it comfortably, three in a pinch.

The run upriver took us past Hippo Rocks, a pool where brown boulders kept rising and sinking in the water. Getting closer, we noticed the boulders had piggy ears and eyes, and blow nose bubbles. They were thousand-pound hippos, the most dangerous animals in Africa. We swung wide around them.

The next landmark was ponderous Steamboat Rock, followed by First Rapids. After that, hard to port, was a wide sandbank called The White Cliffs of Dover. It was streaked with "slides" where big crocodiles slipped into the stream. Past the cliffs came the Flotilla, with Croc Rock in the middle. Then there was Second Rapids, the Gorge and last, Third Rapids.

"We won't go through there. It'd bounce us all out of the boat," Butch warned.

The banks here were volcanic basalt shaped like chunks of thick, dark chocolate that had been chopped with a cleaver.

One angling strategy was to drift along the bank and cast toward shore. Another method was to float the center and cast into deep pools, count 20 to sink the lure, then reel back slowly. I flexed my baitcasting rod and cast a Mepps Willow Leaf #2 attached to 35-pound Spiderwire tipped with an 8-inch Orvis Pre-Looped Bite Guard. Without steel, any tigerfish is history.

In a pre-trip fax Butch had told me, "Cut the treble hooks off the Mepps. Tigerfish crush treble hooks into a ball. Put on good quality spilt-rings and single 2/0 or 3/0 hooks." To his rig, Butch added a split-shot or two, a length of piano wire and a fresh fish filet.

My respect for tigers grew quickly. We floated through the Gorge and I cast to the rocks. A fish exploded like a grenade. It socked the lure like no other freshwater fish I'd ever felt. Shocking! Vicious! It dashed downriver with my reel screaming. A little tension and back he came as if to attack the boat. Up in the air, then plunging like a spear into the river. Airborne again. Head-shaking. Lure-rattling. Alongside the boat but not subdued. Glaring, full of hate. Released, he charged away like he was never hooked, never played, never tired.

We were on the water mornings and evenings for three days, and our group managed to break four rods, lose dozens of fish and rip off countless lures. Butch caught and released about 12 tigers and his heaviest was nine pounds. I had a lot of hookups and boated ten fish, one over six. Murray got quite a few. His best weighed seven pounds, nine ounces.

That fish is a good story: We left Murray casting off Croc Rock while we went upstream to float down. When we got back he held up his seven-pounder and told us how tough it had been to land it. No net. No gig. No nothing. As he reeled in the fish, he kept looking down at his bare hands and repeating to himself. "Don't handle it like a bass. You can't lip-land this fish. Never!"

Murray grabbed the short wire leader and slid the fish onto shore, being very careful not to expose any part of his tender anatomy to the tiger's merciless set of choppers.

O ur adventure on the river ended with a commercial breakfast and hearty handshakes. Then Butch, Tim and I were off to Lake Kariba and the town of Binga, a small settlement with three harbors devoted to commercial fishing and pleasure boating. It's the home port for a fleet of houseboats popular with vacationing locals, South African families and anglers who have a week or more to explore Lake Kariba. One of the world's largest reservoirs, Kariba is 180 miles long and 25 miles across at its widest point. It was created by damming the mighty Zambezi, Africa's fourth largest river, stretching 1,600 miles from inland mountains to the Indian Ocean. Ten thousand men worked four years to construct the dam, 1,279 feet-long and 282- feet-high. It was completed in 1958 and produces hydroelectric power for both Zimbabwe and Zambia.

The guest house at Binga was fabulous. Built on a ridge about 500 feet above the water, it occupied roughly six landscaped acres in the middle of untamed bush. There was an azure, figure-eight-shaped swimming pool with 12 stools along a 20-foot bar under a thatched roof. The walls were cement and flat fieldstone. A balcony over the dining room looked out across the lake and scattered islands. We dined at an executive-sized, mahogany conference table flanked by carved Spanish chairs. The staff went all-out for our evening meals. To give you an idea, we had our choice of pork or lamb chops or both with salad, green beans and corn fritters. Dessert was crepe suzettes in an apricot sauce doused with brandy to make it a fiery *flambé*.

Mornings on Lake Kariba went like this: Up at 4:30, coffeed, toasted and out by 5 a.m. Drove 15 minutes down to the boat, loaded the gear and cleared the harbor by 6:30. There was a dim glow in the sky. Out on the lake I counted bright floodlights on 11 Kapenta boats.

Butch explained: "A shoal of Kapenta sardines is lured in by the lights. They swarm on the surface and are scooped up in big dip nets, then dried and bagged. Natives cook a thick gravy and eat the fish on their staple food, a gooey, white, cornmeal paste called zudza."

The stuff looks and tastes like the grits I ate fried and doused with Log Cabin during my kidhood in Kansas and Missouri.

We zoomed out to one of the Kapenta boats and bought a coolerful of sardines, then ran 45 minutes northeast down the lake to the Sengwe River.

# AFRICA

At 7:15 we glided into a bay on Kangamani Island. Butch pointed to where crocodile eyes studded the shore, and we watched three bull elephants parade along the beach. They had paddled a thousand yards out to the island to find thicker grass, sweeter water-weeds and fresher trees to dismantle. After a monastic visit of several weeks, they would swim back and rejoin the herd to see if there were any cows who required their attention. Not a bad lifestyle.

Butch told us some of his life story to pass time between strikes. He started tigerfishing as a boy and still entered the tournament at Binga where 40 boats and 200 anglers team up annually. His team had won each of the last three years. Butch had a degree in zoology and botany from Rhodes University in South Africa. He became a ranger for the Zimbabwe Wildlife Department and later a warden for the Forestry Commission.

A slim, 6-foot-3 with a ruddy complexion and light brown hair, Butch was one of the founders of Campfire, a program that educates local people on the value of their natural resources, be it elephants or tigerfish.

"When we bring guests to a lodge, about twenty-five percent of the fee goes to the tribespeople," Butch explains. "It makes them realize the animals that have been around them for ages are actually worth something. In the past, wild animals belonged to the state. Now they don't. They belong to the people. It's a great program, and I think it will be a success. Our progress is being watched by other countries in Africa. If it does not work, wildlife everywhere will be highly endangered. If an animal doesn't pay its own way, it'll get poached."

We anchored off a rocky point and idled in the shade of a red-and-white awning. Hooks draped with sardines drifted toward the bottom, where they were lifted up and down. What we call "jigging" in the States, the locals here called *Doba-Doba* fishing.

"When you feel a solid take," Butch told us, "hit hard about five times to bury the hook into that stone jaw."

To lure fish in and turn them on, a wire basket loaded with Kapenta was lowered and swooshed up and down. The idea was, "If you chum, they will come."

After some success, including my eight-pounder, we moved around the point into a bay where the elephants were feeding along shore 60 yards away. Butch and Alec tossed out handfuls of Kapenta and promised a school of tigers would charge in soon and rip up the surface. I was supposed to cast to swirls in the middle of this feeding frenzy and reel in fast.

I waited to see if anything happened. As predicted, the water foamed as a school attacked the chum. I felt a vicious hit, but no hook-up. I whipped the bait back into the water. Another take, a tiger jumped and tossed the lure. They seemed to be nipping at the artificial as they rocketed by at Mach speed. A third hit. This time an underwater run. I jerked to stick the point. He jumped but the hook held. The fish porpoised again and again, then leaped several times in quick succession. Slowly, I eased him to the boat. The Normick digital scale read three pounds, eight ounces.

I rigged my fly rod and tried to connect before the sun set and we had to head for the lodge. No frenzy. No luck. No takers. But we'd had very good fishing. Our Lake Kariba catch went like this: Butch landed a dozen fish, one nine pounds, two ounces on heavy line. I hooked eight and landed six, several in the five-pound range plus my eight-pounder. I was glad to catch any tigers at all. Some people fish for days and get skunked.

From Binga we drove to Hwange's main camp. One writer describes the park as "a great, flat, hot, arid, sandy, bushy stretch of wasteland with no permanent water." He pointed out, "Here, wildlife's survival depends on man's compassion."

"There are about 38,000 elephants in Hwange Park now and its carrying capacity is 14,000," Butch explained. "That's way over double and very worrisome."

Butch took us game-viewing one evening. My list read: lion, warthog, baboon, giraffe, kudu, impala, zebra, wildebeest, Cape buffalo, sable, duiker and elephants. A curious young hyena walked up and sniffed our truck. I could have leaned out the window and petted his head. It was too dark for Tim to shoot the hyena's picture, but he had a collection of slides on every other animal. My collection of mental slides includes a lot of wild beasts, but concentrates on the mean, wonderful, challenging, terrible tiger. He's something else.

# THE SMILE OF DEATH

*With murderous rows of sharp teeth and powerful jaws shaped like a smile, the crocodile is nature's grimmest reaper, a cold-blooded killer that has dominated its watery domain for more than 200 million years.*

*By Ken Kirkeby*

ater beckons to most of the world. The inland bodies: lakes, streams, rivers and ponds, shimmer blue and tempting, the promise of passage, a respite from heat and drought, a shining solace, life-giving. In most parts of the world, that is.

In sub-Saharan Africa, the water can be as inviting but far less kind – malevolent, in fact. In much of Africa the shining waters can explode suddenly and seize you. They can draw you down in a horrible convolution of maligned head and teeth – a great serrated trap sprung, unsprung and springing again, in fractions of seconds perhaps, tighter and higher up your torso as light-filled water caves in above. There is one great gasp of shock and hopeless reflex to struggle as all goes deeper and darker. The awful twisting and tearing, the muted outrage of your last tortured scream.

# AFRICA

Largest of all reptiles, the crocodile is arguably the deadliest creature ever to walk or swim the face of the earth. Commonly reaching 16 feet in length, Africa's Nile crocodile has, for centuries, been the world's most prolific man-eater. In the 1940s and 50s, when East Africa was still under British rule, Nile crocodiles killed over a thousand people each year. Even today, in the coastal areas of Australia and the Indian subcontinent, saltwater crocodiles kill at least that number annually.

Among supreme predators, the great white shark gets much fanfare, but to those who know it, the crocodile is most dreaded. Both are ancient animals, having changed little since prehistoric times. The great white, however, is a deep-water predator. You pretty much have to be out there looking for one to provoke an attack. With the crocodile it's a little different. Enter almost any African inland water, deep or shallow, and he'll generally find you. Even if you make it to the other side you are not necessarily safe. The crocodile is amphibious. Simply being near water can get you eaten. Native Africans, especially women washing clothes or fetching water, present the easiest opportunity. Basking crocodiles often appear lethargic and slow-moving, yet they're able to instantly extend their legs and reach speeds up to 30 miles-per-hour for a short distance. Crocodile victims seldom see the one that takes them.

Don't get cocky if you're in a boat, either, unless it's a very large one. In his book of African exploration, *Hearts of Darkness*, Frank McLynn writes of a crocodile that attacked a vessel of six-and-a-half tons. As for native canoes, there are more documented cases of attacks than can be counted and possibly a hundred times more that have not. Equally numerous are hands, arms and feet trailing over the gunnels that have been snapped off as well as entire men neatly snatched from their seats.

We've all seen the documentaries of lions singling out a migrating zebra or wildebeest. There is the sudden burst of speed and a dramatic, even sporting, pursuit, to the point where one finds oneself actually cheering for the lion. Nobody ever cheers for the lizard-like blur that clamps down on the muzzle of a watering gazelle. There is only a brief, soundless (if we're lucky) struggle of staggered legs and flying water. Crocodile attacks are highly efficient, but they are never exalting. It's like watching an animal going down a garbage disposal.

Crocodilians are the only order of survivors from the *Archosauria* group, which ruled the earth during the Mesozoic Period. In the last 200 million years, the order has changed little relative to other animals. However, the modern crocodile is really small in comparison to its early ancestors. *Deinosuchus* was a 30-footer that lurked in the shallow water over much of what are now the Americas, and *Phobosuchus*, the granddaddy of them all, exceeded 45 feet and weighed about 15 tons. Both critters lived during the Cretaceous Period, the heyday of the dinosaurs, and it is supposed that the *Phobosuchus* actually preyed on dinosaurs. I've seen the skull of a *Phobosuchus* in New York's Museum of Natural History. It was found in East Texas in 1940 and measures 6 feet long and about 3 1/2 feet across. The word frightening doesn't even apply. *Phobosuchus* clearly had to have been a virtual monster.

Today, there are more than 14 species of *Crocodylidae*. Most are tropical animals inhabiting the Southern Hemisphere. Because it has the widest range, the American crocodile is probably the best known. Found in brackish waters of Florida, the Caribbean, and Central and South America it rarely exceeds 13 feet in length. The Nile crocodile, *crocodylus niloticus*, once ranged throughout Palestine and Egypt, and is still found throughout much of Africa. Largest and most fierce is the Indio-Pacific, or saltwater, croc of *Crocodile Dundee* fame. Known for their voracious appetite, many over 20 feet have been taken by hide hunters. Like the American crocodile they are now protected and, therefore, are not hunted.

Characterized by its long reptilian head, the crocodile differs from our American alligator by a pointed rather than rounded snout. Having 64 teeth, the croc is constantly in the process of replacing lost ones and it will grow about 45 sets in an average lifetime. Also, on either side of the jaw, its fourth mandibular tooth protrudes upward rather than fits into the upper jaw. This difference can be seen clearly when the crocodile closes its mouth. As the lower jaw beneath the eye is upturned, the countenance resembles a sinister smile.

The croc also grows quite larger than the alligator. A crocodile killed in Tanzania in 1905 measured 21 feet and weighed more than 2,300 pounds! More recently, one taken in Uganda was 19 1/2 feet long with a 6 1/2-foot girth.

In their several-year study of the large crocodile population around Lake Rudolf, Kenya, Alistair Graham and Peter Beard measured some

500 specimens taken for research. They found the growth rate for crocodiles to be extremely high in youth to adolescence and slower in later years. Like many animals, crocodiles keep growing until they die, though the greatest growth in old crocs is in their weight. Because of their tremendous number at Lake Rudolf, the crocodiles did not grow quite as big as in other areas; thus, the world's largest are generally found where populations are smaller.

Graham and Beard found it difficult to determine the exact age of crocodiles. They surmised that about 40 years was the upper age limit for most of the Lake Rudolf population, but that certain animals could live as long as 70. The oldest croc ever recorded was a zoo-kept specimen of 50.

As with most crocs, those in Lake Rudolf prey mostly on fish, especially the large Nile perch, which can reach several hundred pounds. Elsewhere in Africa, rivers and waterholes provide a steady supply of drinking and crossing animals, both wild and occasionally domestic. Waterholes are the ideal setup to take grazing game. The unknowing animal bends to drink and the waiting croc lunges, swiftly clamping down on the prey's muzzle and dragging it into deeper water to drown. The enormous conical teeth make the hold inescapable. Lacking grinding teeth, the crocodile rolls quickly, tearing off limbs and chunks small enough to swallow. The crocodile is also adept at using its tail either to sweep prey off a riverbank or to corral fish in shallow areas where they become easier to catch.

The crocodile's land prey can be anything up to the size of a giraffe, but buffalo and young hippos are quite common. If the skin is too tough for the crocodile to break, he will store it in an underwater cache until it rots sufficiently to be consumed. At a game crossing on Kenya's Mara River, Leonard Lee Rue witnessed so many wildebeests killed by the crocodiles that they couldn't eat them all.

On my first African safari I was amazed to discover that even the smallest waterhole can support a croc or two. One afternoon I sneaked up on what looked like a puddle of about ten feet across and possibly 18 inches deep, where two reptilian eyes and a mean little snout faced the other way. I took a picture. At the sound of the shutter, the water erupted so quickly I nearly fell over backwards, but not before I snapped another. I have the photos next to each other in an album. One of a puddle with bumps, the other of flying water and angry crocodile. Small water, small croc, I concluded, but after that I gave even the smallest ponds ample quarter.

Crocodiles live where they make their living best, be it fish, fowl or migrating plains game. If the food source dissipates, they will attempt to move, though they must make it to another waterhole before the sun can parch their skin. Their bulky bodies build up tremendous heat, and a frequent sight among river travelers is the rows of crocodiles basking on shore with their huge mouths agape. This is not a threatening gesture, but serves to dissipate body heat like a panting dog.

Among Graham and Beard's many experiments were attempts to trap crocodiles alive. Underestimating their tremendous strength, Beard purchased a shark net. If the net could hold 500-pound sharks, he deduced, it could do the same for crocs of equal weight. On their first try, several medium-sized specimens quickly tore holes and escaped. "It might have been a spider's web for all of the trouble these crocs had tearing their way loose," Beard lamented.

The crocodile's raw power is astounding. And he is absolutely fearless. He has little reason not to be, having no other animal as a natural predator. The lion, formidable alone, often hunts in groups, yet the crocodile seldom finds it necessary to team up with another croc. Certainly, frenzies occur similar to what Lee Rue witnessed with the crossing wildebeest, but Graham and Beard saw curious little competition among crocodiles for prey. The crocodile is basically a solitary predator and seldom fights with its own kind, even over a mate.

Most crocs breed near the end of the year, with the male performing ceremonial courtship maneuvers as he approaches receptive females. Once bred, the female eventually builds a nest and lays her eggs, seldom venturing far away. This is possibly the phase at which many boats have encountered unprovoked attacks – by protective mothers. After hatching, she will continue to guard her young against predators, including adult crocodiles, for two more years.

Sexual maturity comes between eight and ten years. Gender is indistinguishable and can only be determined by probing a specimen's underside. Unique body features include eyes set high on the head and a valve that prevents water from entering the nose – both enabling the crocodile to remain almost entirely submerged until a meal presents itself. Their sense of smell is exceptionally keen as is their vision both in and out of the water.

As adults, Nile crocodiles live in large communities of up to a hundred animals. In recent years many crocodile attacks have been in lakeside areas where the human population is growing ever closer to the crocodiles. Incidents on Lake Victoria, Africa's largest freshwater lake, occur frequently. In March of this year, after 40 people had been killed over a seven-month period, the Uganda Wildlife Authority began an operation to cull predatory crocs on their side of Victoria. In the narrow country of Malawi, east of Zambia, BBC News reported two years ago that crocodiles protected by the CITES treaty were killing at least two people every day! The survey found that the dramatic increase in crocodile numbers had depleted the animals' usual food sources, causing much greater predation on humans and livestock. The survey pointed out that it is likely the death toll is even higher as fatalities had become so commonplace that people no longer reported them to authorities.

The most devastating crocodile attack in history was not in Africa, but in Burma by saltwater crocodiles. Toward the end of the Second World War, British troops cornered about 1,000 Japanese soldiers on Ramree Island. The Japanese attempted to escape through the swamps. Many were already wounded and the smell of blood was heavy in the mire and mangrove thickets. As the tide began to ebb, the crocodiles moved in among the struggling men. It is likely the crocodiles had become accustomed to the sound of gunfire, associating it with corpses, and were summoned by the shots. In the morning only 20 of the original 1,000 Japanese were left to surrender to the British. That night of February 19-20, 1945, marked the most harrowing and deliberate attack on humans by animals of any kind.

P robably the first commercial hunter of Nile crocodiles was the restless son of a South African tobacco farmer. Just returned from World War II, Bryan Dempster was assured a decent living on the family kraal and had recently married. Years earlier, as a boy of only 8, he had killed a crocodile on the Zambezi while hunting with his father. One evening they had heard a tribesman's story of losing his wife and nursing child to a big croc at the river's edge. They decided to hunt it. They shot a hippo to serve as bait and slept on the riverbank less than 20 yards away. Father and son woke to a loud thrashing as two pair of 12-footers ravaged the carcass. The hunters slipped silently to the river, closing to within five yards of the ruckus. Thrilled beyond all he could imagine, young Bryan and his father watched for ten minutes that which few humans had ever before witnessed. A feeding pair would seize the hippo and somersault backwards, tearing chunks loose and devouring them with a series of swallows as another pair moved in to feed. There was no fighting among them, just a morbid reptilian ritual of waiting, moving in to feed and retiring back to consume. Shivering with excitement, the boy moved closer and, at his father's cue, leveled his old .303, nearly touching the muzzle to a croc's head. Father and son fired simultaneously, and both were splashed as two crocs reacted, slumped and died.

The memory of that night never left Dempster. He announced to his family and new bride that he was headed to the Zambezi to hunt crocodile skins for the market. He purchased what equipment he could afford in Durban and set out in December of 1947 along with two good Zulu men: Joseph, his best friend since childhood and Joseph's cousin, Albaan.

It was tough going. Dempster's first mistake was to start at the height of the wet season. Rain and wind pelted their small boat in a storm and the swollen river grew rough. Trying to make it to shore, they ran aground on a submerged sandbank. Joseph and Albaan jumped over to push while Bryan steered. Instantly Joseph was trapped in quicksand and nearly sunk from sight. Dempster and Albaan were just barely able to pull him out and the expedition finally made it to the riverbank.

When the weather cleared, the men were encouraged by the number of crocodiles they began to see, but efforts to shoot them from the boat proved useless. The crocs simply slid into the water before Dempster could speed close enough to shoot. He tried to stalk them on land, but even after crawling through available cover and heeding the wind, he was only able to get within 200 yards or so – too far to hit the vital brain. The rain started again. There were clouds of gnats, endless stalking and poor meals. There was failure after failure. Then Dempster came down with typhoid. It took him two weeks in a Livingstone hospital to recover. During that time he realized that hunting by day was pointless; the crocodile had to be hunted at night.

His hunting then began a new challenge of navigating the Zambezi in darkness. The river meandered sharply and the narrow channels twisted through it like a maze. Sandbanks stopped the boat and sheared propeller pins. The men learned to follow the reeds along the river's edge and, as their night experience grew, Dempster began to take crocodiles, drifting close as he found their eyes in his lamp. The group was harvesting about three crocodiles each night until a rogue hippo attacked the boat, crushing it to pieces and turning to kill Albaan in his massive jaws.

Nearly wiped out by the hippo attack, Dempster was determined to carry on. He sold his skins and purchased a Brno 8x60 rifle, more powerful than his old .303, and an aluminum boat. Dempster and Joseph set out again for the river, this time to where he'd heard there were many crocodiles in the 300-mile stretch from Victoria Falls to the Mozambique border.

It was this second expedition where Bryan perfected his hunting method. He would bait the crocs with hippos as he had done with his father long ago. That way he could enlist the help of local natives who were given any leftover hippo meat. Dempster's luck changed for the better and he began to take as many as five animals a night without peril.

Then, after a certain successful night's hunt, as the men started back in the early morning twilight, Joseph whistled and pointed to the riverbank. There, sleeping, lay the largest crocodile any of them had ever seen. It seemed to be well more than 20 feet! Dempster signaled for Joseph to turn the boat toward the great croc. The wind was coming up and the river had turned choppy, but Dempster moved up to the bow and readied his rifle. No more than six feet from the tail, he aimed for the croc's brain and squeezed. As he did, the boat's bow rose slightly with a wave, causing his bullet to miss the vital spot. Poorly hit, the croc reared straight up on its tail and somersaulted backwards. The men had no time to react and the enormous animal crashed down on the boat like a falling tree.

When Dempster regained consciousness he was in the river, floating down a particularly fast area. Joseph was close by, his eyes wide with fear. The two struggled to a point of land and crawled ashore. The boat was nowhere in sight and all of their equipment was lost. The next day a Sena tribesman found the dingy, but the great weight of the croc had demolished it.

Again, Dempster reoutfitted and returned to the river. He even experimented with a metal trap, which the crocodiles mangled to ribbons. There appeared to be no easy way, but he and Joseph had become skillful, drifting downriver to four or five hippo baits each night and taking as many crocs. In time the rigors of croc hunting took its toll on Dempster. Bouts of malaria recurred and rheumatic aches became constant. His shoulder was so chronically sore that he came to dread firing his rifle. Finally, with the help of a tannery owner, he began a crocodile farm to raise his own skins and gave up commercial hunting.

Today, sportsmen can hunt crocodiles in most countries of southern Africa. Usual methods are by opportunity when hunting other animals, by baiting, or from either a boat or blind. The SCI record is a 17-foot, 8-inch animal killed in Tanzania. An 18-footer taken earlier this year in Zimbabwe is currently pending approval for the new number one. Both animals were taken with a rifle. The present bow record is a 13-foot specimen taken in Zambia.

The crocodile can be a difficult trophy to kill. My friend, Paul Hamner, recently hunted one in Zimbabwe – an agonizing, two-hour stalk through swampland in which he, the PH and trackers crept barefoot to a secluded upwind pool where the biggest croc lay half out of the water. Paul squeezed off a neck shot – six inches behind the jaw – as instructed. Instantly, the croc swapped ends and submerged. Thinking the animal fatally hit, the PH suggested they wait a few days for internal gas to float the carcass back up.

After the second day, to everyone's amazement, the very same crocodile appeared in his former position at the edge of the pool. Except for the bullet slightly forward of the intended area, the croc appeared unaffected. The group repeated their long stalk, this time circling behind the croc, to where Paul was able to dispatch it with a brain shot. It is an exceptional specimen, all sleek reptilian lines and macabre smile – a truly fine representation of the world's most deadly predator.

# APE-MAN OF AFRICA

*In the late 1920s a fearless adventurer sets out to film and capture wild gorillas in the forests of equatorial Africa.*

*By Ben Burbridge*

y interest in the gorilla was first stirred by Du Chaillu's vivid descriptions of these great primates of the west African coast. It was before the age of shattered illusions and I looked out on a very mysterious world. Perhaps unconsciously I was more susceptible then to the realism in the intrepid little French-American's descriptions, and had kindred primeval emotions sympathetic with these roving giant habitants of the African jungles; and certainly, the imagination tends to run riot when contemplating the personality of the gorilla. Disconcertingly manlike, this great ape measures fully six feet in height, weighs upward of 400 pounds, and stands so close to the riddle of human existence that about him arise spontaneously pictures of the caveman and the romantic glamour of the days of gigantic beasts long since extinct.

# AFRICA

The groping through the ages toward knowledge of the origin of our species has created an unreal and fantastic atmosphere around the earliest accounts of gorillas. They were maligned as ferocious creatures that invaded native villages and carried off women to their jungle strongholds. Each skin with its spear-hole in the back, from native deadfall, seems to have been impregnated with germs of exaggeration that multiplied as it drifted down the trade channels to Europe.

Du Chaillu discredited much of the early folklore about the gorilla, but told of his great courage, his manlike aspect, and his terrifying roar as, beating his chest, he advanced upon his foe. In one of his descriptions he dwells upon an incident when his native gunbearer was killed, a gorilla having snatched the rifle from the black's hands and bent it double. Du Chaillu wrote this some 65 years ago, and for just that period of time natural histories have branded his stories as fabrications and have poked fun at his description of roaring and chest-beating gorillas. Some present-day naturalists have gone even further in burning up the ears of the little Frenchman. While the roaring and the chest-beating are accepted, the gorilla by them is described as more or less harmless unless driven to attack in self-defense.

Such a different review of the gorilla's behavior would seem strange were it not that casual observations have small value when the temperamental variations and individuality of gorillas are considered. The animals are remarkably individualized, and facts as well as inconsistencies of behavior appear to defy standardization.

Lions, elephants, buffaloes and rhinos, recognized as capital killers, have an instinctive fear of man. The lower races of men fear the higher. Perhaps the gorilla stands somewhere between. None knows just where instinct ends and reason begins, or what psychological conditions prompt discretion or aggression in the moments of his wrath. In the lone savage the gorilla may instinctively perceive a ready victim, whereas the white man and his attendants, armed with thunder and lead, may look no safer to him than did a handful of Spaniards to the Aztec horde hundreds of years ago.

Misunderstandings and exaggerations seem to dog the very name gorilla, and almost to be synonymous with it.

On my arrival in New York with the young gorilla, Congo, which I recently captured in Africa, a ring of inquisitors from the press crowded around, listening to a story of the damaged and misshapen left thumb and fingers that I got by contact with a young gorilla's teeth in its capture, when a late arrival rushed up and asked the weight of an adult gorilla. He was informed around 400 pounds. My poor hand was never so twisted as the version of the story that appeared in some of the papers next morning, for I was depicted battling hand-to-hand with a huge 400-pound gorilla. During the encounter I choked the animal by thrusting my fist down its throat! Sportsmen usually perform their wildest exploits in the train before reaching the hunting grounds, but here the position was reversed, for mine took place after I had returned home!

It is doubtful if an adult gorilla muzzled could be overcome by a dozen trained prizefighters, but for many reasons he cannot be classed in the top category of dangerous game. Still, because of certain ocular evidence in my possession, I would not care unarmed to pick berries with him in the same patch.

I will not soon forget a certain afternoon on the southeastern slopes of Mount Karissimbi where I was camped, recruiting tribesmen to help capture young gorillas. Half-a-dozen men were needed, but it seemed impossible to get them. The natives were full of stories of the gorilla's ferocity. To kill, yes; but to capture young gorillas they refused point-blank. Oratory was essential, and I had begun a harangue in Swahili, the purpose of which was to convince my native bearers that the gorilla was not dangerous. When I finished, there was dead silence. It seemed that someone had put his foot on the rattle-box. At length the chief stepped from the throng, who squatted in closely wrapped skins, for a drizzling rain snow glimmered on the mountain peak above our forest background.

"The Bwana (Master) says the gorilla is harmless. Look!" He turned with the gesture of a prosecuting attorney who springs on the defense of his star witness. One of the crouching figures limped forward. On his shoulder, thigh and knee were frightful scars. Pointing eloquently to him the chief said simply, "This man went to the forest to cut bamboo for a hut; a gorilla, unprovoked, attacked him."

The gorilla's ferocity or gentleness is of small interest when compared to the problem of human evolution, and my purpose, enduring throughout the many months of weary travel on my two expeditions to the Congo, was to study the gorilla, not to kill him; to learn if he dances as does the chimpanzee; did he talk as certain authorities assert of monkeys? In a word, whether in him brutish or human characteristics predominate. Also I planned to take motion pictures of the gorilla in the privacy of his jungle home and if possible to capture his young. It was an ambitious program, presumptuous perhaps, for it included everything I could think of short of taking back to civilization with me the whole anthropoid tribe.

Far up the picturesque Congo River and back across hundreds of miles of equatorial forests, arise almost in the center of Africa the snow-covered heights of the ancient volcanoes, Mikeno, Karissimbi and Visoke. These grim old sentinels, in altitudes above 14,000 feet, stand in a triangle and form a guard of honor to the 400-odd square miles that the gorilla (*Gorilla beringeri*) claims for his kingdom.

M y first impressions of the gorilla were lasting. We picked up the trail at daybreak and followed the wanderings of a gorilla band through the forest. It was rough going. Joe, a native of the lower Congo, my one English-speaking companion, who had followed me from the mouth of the Congo 2,000 miles distant to this place, helped me lift and push each man bearing the weight of our outfit over boulder and fallen tree-trunk and up the steep precipitous walls that were among the forest obstacles in our path.

At noon we paused for rest at a place in the forest, which was flat enough to get a toe-hold. The rain had begun to trickle through the trees and with it came a glacial damp, edged with penetrating keenness. The heavens darkened, blotting out the frosty peak of Mikeno, and we took advantage of the scant shelter at hand, thinking all was done for the day when from the forest below came a curious rattling sound like the chattering of teeth. It persisted for a dozen seconds, ceased, and was repeated. The men looked at each other and muttered "*Engabe*" (gorilla).

Then came a deeper boom, a dull, resounding rapid striking, a muffled drumming that carried with it a certain sense of power. It was like the sound of strong men rapidly beating a carpet. A terrific roar filled the forest stillness. Again and again it crashed, deep and guttural, in answer to the echoes that were flung back and forth among the assembled peaks. In the accompanying silence it came to me that down there beyond the leafy screen an old man gorilla was looking up at us and voicing in his roars and chest-beats the ape's ancient defiance of humankind, a defiance as old as Africa.

We had been trailing the animals for hours, tugging through the thick shrubbery on hands and knees like boring through an apple. It was exhausting work, for no trail-cutting was allowed. In silence we noted the fresh droppings and presence of a bush fly upon the trail, which spelt the nearness of our quarry. Slowly we crawled through a dense canebrake, beyond which some forest trees extended wide mossy branches over patches of wild celery. Just ahead we could hear the gorilla band moving in the thickets. A little Batwa pointed with his spear. I followed with my eyes the gleaming shaft: 50 feet distant were several gorillas in a vine-grown tree. They had stopped, dead still, watching.

The gorilla, though passing most of his life on the ground, may be decidedly arboreal when it pleases him. I crouched low, assembling my camera. A scream split the silence; the tree seemed full of bounding apes, then they came down the rope-like creepers hand over hand. The men had been cautioned to conceal themselves and to be absolutely quiet. I crouched behind my camera, which was so camouflaged that only the lens showed among the leaves.

No movement broke the tense silence that settled upon the forest as I raised and lowered my helmet from my place of concealment. I repeated it once, twice, thrice. A violent crash in the thicket, like the rapid explosion of giant firecrackers, and up lunged out of the green 30 feet distant a great gorilla. For a moment he sat there transfixed, one huge fist closed around the branch of a tree overhead. Then with slow deliberation he raised himself higher, craning his neck to see over intervening thickets, a half human, half brutish thing, silhouetted against the gloomy forest. His wrinkled old face, framed in bristling hair, expressed intense curiosity. It was a strange introduction the presentation of these two – white man and gorilla – out there in the Congo forest.

The ape, so manlike, seemed gazing from a gloomy cavern; impersonating the Stone Age in a meeting with the steel. It was a vivid picture, tragic to a degree. The sudden movement of another gorilla just below him, and screened from sight, caused the first gorilla to look down.

Perhaps some word passed between them, for as he jerked his head back toward me a fit of passion convulsed his face. The cavernous mouth opened and a thunderous roar filled the forest.

With sudden tremendous power, he tore a limb from the tree and carried it to his mouth, biting off chunks of the hard wood and spitting them out. I sprang up to swing the motion picture camera upon him, but he dropped from sight into the jungle masses and was gone.

# AFRICA

I turned to Joe with the remark, "I thought he was coming that time." Joe arose; his hands were empty. In the excitement attending the stalking of the gorillas we had left our rifles behind!

The most interesting motion picture, and one fraught perhaps with the most excitement, was taken one day as we carried out of the forest two young gorillas we had captured. We thought the gorilla band had gone, and had begun our march campward. A Batwa was leading. Behind him came two men bearing sacks containing the young gorillas; the other men followed. Suddenly, just ahead, a face rimmed in bristling hair peered from the tangle of vivid green. The Batwa and gorilla-bearers fell back. I took the rifle from my gun-boy. A leafy curtain closed over the head as it was withdrawn.

We stood there for a moment looking into the depths of the jungle. No word was spoken; then, from a hundred feet distant came a roar. Back and forth a gorilla plunged in the underbrush. The swaying vegetation showed his progress, his roars broke harshly upon the forest stillness. The camera was assembled quickly. I had treasured this scheme, this trick I intended to use now, and had tried it often, but always it had failed. My gun-boy stepped to the camera; his hand on the crank.

Before me two men with the young gorillas approached the crashing underbrush where the gorilla band was located. The little captive gorillas, in answer to the roars of their parents, screamed shrilly. It was the signal. Both men started running with their squirming bundles. Quick, unheralded, out of the blackness of the jungle charged a great gorilla, reeling drunkenly on short bowlegs. Out of the corner of my eye I saw that Joe was still turning the handle of the motion-picture machine. I glanced back just in time, for the gorilla was almost upon me. He was so close that in self-defense I had to press the trigger of the rifle that covered him. There was but a single shot, and as he fell, an answering roar to the explosion of the .405 came from the gorillas behind him. Momentarily they paused, thunderstruck by what had happened, peering upon the still figure of him who had been their master. Then one by one they disappeared in the forest.

I had seen many gorillas and was impressed by their power and size, but I was astonished at the proportions of this hairy giant as he lay dead in the lap of Mikeno, a throne where he had so long been king. I was sorry, very sorry, for I did not want to destroy this magnificent creature that had fought for his young. He must have weighed 400 pounds, and was covered with long black hair that faded to a light tan upon his neck. His face, which a moment before had been convulsed, horrible to see, now was placid, almost kindly in the repose of death. Huge, powerful shoulders buttressed the bullet head and tapered to loins and short bowlegs. He was plastered all over with great gnarled muscles. His strength must have been enormous.

I looked at one great fist clutched in death as though in menace. It would easily have filled a gallon measure. His foot was 12 inches from heel to toe. He was 5 feet, 11¾ inches standing upright. A fighting force in single-handed combat that could not be computed.

My men gathered around emitting guttural expressions of wonderment. Even in death his presence commanded caution. They touched him gingerly with their spears.

Above, filtering through the forest, the sun broke at last. Feeling as if I had killed a man, I photographed, then skinned him hurriedly. Scarcely had we finished when the storm clouds ever lurking around the summit of Mikeno and Karissimbi came lowering and muttering like gods displeased with an evil deed.

We hurried down the mountainside with the little gorillas squirming between the carrying poles. It was midday. Camp was far distant. The rain seeped icily through the matted roof above. Each headland warmed by the distant fires of Namlagira died in the brighter lightning flashes that occasionally illuminated our surroundings.

But my men were happy. The slavish grind was over. They were going back to their homes wealthy, back to the savage orgies that awaited. I was dead tired. I had of late weeks always been so, but now the intoxication of success engendered buoyant hopes and thoughts that put life into a lagging engine that was all but worn out. For I had accomplished what had never been done before, something that would be of inestimable value. Besides taking motion pictures of wild gorillas, I had captured many of their young!

*These excepts are from Ben Burbridge's 1928 book,* Gorilla – Tracking and Capturing the Ape-Man of Africa, *published by The Century Company.*